GUI Bloopers 2.0

Common User Interface Design Don'ts and Dos

The Morgan Kaufmann Series in Interactive Technologies

Series Editors:

- Stuart Card, PARC
- Jonathan Grudin, Microsoft
- Jakob Nielsen, Nielsen Norman Group

GUI Bloopers 2.0

Common User Interface Design Don'ts and Dos

Jeff Johnson

UI Wizards, Inc.

AMSTERDAM · BOSTON · HEIDELBERG · LONDON
NEW YORK · OXFORD · PARIS · SAN DIEGO
SAN FRANCISCO · SINGAPORE · SYDNEY · TOKYO

Morgan Kaufmann Publishers is an imprint of Elsevier

MORGAN KAUFMANN PUBLISHERS

Publisher	Denise E.M. Penrose
Executive Editor	Diane Cerra
Publishing Services Manager	George Morrison
Senior Production Editor	Dawnmarie Simpson
Assistant Editor	Mary E. James
Production Assistant	Lianne Hong
Cover Design	Dennis Schaefer
Cover Illustration	Melissa Walters
Composition	SPi
Copyeditor	Valerie Koval
Proofreader	Phyllis Coyne et al. Proofreading Service
Indexer	Broccoli Information Management
Interior printer	Sheridan Books
Cover printer	Phoenix Color, Inc.

Morgan Kaufmann Publishers is an imprint of Elsevier.
30 Corporate Drive, Suite 400, Burlington, MA 01803, USA

This book is printed on acid-free paper.

Library of Congress Cataloging-in-Publication Data
Johnson, Jeff, Ph. D.
  GUI bloopers 2.0 : common user interface design don'ts and dos / Jeff Johnson.
    p. cm.
  Originally published: San Francisco : Morgan Kaufmann Publishers, under title: GUI bloopers, 2000.
  Includes bibliographical references and index.
  ISBN 978-0-12-370643-0 (pbk. : alk. paper) 1. Graphical user interfaces (Computer systems)
I. Title.
  QA76.9.U83J63 2007
  005.4'37–dc22

                                                                                    2007012860

ISBN: 978-0-12-370643-0

For information on all Morgan Kaufmann publications, visit our Web site at www.mkp.com or
www.books.elsevier.com

Printed in the United States of America.
07 08 09 10   5 4 3 2 1

Contents

Acknowledgments

I could not have written this book without the help and support of many other people.

First I would like to thank my wife and friend Karen Ande for her love and support while I was working on this book.

I would also like to thank the reviewers of the first draft, who made helpful comments and suggestions: Sara Bly, Bob Carpenter, Ed Chi, Susan Fowler, Jesse Heines, Robin Kinkead, and Innosanto Nagara. Many colleagues sent me examples of bloopers, especially Tim Bell, Michael Bell, Cathy de Heer, Roland Dumas, Simon Edwards, Susanne Jul, Ellen Isaacs, Victor Stanwick, and Marcin Wichary. Cathy de Heer also helped identify parts of the first edition that needed updating. Comments about the first edition posted by readers at bookseller Web sites also helped guide the changes.

The book also was helped immeasurably by the care, oversight, layout and organization advice, logistical support, and nurturing provided by the staff at Morgan Kaufmann Publishers, especially Diane Cerra, Dawnmarie Simpson, Mary James, and Valerie Koval.

Finally, I would like to thank my clients and former employers. Without them, this book would not have been possible … or necessary.

Introduction

Why was this book updated?

The first edition of this book was written in 1998 and 1999. The common application platforms then were MacOS9, Windows98, Windows NT, early versions of Java Swing, and Unix or Linux with CDE/Motif. Although many of the bloopers covered in the first edition are as common now as they were in the late 1990s, the book was starting to look out of date because the blooper *examples* were all from the last century. To look current, the book needed new examples.

A second reason for a new edition was that some bloopers that were common in 1999 have become less common, and new common bloopers have taken their place. A higher proportion of new applications these days are Web based, so it became important to discuss bloopers that are common in Web applications.

A third motivation for an update was that I have developed better ways to explain some of the bloopers and how to avoid them. I also have a clearer understanding of the basic UI design principles underlying the bloopers.

A final reason for revising the book is that readers of the first edition have provided a lot a feedback about what they liked and didn't like, in review articles published in magazines, comments posted in online discussion groups and on the book's pages at online booksellers, and e-mail sent to me and to the publisher. I and the publisher decided it was time to build on the first edition's strengths and correct some of its weaknesses (see Appendix B: How this book was usability tested).

Why is this book needed?

Throughout the software industry, software engineers develop user interfaces with little—sometimes no—support or guidance from professional UI designers. Some software is developed by individual freelance programmers who lack training in designing GUIs or access to people who have such training. Even in large development organizations, there may be no one with UI design training. Finally, some companies do have UI professionals, but not enough of them to cover all the development projects needing their skills.

The marketplace of software products, software-controlled appliances, and online services is therefore full of software designed entirely by people who are professional developers, but UI amateurs. Such software is a drag on the success of the entire industry.

I often review or test software that was developed by people who have little UI design experience. Such software is typically full of design errors. Many of these errors are common.

This suggested that a book focused on design errors and how to avoid them might be more effective than other UI design books have been, or at least a useful complement to such books. Accordingly, this book presents design guidelines in reverse: here's a common error; here's how to avoid it.

Not all bloopers that hurt software usability are made by programmers. Many software development organizations commit errors at the *management* level that negatively affect the UIs they develop. These management errors are in many ways more serious than concrete GUI design errors because they affect more projects and are harder to correct. In Chapter 8, I describe those sorts of errors and explain how to avoid them.

The main goal of this book is to help GUI developers and designers become better at catching their own design mistakes and at avoiding them altogether.

It would be great if the real world had error dialog boxes. They would pop up out of thin air in front of your face whenever you made a mistake. They would be a great way to train software developers and their managers to recognize when they had committed, or were about to commit, a blooper. Since there are no error dialog boxes in the real world, we need to program them into developers' heads. I am hopeful that this book will help with some of that programming.

What is a GUI blooper?

This book describes "bloopers" (that is, mistakes) that software developers frequently make when designing graphical user interfaces (also known as GUIs). The bloopers in this book do not cover all of the mistakes GUI designers could make, or even all of the mistakes I have seen. Believe me, in over two decades of working as a user interface professional, I've seen some design mistakes that were simply *amazing*—true "howlers," as some of my colleagues call them.

To get into this book, it wasn't enough for a design mistake to be a howler. It also had to be common. There is little value in warning software developers away from very rare or application-specific mistakes, no matter how horrible the errors may be. On the other hand, there is great value in warning developers away from errors that many developers make.

Bloopers are not just specific examples of design errors I have seen in software. The bloopers are mistakes that developers make over and over and over again. The examples serve only to illustrate the bloopers—to make them more concrete.

Therefore, this book is not just a collection of UI "outtakes"—embarrassing mistakes software developers have made. My aim is *not* to provide a parade of UI howlers that embarrass their developers and cause readers to laugh, shake their heads, and wonder how any designer could be so dumb. My purpose is to help GUI designers and developers learn to produce better GUIs.

The bloopers in this book are described and, where possible, illustrated using screen images captured from real products and online services, made-up screen images, and stories from my experience. With each blooper is the design rule that developers should follow to avoid the blooper. Like the bloopers, design rules are often illustrated by examples, both real and made up.

The bloopers in this book are classified into seven categories: GUI control, navigation, textual, interaction, graphic design and layout, responsiveness, and management.

Figures that show bloopers are marked with a "thumbs down" symbol. Those that show *avoiding* bloopers are marked with a "thumbs up" symbol. Images that have no symbol are neutral, provided just for information.

How were the bloopers compiled?

The bloopers in this book were sampled from over three decades of experience designing, critiquing, and testing UIs for software products. They were compiled from UI reviews, usability test reports, design guidelines documents, and classes prepared for employers and consulting clients. Several were sent by colleagues.

Very few examples that identify a product or a software company come from my consulting clients. I usually work for clients under nondisclosure agreements that prevent me from revealing details of what was developed, even for software that never made it to the market. Therefore, in most of the stories in this book, the names of companies and specific products are altered or withheld. For the same reason, the screen images showing bloopers come mainly from commercially available software and Web sites developed by companies other than my clients. However, I did obtain permission in a few cases to use real names and screen images when discussing client software.

Finally, some of the screen images that illustrate bloopers in this book were made up—created specifically for this book in order to depict certain bloopers clearly.

How is the book organized?

Chapter 1, First Principles, presents nine basic UI design principles that underlie both the bloopers and the design rules for how to avoid bloopers.

The remaining chapters describe and illustrate common bloopers software developers and their managers make that make software difficult to use. Each chapter focuses on a different type of blooper: GUI control bloopers, navigation bloopers, textual bloopers, graphic design and layout bloopers, interaction bloopers, responsiveness bloopers, and management bloopers.

Who should read *GUI Bloopers 2.0* and how should they use it?

The main intended audience for this book is developers who develop software or Web sites with little or no guidance or feedback from UI professionals. For such readers, this book is intended to serve both as a tool for self-education and as a reference. It is intended to supplement—not replace—UI design guidelines for specific GUI platforms.

A second target audience is managers of software development teams. It is for their benefit that the book includes a chapter on management bloopers.

A third target audience is UI designers, especially those who are new to the profession. For them, this book supplements the standard references and textbooks on UI design and evaluation by warning against common design errors, with real examples.

The three different types of readers will probably want different information from this book.

GUI programmers will probably want to start with the specific bloopers: GUI component, navigation, textual, and graphic design and layout. You can start with Chapter 1, First Principles, before reading about the bloopers, or you can go back and read the principles when they are relevant to a blooper you are reading. After those chapters, read the chapters on interaction and responsiveness bloopers. You can read the management bloopers and appendices if you have time or interest.

For software managers, the chapter on management bloopers is the most important. Following that, in order of importance, are textual bloopers, responsiveness bloopers, and interaction bloopers. Chapter 1, First Principles, may be of interest if you have a background or interest in UI design and human–computer interaction. You can probably skip the chapters on GUI control, navigation, and graphic design and layout completely. You can just tell your programmers and designers to "read those sections and do what Johnson says." :-)

New UI professionals should start by skimming the glossary (Appendix A) and reading Chapter 1, First Principles. Then skim the chapters on GUI control, navigation, and textual bloopers mainly to see what is in them; you can revisit specific bloopers in those chapters later as needed. The chapters on interaction, responsiveness, and management bloopers are highly recommended for new UI professionals. You may be interested in reading Appendix B to see how this book was improved through usability testing. Table I.1 summarizes these recommendations.

GUI-Bloopers2.com

Supplementing the book is a Web site, www.gui-bloopers.com. There, you will find:

- *GUI Bloopers 2 checklist:* a terse list of all the bloopers in the book, suitable for printing. Use it to check software before release.
- *Web Appendix: Color Bloopers:* two bloopers about poor use of color that could not be included in the book because it was not printed in color.
- *More bloopers:* additional bloopers not included in the book, starting with bloopers that didn't quite make the book's "final cut." This collection may be extended over time based on submissions from readers (info@uiwizards.com).

Table I.1   *Type of reader*

GUI programmer	New UI professional	Development manager
(First Principles)	Appendix A: Glossary*	Management Bloopers
GUI Control Bloopers	First Principles	Textual Bloopers
Navigation Bloopers	GUI Control Bloopers*	Responsiveness Bloopers*
Graphic Design and Layout Bloopers	Navigation Bloopers*	Interaction Bloopers*
Textual Bloopers	Graphic Design and Layout Bloopers*	(First Principles)
Interaction Bloopers	Textual Bloopers*	(Appendix A: Glossary)
Responsiveness Bloopers	Interaction Bloopers	
(Management Bloopers)	Responsiveness Bloopers	
(Appendices)	Management Bloopers	
	(Appendices)	

Parentheses indicate optional.
*Skim.

- *Sample chapter:* a chapter selected from the book, available for free download.
- *Purchase function:* a way to buy the book from the publisher.
- *More:* additional content may be provided, depending on what readers request and the author and publisher decide makes sense to provide.

First Principles

Introduction

This book describes common user-interface bloopers found in software-based products and services and provides design rules and guidelines for avoiding each one. First, though, it is useful to lay the foundation for the discussion of bloopers by describing the basic principles for designing effective, usable user interfaces.

The nine basic principles in this chapter are *not* specific rules for designing graphical user interfaces (GUIs). This chapter does *not* explain how to design dialog boxes, menus, toolbars, Web links, etc. That comes later in this book, in the rules for avoiding bloopers.

The nine basic principles represent the cumulative wisdom of many people, compiled over several decades of experience in designing interactive systems for people. The principles are also based on a century of research on human learning, cognition, reading, and perception [Card et al., 1983; Norman and Draper, 1986; Rudisill et al., 1996]. Later chapters of this book refer to these basic principles to explain why certain designs or development practices are bloopers and why the recommended remedies are better.

"Usable"—not just easy to learn

The term "usable" means more than just easy to learn. Ease of learning is an important component of usability, but it is the *least* important of three components. To be usable, a product also has to be quick to use and relatively error-free. Most importantly, it must *do what the user wants*. Keep this in mind as you read this book. Usability refers to three different components: the product does what you need it to do, it does that quickly and safely, *and,* last, it is easy to learn. Violins are hard to learn, but they have survived for hundreds of years with little change because they supply the other two more important components of usability.

More comprehensive explanations of UI design principles are presented in several books, e.g., Smith and Mosier [1986], Cooper, Reimann, and Cronin [2007], Isaacs and Walendowski [2001], Raskin [2000], Shneiderman and Plaisant [2004], and Tidwell [2005].

Basic Principle 1: Focus on the users and their tasks, not on the technology

This is Principle Numero Uno, the Main Principle, the mother of all principles, the principle from which all other user interface design principles are derived:

Focus on the users and their tasks, not on the technology.

Now that you've read it, we're done, right? You now know how to design all your future software, and nothing more needs to be said.

I wish! Alas, many others have stated this principle before me, and it doesn't seem to have done much good. And no wonder: it is too vague, too open to interpretation, too difficult to follow, and too easily ignored when schedules and resources become tight. Therefore, more detailed principles, design rules, and examples of bloopers are required, as well as suggestions for *how* to focus on users, their tasks, and their data.

What does "focus on users and their tasks" mean? It means starting a software development project by answering several questions:

- For whom is this software being designed? Who are the intended users? Who are the intended customers (not necessarily the users)?
- What is the software for? What activity is it intended to support? What problems will it help users solve? What value will it provide?
- What problems do the intended users have now? What do they like and dislike about the way they work now?
- What are the skills and knowledge of the intended users? Are they motivated to learn? How? Are there different classes of users, with different skills, knowledge, and motivation?
- How do users conceptualize the data that the software will manage?
- What are the intended users' preferred ways of working? How will the software fit into those ways? How will it change them?

It would be nice if the answers to these questions would fall out of the sky into developers' laps at the start of each project. But, of course, they won't. The only way to answer these questions is for the development team to make an explicit, serious effort to do so. That takes time and costs money, but it is crucial, because the cost of not answering these questions before starting to design and develop software is much, much higher.

Understand the users

Several of the questions listed above are about the intended users of the software: Who are they? What do they like and dislike? What are their skills, knowledge, vocabulary, and motivation? Will they be the ones who make the decision to buy the software, or will someone else do that? These questions are best answered using a process that is part business *decision,* part empirical *investigation,* and part *collaboration.*

Decide who the intended users are

Early in development, you need to decide who you are developing the software for. It is tempting to say "everyone": most developers want the broadest possible market. Resist that temptation! Software designed for everyone is likely to satisfy no one. Choose a specific primary target population as the intended user base in order to focus your design and development efforts, even if you believe that the software will also have other types of users.

In reaching this important decision, confirm that your target user base is aligned with your organization's strategic goals. Seek input from the marketing and sales departments, because it is they who are usually responsible for identifying and categorizing customers. However, remember that Marketing and Sales focus on *customers* of the product or service, whereas you need to understand the *users*. A product's customers and its users are not necessarily the same people, or even the same type of people, so Marketing and Sales' ideas about who the product is aimed at may have to be filtered or augmented in order to be useful to you.

Investigate characteristics of the intended users

Understanding the users also requires *investigation*. This means making an effort to *learn* the relevant characteristics of potential users. Surveying potential users helps you find specific populations whose requirements and demographics make them an attractive target market. After identifying a primary target user population, learn as much as possible about that population.

How do you gather information about the intended users? By talking with them, inviting them to participate in focus groups, observing them in their "natural" environment, talking to their managers, or reading about their business.

"Darn these hooves! I hit the wrong switch again! Who designs these instrument panels, raccoons?"

Users: Not just novice vs. experienced

Software developers often think of their intended users as varying on a continuum from computer "novice" to "expert." People who have never used a computer are on the novice end; professional computer engineers are on the expert end. With that assumption, figuring out who the users are for a particular application is largely a matter of determining where they fall on the continuum.

However, the continuum is wrong. No such continuum exists. A more realistic and useful view is that the intended users can be placed along three independent knowledge dimensions:

- *General computer savvy:* how much they know about computers in general
- *Task knowledge:* how facile they are at performing the target task, e.g., accounting
- *Knowledge of the system:* how well they know the specific software product, or ones like it

Knowledge in one of these dimensions does not imply knowledge in another. People can be high or low on any of these dimensions, independently. This explains situations such as the following:

- A long-time C + + programmer doesn't know how to program his DVR.
- An experienced Linux system administrator struggles with Microsoft Word, while an office secretary who has never even heard of Linux handles Word with ease.
- Computer novices and experts alike get lost in an online travel agency's Web site.
- A programmer with no accounting experience has trouble learning to use an accounting package, while an experienced accountant with no programming experience learns it easily.

When creating user profiles, position the target user types along each of the three dimensions, rather than on a single novice-to-expert scale. The users' motivation is also a factor: *why* would they learn and use the software? Is it a job requirement, or is the software for home use, used at the customer's discretion? Are there alternatives?

Collaborate with the intended users to learn about them

Finally, understanding the users is best accomplished by working with them as *collaborators*. Don't treat users only as objects to be studied. Bring some of them onto your team. Treat them as experts, albeit a different kind of expert than the developers. They understand their job, experience, management structure, likes and dislikes, and motivation. They probably don't understand programming and user interface design, but that's OK—others on your team do. A useful slogan to keep in mind when designing software is:

Software should be designed neither *for* users nor *by* them, but rather *with* them.

Bringing it all together

The goal of this three-part process—decision, investigation, and collaboration—is to produce *profiles* that describe the primary intended users of the software. The profile should include information such as job description, job seniority, education, salary, hourly versus salaried, how their performance is rated, age, computer skill level, and relevant physical or social characteristics. With such a profile in hand, developers know what they are aiming at. Without it, they are, as Bickford [1997] says: "target shooting in a darkened room."

Some designers go beyond constructing profiles for the intended users of an application. Cooper [1999] advocates making user profiles concrete by elaborating them into fleshed-out *personas:* characters with names, vocations, backgrounds, families, hobbies, skills, lifestyles, and realistic complexities. This is similar to the practice among novelists and scriptwriters of writing "backstories" for every significant character in a book, movie, or play. A character's backstory helps ground decisions about what that character would and would not do. Similarly, the personas in Cooper's design methodology help ground judgments about the designs a particular user type would find easy, difficult, annoying, fun, useful, useless, etc. Because most products have more than one type of user, it helps to develop and use a range of personas covering the most important user types.

The trick is to build profiles and personas from real data obtained from prospective users. User profiles and personas based on pure armchair speculation would not help inform design decisions and so would add no value.

Understand the tasks

As with understanding your users, understanding your users' tasks should be a three-part process: part business *decision,* part empirical *investigation,* and part *collaboration.*

Decide what set of tasks to support

Understanding the intended tasks is partly a business decision because no organization is completely open-minded about what applications to develop. No organization is going to pick a group of potential customers purely at random, figure out what they need, and design a product to fill that need. Instead, decisions about what to offer are strongly influenced—one might even say "predetermined"—by:

- the organization's strategic goals, reflecting the interests of its founders, top management, and shareholders;

- the expertise of its employees;
- its past history;
- its assets, processes, and infrastructure;
- its perception of market opportunities and niches;
- new technologies developed by researchers.

The last bullet above, "new technologies developed by researchers," is especially important. In the computer and software industries, decisions about what products or services to bring to market are often more influenced by technological "push" than by "pull" from the marketplace [Johnson, 1996a]. Whether this is good or bad is a subject of debate. Norman [1998] argues that it is often good for emerging markets, but usually bad for mature ones.

Regardless of which factors apply to your situation, you should decide in advance what general application area to target, such as document creation and management, information retrieval, banking, music, home finance, or airline reservations. This decision combines with the decision about the primary target user base to yield a fairly specific product category, such as document editing software for technical writers or banking software for bank tellers.

As with identifying the target users, seek confirmation that the target task domain of the product or service is in line with strategic goals. Again, you should seek input from the marketing and sales departments, because it is they who are usually responsible for identifying market opportunities and because they often have at least a secondhand understanding of the work the intended users do.

Investigate the intended tasks

Once you've chosen a product category, the empirical *investigation* part of "understanding the tasks" comes into play. Before starting to design or implement anything, learn as much as you can about exactly how the intended users do the tasks that the software is supposed to support. This is called conducting a "task analysis." The goal of a task analysis is to develop a thorough understanding of the activities the software will support.

The best way to conduct a task analysis is for you and other members of the development team to talk with and observe people who either will be users or are similar to the intended users. These interviews and observation sessions are usually concerned with understanding how people perform a task *before* a new product or service is introduced. A few new products radically change how people perform tasks or create entirely new ones. In such cases, interviewers describe and/or show the product and ask participants to *speculate* on how they would use it. In either case, you can interview people individually or in groups, face to face or by telephone or e-mail, in the usage setting or apart from it.

It is important to both interview users and observe them working. The two techniques are complementary. Interviews and focus groups provide explanations, rationales, goals, and other information that cannot be directly observed. However, interviews may also pro vide *mis*information, such as how a process is *supposed* to (but doesn't) work or what the user thinks you want to hear. Observation, on the other hand, lets you see what actually happens, but requires you to interpret what you see. If you are unfamiliar with the task domain—and you probably are; otherwise you wouldn't need to learn about it—your ability to interpret correctly what you observe will be limited.

It is possible to interview and observe simultaneously: you can interview potential users at their workplaces, encouraging them to answer questions-not only verbally, but also by demonstrating how they work. Remind people to explain what they are doing as they work; otherwise they may just work silently or mumble inaudibly. Ask questions if necessary.

You can also interview managers. This provides another useful perspective on the same tasks. However, interviews of users' managers must be interpreted carefully: managers often describe how work is *supposed* to be done rather than how it really is done.

 Example task-analysis questions

For a research project, a colleague and I conducted a task analysis of how people prepare slide presentations [Johnson and Nardi, 1996]. We interviewed people in their offices, encouraging them to both talk about and demonstrate how they work. The interview questions are excerpted below (and provided in full in Appendix C). The interviewers allowed the conversation to flow naturally rather than strictly following the list of questions, but made sure all the questions had been answered.

1. What is your role in producing slide presentations?
    1.1   Do you produce slides yourself or do you supervise others who do it?
    1.2   How much of your total job involves producing slide presentations?
    1.3   For whom do you produce these slide presentations?
    1.4   What quality level is required for the slides?
    1.5   Do you (your department) follow slide formatting standards?
2. What software do you use to create slide presentations?
    2.1   Who decides what software you use for this?
    2.2   Do you use one program or a collection of them?

    2.3 Do you use general-purpose drawing software or slide-making soft-ware?

    2.4 What do you like and dislike about each of the programs you use?

    2.5 What other software have you used, tried, or considered for making slides, either here or in previous jobs?

3. What is involved in making slides?

    3.1 Describe the complete process of producing a presentation.

    3.2 Do you reuse old slides in new presentations?

    3.3 How do you (your department) organize and keep track of slides and presentations?

Collaborate with users to learn about the tasks

Collaborating with users is even more important for understanding the tasks than it is for understanding the users. The limitations of both interviews and observation make it risky to rely upon conclusions obtained by either method alone. These limitations can be overcome by introducing two-way feedback into the task discovery and analysis process. Don't just collect data from users; present preliminary analyses and conclusions to them and solicit their reactions. In such a process, you won't be the only one who learns; users also gain a greater awareness of how they work and about what sorts of technology might help them work better. In return for the effort required to establish a collabora-tive working relationship, you will get more reliable data from the users.

Detailed advice on enlisting the help of users to understand their tasks bet-ter is provided in an article by Dayton et al. [1998] and books by Greenbaum and Kyng [1991] and Courage and Baxter [2004].

Bringing it all together

Fortunately, analyzing tasks requires much the same activities as investigating users. Although the two investigations were discussed separately here in order to explain each one better, most developers conduct them at the same time, in the same interview and collaboration sessions. This synergy is useful because access to prospective users is usually limited (Blooper 68, page 362).

A well-done task analysis answers some fairly detailed questions. They are:

- What tasks does the person do that are relevant to the application's target task area?

- Which tasks are common, and which ones are rare?

- Which tasks are most important, and which ones are least important?

- What are the steps of each task?

- What is the result and output of each task?
- Where does the information for each task come from, and how is the information that results from each task used?
- Which people do which tasks?
- What tools are used to do each task?
- What problems, if any, do people have performing each task? What sorts of mistakes are common? What causes them? How damaging are mistakes?
- What terminology do people who do these tasks use?
- How are different tasks related?
- What communication with other people is required to do the tasks?

Consider the context in which the software will function

Engineers often view what they are designing as if it were the only thing in the universe. They don't consider the context in which the technology will be used or what the users' total experience will be in using the technology in that context.

Sometimes, even people who purchase technology fall prey to technocentric tunnel vision. They have a problem and hope that, by acquiring and using some technology, they can fix it. Wishful thinking often predisposes people to see a problem as simpler than it really is, that is, easily correctable with technology. It also often makes them gullible to the often inflated claims of technology manufacturers and vendors.

Engineers and technology consumers manifest technocentric tunnel vision simply because they are human. People focus on their own (or their organization's) goals and desires and often fail to notice other things in the environment that influence the outcome of applying technology to a problem.

Consider a person who designs a car alarm or who buys one. The designer focuses on creating a device that signals when a car is being burglarized or vandalized. The consumer focuses on protecting his or her car. Neither considers that the alarm has to work in an environment in which many other people have car alarms and in which things other than break-ins trigger the alarm. When an alarm sounds, it is difficult to know whose car it is and impossible to know if it signals a break-in. Only rarely will it be a break-in. An otherwise good product idea fails to provide value because the designer and the consumer didn't consider the larger picture.

Technocentric tunnel vision, applied to an office containing a computer, sees the office as a darkened room with a spotlight on the computer (Figure 1.1). Users come into the spotlight, use the computer, and leave, disappearing

Figure 1.1

Viewing the computer alone, without its context.

back into the darkness. The things people do with the computer are seen as disconnected, and the things they do without it would be invisible. Using the computer, people view, create, and edit documents and spreadsheets; read and send e-mail; visit or create Web sites, etc. Where does the input come from? Unimportant. What is the output used for? Irrelevant.

In fact, the computer is embedded in a work context. A better way to view an office is as a collection of light paths flowing into, through, and out of the office (Figure 1.2). In each light path is a person. Some of the paths intersect the computer; others don't. The paths represent the flow of information, communication, and work; they show where it comes from and where it goes. Instead of asking "What should this product do?" you should ask, "What does this *office* do?" "How does it do it?" and "What software would support doing that better?"

When designers of a software application don't consider the context in which the application will be used, the application's users often find themselves typing data into it that just came out of another computer program. The application's designers didn't think about where the data would come from and so didn't design their application to take input directly from the other program.

To understand the context in which a planned software application will be used, you must study that context. That means talking to prospective or representative users, observing them, and analyzing the collected data. Advice on how to do this is provided by Holtzblatt et al. [2004].

Figure 1.2

Viewing the computer in its context: the office and tasks in which it is used.

Basic Principle 2: Consider function first, presentation later

Many GUI developers—even many UI designers—begin by deciding what their application's UI will look like. Some sketch designs on paper or with computer drawing tools. Some use interactive development tools to lay out displays and controls. Some begin hacking implementation code.

Don't do that! Starting by worrying about appearances is putting the cart before the horse. It is tempting, but usually a mistake. It results in products that lack important functionality, contain unneeded functionality, and are difficult to learn and use.

What it does **not** mean

Warning: "Considering function first, presentation later" does *not* mean "design and implement the functionality first and worry about the UI later." That misinterpretation matches the approach many developers use. It seldom produces successful software.

The UI of a software application is not just about the software's presentation. It embodies design decisions that extend down deep into the architecture, such as what concepts are exposed to users, how information is structured, back-end functionality, and customizability. The user interface therefore cannot successfully be tacked on at the end of implementation.

What it **does** *mean*

Principle 2 should be interpreted this way: A software application embodies certain concepts and relationships between concepts. Designers should fully define the concepts and their relationships before they design how to present the concepts to users.

Stated more concretely: don't jump right into GUI layout. Before sketching screens, choosing and laying out controls, cutting foam prototypes, or writing code, developers should focus on answering the task-related questions given under Principle 1 and then the following questions:

- What concepts will be visible to users? Are they concepts that users will recognize from the task domain, or are they new? If new, can they be presented as extensions of familiar concepts, or are they foreign concepts imported from computer science?

- What data will users create, view, or manipulate with the software? What information will users extract from the data? How? What steps will they use? Where will data that users bring into the software come from, and where will data produced in it be used?

- What options, choices, settings, and controls will the application provide? This is not about how to present controls (e.g., as radio buttons, menus, sliders). It is about their function, purpose, and role in the software (e.g., day of the week, dollar amount, e-mail address, volume level). It is about what options the software provides.

Develop a conceptual model

Once a development team has answered the above questions, it is important to capture and organize that knowledge in a way that aids UI design. A recommended way is to design a *conceptual model* for the software.

What is a conceptual model?

A conceptual model is the model of an application that the designers want users to understand. By using the software and perhaps reading its documentation, users build a model in their minds of how it works. It is best if the model that users build in their minds is like the one the designers intended. That is more likely if you design a clear conceptual model beforehand.

Developing a conceptual model before designing a user interface is hard: it is tempting to jump right into discussing user interface concepts, such as control panels, menus, and data displays. The temptation is exacerbated by the tendency of sales and marketing people to state functional requirements in terms of window layout and mouse clicks. When marketing requirements are stated in UI terms, gracefully but firmly decline them, and demand requirements stated in terms of the task: the problems users face and the goals they wish to achieve.

A conceptual model is not a user interface. It is not expressed in terms of keystrokes, mouse actions, dialog boxes, controls, or screen graphics. It is expressed in terms of the concepts of the intended users' tasks: the data users manipulate, how the data is organized, and what users do to the data. A conceptual model explains, abstractly, the function of the software and what concepts people need to be aware of in order to use it. The idea is that by carefully crafting an explicit conceptual model, and then designing a UI from that, the resulting software will be cleaner, simpler, and easier to understand.

> As simple as possible, but no simpler—*Albert Einstein*

One goal, when developing a conceptual model for a planned software application, is to make it as simple as possible. The fewer concepts it has for users to master, the better, as long as it provides the required functionality. For designing computer software, as in many things, remember this:

> Less is more—*Mies van der Rohe*

For example, in an application that gives driving directions, are "turn northeast" and "turn southwest" needed, or are "turn left" and "turn right" enough?

Task focused

Keep the conceptual model focused on the tasks, with concepts that will be familiar to users. Leave foreign concepts out.

The more direct the mapping between the system's operation and the tasks it serves, the greater the chance that your intended conceptual model will be adopted by the users [Norman and Draper, 1986]. For example, imagine that you are designing software for creating and managing organization charts. Is an organization chart:

(A) a structure of boxes, box labels, box layout, and connector lines or

(B) a structure of organizations, suborganizations, and employees?

Model B maps more directly to the tasks of most people who create and use organization charts and so will be easier for them to master. In contrast, Model A focuses on the graphic appearance of organization charts, rather than on their function and semantic content. Model A might be a suitable model for graphic designers, but it won't be suitable for anyone else.

Computer-based systems often provide new capabilities. This is usually true of tasks that were not previously computerized, but can also be true for those that were. As a result, foreign concepts often creep into the conceptual model. For example, paper appointment books can't actively remind users of events, but computer-based appointment books can.

However, each new concept comes at a high cost, for two reasons:

- It adds a concept that task experts will not recognize and so must learn.
- It potentially interacts with every other concept in the software. As concepts are added, the complexity of the system rises not linearly, but *exponentially*!

Therefore, additional concepts should be resisted, and admitted into the conceptual design only when they provide high benefit and their cost is minimized through good UI design. Remember: Less is more!

Perform an objects/actions analysis

The most important component of a conceptual model is an objects/actions analysis. This specifies all the conceptual objects that an application will expose to users, the actions that users can perform on each object, the attributes (user-visible settings) of each type of object, and the relationships between objects [Card, 1996; Johnson and Henderson, 2002].

The software's implementation may include objects other than those listed in the conceptual model, but if so, those extra objects should be invisible to users. Purely implementation objects and their associated actions—such as a text buffer, a hash table, or a database record—do not belong in a conceptual model.

The objects/actions analysis, therefore, is a *declaration* of the concepts that are exposed to users. Follow this rule: "If it isn't in the objects/actions analysis, users shouldn't know about it."

Example objects/actions analyses

If we were designing software for managing checking accounts, the objects/actions analysis would, if task based, include objects like *transaction, check,* and *account*. It would exclude non-task-related objects like *buffer, dialog box, mode, database, table,* and *string*.

A task-based conceptual model would include actions like *writing* and *voiding* checks, *depositing* and *withdrawing* funds, and *balancing* accounts, while excluding non-task-related actions like *clicking* buttons, *loading* databases, *editing* table rows, *flushing* buffers, and *switching* modes.

In a task-focused conceptual model, the attributes might be as follows:

- Checks have a *payee*, a *number*, *memo* text, and a *date*.
- Accounts have an *owner* and a *balance*.
- Transactions (deposits and withdrawals) have an *amount* and a *date*.

A checking account conceptual model in which *accounts* included attributes from computer technology, such as *encryption type*, would not be task focused. That would detract from the usability of the software, no matter how much effort went into designing the user interface.

Consider how recurring transactions are handled in Quicken.[1] Quicken's designers recognized that transactions that recur often—such as paying the power bill each month—must be easy and fast to record. Wisely, they didn't satisfy this by adding an explicit concept of *transaction templates*, with facilities for creating, managing, and reusing them. Instead, Quicken users enter a transaction as a one-time event, then tell Quicken to save it in a "Quick-fill Transaction" list. Users reenter recurring transactions simply by clicking on them in the list, then filling in the variable amount. Thus, Quicken's designers added support for recurring transactions without burdening the UI with excess conceptual baggage.

The objects, actions, and attributes for modeling checkbook management may seem obvious, so let's consider a domain for which the objects/actions analysis may seem less clear-cut: customers posting comments about products at an online store. Suitable objects in this domain might include *customers*, *products*, customer *comments*, and *responses* to comments. Actions on products would include *viewing* and *adding comments*. Actions on comments would include *viewing* and *responding* and, for a user's own comments, *editing*. The attributes of a comment might include the *title*, the customer's *name*, and the posting *date*. Comments on a product could be organized as a branching structure of comments and responses, but that might be more complex than necessary; a simple list of comments for a given product might be good enough. These issues can be decided without saying anything about how the GUI will look or even whether the UI is graphical or speech.

For a discussion of how objects/actions analysis helps designers achieve design simplicity, see Appendix C.

Object relationships

One important role of objects/actions analysis is to define and represent relationships between objects. Conceptual objects may be related to each other in several ways.

---

1. Bank account management software from Intuit.

A task domain's objects usually form a *type hierarchy* in which some objects are more specific *types* of others. For example, a *checking account* is one type of *bank account,* a *digital camera* is one type of *camera,* and a *fixed-rate mortgage* is one type of *mortgage.* Making the type hierarchy clear in the conceptual model helps you understand it and determine how best to present it to users. It can help you notice actions common across objects, which can be designed as generic actions (see also Basic Principle 3). This, in turn, makes the command structure easier for users to learn: instead of a large number of object-specific commands, a smaller number of generic commands apply across objects.

For example, imagine an application for scheduling Meetings and Parties. If a Party is a special type of Meeting, the UIs for creating them should be similar or identical, so after learning how to create one of them, users will already know how to create the other. Similarly, rescheduling, editing, deleting, printing, and other functions might have similar UIs for both Meetings and Parties.

Depending on the application, objects may also be related by *part/whole* hierarchies, in which some objects are *parts* of others, and *containment* hierarchies, in which some objects can *contain* others. For example, a heading is *part* of a document, and a photo album *contains* photos.

Finally, concepts in a task domain vary in *importance*: users encounter some more frequently than others. For example, checking accounts are more common than trust accounts, and recording transactions in a checking account is much more common than opening a new account. The relative importance of concepts can be used to focus the design (see Basic Principle 4).

Listing a conceptual model's objects and actions according to the type, part/whole, and containment hierarchies, as well as their relative importance, greatly facilitates the design and development of a coherent, clear, easy to learn user interface.

Develop a lexicon

After the objects/actions analysis, the next most important component of a conceptual model is a *lexicon*[2] defining the terminology to be used throughout the software and its documentation. Once the team agrees what each user-visible concept in the software is, the team should also agree on what to *call* that concept.

The entire team develops the lexicon, but it is best managed and enforced by the team's technical writer. Whoever manages the lexicon should constantly be on the lookout for inconsistencies in what things are called. For example:

---

2. Also sometimes called a *nomenclature* or *vocabulary.*

> "Yo, Rajiv. We called this thing a 'slot' in this dialog box, but we call it a 'cell' everywhere else. Our official name for them is 'cell', so we need to fix that inconsistency."

Software developed without a lexicon often suffers from two common user interface "bloopers": (1) multiple terms for a given concept and (2) the same term for different concepts (Blooper 22, page 153).

It is also the lexicon manager's role to be on the lookout for user-visible concepts in the software or documentation that aren't in the lexicon, and to resist them. For example:

> "Hey Sue, I see that this window refers to a 'hyperconnector'. That isn't in our conceptual model or lexicon. Is it just the wrong name for something we already have in our conceptual model, or is it something new? And if it's something new, can we get rid of it, or do we really, really need it?"

For more detail on how to construct a conceptual model, see Johnson and Henderson [2002]. Most industry-standard style guides for specific GUI platforms also provide advice on devising conceptual models.

Write task scenarios

Once a conceptual model has been crafted, developers can write use cases or task scenarios depicting people using the application, using only terminology from the conceptual model. These scenarios can be used in product documentation, product functional reviews, and usability test scripts. For the checkbook application, for example, developers could write scenarios such as:

> "John uses the program to check his checking account balance. He then deposits a check into the account and transfers funds into the checking account from his savings account."

Note that this scenario refers to task objects and actions only, not to specifics of any user interface. The scenario does not indicate whether John is interacting with a GUI on a personal computer, a pen-based interface on a PDA, or a voice-controlled interface over a telephone.

Base UI design on the conceptual model

The user interface should be based on the conceptual model. It translates the abstract concepts of the conceptual model into concrete presentations, controls, and user actions. Scenarios can then be rewritten at the level of the user interface design. For example:

"John double-clicks on the icon for his checking account to open it. The account is displayed, showing the current balance. He then clicks in the blank entry field below the last recorded entry and enters the name and amount of a check he recently received."

Objects/actions analysis can kick-start development

If you are a programmer, you may have noticed the similarity between the objects/ actions analysis described here and the object-oriented analysis that is a common early step in software engineering. Although objects/actions analysis is restricted to *user-understood* concepts, while object-oriented analysis is not, developers can treat the objects/actions analysis as an initial design for an implementation object model and can begin implementing it—even before a user interface is specified. Therefore, developing a conceptual model is not purely an added cost for a project; it produces outputs that can *save* costs during development.

Conceptual model focuses design process

Because almost everyone on a development team has a stake in the conceptual model, it serves as a coordination point for the team. This has one very strong implication:

■ Unilateral changes that impact the system's conceptual model are not allowed.

For example, if a programmer believes a new concept needs to be added to the software, she must first persuade the team to add it to the conceptual model; only then should it appear in the software. Similarly, if a documenter feels the need to introduce an additional concept to explain the system, that change must be reflected first in the official conceptual model (with the team's agreement); only then can it appear in the documentation.

The process isn't linear.[3] As design proceeds from conceptual model to user interface to implementation, downstream efforts will almost surely reveal problems in the conceptual model that must be corrected. Early low-fidelity prototypes and lightweight usability tests can accelerate this by allowing evaluation of the conceptual model as well as the UI.

Resist the temptation to treat the conceptual model document as "ancient history" after an initial UI has been designed from it. If you don't keep the conceptual model document current as you improve the design, you will regret it in the end, when you have no single coherent high-level description on which to base user documentation, training, and later system enhancements.

---

3. Especially in the era of Agile development methods, which place value on a highly iterative design–test cycle.

Summary: Benefits of developing a conceptual model

Starting a design by devising a conceptual model has several benefits:

■ *Task focus:* Devising a conceptual model forces designers to consider the relevance to the task of each user-visible concept and the relationships between objects. When these issues have been thought through before the UI is designed, it will map more naturally onto users' tasks.

■ *Consistency:* Enumerating the objects and actions of an application's supported task allows you to notice actions that are shared by many objects. The design can then use the same user interface for operations across those objects. This makes the UI simpler and more consistent and thus easier to learn.

■ *Importance:* Listing all user-visible concepts allows you to rate their relative importance. This impacts both the UI design and the development priorities.

■ *Lexicon:* A conceptual model provides a product lexicon, a dictionary of terms for each of the objects and actions embodied in the software. This fosters consistency of terminology, not only in the software, but also in the product documentation.

■ *Scenarios:* A conceptual model allows the development team to write task-domain-level scenarios of the product in use. Those scenarios are useful in checking the soundness of the design and also in documentation, in functional reviews, and as scripts for usability tests.

■ *Kick-start development:* An objects/actions analysis provides an initial object model—at least for objects that users encounter. Developers can start coding it even before the UI is designed.

■ *Focus team and process:* The conceptual model serves as a focal point for all development team members and other stakeholders to discuss and continually evaluate the design.

Basic Principle 3: Conform to the users' view of the task

Software user interfaces should be designed from the users' point of view. You cannot do that if you don't know what the users' point of view is. The best way to discover the users' point of view is to follow Basic Principle 1: talk with representative users, observe their work, and collaborate with them to perform a task analysis.

Conforming to the users' view has several subprinciples.

Strive for naturalness

A task analysis lets you see what belongs "naturally" to the target task domain and what activities are extraneous, artificial, "unnatural."

Don't make users commit unnatural acts

Unnatural acts are steps users have to perform that have no obvious connection to their goal. Software that makes users commit unnatural acts strikes them as arbitrary, nonintuitive, and amateurish, because unnatural acts are difficult to learn, easy to forget, time consuming, and annoying. Too many software applications force users to commit unnatural acts (Figure 1.3).

An example: Playing chess

As an example of how performing a task analysis can help clarify what actions are natural, consider the game of chess. An important action in playing chess is moving a chess piece to a new board position. To move a piece, what must be specified? Think about this for a few seconds. Answer the question in your own mind first, then read on.

    Moving a piece in a chess game requires indicating: (a) which piece is to be moved and (b) where it is to be moved. I'm not talking about the user interface

Figure 1.3

Forcing users to commit unnatural acts.

of a chess program. I'm talking about the task of *playing chess,* whether it is played on a computer, on a wooden chess board, by mail, or by Internet. Wherever, whenever, and however chess is played, moving a piece requires specifying the piece to be moved and where it is to be moved.

Now, let's consider a computer chess program. If a chess program requires users to specify *anything* other than the piece to be moved and the destination square, it is requiring unnatural acts. What sorts of unnatural acts might a computer chess program require? Here are some:

- *Switching to Move mode:* The software might have a mode for specifying moves and a mode for typing messages to the other player. If the software is always in one of these modes, users will often forget to switch modes and will either type moves when in Message mode or type messages when in Move mode. (For more on modes, see Blooper 48, page 269.)

- *Assigning a move name:* Perhaps the software requires users to name each move so that there is a way to refer back to it later.

- *Stating a move reason:* Perhaps the software asks users to record their reason for each move, to provide a record that can be used in later postmortem analyses of the outcome.

- *Specifying which game this move is for:* Perhaps the software supports playing multiple games at once. The user must identify the game in addition to the piece and destination.

Moving a piece in chess should be a simple operation, but software can easily complicate it by adding extra, unnatural steps. Similar analyses can be performed for the other operations provided by a chess program. The ideal is for *all* operations in the program to be as free as possible of actions that are foreign to playing chess.

As another example, a photo management application would presumably provide at least the following operations: download photos from camera, review photo inventory, display photos, delete photo, create photo album, copy photo into album. These operations could be analyzed to determine what their "natural" inputs are. Software designers should perform this analysis on all of important operations of every application they design.

Imposing arbitrary restrictions

Another way in which software can violate users' sense of naturalness and intuitiveness is by imposing arbitrary or seemingly arbitrary restrictions on users. Examples of such restrictions include:

- limiting person names to 16 characters;
- allowing table rows to be sorted by at most three columns;

- providing Undo for only the last three actions;
- requiring a fax number in all address book entries even though some users don't have fax machines.

Arbitrary restrictions, like unnatural acts, are hard to learn, easy to forget, and annoying. A product with many arbitrary restrictions won't have many satisfied users. Obviously, size and length restrictions are more bothersome the more people bump into them. If a limit is so large that users never encounter it, it isn't really a problem. For examples of bloopers involving arbitrary restrictions, see Blooper 41, page 242.

Use users' vocabulary, not your own

Software applications are infamous for being full of technobabble: jargon that computer engineers understand but most users do not. Even when terms in computer software come from users' standard vocabulary, the terms are often redefined to have specific technical meanings; users don't understand this either. An overabundance of technobabble is one of the enduring shames of the industry (Figure 1.4). For more on this issue, see Blooper 26, page 173.

When writing text for the software or its documentation, avoid computer jargon. As described in Basic Principle 3, you should create a project lexicon. The lexicon should name every concept (object, action, or attribute) that users can encountered. The terms in the lexicon should match the conventional terminology from the task domain. Once the lexicon has been developed, text in the software or in the documentation should conform strictly to it.

Figure 1.4

Exposing users to technobabble.

Keep program internals inside the program

Software users are not interested in how the software works. They just want to achieve their goals. Details of the software's internal workings should therefore remain internal—out of sight and out of the users' minds. This sounds reasonable, but in fact exposing software internals to users is a very common user interface blooper (Blooper 40, page 241).

By now you know that you should develop a conceptual model before designing a user interface. The conceptual model indicates which concepts to expose to users. The user interface of an application should represent only concepts that are required to support the intended tasks. Hide all other concepts, including general computer technology concepts and those pertaining only to the implementation.

Find the correct point on the power/complexity trade-off

There is usually a trade-off between power and usability. Every feature, function, or capability in an application needs a way for users to invoke or control it. Unfortunately, our industry pays too much attention to lengthy feature lists and not enough to the price one pays for power.

Software developers tend to believe "the more options, the more controls, the more power, the better" (Figure 1.5). In contrast, most people who use computer software want just enough functionality to achieve their goals—no more, no less. Most people learn to use only a few of the features of a software application and ignore the rest. Some features are ignored because they are too complicated to be worth learning. Sometimes the obstacle isn't the complexity of a particular feature, but rather the sheer quantity of things to learn. The mere presence of less important features can make more important ones less likely to be learned and used.

The problem facing you as a software developer is finding the optimal point in the trade-off between power and complexity. To do that, you must talk with and observe representative users, maybe even bring some onto your team. Otherwise, you are just guessing.

Once you know how much functionality users need, you can also use one or more of these design techniques for reducing complexity:

- *Sensible defaults:* Make sure that every setting in an application has a default value. Users should be able to leave all or most of the settings at their default values and still get a reasonable result. This allows users to ignore most of the settings most of the time.

- *Templates or canned solutions:* Instead of making users start every task from scratch, provide partial or complete solutions for users to start from

Figure 1.5

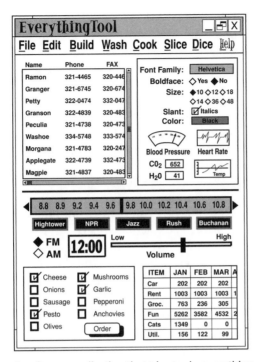

A software application that tries to do everything.

and modify if necessary to satisfy their specific goals. This approach allows users to bypass most of the software's functionality. They can get useful results without knowing how to produce results from scratch.

- *Guided paths–wizards:* New users often seek someone to guide them through the steps of complex tasks. Applications can provide this by offering "wizards": predefined sequences that guide users step-by-step through complicated processes, with clear instructions and choices specified mainly through menus instead of text fields. As long as a user wants what one of the wizards produces, wizards are a great way to reduce complexity.

- *Progressive disclosure:* Hide detail and complexity until the user needs it. Deactivate controls and hide menubar menus[4] until they are relevant. Hide seldom-used settings, or controls requiring advanced knowledge of the software, under panels labeled "Details" or "Advanced." Assign names to combinations of settings, allowing users to work with the named combinations instead of all the individual settings. For example, paragraph styles in document editors allow users to define collections of formatting properties to apply all at once to text paragraphs.

---

4. *Note:* Hide menus, not menu items. Disappearing menu items is a blooper (Blooper 8, page 89).

- *Generic commands:* Use a small set of commands to manipulate all types of data. A carefully chosen set of generic commands, mapped onto all of the types of data in an application, can reduce the required number of commands. Most of what people do with computers can be expressed in terms of these nine generic commands: Create, Open, Move, Copy, Save, Delete, Print, Show/Edit Properties, and Follow Link. As described in Basic Principle 2, starting by developing a conceptual model can show which actions are common across objects and therefore could be provided through generic commands.

- *Task-specific design:* Support a small set of tasks very well. Instead of offering users big feature-rich programs that attempt to support a wide range of tasks, offer them a collection of small specialized programs, each of which supports one task extremely well. For example, instead of developing a single generic document editor that can be used for creating everything from song lyrics and to-do lists to corporate financial reports and slide presentations, develop several simple, task-specific editors. This approach has been used successfully for household tools and appliances, including information appliances. It is more successful when task-specific applications and appliances can share information. For a more complete discussion of the advantages and disadvantages of task-specific software applications, see Nardi and Johnson [1994] and Johnson and Nardi [1996].

- *Customizability:* Make the UI customizable, so customers can adjust it to emphasize the functionality they will use and deemphasize or hide the rest. Allow users—or local developers acting for users—to set defaults, define macros, create templates, and otherwise customize the software for their specific requirements. For example, users at a company may need only 10 of 50 possible toolbar buttons, so the rest can be removed (and left as menu commands). However, customizability is risky: it tries to transfer some of the responsibility for simplifying the UI to users. The attempt may fail: users may not want to do that. Even when customizability succeeds, it is rarely because users embrace and exploit it. Most users ignore customizability completely. Rather, it is usually because value-added resellers, local system administrators, or a few power users customize the system for everyone else.

Basic Principle 4: Design for the common case

In any task domain, users will have goals ranging from common to rare. Design your application to recognize this range.

Make common results easy to achieve

If a user's goal is predictable and common, the user shouldn't have to do much to achieve it. Unusual goals may require more effort to achieve. Stated more formally: The amount users should have to specify in order to achieve a desired result should *not* be proportional to the complexity of the result. It should be proportional to how much the desired result *deviates* from what is common.

If a man goes into a restaurant every day for dinner and always orders the same thing, he can just say, "I'll have the usual." Perhaps he usually has a steak. Perhaps he usually has a wilted spinach and Belgian endive salad topped with curried free-range chicken, goat cheese, organic walnuts, and a basil–artichoke–mustard dressing. Regardless of whether his usual dinner is simple or complicated, he can just order "the usual." If on a particular day he wants a little change from his usual meal, he can specify it as a *change,* for example, "I'll have the usual with the sauce on the side." However, if he ever decides to order something out of the ordinary, he has to tell the waiter what menu item he wants and indicate his choices for all of its options.

Returning now to computer software, suppose someone is preparing a presentation and wants slides containing bullet-point text and simple business graphics, all conforming to the company's standard format. The slide preparation program should make that a snap—just plug in the content and the slides are done. However, it may take significant work—including help from graphic artists—to prepare a presentation containing fancy, unusual charts, dissolves, animations, or other visual effects or one that deviates from the company's standard format.

There are four ways to make common tasks easy. All were mentioned under Basic Principle 3 as ways of reducing UI complexity: sensible defaults, catalogues of templates or "canned" solutions, wizards, and customizability. The bottom line is that users should be able to get a lot without specifying much. Do a little; get a lot. That's what users want.

Two types of "common": "how many users?" vs. "how often?"

Interactive systems typically offer many features—different things users can do. When designing the user interface for a feature, it makes sense to factor in how commonly used the feature is. The UI for a very commonly used feature would be designed differently than that for a rarely used one.

But what does "common" mean for software features? It can mean either:

- *How many users* will need the feature? Will it be used by all or nearly all users, the majority, a significant minority, or almost none?
- *How often* will users need the feature? Will those people who need the feature use it every few seconds, minutes, hours, days, weeks, months, or years?

The optimal UI for a feature depends on *both* factors: how many users need it *and* how often they need it. This design principle is described fully by Isaacs and Walendowski [2001], Chapter 6. For convenience, I will summarize the design rules.

The more frequently a feature will be used, the fewer clicks it should require

Features that users use repeatedly at short time intervals should not require much user input to invoke and control. They should require very few keystrokes and clicks. Some features are needed so frequently that they should require *no* clicks. For example, to check the time while using your PC, you don't click anything; you just look at the clock display. In contrast, users tolerate more clicking and keystrokes for features they use less frequently. For features that people use once or twice a year—e.g., setting installation or configuration options—minimizing keystrokes is completely irrelevant compared to ease of remembering and clarity of instructions.

The more users will use a feature, the more visible it should be

The greater the percentage of users who will need a function, the more visible and prominent it should be to ensure that everyone finds it. If all users will use a feature, it's OK for it to take up screen space; it needs to be right out front. Actions that few users will need can be less prominent—maybe just hinted at in the UI; maybe even hidden, e.g., behind "Advanced" switches, special function keys, or key combinations.

Combinations: frequent by many, frequent by few, infrequent by many, infrequent by few

Interesting design issues arise when the two dimensions of "commonness" are considered together. For simplicity, we divide each dimension into only two levels: high and low. How does one design a UI for a feature that is used often by most users? How would that compare to the UI for a feature used rarely by most users, often by few users, or rarely by few users? We can construct a 2 × 2 matrix that gives the design guidelines for the four cases (Table 1.1).

Design for core cases; don't sweat "edge" cases

The "rarely by few" cell of the matrix may not be worth wasting much design effort on. Alan Cooper [1999] argues precisely that. He points out that programmers are trained to handle *all* cases that can arise in a software system and so often spend inordinate amounts of time and effort designing GUIs that cover low-probability cases as well as higher probability ones. That, Cooper says, hurts usability in two ways:

Table 1.1   Desired UI characteristics for features depending on use frequency and number of users

		More visible ↔ *Less visible*	
Fewer clicks		**By most**	**By few**
	Frequently	Highly visible; few clicks	Barely visible; few clicks
↕	**Rarely**	Barely visible; more clicks OK	Hidden; more clicks
More clicks			

- It takes development time and resources away from designing good UIs for the common cases.
- It burdens the entire UI with having to cover "edge" cases as well as common ones.

Cooper recommends designing UIs to optimize for common cases (for both definitions of commonness) and more or less ignoring improbable or optional cases. For rare users who might occasionally need one of those functions, an ad hoc UI can be tacked on. The main point is to focus development resources on the important features. Microsoft's UI designers agree:

> The core scenarios—the primary reasons people use your ... program—are far more important than the fringe scenarios—things people might do but probably won't. Nail the basics! (And if you do, users will overlook fringe problems.)— *Windows Vista User Experience* [Microsoft Corporation, 2006]

Basic Principle 5: Don't distract users from their goals

The human mind is very good at multitasking. We often do many tasks at once, for example, talking on the phone while beating an egg while keeping watch on our child, all while tapping a foot to a song we heard on the radio earlier this morning.

However, our ability to multitask is limited mainly to activities that are well learned or based on perceptual and motor skills. One way to categorize activities that we can multitask is "stuff we already know how to do." In contrast, working out solutions to novel problems is an activity that human minds cannot multitask effectively. Problem solving—stuff we don't already know how to do—requires concentration and focused attention. We're pretty much limited to solving one novel problem at a time.

Software systems should not distract users from their own tasks and goals. Don't make people actively think about the software they are using. Operating the software should be in the background, not the foreground, of users' consciousness. User interfaces that force users to stop thinking about their own goals and think about the UI are design failures. This design guideline is stated well in the title and content of Steve Krug's Web design book *Don't Make Me Think* [Krug, 2005]. It is as applicable to desktop applications and information appliances as it is to Web sites.

The damage caused when software distracts users from their primary goals goes beyond simply consuming mental bandwidth. It also yanks the user's mind out of the original task context, switching it into the "operate the program" context. After the user solves the software problem, mentally reconstructing the original task context can take significant time.

Don't give users extra problems

People have plenty of their own problems in the domains of their work, their hobbies, and their personal lives. That's partly why they use computer products and services: to help them solve those problems and achieve their goals. They don't need or want to be distracted from those problems and goals by extra problems imposed by computer products and services. For example:

- A student wants to put a picture on his Web site, but the picture is in TIFF format rather than the required GIF or JPEG graphics format. His graphics software won't convert images from TIFF to GIF or JPEG; it will only convert from BMP format to GIF. He's stuck.

- A teacher tries to look up facts about another state's government. He points his Web browser to the state's official Web site, but it tells him that the site requires a browser different from the one he has. It provides a link to download the required browser, but the browser provided there is incompatible with his computer. He starts to wonder if he really needs those facts.

Software should let users focus their attention on their own problems and goals, whatever they may be: analyzing financial data, looking up job prospects on the Web, keeping track of friends' birthdays, viewing a relative's vacation photos, and so on. Software should support problem solving *in the target task domain*, but it should minimize or eliminate the need for users to spend time problem solving *in the domain of computer technology*.

Don't make users reason by elimination

Minimizing the need for problem solving in the domain of computer technology includes not requiring users to figure out how software works by a process of elimination. Users should not have to go through thought processes such as the following:

- "I want page numbers in this document to start at 23 instead of 1, but I don't see a command to do that. I've tried the Page Setup settings, the Document Layout settings, and the View Header and Footer commands, but it isn't there. All that's left is this Insert Page Numbers command. But I don't want to *insert* page numbers: the document already has page numbers. I just want to change the starting number. Oh well, I'll try Insert Page Numbers because it's the only one I haven't tried."
- "Hmmm. This checkbox is labeled 'Align icons horizontally.' I wonder what happens if I *un*check it. Will my icons be aligned vertically, or will they simply not be aligned?"
- "This online banking service is asking me for a 'PIN.' But the card they sent me has a 'password.' I wonder if that's it? They haven't sent me anything called a 'PIN.'"

The functions of controls, commands, and settings in a user interface should be clear and obvious. Figuring out how to use software should not require reasoning by elimination.

Basic Principle 6: Facilitate learning

A common complaint about software applications is that they are hard to learn. Learning takes time; the more a user has to learn in order to use a product or service, the longer it will be before that user can be productive. Time is money. Furthermore, if users are not *required* to learn to use an application (e.g., because of their job), they may simply not bother. User interfaces should therefore be designed to facilitate learning. The user interface of an application can facilitate learning in several different ways.

Think "outside-in," not "inside-out"

Software developers often design as if they assume that the users will automatically know what the developers intended. This is inside-out thinking. When developers design software, they know how it works, what information is displayed in what place and at what time, what everything on the screen means, and how information displayed by the software is related. Most designers think inside-out: they use their own knowledge of the software to judge whether the displays and controls make sense. They assume that users perceive and understand everything the way the designer intended it to be perceived and understood.

The problem is, users *don't* know what the designer knows about the software. When people first start using a software product, they know very little about how it works or what all that stuff on the screen is supposed to mean. They do not know the designer's intentions. All they have to base their understanding on is what they see on the screen and, perhaps, what they read in the software's documentation.

Example: Textual ambiguity

Thinking inside-out is a problem that is not limited to software developers. Newspaper headline writers sometimes commit the same error when they fail to notice that a headline they've written has interpretations other than the one they intended. Some examples:

Crowds Rushing to See Pope Trample 6 to Death

Drunk Gets Nine Months in Violin Case

Red Tape Holds Up Bridge

Nurse Helps Dog Bite Victim

New Vaccine May Contain Ebola

Two Ships Collide, One Dies

Farmer Bill Dies in House

Example: Ambiguous button label

Figure 1.6

Ambiguous key label: "Do It" or "DoIt"?

A famous example of textual ambiguity in a computer system—and inside-out thinking by the designers—is a LISP workstation, circa 1985, that had a key on its keyboard labeled "DoIt," as in "do it." The key was labeled in a sans serif font, in which lowercase "L" and uppercase "I" characters looked alike (Figure 1.6). The designers of this keyboard apparently assumed that users would read the label as intended, but predictably, some users read it as "Dolt" and wondered why anyone would press that key.

Figure 1.7

Graphical ambiguity: antenna or martini glass?

Example: Graphical ambiguity

Graphic designers are thinking inside-out if they assume that an icon they've drawn will "naturally" convey the intended meaning to users. Designers at one of my client companies were surprised when usability testing showed that most test participants thought an antenna symbol for a Transmit function was a martini glass with a swizzle stick in it (Figure 1.7).

Similarly, a colleague told me: "There is an icon in Lotus Notes that everyone at my company refers to as 'the lollipop.'" A case study of designers mistakenly expecting users to instantly recognize and understand icons created for a computer game is described by Johnson [1998].

The right way to design: Think outside-in

Thinking outside-in when designing a UI means making sure it makes sense to people who do *not* know everything you know about it. This doesn't mean you should assume users are stupid. They probably know more than you do about the software's supported tasks. What users don't know is your *intentions*. They don't know the intended meaning of the various parts of the display. They don't know what depends on what.

If your intended users misperceive or misunderstand your design, they may have an immediate problem, but you will have the more serious and longer term problem: unsatisfied users and diminished sales. You therefore must make sure the UI makes sense, not to *you*, but to *them*.

Consistency, consistency, consistency

User interfaces should foster the development of usage *habits*. When using interactive software and electronic appliances, users want to fall into unconscious habits as quickly as possible. They want to be able to ignore the software or device and focus on their work. The more consistent the software is, the easier it is for users to do that.

Consistency avoids "gotchas"

Software that is full of inconsistencies, even minor ones, forces users to keep thinking about it, detracting from the attention they can devote to their task. This sort of software is full of "gotchas": it's constantly saying to the user "Aha! Gotcha! Stay on your toes, buster, or I'll getcha again." You should try to minimize the number of "gotchas" by striving for a high degree of user interface consistency.

When beginning a design, develop a conceptual model and perform an objects/actions analysis to expose operations that are common to many different types of objects. This allows the design to make use of generic commands (see Basic Principle 3) or at least to use highly similar UIs for similar but distinct functions. When adding new features to an application, reuse user interfaces from other parts of it instead of inventing new ones for each new feature.

The alternative is to provide a bewildering array of different ways of doing more or less the same thing in different contexts. For example, the user interface for deleting items often varies depending on what is to be deleted (Figure 1.8).

Dangers of naive consistency

Exhorting software developers to make user interfaces "consistent" is somewhat risky: it could do harm as well as good. Why? Because, consist-

Figure 1.8

Various Delete commands.

ency is a more complex concept than many people realize. In particular, consistency is:

- *Difficult to define:* Many experts have tried without success.
- *Multidimensional:* Items that are consistent in one dimension (e.g., function) may be inconsistent in another (e.g., location).
- *Subject to interpretation:* What seems consistent to one person may seem inconsistent to another.

Some designers either are unaware that users might see things differently or believe that they can define consistency for users. Some astonishingly bad designs have been produced in the name of consistency. Examples include software applications in which everything is controlled by data-entry forms, or by hierarchies of menus, even though forms or menus may not be the best way to control all the functions. Grudin [1989] even suggests that consistency is so ill defined and easy to misapply that it should be abandoned as a UI design principle.

Consistency is good anyway

Consistency can certainly be misapplied in UI design, but that doesn't mean we should abandon the concept. Just because we don't have a formal definition of consistency doesn't mean that the concept is useless. It clearly has value to software users, even though their ideas of what is and is not consistent may not match those of UI designers. Users search for consistency along the dimensions that are relevant to them. They are so anxious to disengage their conscious mind from the task of controlling the computer—to free it to focus on their own problems—that they make up consistency even when it is absent.

For example, programmers might argue: "Yes, most items on this computer are opened by double-click, but this application is different because items can only be opened, not selected, so a single-click should open them." So they design it that way, and users *double*-click to open items anyway and also accidentally open items (with a single-click) they didn't mean to open.

Computer users gladly expend *physical* effort to reserve *mental* effort for working on their own tasks. For example, a usability test participant once said, after completing a task:

"I was in a hurry so I did it the long way."

Making consistency user-centered

Instead of abandoning consistency as a UI design goal, we must make it more *user*-centered. When interviewing or observing users, try to determine how *they* perceive consistency. What aspects of their current tools seem consistent and inconsistent to *them?*

Test sketches or other prototypes on representative users, and watch for aspects of the UI that users perceive as inconsistent. The consistency of a user interface should be evaluated based not on how "logical" it seems to designers and developers, but rather on how predictable it is to *users*.

Provide a low-risk environment

People make mistakes. A software application that is risky to use is one in which it is too easy for users to make mistakes, does not allow users to correct mistakes, or makes it costly or time consuming to correct mistakes. People won't be very productive in using it; they will be wasting too much time correcting mistakes. Such software will not be popular.

Even more important than the impact on time is the impact on learning. A high-risk situation, in which mistakes are easy to make and costly, discourages exploration: people will tend to stick to familiar, safe paths. When exploration is discouraged, learning is severely hampered. A low-risk situation, in which mistakes are hard to make or easy to correct, reduces stress and encourages exploration, and hence greatly fosters learning. In such situations, users aren't so hesitant to try new paths: "Hmmm, I wonder what *that* does."

Basic Principle 7: Deliver information, not just data

Computers promise a fountain of information, but deliver mainly a glut of data … most of it useless. Data is not information. People extract information from data.

If I want to know whether my colleague is in his office, all I want is one bit of information: yes or no, true or false, 1 or 0. But I can get the answer in a variety of ways, involving the transfer of widely different amounts of data. I can:

- send him an e-mail and wait to see if he replies (several hundred bytes, including mail headers),
- call him on the phone and listen to see if he answers (kilobytes of audio),
- visit his Web site and view an image from the Web cam in his office (megabytes), or
- knock on the wall between our offices and listen to whether he knocks back (analog signal).

Regardless of the method used and the amount of *data* transferred, I receive only one bit of *information,* assuming that all I care about is whether Bill is in his office.

Software applications often treat data as if it were information. They put it all in your face and make you figure out what it means. Software should focus users' attention on the important data and help them extract information from it.

Design displays carefully; get professional help

Basic Principle 2 says, "Consider function first, presentation later," but there comes a time in every software development effort when you must consider how to present the software's controls and status as well as the users' data. When that time comes, you should consider screen design seriously and carefully. Your goals:

- *Visual order and user focus:* A successful UI doesn't just present. It directs users' attention toward what is important. For example, find the selected text in each of the computer screens in Figure 1.9. The large amount of contrast

Figure 1.9

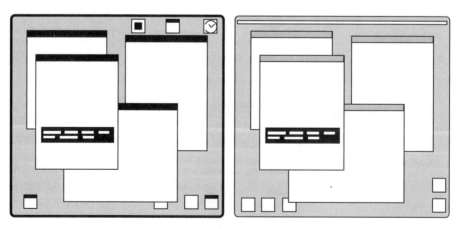

The amount of high contrast on the screen can make it hard or easy to spot the selected text.

on the screens of many computer systems (the left screen) makes it hard for users to spot the important information. The current selection should be the users' main focus; it is the object of the next operation. The screen on the right shows how the display of the Apple Macintosh minimizes contrast on the screen in order to focus attention on the current selection.

■ *Scannability:* Computer users rarely read the screen carefully; they usually scan it quickly looking for anything matching their goals. Therefore, design screens to be easily scannable. Instead of long paragraphs of prose text, break information up into headings, bullets, lists, and tables. Display information graphically where possible. Keep link labels short.

■ *Match the medium:* One mark of a poorly designed UI is failing to match the design to the limitations of the presentation medium. Examples: window systems for 2-inch screens, visual metaphors presented aurally through a phone, point-and-click GUIs on devices that have only arrow keys, subtle colors on a display that can't render them well. Well-designed user interfaces match the medium in which they are presented.

■ *Attention to detail:* Success is in the details. Nowhere is this more true than in the design of information displays. Hiring UI and graphic designers may seem expensive, but they bring an eye for detail that few other developers can provide and thus repay their cost. In cases in which programmers must design without the support of design specialists, at least assign the UI to people who are sticklers for detail. The alternative is many of the bloopers described in this book, incoherent displays, design inconsistencies, indecipherable symbols, and a generally unprofessional appearance, which may result in a less successful product.

Development managers should get the right people for the job. You would not hire a plumber—even a skilled one—to repair your car. Yet many software development teams expect GUI programmers to design screens as well as implement the GUIs. Many assign GUI programming to student interns and new hires and use graphics created by programmers or managers. The problems this sort of corner-cutting can cause, and how to avoid them, are described in detail under Blooper 64, page 331.

The screen belongs to the user

Early in the history of GUIs, researchers discovered that it is usually a bad idea for software to unilaterally move controls and data around on the screen. This includes having the software:

■ jump or "warp" the mouse pointer to new positions,

■ move controls to the pointer,

■ reposition, stretch, or shrink windows.

Such attempts to be helpful and efficient disorient and frustrate users more than they help. They interfere with users' perception of the screen as being under *their own* control.

The operative GUI principle is "The screen belongs to the user." Graphical user interfaces are supposed to be based on direct manipulation of data by users, and that is what users expect. When software changes too much on its own initiative, users become disoriented and annoyed.

Consider the screen pointer. Moving it requires hand–eye coordination. After someone has learned to use a mouse or touchpad, moving the pointer becomes a reflex—controlled more by "muscle memory" than by conscious awareness. Users' conscious minds are freed to think about the tasks they are trying to accomplish. Automatic, unilateral movement of the pointer by the software disrupts hand–eye coordination, causing disorientation and yanking users' consciousness back to the task of controlling the pointer. Users aren't sure which pointer movements resulted from their actions versus those of the computer.

The principle covers more than just screen pointers, windows, and controls. It includes desktop icons, lists of items, and other types of data that people manipulate. Software should not "help" users by rearranging their data for them. It should let users arrange and manage their data themselves. Bloopers caused by violating this principle, and how to avoid them, are discussed under Blooper 49, page 277.

Preserve display inertia

Closely related to the principle that *the screen belongs to the user* is the principle of *display inertia*.

When software changes a display to show the effect of a user's actions, it should try to minimize what it changes. Small, localized changes to the data should produce only small, localized changes on the display. When a user changes something on the screen, as much of the display as possible should remain unchanged.

Failing to confine display updates to what has actually changed can disorient users. For example, if someone edits the name of a file listed in a folder, it would be very disorienting and annoying if the file constantly jumped around to different alphabetical positions as the name was being edited. Therefore, most file managers leave the file temporarily where it is until users indicate that they are done by pressing Enter or moving the selection elsewhere.

Similarly, if a user edits a field in a Web form or a word on a Wiki page, it would be poor UI design for the entire page to refresh, possibly scrolled to a different position in the browser. Users would have to examine the page carefully for confirmation that what they edited was the only thing that changed.

This problem used to be common on the Web, but fortunately, the ascendancy of AJAX[5]-based Web UIs is reducing its frequency daily.

When large changes in the display are necessary (such as repaginating or swapping the positions of branches in a diagram), they should not be instantaneous. Rather, they should be announced clearly and carried out in ways that:

■ foster users' perception and comprehension of the changes and

■ minimize disruption to users' ability to continue working.

Basic Principle 8: Design for responsiveness

Over the past four decades, much evidence has accumulated suggesting that responsiveness—a software application's ability to keep up with users and not make them wait—is the *most* important factor in determining user satisfaction. Not just *one* of the most important factors—*the* most important factor. Study after study has found this [Miller, 1968; Thadhani, 1981; Barber and Lucas, 1983; Lambert, 1984; Shneiderman, 1984; Carroll and Rosson, 1984; Rushinek and Rushinek, 1986]. The findings of all these studies are well summarized by Peter Bickford in his book *Interface Design* [1997]:

> Many surveys have tried to determine what it is about a computer that makes its users happy. Time and time again, it turns out that the biggest factor in user satisfaction is not the computer's reliability, its compatibility with other platforms, the type of user interface it has, or even its price. What customers seem to want most is speed. When it comes to computers, users hate waiting more than they like anything else.

Bickford goes on to explain that by "speed," he means *perceived* speed, not actual speed:

> Computers actually have two kinds of speed: … real (machine) speed and … perceived speed. Of these two, the one that really matters is perceived speed. For instance, a 3-D rendering program that saves a few moments by not displaying the results until the image is complete will inevitably be seen as slower than a program that lets the user watch the image as it develops. The reason is that while the latter program's users are watching an image form, the first program's users are staring impatiently at the clock, noticing every long second tick by. Users will say that the first program ran slow simply because the wait was more painful.

---

5. Asynchronous Javascript and XML: an implementation technique enabling updates to small parts of Web pages.

Research also suggests that improving the responsiveness of software not only increases user satisfaction, it also can improve users' productivity [Brady, 1986] (Figure 1.10).

What is responsiveness?

Responsiveness is related to performance, but different. Interactive software can have high responsiveness despite low performance, and it can have low responsiveness despite high performance. Performance is measured in terms of computations per unit time. Responsiveness is measured in terms of compliance with human time requirements and, ultimately, user satisfaction.

Responsive software keeps up with users even if it can't fulfill their requests immediately. It provides feedback to let users know what they are doing and what it is doing and prioritizes the feedback based on *human* perceptual, motor, and cognitive deadlines.

Software that has poor responsiveness does not do these things. It doesn't keep up with users. It doesn't provide timely feedback for user actions, so users are unsure of what they have done or what it is doing. It makes users wait at unpredictable times and for unpredictable periods. It limits—sometimes severely—users' work pace. Here are some specific examples of poor responsiveness:

- Delayed feedback for button-presses, scrollbar movement, or object manipulations
- Time-consuming operations that block other activity and cannot be aborted
- Providing no clue as to how long lengthy operations will take

Figure 1.10

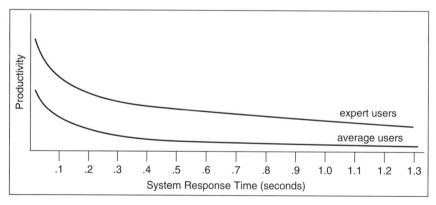

Effect of response time on user productivity [Brady, 1986].

- Jerky, hard-to-follow animations
- Ignoring user input while performing "housekeeping" tasks users did not request

These problems impede users' productivity and frustrate and annoy them. Unfortunately, despite all the research showing that responsiveness is critical to user satisfaction and productivity, a lot of software in today's marketplace has poor responsiveness.

Responsiveness on the Web: Poor but improving

The rise of the Web in the early 1990s was a great leap forward in communication and commerce, but a great leap *backward* in responsiveness. This was due partly to limited communication between Web browsers and servers. Basic HTML can update only entire pages at a time and is slow to do so, greatly limiting Webware's ability to provide timely feedback for user actions. For example, static Web forms can't check the validity of users' input as often as can forms in desktop applications, making it hard to provide timely error messages. Providing more subtle and immediate feedback requires Java or scripting-language code on the browser side, which can be costly to develop.

Poor responsiveness of Webware is also due partly to ignorance among Web designers and developers about the need for responsiveness and how to achieve it on the Web. In the late 1990s and early 2000s, exhorted by Web design gurus (e.g., Flanders and Willis [1998], Nielsen [1999d], King [2003]), many Web designers learned to improve the performance and responsiveness of their sites and applications using a variety of methods, which are described in Chapter 7 (Responsiveness Bloopers).

However, even with the recommended performance-enhancement methods, Webware until recently could not come close to the responsiveness and interactivity of desktop software applications or even that of most nineties-era client-server applications. This was highly unsatisfactory because the public Web is highly competitive. Users of desktop computer applications are somewhat "captive" because of the cost and effort of obtaining and installing applications. Users of intranet Web applications are fully "captive" because they have to use whatever their employer provides. In contrast, on the public Web, users are rarely captive. If they get frustrated with the responsiveness of an e-commerce Web site, they just hit Back and are gone, possibly to a competitor.

Enhancements in browser–server communication, along with programming techniques that exploit them (collectively referred to as Asynchronous Javascript and XML—AJAX), are closing the responsiveness gap between Web applications and desktop applications [Garrett, 2005]. However, until AJAX methods are refined and widely adopted, the gap will remain.

Designing for responsiveness

To be perceived by users as responsive, interactive software must:

- acknowledge user actions instantly, even if returning the answer will take time;
- let users know when it is busy and when it isn't;
- free users to do other things while waiting for a function to finish;
- animate movement smoothly and clearly;
- allow users to abort lengthy operations they don't want;
- allow users to judge how much time operations will take;
- do its best to let users set their own work pace.

For bloopers that hurt responsiveness, and principles and techniques for avoiding those bloopers, see Chapter 7.

Basic Principle 9: Try it out on users, then fix it!

Most people in the computer industry have heard the saying "Test early and often." Although there are many different kinds of testing to which computer software and hardware can be subjected, the kind that is relevant to this book is *usability* testing—trying a product or service out on people who are like the intended users to see what problems they have in learning and using it. Such testing is extremely important for determining whether a design is successful, that is, whether it helps users more than it hinders them.

Test results can surprise even experienced designers

Developers can learn surprising things from usability tests. Sometimes the results can surprise even user interface experts.

I usually review the UI of software products or services before testing them on users. Reviewing the UI beforehand gives me an idea of how to design the test, what sorts of problems to look for, and how to interpret the problems I see users having. However, conducting the test almost always exposes usability problems I hadn't anticipated.

For example, a company was developing software for analyzing the performance of server clusters. The software could plot the performance of a cluster of servers as a function of the number of simultaneous users. Users could specify the type of plot they wanted: bar, line, etc. A thumbnail image represented the currently selected type of plot. Surprisingly, usability tests showed that many users thought the small thumbnail images of plot types were the actual data plots! It is always useful to test; you never know what you will learn, but you *will* learn something that will help you improve your software.

Schedule time to correct problems found by tests

Of course, it isn't enough just to test the usability of a product or service. Developers must also provide time in the development schedule to correct problems uncovered by testing. Otherwise, why test?

Testing has two goals: Informational and social

Usability testing has two important but different goals: one informational, the other social.

Informational goal

The informational goal of usability testing is the one most people are familiar with: find aspects of the user interface that cause users difficulty, and use the exact nature of the problems to suggest improvements. This goal can be accomplished with a wide variety of testing and data-collection methods, some expensive and time consuming, some cheap and quick.

Social goal

The social goal of usability testing is at least as important as the informational goal. It is to convince developers that there are design problems that need correcting. Developers often resist suggestions for change, partly because of the time and effort required and partly because the need to improve a design suggests that whoever designed it did a poor job. To achieve testing's social goal, it is most effective to have developers watch usability tests, either live or on video.

Developers can become agitated while watching a user who is having trouble with the software (Figure 1.11). Therefore, when developers observe tests in person, it is important to explain to them the need to observe *passively*.

Emphasizing the social goal of usability testing has benefits beyond convincing developers to fix usability problems. It also makes developers more accepting of the idea that usability testing is an essential development tool rather than a way to evaluate GUI developers. Programmers who initially resist usability testing often become "converts" after witnessing a few (painful) tests. In later projects, they actively solicit usability tests as a way to get feedback.

Figure 1.11

Developer watching videotape of usability test.

There are tests for every time and purpose

Many people in the computer industry have the mistaken impression that usability testing is conducted when a software product or appliance is nearly ready to ship, using elaborate testing facilities and equipment. In fact, there are many ways to do usability tests, each having its benefits and drawbacks.

Usability tests can be categorized along two independent dimensions: (1) the point in development at which testing occurs and (2) the formality of the testing method (see Appendix E). Tests can be conducted before any code is written, when the software has been only partially implemented, or after the software is almost done. Testing methods can be informal, quasi-formal, or formal. Interviews, surveys, naturalistic observations, and field studies are "informal." Tests in which users perform prescribed tasks and in which both qualitative and quantitative data is collected are "quasi-formal." Studies measuring mainly quantitative data and requiring statistical analysis (often comparing different designs) are "formal." Any combination of implementation stage and formality is possible.

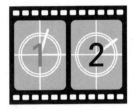

GUI Control Bloopers

Introduction

Most software applications and many Web sites are built using graphical user interface (GUI) development tools. Such tools provide a set of controls—also known as *widgets*—for building GUIs. The controls include text and number fields, checkboxes, radio buttons, sliders, menus, scrollbars, buttons, knobs, dials, meters, and various types of windows.

GUI tools are supposed to make it easier and faster for programmers to develop GUIs. However, the help they provide is limited by several flaws:

- *Too low level:* GUI toolkits provide low-level building blocks to allow maximum flexibility in what can be built. But that is misguided: it makes developing applications tedious, time consuming, and error prone. It makes common, ordinary UIs just as hard to implement as highly unusual ones; the common case suffers to allow for the rare case. Some toolkits are low level because the toolkit developers lacked the time, motivation, or skill to design high-level building blocks covering the desired range of GUIs.

- *Too unguided:* GUI toolkits allow programmers to build GUIs that violate design guidelines. They don't help guide programmers toward good designs. Most toolkits claim to support a GUI standard—such as Windows or MacOS—but make it just as easy to violate the standard as to adhere to it. They allow designers to make poor choices, like using the wrong control for a setting. A control may look nice, but that's a minor detail if it's the wrong control or behaves unexpectedly.

- *Too focused on appearance:* Most GUI tools require developers to spend too much time fiddling with the appearance and layout of their GUIs. Are the labels for settings aligned properly? Should a number be presented as a digital readout or a position on a dial? Should a choice be presented as radio buttons or a menu? What font should be used in a text field? These are mere presentation issues—the "low-order" bits of GUI design. The important issues are the *semantics* of the UI, such as whether a setting is a *date*, a *filename*, a *volume level*, or a choice between *fonts*. Decisions about presentation will change from day to day or even hour to hour as the design evolves and so should not require recoding. Changing the presentation of a choice from radio buttons to a dropdown menu should require changing only an attribute, not ripping out radio button code and replacing it with dropdown menu code. Time spent fiddling with presentation would be better spent learning about users, tasks, and work flow and planning appropriate functionality.

The primitiveness of most GUI tools is a problem because many GUIs are not designed by UI professionals. Rather, they are quickly assembled on tight deadlines by programmers who lack the UI expertise necessary to compensate for the lack of guidance from the toolkits.

The result is that many GUIs are full of design errors. Some errors are semantic and can be detected only by people who understand the application's target users and tasks. However, many GUI design errors would be easily detected by most UI professionals, even those unfamiliar with the users and tasks. Such errors are GUI control bloopers. They fall into two categories:

1. Using the wrong GUI control
2. Using a control incorrectly

GUI control bloopers harm usability. They also give customers an impression of a shoddy, unprofessional product, especially when a GUI has many of them. Fortunately, they are fairly easy for usability experts to spot. They are also concrete and relatively easy to explain. Finally, they are usually easy to correct unless they are due to limitations of the GUI tools used to build the software. This chapter describes the most common GUI control bloopers, with design rules for avoiding them.

Using the wrong control

The first category of GUI control bloopers concerns situations in which controls comprising the UI are not the right ones.

Blooper 1: Confusing checkboxes and radio buttons

All GUI toolkits provide controls for choosing one of several possible values, for example, *Text Font:* {*Times, Helvetica, Courier, New York*}. One such control is called "choice buttons" or "radio buttons." Radio buttons display options as an array of buttons. When users choose one by clicking on its button, it is highlighted. Only one option can be chosen at a time; clicking another option highlights it and deselects the previous one. These controls are called radio buttons because they are like the buttons on car radios that select one of several stations. On computers, radio buttons usually appear as a group of labeled round dots. One button is highlighted as the setting's current option.

Some GUI toolkits treat each individual radio button in a choice as a separate control, requiring programmers to "wire" them together so that choosing one deselects the previous selection. Other toolkits treat a set of radio buttons as one control, prewired to be mutually exclusive.

GUI toolkits also provide controls for simple On/Off, True/False, or Yes/No settings, for example, *Automatic spell-checking:* {*OFF, ON*}. The most common of these is a "checkbox": a box that is empty when OFF and contains a checkmark or X when ON. Clicking a checkbox toggles it between ON and OFF. Each checkbox is a separate control. Checkboxes can be grouped, but each checkbox should be independent of the others.

Figure 2.1

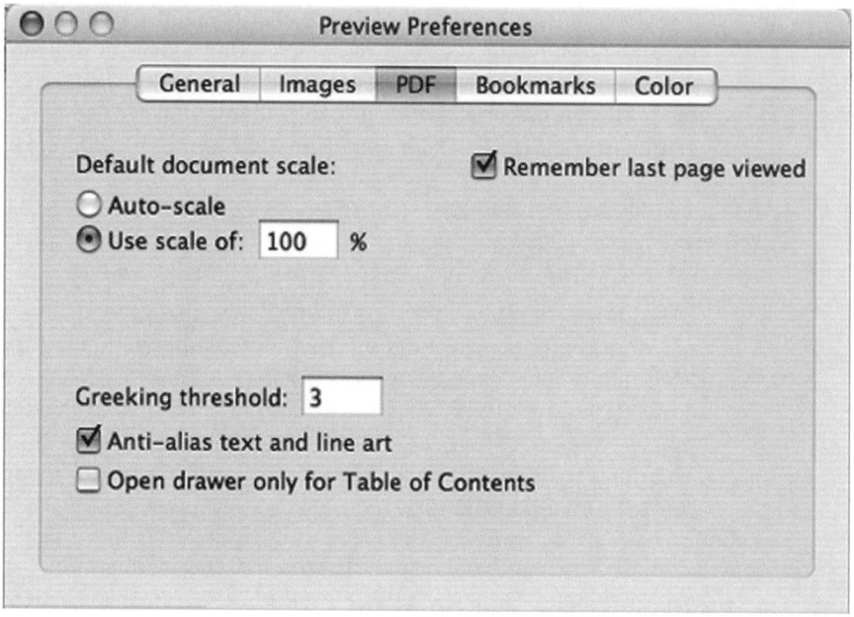

Apple Preview Preferences window: radio buttons and checkboxes.

An example of both radio buttons and checkboxes is provided by the Preferences window of Apple's Preview software (Figure 2.1).

A common blooper is to confuse checkboxes and radio buttons. Some GUI toolkits treat checkboxes and radio buttons as variants of a single control type— *toggle button*—based on their somewhat similar appearance. The toggle button control is turned into a radio button or a checkbox by setting attributes. If you forget to set the attribute or set it incorrectly, the GUI will have the wrong control. However, programmers confuse radio buttons and checkboxes even when their toolkits treat them as distinct. Whatever the reasons, confusion between radio buttons and checkboxes manifests itself in three different ways.

Variation A: Single radio button

The most common variation of this blooper is a lone radio button—a radio button misused as a checkbox. An example comes from the online form for registering for courses at Forrester Research (Figure 2.2).

The "lone radio button" error occurs for four different reasons:

1. An inexperienced programmer doesn't know the difference between radio buttons and checkboxes.
2. The GUI toolkit provides a generic toggle button and the programmer sets its attributes incorrectly.

Figure 2.2

Gigaweb.com/events/register: Forrester Research course registration page has one radio button. Also, the indicated cost is incorrect.

3. Some options in a set of radio buttons are eliminated due to a change in functional requirements. Only one option remains, but no one redesigns the UI to reflect that.

4. The number of options in the choice varies depending on circumstances. The software does not treat the "one option" case as special.

Online travel agency Travelocity.com exhibits Reason 4. If customers book a flight too near the departure date to allow confirmation to be mailed to them, Travelocity offers only one ticketing option, electronic, but still presents it as a "choice" of one option (Figure 2.3).

Whatever the reason, a single radio button is a design blooper.

Variation B: Checkboxes as radio buttons

Using checkboxes where radio buttons should be used is almost as common.

Long Island University's online application form used to have checkboxes where it should have had radio buttons. Applicants could apply for multiple school terms simultaneously and answer both "Yes" and "No" to questions (Figure 2.4).

Figure 2.3

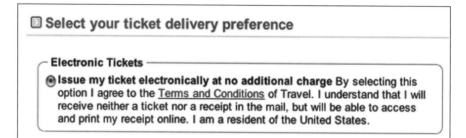

Travelocity.com: when only one option is available, it is presented as a "choice" of one.

Figure 2.4

For which term are you applying?

☑ Fall ☑ Spring ☑ Summer [   ] Year

Do you wish dormitory accommodations? ☑ YES ☑ NO

Have you previously attended or applied to The Brooklyn Campus of L.I.U.? If yes, when?

[   ]

Do you intend to apply for financial aid?
☑ YES ☑ NO

Are you a veteran of the United States Armed Forces?
☑ YES ☑ NO

LIU.edu: checkboxes misused as radio buttons.

Figure 2.5

24. Does your employer provide matching gifts to double employee donations to environmental or educational organizations?

Y	N	Don't know
☑	☑	☑

Earthwatch.org and SurveyMonkey.com: checkboxes misused as radio buttons.

More recently, Earthwatch.org sent a SurveyMonkey.com survey to its members in which one question wrongly used checkboxes instead of radio buttons (Figure 2.5). Someone at Earthwatch, in developing the survey using SurveyMonkey's tools, chose the wrong control for this question.

The main reason for this variation of the blooper is ignorance: the developers did not know the difference between checkboxes and radio buttons or how to display radio buttons.

Variation C: Mutually exclusive checkboxes

A third variation of this blooper is "wiring" checkboxes together so only one can be ON at a time, making them behave like radio buttons (Figure 2.6).

Figure 2.6

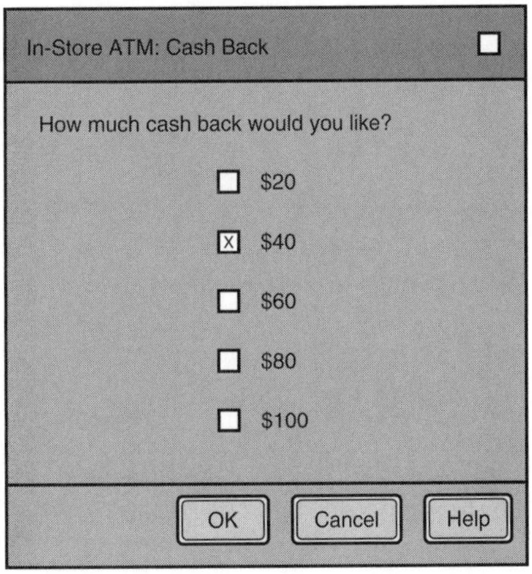

Blooper: mutually exclusive checkboxes.

This error can occur when a GUI toolkit treats radio buttons and checkboxes as variants of a generic toggle button control. The default appearance is usually a checkbox. A programmer may wire the buttons together to be mutually exclusive, but forget to set the attribute to make them appear as radio buttons.

The error can also occur if a programmer changes independent ON/OFF settings to be mutually exclusive to accommodate a change in the software's functional requirements, but neglects to change the checkboxes into radio buttons. This is more likely with toolkits that treat radio buttons and checkboxes as *different* controls.

Developers may also commit this error because of implementation constraints. A medical chart application might be able to show eight categories of patient data, but only one category at a time fits on its small screen. A developer might present this as eight "show/hide" checkboxes—one for each data category. With a larger screen, the checkboxes could be independent, but with the small screen, they might be "wired" so only one could be ON at a time.

In the font controls of Microsoft Word and PowerPoint (for MacOS X) some checkboxes behave normally, while others behave like radio buttons. The Superscript and Subscript checkboxes are actually one setting: checking one unchecks the other (Figure 2.7). In Word, the Small caps and All caps checkboxes are also not independent.

There are two possible reasons for these designs:

1. The designers may have placed more importance on appearance than on usability and functional correctness. The panel *looks* better when all the settings are checkboxes than it would if the panel had both radio buttons and

Figure 2.7

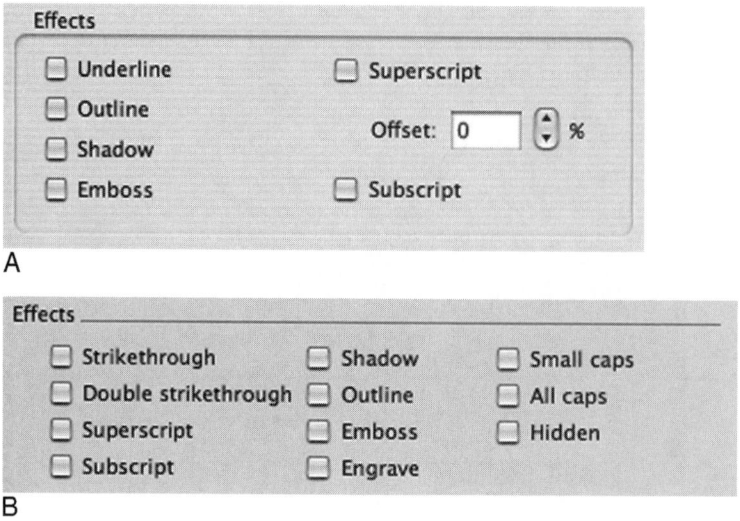

A

B

Some checkbox pairs are not independent. (A) PowerPoint. (B) Word.

checkboxes. This is a poor reason: user-interface clarity is more important than some simplistic notion of aesthetics. How well a UI conveys its function to users is part of its aesthetic merit.

2. The Small caps/All caps setting really has three options: small caps, all caps, and *neither*. This could be represented by two radio buttons, both initially OFF, but that would not allow users to return to "neither." Representing the three options correctly requires *three* radio buttons. The designers may have used two checkboxes to avoid having three radio buttons. The same is true for the Superscript/Subscript checkboxes. The problem with this reasoning is that two checkboxes don't accurately represent three options either. Users expect checkboxes to be independent, so a pair of checkboxes represents *four* options, the fourth being "both." Therefore, using checkboxes to avoid an awkward set of radio buttons is simply replacing one GUI design problem with another. Furthermore, nonindependent checkboxes is a *worse* blooper than radio buttons that have no default value.

Whatever the reason, "wiring" checkboxes together into mutually exclusive groups is wrong.

Avoiding Blooper 1

Checkboxes and radio buttons are suited to different types of settings.

Radio buttons

Radio buttons are for presenting one-from-*N* choices. They are best suited when two conditions hold:

1. The number of options is fixed and small: between two and eight.[1]
2. Enough space is available on the panel to display all of the options.

Radio buttons always occur in sets of at least two; a single radio button is not a valid control.

Long Island University recently revised their online application form. Along with other changes, they replaced the erroneous checkboxes with radio buttons (Figure 2.8).

Figure 2.8

Avoiding the blooper: LIU.edu online application, corrected to use radio buttons.

Other choice controls

Radio buttons require a lot of space because all their options are displayed. Most GUI and Web toolkits also provide choice controls that require less space. Which one is best depends on the number of options.

▪ *Dropdown menus:* also called "option" menus. They display their value and present a menu of possible values when clicked ON (Figure 2.9). Dropdown menus are distinct from "pulldown" menus, which are menus consisting mainly of *commands* accessed from a menubar. Dropdown menus are best suited when space is limited and the number of options either is greater than eight or changes at runtime.

Figure 2.9

Dropdown menus. (A) Microsoft Windows Vista. (B) MacOS X.

---

1. Although, in special cases, carefully designed arrays of radio buttons can be used to present more choices.

■ *Scrolling list boxes:* These display a list of options and allow users to select one or more (Figure 2.10). Like radio buttons, scrolling list boxes consume significant space, but their scrollability allows more options than can comfortably be presented with radio buttons. Like dropdown menus, scrolling list boxes are useful when the list of options can change.

Figure 2.10

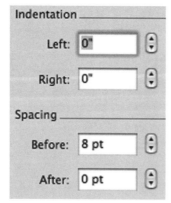

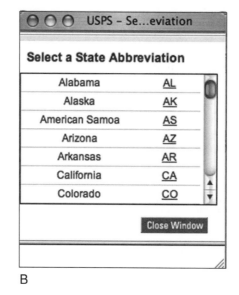

A   B

Scrolling list box. (A) Microsoft Word, font sizes. (B) USPS.gov, state chooser.

■ *Spin boxes:* also known as "cycle buttons." They display the current option and switch to the next option when clicked ON (Figure 2.11). Cycle buttons are suited to presenting choices in limited space with few options

Figure 2.11

Microsoft Word: cycle buttons, a.k.a. "spin boxes," in the Paragraph Format dialog box.

Checkboxes

Checkboxes represent ON/OFF settings (Figure 2.12A). They should be independent of each other. Checkboxes *can* be grouped to present related ON/OFF settings (Figure 2.12B).

Occasionally checkboxes are used in groups to present controls for selecting a limited subset of the available options (Figure 2.13). Such cases present a dilemma: checkboxes are supposed to be independent, yet the group of checkboxes has to limit the number of selected options.

Two solutions have been found in usability tests to work, with the first being preferable:

- Refuse to turn options ON when that would exceed the group maximum. Notify users by beeping, displaying an error message, or both.
- Allow users to turn any number of items ON, and inform them *later* that the number of selected options exceeds the maximum. For example, display an error message when the user clicks OK or Apply on the enclosing dialog box.

An approach that definitely does *not* work is to uncheck an already checked option when a user selects one that would exceed the maximum. Among other things, users would wonder: "Why did it turn *that* one OFF instead of another one?"

Figure 2.12

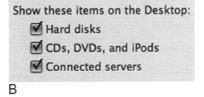

Good checkboxes. (A) Apple Preview Print dialog. (B) MacOS X Preferences.

Figure 2.13

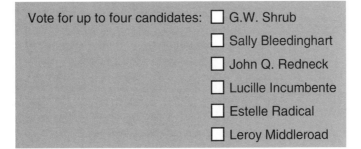

Group of related checkboxes of which a limited number can be checked.

Advice for choosing GUI toolkits

When choosing a GUI toolkit, developers should look for ones that:

- treat checkboxes and radio buttons as distinct control types;
- treat a group of radio buttons representing a choice as a single control;
- treat radio button sets, dropdown menus, and scrolling lists as different presentations of a single one-from-*N* choice control type [Johnson, 1992] (Blooper 69, page 365).

Blooper 2: Using a checkbox for a non-ON/OFF setting

Checkboxes are sometimes used to display a choice between two options that aren't clear opposites. Assume a color setting has two possible values: red and green. Some developers might present this as a checkbox because it is easy and saves space (Figure 2.14). The problem is that users can't tell what *unchecking* the box would mean.

A programmer at one of my client companies committed a more subtle version of this blooper. The application he was developing had a command toolbar. The program could display its toolbar horizontally under the menubar or vertically along the left edge of the window. He presented the choice using a checkbox (Figure 2.15). By default, the program displayed a horizontal toolbar, so the checkbox was checked. The programmer assumed that users would realize that unchecking it would display the toolbar vertically. The programmer *knew* what the options were, but users might *not* know and could easily assume that unchecking the checkbox would *hide* the toolbar. They might learn eventually what unchecking the box did, but users should not have to Figure out how software works by a process of elimination (Basic Principle 5, page 35).

Figure 2.14

Color: ☒ Red

Blooper: checkbox for choice of two nonopposite values.

Figure 2.15

☒ Horizontal Toolbar

Blooper: checkbox for choice of two nonopposite values.

More or less the same blooper occurs in Sybase's PowerBuilder, an interactive GUI-building tool (Fig 2.16). Ironically, PowerBuilder's misuse of a checkbox occurs in a panel for setting the properties of radio buttons in a GUI.

Most of the checkboxes in this panel are OK. It is clear what the opposite of "Visible" is. However, the one labeled "LeftText" should not be a checkbox because it isn't obvious what the *opposite* is—it could be "LeftGraphics." This checkbox is ambiguous even when users know that it controls the placement of the label on a radio button. If "LeftText" is checked, the radio button's label will be on the left, but what does *unchecking* it do? PowerBuilder users have to know that PowerBuilder positions labels only on the left or right of radio buttons.

An even more confusing example of a misused checkbox comes from an application I reviewed. The label names *both* options (Figure 2.17). You can't tell which option is selected when you uncheck *or* check the box.

Figure 2.16

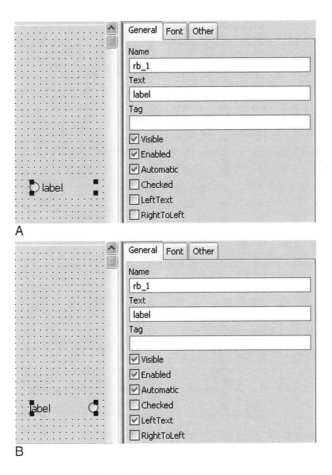

Sybase Powerbuilder: "LeftText" checkbox not clear opposite. (A) Unchecked. (B) Checked.

Figure 2.17

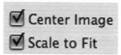

Blooper: checkbox for choice of two nonopposite values.

Avoiding Blooper 2

Checkboxes are unsuitable for settings that have two nonopposite values. Use them only for binary settings for which the two values are natural, obvious opposites, such as On/Off, True/False, Color/B&W, or Present/Absent. That way, one label labels the entire setting, labels the ON value, and makes clear what the *opposite* value is.

Examples

Correct uses of checkboxes can be seen in Apple Preview's Print dialog box (Figure 2.18). It is clear what the opposite of each one is: *"Don't* center image" and *"Don't* scale to fit."

If a two-valued setting does not fit the criteria for being presented as a checkbox, it should be presented as radio buttons or a dropdown menu, so users can see both values. The toolbar orientation setting in Figure 2.15 should have been two radio buttons. Adobe Photoshop does exactly that in its New Guide dialog box: users choose whether a guiding line to be overlaid on an image is horizontal or vertical (Figure 2.19).

Figure 2.18

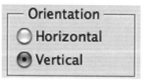

Apple Preview Print dialog box: checkboxes with clear opposites.

Figure 2.19

Photoshop: two-valued choice presented as radio buttons, so both values are visible.

PowerBuilder's confusing "LeftText" checkbox

The PowerBuilder checkbox setting in Figure 2.16 would be clearer if it were either a pair of radio buttons or a dropdown menu (Figure 2.20).

Figure 2.20

PowerBuilder's "LeftText" setting (Figure 2.16) should be radio buttons or a dropdown menu.

Blooper 3: Using command buttons as toggles

Most GUI toolkits provide a command button control (also called *action buttons*). Command buttons invoke an action or trigger an event.

Command buttons are sometimes misused as toggle controls. Pushing the button once toggles something ON or switches to an alternate mode; pushing it again toggles something OFF or returns to the original mode. Command button toggles are bad UI design: they mislead users. Users can't predict by looking at them how they'll behave; they have to try them (Figure 2.21).

Command buttons serving as toggles usually don't show their current state. A developer may think the control need not show its state if the state is shown elsewhere in the UI, e.g., the button is "Show Medical History" and the medical history is either shown or not.

Consider a toolbar from the main window of the music accompaniment program Band in a Box (Figure 2.22). Most of the buttons on this toolbar initiate commands, but the "Lyrics" button toggles between displaying or hiding a field for the user to type lyrics into, and the "Notation" button toggles between displaying a tune as music notes or as a chord chart. Neither of these two button labels changes when toggled.

These buttons look like commands, but are toggles. Their behavior is unexpected and so is an arbitrary fact about Band in a Box that users must learn.

You may agree that command button toggles with static labels are bad, but feel that command button toggles are OK when their labels change to indicate their state. For example, a button labeled "Show Data" could change to "Hide

Figure 2.21

Blooper: command buttons misused as toggles (ON/OFF switches).

Figure 2.22

Band in a Box: "Lyrics" and "Notation" buttons are command buttons misused as toggles.

Figure 2.23

| Print... | Next Page | Prev Page | Two Page | Zoom In | Zoom Out | Close |

Kodak Picture Disk: "Two Page" button is a toggle. Clicking changes label to "One Page."

Data" after being pushed. This doesn't help. Many users won't notice the label change. More importantly, switching the label forces users to Figure out if the label shows the *current* state or the state that will result when the button is pushed. For example, in a nuclear power plant, if a command button toggle reads "Fuel rods IN," are the fuel rods in, or will clicking the button *put* the fuel rods in? If the fuel rods aren't visible from the control room, user confusion about the meaning of the button label is very likely and could cause a disaster.

The Print Preview window of Kodak's Picture Disk has a command button toggle that changes its label (Figure 2.23). In the window's toolbar, most of the buttons invoke commands, but the "Two Page" button toggles the display between showing one page (photo) at a time and showing two pages side by side. The button label shows what mode it will *change* to when clicked. When Print Preview is showing one page, the button is labeled "Two Page"; when Print Preview is showing two pages, the button is labeled "One Page." Clear? A pair of radio buttons would make the setting much clearer.

The more primitive the GUI toolkit being used, the more limited the selection of built-in control types. This puts more pressure on programmers to use the command button for all types of controls, which, in turn, makes misusing them more likely.

Avoiding Blooper 3

Command button controls in GUI toolkits are for invoking commands or initiating events. They appear pressed only briefly, but revert to an unpressed appearance. They have no persistent state (Figure 2.24).

ON/OFF settings should be presented using checkboxes or other types of toggle controls. Some GUI toolkits provide special-purpose toggle controls (Figure 2.25), such as Expand/Contract switches for opening and closing auxiliary data panels or rocker switches that look like physical light switches. Some toolkits let developers define variants of built-in controls that retain the behavior of the control but have a different appearance. This can be used to create special-purpose toggle buttons.

Figure 2.24

| Print... | Paste | Compile |

Command buttons.

Figure 2.25

 changes to

Specialized toggle buttons.

Blooper 4: Using tabs as radio buttons

Many GUI toolkits provide a tabbed panel control (also called tabbed pane or notebook) for cases in which a GUI has more settings or data displays than can be shown at once. Tabbed panels simulate tabbed cards such as those in a recipe box. They consist of superimposed panels, displayed one at a time, with labeled tabs along one edge corresponding to the panels. When a user clicks on a tab, the corresponding panel comes to the "front" of the stack. Tabbed panels are a way to organize a lot of information and controls into a relatively compact space.

The blooper

Tabs are often misused as radio buttons: to present choices that affect what the application will *do,* rather than just to choose which panel is displayed.

For example, suppose you were designing a dialog box for a document editor's Save As function (Figure 2.26). The Save As dialog box prompts users for a destination file name and other parameters and, when the user clicks OK, saves the

Figure 2.26

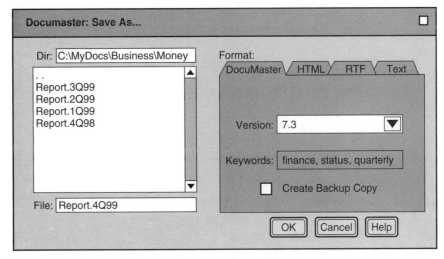

Blooper: tabs misused as a value setting, rather than just for navigation.

document. This dialog box lets users choose a format for saving the document: the document editor's own format, HTML, Rich Text Format, or plain text. You might design the Save As dialog box to display a set of tabbed panels—one for each available data format. You might expect users to click the tab for the desired format, set that panel's format-specific settings, and then click the "OK" button.

The problem is that this design violates users' expectation that tabs are just for switching between panels. In this dialog box, the format used to save the document depends on whichever tab panel happens to be "in front" when the user clicks OK. Most users would be confused and annoyed by this. Some might click on a tab, look at the settings there and set some, then click on another tab, look at the settings there, decide not to do anything on that tab panel, then click OK, and be dismayed when the program uses the file format corresponding to the last tab panel viewed. Users would also be annoyed that data they entered on one of the tab panels was ignored simply because that panel was not in front when they clicked OK.

A common excuse

A common excuse for using tabs as settings is that other choice controls, such as radio buttons and dropdown menus, are used for both navigation and data settings. These are cases in which changing a radio button or dropdown menu's value causes other settings to appear or disappear (Figure 2.27). According to this excuse, tabs are just another choice setting.

Yes, radio buttons and dropdown menus sometimes control the presence or absence of other settings. Yes, tabs are a kind of choice setting. However, using tabs for more than navigation violates users' expectations, and it is *those* expectations that matter. Users don't like it when changing tabs changes data or affects the application's behavior. They don't like it when the settings on a tab panel go into effect just because they switched to another panel. Users' expectations about radio buttons and menus are more flexible than their expectations about tabbed panels.

Navigation vs. progressive disclosure

Radio buttons or menus that affect the visibility of other settings are not mainly navigatory. They are instances of the well-established UI design principle of

Figure 2.27

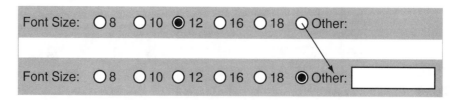

The "Other" text field appears only when radio buttons are set to "Other."

"progressive disclosure": hiding detail until it is relevant (Basic Principle 3, page 26).

For example, consider a dialog box for setting text font properties. Font size could be set with radio buttons or a dropdown menu. The choices might include "Other" with a text field so users can specify unlisted font sizes. That text field could be hidden until the font size choice is set to "Other." This font size setting is not for navigation; it is an application setting. It has the *side effect* of changing the visibility of the "Other" text field.

Avoiding Blooper 4

Tabs are purely *navigation* controls. They affect where the user is in the application: which settings are visible. They are not supposed to *be* settings. Choosing one panel of a set of tabbed panels to display should not affect the application's data or have consequences for its subsequent behavior. Correct use of tabbed panels is shown in the Mouse Properties dialog box of Microsoft Windows (Figure 2.28).

The Save As ... dialog box discussed earlier (Figure 2.26) would make more sense to users if the tabs were replaced by a dropdown menu or radio buttons, with a labeled group box to display the format-specific settings (Figure 2.29).Users would then be much more likely to interpret the Format choice as an application setting determining how the file is saved.

Figure 2.28

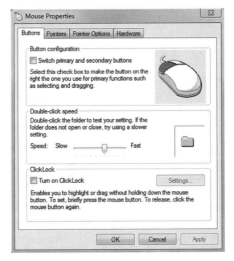

Microsoft Windows Vista Mouse Properties: tabs used for navigation only.

Figure 2.29

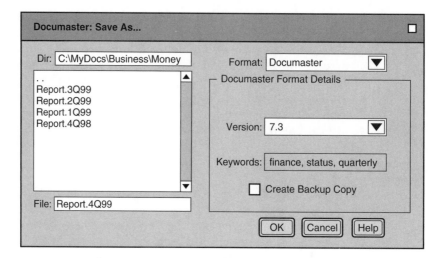

Menu used for navigating between different groups of settings.

Blooper 5: Too many tabs

An important purpose of tabbed panels is to save space by overlaying different control or information panels so they share the same screen real estate. Tabbed panels provide a user interface for this that capitalizes on users' familiarity with tabbed sheets, notebooks, and folders.

However, tabs themselves require significant space. It doesn't take many tabs before the available space along one edge (usually the top) of a stack of panels is full. Bloopers occur when tabs are "scaled" beyond that limit. There is no good solution, even though many have been tried.

Variation A: Wagging the dog

One false solution is to widen the panel to allow more tabs. But each tabbed panel has only a certain amount of controls or data to display, so widening the panel space can result in wasted space on many of the panels in the set (Figure 2.30). If you do that, you've crossed the line from using tabs to save space to wasting space to use tabs. The tail is wagging the dog.

Variation B: Tabs to the left of us, tabs to the right of us, tabs all around us!

A second false solution is to put tabs on more than one edge, e.g., down the left or right side of the panel. And why stop there? Why not run 'em across the bottom, too (Figure 2.31)! People never see this in the physical world, but who cares? This is a computer screen; we can do whatever we want, right?

Figure 2.30

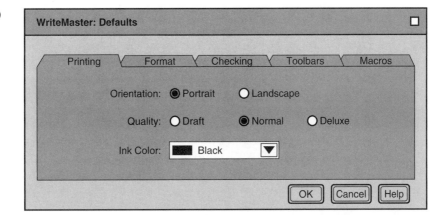

Too many tabs make each panel wider than its content requires, wasting space.

Figure 2.31

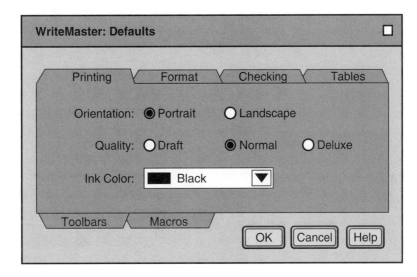

Too many tabs, so tabs are placed both above and below the tabbed panel.

The problem is that users perceive such a panel as a hierarchy, with the tabs across the top as main categories and those across the bottom or side as subcategories. They will. Try it. In addition to that usability problem, displaying tabs on several edges of the panel looks awful.

Variation C: Shrt lbls

Some designers decrease the width of each tab by abbreviating the tab labels, for example, using "PS" instead of "Postscript" (Figure 2.32). This sacrifices

Figure 2.32

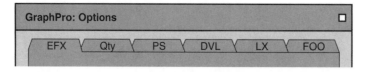

Too many tabs, so tab labels are abbreviated; users must learn what they mean.

clarity to achieve narrower tabs and so is another case of the tail wagging the dog. It also may not work in all languages.

Another way to narrow tabs is to break their labels into two lines (Figure 2.33). This is not so bad, but some GUI toolkits support only one-line tab labels. This approach also works only when labels have more than one word; breaking words into two lines makes them hard to read. It also may not work in all languages. Finally, a mix of one-line and two-line labels looks bad.

Variation D: Dancing tabs

The most popular false solution is to display multiple rows of tabs. It's as if the user were looking down at a file drawer of tabbed manila folders, seeing the tabbed tops of all the folders from the front to the back of the drawer. It's a nice idea, but it has a serious flaw.

When tabs are in multiple rows, selecting a tab from any row other than the first row not only displays its panel but also usually shifts that tab's row so it is now the *first* tab row. If you click on a tab in the second row, that row instantly moves—right out from under your pointer—to the first row. Meanwhile, the row of tabs that was first either swaps with the row you clicked on or shifts to the back row.

Microsoft Windows Media Player's Options window has two rows of tabs. When the Rip Music tab is displayed, the Privacy tab is in the back row (Figure 2.34A). Clicking on the Privacy tab brings its row to the front, moving the other row to the back (Figure 2.34B).

This briefly disorients users. They click on a tab and it seems to vanish. Consciously, they know what happened, but their unconscious mind is briefly

Figure 2.33

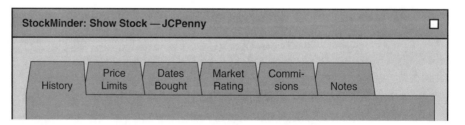

Too many tabs, so some tab labels are made using two lines.

Figure 2.34

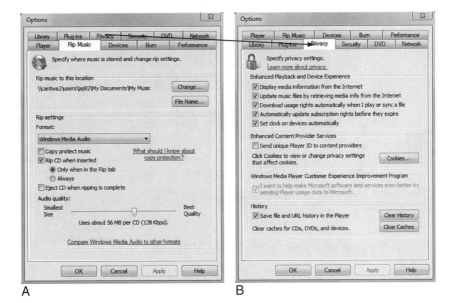

A   B

Windows Media Player: dancing tabs. Clicking Privacy tab swaps the two tab rows.

disoriented and their eyes flit involuntarily around. After a half-second, their conscious mind kicks in and they find the tab again.

Users do not get over this brief disorientation caused by dancing tabs. Their previous and continuing experience with single rows of tabs (as well as with tabs in the physical world) supports their expectation that tabs stay put when selected. There is no question: people *do not like* multiple rows of tabs.

If dancing tabs disorients users, it might seem that you could fix that by simply not moving a selected tab's row to the front. However, then the tabs wouldn't look connected to the displayed panel, making it hard for users to see which tab is selected.

Avoiding Blooper 5

To avoid this blooper, follow these rules of thumb.

Keep the number of tabs small

If you have so many panels that their tabs won't fit into a single row, the real problem is that you have too many panels. Reorganize them into fewer panels, requiring fewer tabs.

The WestCiv.com Web site uses tabbed panels. The large amount of information available at the site has been organized into a manageable number of tabbed panels (Figure 2.35).

Figure 2.35

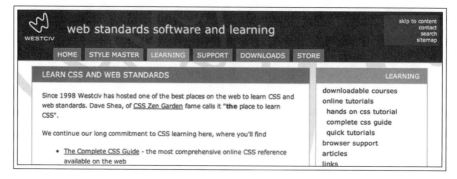

WestCiv.com: one row of tabs.

Use another control instead of tabs

Another way to avoid too many tabs is not to use tabs. Use radio buttons, dropdown menus, or scrolling lists for switching between alternative displayed panels.

In 1999 Amazon.com categorized all of its products into one row of tabs (Figure 2.36), but eventually the number of categories grew too large for tabs to be a good way to present them.

By late 2006, Amazon had 35 product categories, too many to present comfortably as tabs. Instead, their home page has three tabs, one of which reads "See All 35 Product Categories" (Figure 2.37). When the pointer is over this tab, a pop-up window appears with links for all the categories. Clicking on the tab takes users to a page displaying all the categories.

In late 2003, the many functions of NetScanTools 8.0, a network administration product, were organized into a monstrous array of dancing tabs (Figure 2.38A). Three years later, version 10.0 presented its functions as a much more sensible scrolling list (Figure 2.38B).

Figure 2.36

Amazon.com (1999): site's many products organized into eight categories, shown as tabs.

Figure 2.37

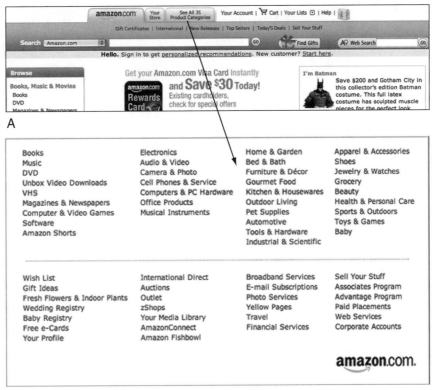

A

B

Amazon.com (2006). (A) 35 categories—too many for tabs. (B) Categories in pop-up, not tabs.

Widen panel slightly

If a set of tabs is just a *little* too wide to fit in one row across the available space, you can widen the entire panel, at the cost of wasting some of the space that tabs are intended to save. This approach should be used only as a last resort for the reasons described under Variation A (above) and then only if the extra horizontal space required is very small.

Never use dancing tabs

Multiple rows of tabs, with their unavoidable shifting tab rows, should never be used. They violate two separate long-standing GUI design principles: (1) the screen belongs to the *user* and (2) preserve screen inertia (Basic Principle 7, page 41, and Blooper 49, page 277).

Figure 2.38

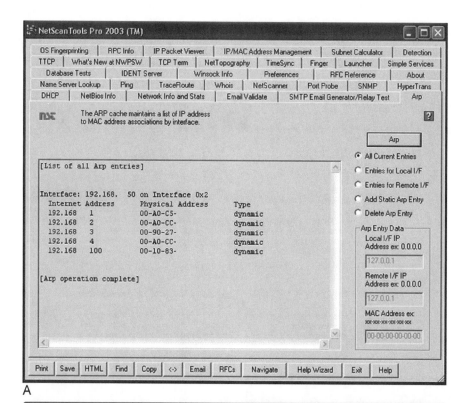

A

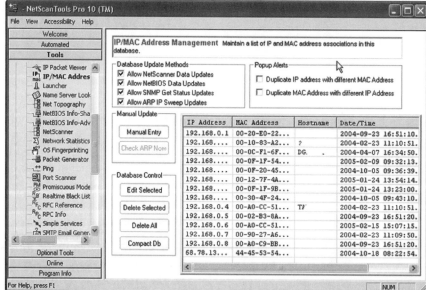

B

NetScanTools. (A) Version 8 (2003), organized by tabs. (B) Version 10 (2006), organized by scrolling list.

Blooper 6: Using input controls for display-only data

A blooper that has become common in recent years is using input controls—checkboxes, radio buttons, text fields, etc.—to present data users cannot change. This refers to controls that are *never* editable, *not* to ones that are temporarily inactive (grayed).

The auction site uBid.com's "Email Us" form commits the blooper twice (Figure 2.39). First, it uses checkboxes to mark "Required" fields. Users can't

Figure 2.39

Email Us

Emailing uBid is a quick and easy way to receive a prompt response to your inquiry. Simply below and click the "submit" button.

1. Select your Subject:

    Bidding/Account
    Shipping/Order Problems
    Website Questions
    General
    Product Problems
    Billing Inquiries
    Feedback

Then, select a Request:

    Feedback

2. Please provide your information: Required

First Name:		☑
Last Name:		☑
Email Address:		☑
Email Address (twice for verification):		☑
Login:		☐
Order Number:		☐
Lot Number:		☐
Service Request/Coupon Number:		☐

Special Instructions:

> We would like to hear the things that aren't working or need improvement, and the things that you really enjoy. If you are making suggestions or comments that do not require a response, you may not receive a reply (though we try our best to get back to

3. Enter your message in the box below:

uBid.com: input controls misused to display noneditable data. Checkboxes mark required fields. "Special Instructions" text area displays noneditable instructions.

change these checkboxes; they are only indicators. Farther down the form is a text box labeled "Special Instructions." These are instructions for filling out the form. They are in a text-entry box like the one below it, but are not editable.

Part of the problem is that some GUI toolkits allow controls to be set to "noneditable." This encourages developers to misuse editable-looking controls to display noneditable data.

Noneditable text fields

Text fields are the input controls most commonly misused for presenting noneditable data. An example occurs in Microsoft Windows' Regional and Language preferences window. The "Samples" text fields show the data formats for the language and region currently shown in the menu (Figure 2.40).

Reasons for the blooper

GUI developers typically commit this blooper for one of several different reasons:

Figure 2.40

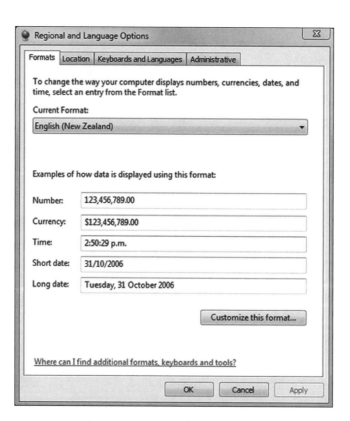

Microsoft Windows' Regional and Language Options has text fields that are not editable.

1. *Setting editability but not appearance.* Input controls in most GUI toolkits have an attribute that controls their editability. Unfortunately, many toolkits do not automatically change the appearance of noneditable controls: they continue to look editable unless programmers explicitly set appearance attributes, such as border visibility or interior background color. Predictably, programmers often set a control to noneditable and don't change its appearance attributes. The result is this blooper.

2. *The GUI toolkit let me do it, so it must be OK.* Many programmers don't know the guidelines (because they haven't seen any) and assume that if a GUI toolkit lets them do something, it must be OK. Bad assumption!

3. *But I made it inactive.* Most GUI toolkits allow controls to be set to *inactive:* they don't respond to user actions until they are again set to *active.* Inactive controls look grayed-out. However, *noneditable data* is different from *inactive input control* and should look different. When GUI toolkits do provide both an active/inactive attribute and an editability attribute on controls, some programmers don't know which one to use and use the wrong one.

4. *Labels are only for labels, right?* The fourth reason comes from misleading control names. Most GUI toolkits have a control for displaying noneditable text on a panel. Alas, many toolkits call this a "label." This suggests that the control should be used only for text that labels something. That, in turn, suggests that text that *doesn't* function as a label, such as read-only data, should be displayed using *another* control. The only other candidate for displaying text is a noneditable text field. Hence, the blooper. In some GUI toolkits, noneditable text controls have better names: "text item," "static text," or "text."

5. *It has to look the same as the editable screen.* Applications may display the same data in several places, but it is editable in only *some* places. In such cases, developers sometimes display all of the values as text fields for "consistency." This is consistency from a developer's point of view. To users it is *in*consistent.

6. *It **is** user-editable—just not directly.* Perhaps users *can* edit the data, but only by bringing up an Edit window, not by clicking and typing in the field itself. National Geographic Trip Planner provides an example (Figure 2.41).

Figure 2.41

National Geographic Trip Planner: trip Origin and Destination fields look like directly editable text, but are only indirectly editable via "Select a City..." buttons and dialog boxes.

7. *The data varies.* The final reason for noneditable data in editable-looking controls is that the data in the controls varies. The uBid.com "Email Us" page is used for several purposes: requesting Customer Support, reporting Web site problems, etc. The required fields and special instructions vary between different uses of the form. Because of this, the designers of this page probably felt it was OK to use non-user-editable checkboxes for marking required fields and a non-user-editable text area for containing the special instructions. Wrong! Just because the data varies does not excuse the use of controls that mislead users.

Avoiding Blooper 6

Noneditable data should never be displayed in a control that looks editable or operable.

Checkboxes, radio buttons, menus, sliders, and the like should never be used for noneditable data because they look operable. Even if they are inactive (grayed), they look like they can somehow be made active, and users will waste time trying to do so.

Avoid noneditable text fields unless they can be displayed without a border, like a label (Figure 2.42). Users don't distinguish bordered noneditable text fields from temporarily deactivated ones. When textual data is display-only, it should be displayed using a text (label) control.

Figure 2.42

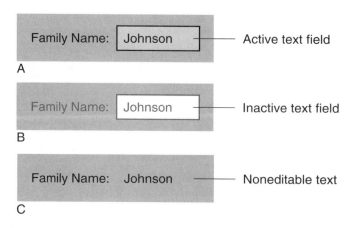

Active, inactive, and noneditable text fields.

Some examples of avoiding the blooper

A bit of image editing shows how uBid.com (Figure 2.43A) and the Windows' Regional and Language Options window (Figure 2.43B) would look if they used static text controls rather than noneditable radio buttons and text fields.

Figure 2.43

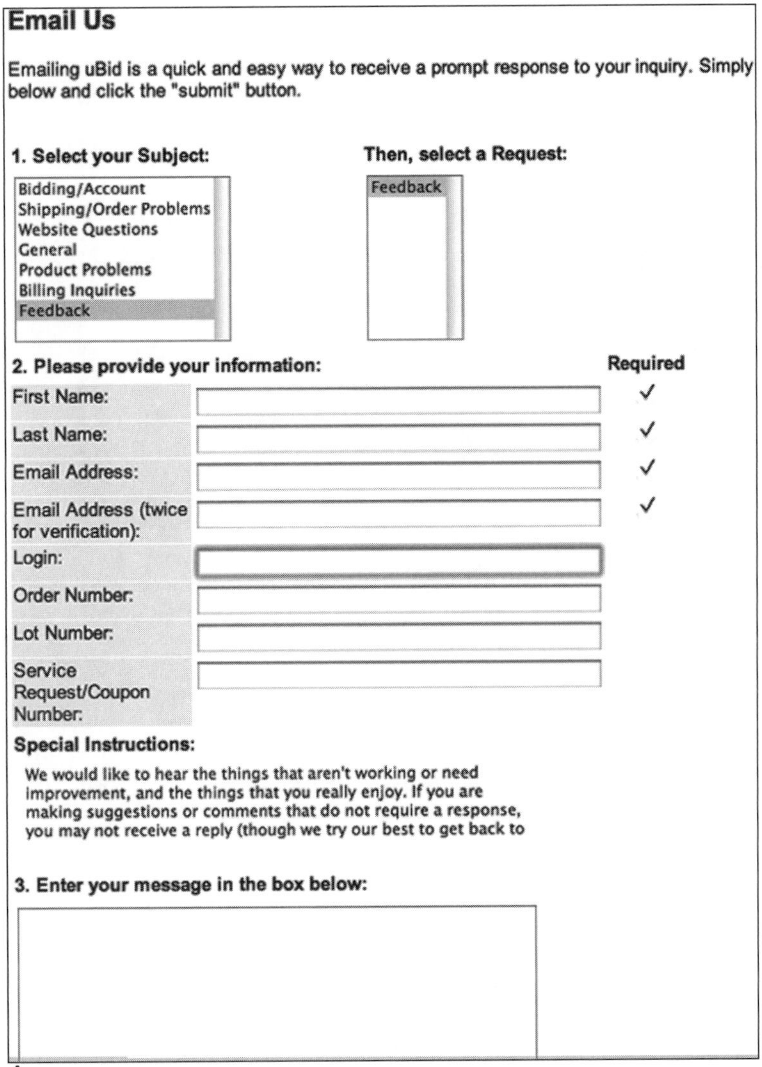

Email Us

Emailing uBid is a quick and easy way to receive a prompt response to your inquiry. Simply below and click the "submit" button.

1. Select your Subject: **Then, select a Request:**

Bidding/Account
Shipping/Order Problems   Feedback
Website Questions
General
Product Problems
Billing Inquiries
Feedback

2. Please provide your information: **Required**

First Name:		✓
Last Name:		✓
Email Address:		✓
Email Address (twice for verification):		✓
Login:		
Order Number:		
Lot Number:		
Service Request/Coupon Number:		

Special Instructions:

We would like to hear the things that aren't working or need improvement, and the things that you really enjoy. If you are making suggestions or comments that do not require a response, you may not receive a reply (though we try our best to get back to

3. Enter your message in the box below:

A

Correction of bloopers at uBid.com and on Microsoft Windows Regional & Language Options. (A) Corrected uBid form has noneditable text checkmarks and instruction text directly on the background.

(Continued)

Figure 2.43

(Continued)

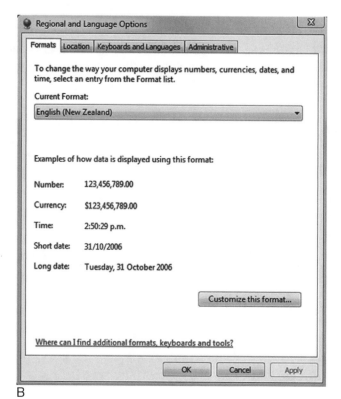

B

(B) In Windows Regional and Language options, text fields were replaced with text "labels."

Microsoft Office applications has a window that displays document properties. Some of the properties are editable and some aren't. Office correctly displays editable properties in text fields (Figure 2.44A) and noneditable data as text "labels" (Figure 2.44B).

A necessary evil: scrolling text boxes for long noneditable texts

One situation in which noneditable text fields seem a necessary evil is when long texts must be presented on relatively short software screens or Web pages. Common examples are:

- received e-mail messages displayed by e-mail software;
- software license agreements displayed during installation of desktop software;

Figure 2.44

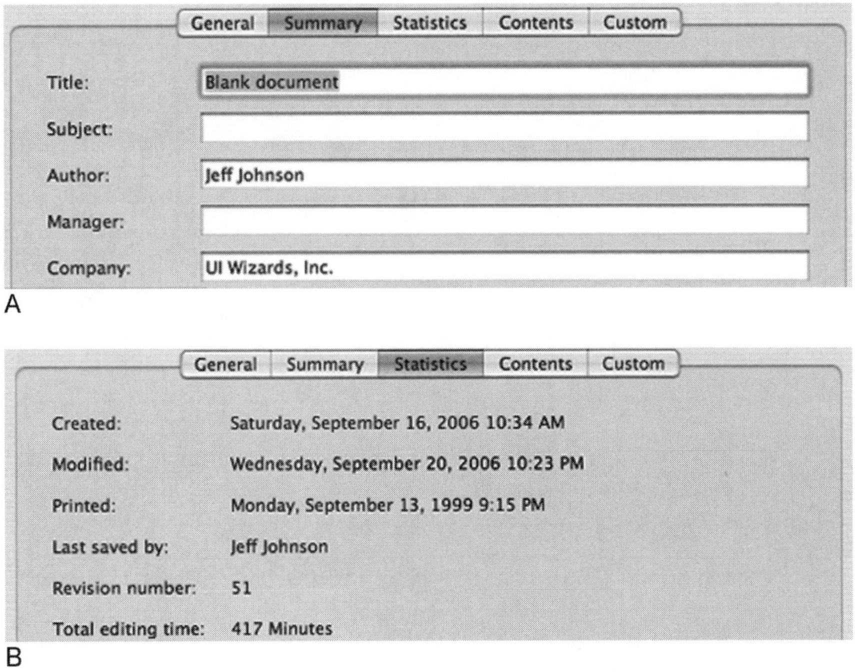

| General | Summary | Statistics | Contents | Custom |

Title: Blank document

Subject:

Author: Jeff Johnson

Manager:

Company: UI Wizards, Inc.

A

| General | Summary | Statistics | Contents | Custom |

Created: Saturday, September 16, 2006 10:34 AM

Modified: Wednesday, September 20, 2006 10:23 PM

Printed: Monday, September 13, 1999 9:15 PM

Last saved by: Jeff Johnson

Revision number: 51

Total editing time: 417 Minutes

B

Microsoft Office Document Properties: correctly displayed data. (A) Editable. (B) Noneditable.

■ usage policies, user agreements, contracts, and other legal documents displayed by membership and e-commerce Web sites.

In all these cases, the text is too long to fit onto the window or page, so it must be displayed in a scrolling control. An example comes from Lego's Web site (Figure 2.45).

Software license agreements, service contracts, and other legal documents are so clearly *not* editable that few people try to type into them. However, nearly every computer user has tried to edit a received e-mail message. The e-mail program Eudora displays an error message when a user tries to do that without first making the message editable.

This is acceptable because trying to type into a received e-mail message or a license agreement is not a costly "error" for users: the feedback—no effect of typing or an error message—is immediate and painless. On the other hand, a control panel or data-entry form full of editable-looking noneditable text fields displaying short texts is not acceptable: it potentially fools many users several times per page, and for what?

Figure 2.45

Lego.com: scrolling text area displays long noneditable legal document.

Blooper 7: Overusing text fields for constrained input

The text field is the most heavily used interactive control in GUIs. It is over-used. Users of desktop applications and e-commerce Web sites are often forced to use text fields to enter highly constrained data such as time of day, volume levels, dates, telephone numbers, postal codes, money amounts, and numbers of dependent children.

Text fields are too unstructured for constrained data. They give users little guidance about the format of valid data and scold users for invalid values after the values have been entered. Error messages would not be needed if the input control allowed users to enter only valid data.

Customer registration forms at Agilent.com and Algorithmics.com ask registrants for their home state or province. Instead of providing menus of U.S. states and Canadian provinces, they both use text fields for that data (Figure 2.46), almost guaranteeing entry errors.

Myth: Text fields are easier to code

A common excuse for using text fields is that they are easier to code than data-type-specific input controls. Even ignoring the problem that ease of programming shouldn't take priority over ease of use, the excuse is poor because it is simply false.

Using a text field for structured data requires you to find or write a parser for the field to check that entered values are valid. The parser may accept a variety of formats or it may accept only one format (Blooper 9, page 94). However, if the control were specialized for the type of input, no parser would be needed.

Figure 2.46

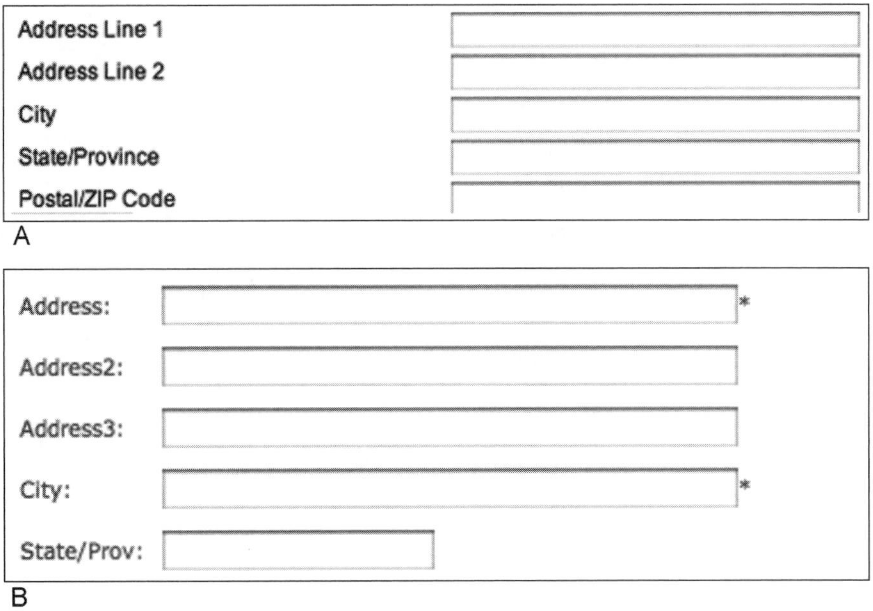

Address Line 1	
Address Line 2	
City	
State/Province	
Postal/ZIP Code	

A

Address:	*
Address2:	
Address3:	
City:	*
State/Prov:	

B

Registration forms use text field for state/province. (A) Agilent.com. (B) Algorithmics.com.

Many programmers are biased toward immediately thinking of any data input problem in terms of a text field and a parser. This is because most programmers learn their craft in school by writing text-processing programs—not GUI programs—as class assignments.

A major source of the blooper: TTY-to-GUI conversions

Overuse of text fields is especially common in software that was converted to the GUI style of interface from older, pre-GUI software that had a user interface based on textual prompts, typed commands, and command-line arguments. Such pre-GUI interfaces were commonly called "glass teletype" or "TTY" user interfaces. Alas, not all TTY-to-GUI conversions have been carried out carefully. Some have been done very quickly, with little consideration of how the GUI should differ from the TTY user interface.

The result is a "TTY GUI": a user interface that essentially recreates a glass teletype UI using GUI controls. It consists of panels of text fields into which users type data (Figure 2.47). Where the TTY user interface had a data prompt (e.g., "Enter appt. name:"), the GUI has a labeled text field. In TTY GUIs, the text field reigns supreme; other GUI controls—sliders, radio buttons, and so on—rarely appear. TTY GUIs miss the whole point of GUIs.

Figure 2.47

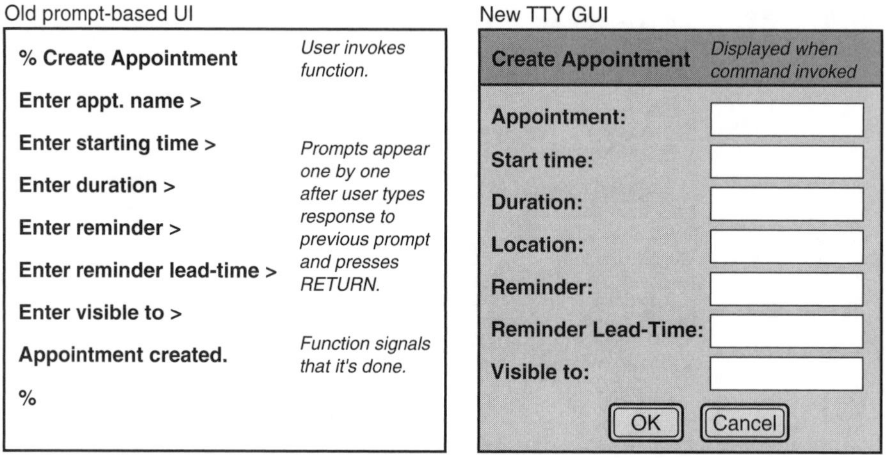

Old prompt-based UI

% Create Appointment	*User invokes function.*
Enter appt. name >	
Enter starting time >	*Prompts appear one by one after user types response to previous prompt and presses RETURN.*
Enter duration >	
Enter reminder >	
Enter reminder lead-time >	
Enter visible to >	
Appointment created.	*Function signals that it's done.*
%	

New TTY GUI

Create Appointment	*Displayed when command invoked*
Appointment:	
Start time:	
Duration:	
Location:	
Reminder:	
Reminder Lead-Time:	
Visible to:	
	OK Cancel

Blooper: simple-minded TTY-to-GUI conversions often yield GUIs that overuse text fields.

Avoiding Blooper 7

Use text fields sparingly

Text fields should be used only for data that really is unstructured, free-form text. Examples of such text are names of people, user-defined passwords, comments, and transaction reasons. Examples of data that is *not* completely free-form are telephone numbers, Social Security numbers, dates, state, city, and font family.

Alternatives to text fields

Most GUI toolkits supply specialized input controls that you can use instead of text fields for collection of highly constrained data from users. You can also build input-specific controls from simpler ones.

Many automatic teller machines (ATMs) in the United States use special "dollar amount" entry controls for specifying withdrawals, deposits, or transfers. ATM users who want to deposit $35.75 do not have to type "$35.75" or even "35.75". They just type "3575" and the ATM puts the decimal point in the right place. The first digit, "3", appears as 0.03 until the next digit "5" is entered, etc. This works.

Another approach is to use multiple text fields—one for each part of the data. This eliminates the need for users to type punctuation characters and reduces the chance of syntax errors. For example, telephone number fields can be broken into several fields: country code, area code, exchange, and final digits. Dates can be segmented into day, month, and year. Labels between the fields can provide "built-in" punctuation (Figure 2.48). For this approach to work, the

Figure 2.48

For structured data, use structured (segmented) text fields.

details must be just right. The Tab key of course advances the input focus to the next field. Backspacing to previous fields must also be allowed. In most cases, the input focus should advance automatically once enough characters have been entered, but this may not be what users expect in some applications.

Southwest Airlines's Web site uses this approach to increase their chances of getting valid e-mail addresses from customers (Figure 2.49).

A more sophisticated, but preferable, alternative to text fields is to use data-type-specific controls that match the data's structure and constrain the input to valid values. You can use a slider for a number between 1 and 100, a digital clock for a time, radio buttons for a small number like number of dependents, or a scrolling menu of states for a State field (Figure 2.50). After all, the "G" in "GUI" stands for "graphical," not "textual."

Figure 2.49

E-mail Address: fred @ bedrock . com

SWA.com: segmented input field for e-mail address.

Figure 2.50

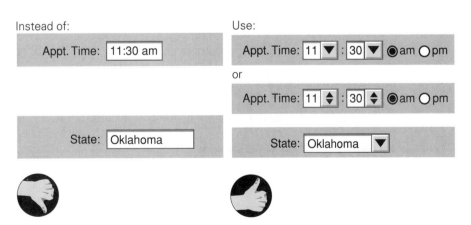

For structured data, use structured controls, with which users can input only valid data.

Figure 2.51

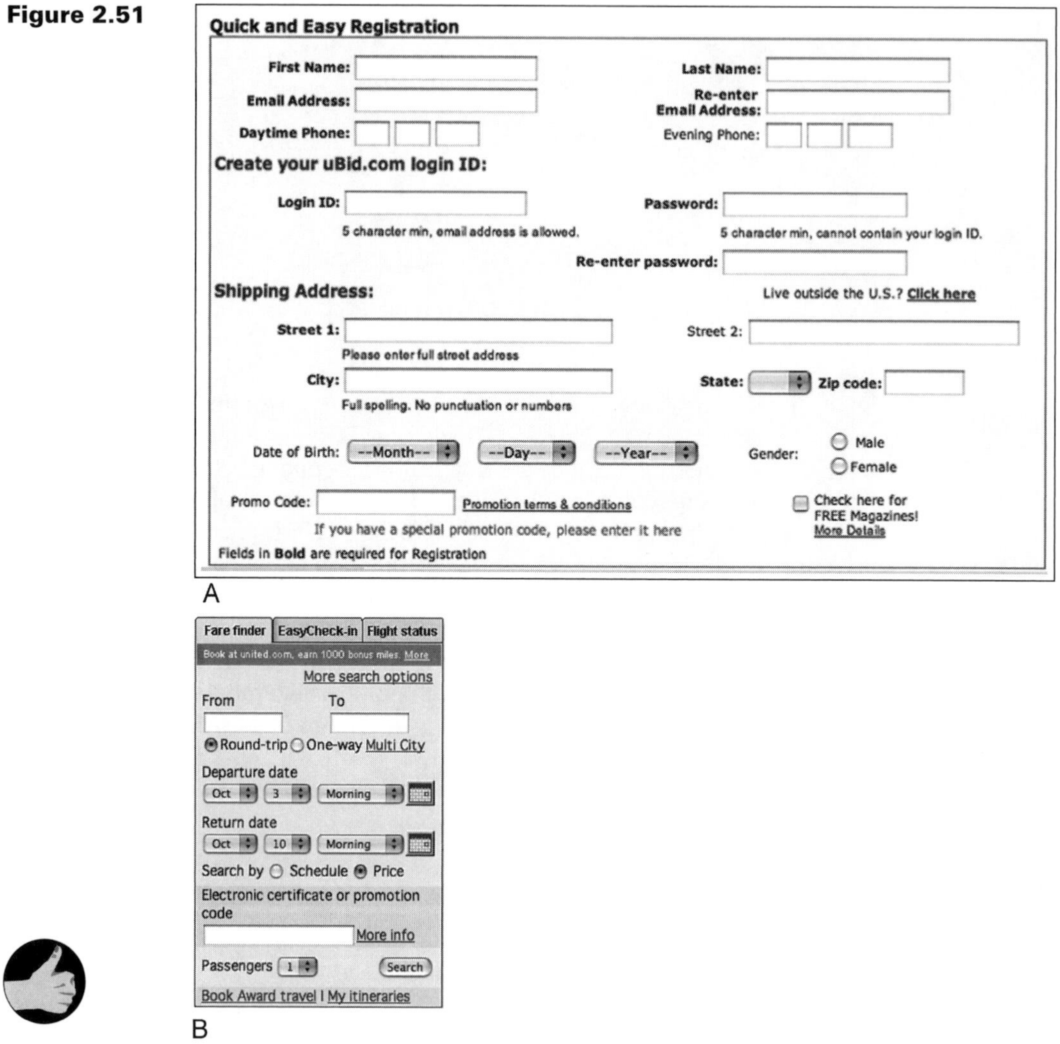

Quick and Easy Registration

First Name: _____   Last Name: _____

Email Address: _____   Re-enter Email Address: _____

Daytime Phone: ☐ ☐   Evening Phone: ☐ ☐ ☐

Create your uBid.com login ID:

Login ID: _____   Password: _____

5 character min, email address is allowed.   *5 character min, cannot contain your login ID.*

Re-enter password: _____

Shipping Address:

Live outside the U.S.? <u>Click here</u>

Street 1: _____   Street 2: _____

Please enter full street address

City: _____   State: [▾] Zip code: _____

Full spelling. No punctuation or numbers

Date of Birth: [--Month-- ▾] [--Day-- ▾] [--Year-- ▾]   Gender: ○ Male ○ Female

Promo Code: _____ <u>Promotion terms & conditions</u>   ☐ Check here for FREE Magazines! <u>More Details</u>

If you have a special promotion code, please enter it here

Fields in **Bold** are required for Registration

A

| Fare finder | EasyCheck-in | Flight status |

Book at united.com, earn 1000 bonus miles. <u>More</u>

<u>More search options</u>

From   To
_____   _____

⦿ Round-trip ○ One-way <u>Multi City</u>

Departure date
[Oct ▾] [3 ▾] [Morning ▾] 📅

Return date
[Oct ▾] [10 ▾] [Morning ▾] 📅

Search by ○ Schedule ⦿ Price

Electronic certificate or promotion code
_____ <u>More info</u>

Passengers [1 ▾]   (Search)

<u>Book Award travel</u> I <u>My itineraries</u>

B

Structured input controls for entering structured data. (A) uBid.com. (B) United.com.

The customer registration form at uBid.com (Figure 2.51A) and the flight search form at United.com (Figure 2.51B) use specialized controls for structured data rather than forcing users to type data into text fields.

Using controls wrongly

The first seven bloopers were cases of using the wrong control. The next five are cases of using controls badly: the control may be appropriate, but something is wrong with how it functions.

Blooper 8: Dynamic menus

In most GUI-based applications, a menubar displays most or all of the application's commands, organized by category, e.g., File, Edit, View, Tools, Window, Help. In MacOS, the menubar for the currently active application is at the top of the screen. In Windows and most Unix-based window systems, each application's menubar is at the top of its main window.

GUI developers sometimes try to reduce the size and complexity of menubar menus by adding and removing items based on the state of the application. Commands are shown in the menus only when they are applicable. Figure 2.52 shows a hypothetical e-mail program's Edit menu in which the commands depend on the users' current activity.

This may seem helpful, but it isn't. It confuses users: if they scan the menus at different times, they will find different menu items. If users haven't learned the software very well yet and don't know what depends on what else, they may not understand why some commands are present at some times but not others. They may not initially even realize that the menus change.

Users faced with software applications that commit this error are often heard complaining as they search in vain through the menus: "Where the heck *is* that Edit Formula command? I *know* I saw it here somewhere."

Figure 2.52

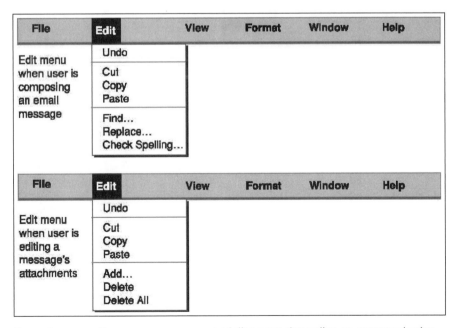

Dynamic menus: items on menu appear and disappear depending on current selection.

For example, a usability test of a client's application yielded the following observation:

> Some test participants were disoriented by the fact that Results—View choices disappear from the View menu when no Project is open. Similarly, there is a top-level menu label that appears and disappears depending on what view is selected.

A product that commits this blooper is Sybase's PowerBuilder, an interactive GUI-building tool. The File menu has more items when the Database Reader tool is being used (Figure 2.53).

Microsoft Office is infamous for adding and removing commands from menus based on how often the commands have been used recently (Figure 2.54). Most Office users turn this feature OFF if they can Figure out how.

Dynamic menus are a symptom of a more general error many software developers make: thinking *inside-out* instead of *outside-in* (Basic Principle 6, page 37). Thinking inside-out is using one's own knowledge of the software

Figure 2.53

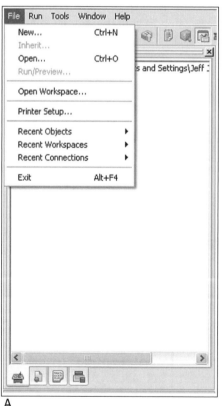
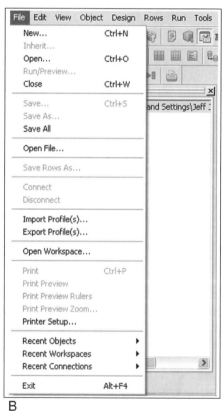

A   B

Sybase PowerBuilder: menu items appear and disappear depending on state of program.

Figure 2.54

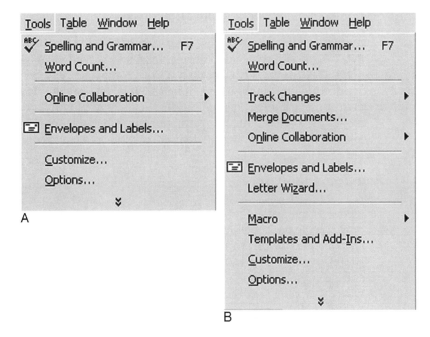

Microsoft Office: "smart menus" feature adds and removes menu items based on recent use.

to judge whether the displays and controls make sense. Thinking outside-in requires thinking like a user: assessing the meaning of the displays and controls based on what a *user* can be assumed to know. Dynamic menus are based on the assumption that users know or quickly learn how and why menu items appear and disappear. That assumption is wrong.

Most applications

Applications that do *not* support plug-in applications or compound documents have no good excuse for having dynamic menus. These are applications that either:

- have modes, with different menubar commands being available in different modes, or
- support several different built-in data types, with different commands available depending on the type of data that is currently selected.

Developers of such applications mean well: they are trying to help users by restricting what commands are available in different situations. The problem is that adding and removing menu commands confuses users. It is much less confusing to activate and deactivate commands, graying out ones that are not currently applicable.

Compound document applications

Applications that support plug-ins or compound documents—using the CORBA, .NET, or JavaEE protocols—have an excuse for dynamic menus: their developers don't know in advance what all the commands will be. Some commands are provided by plug-ins for editing specific types of data. This is why dynamic menus are common in applications that allow plug-ins or compound documents. However, there are alternatives (see below), so dynamic menus are a blooper even for applications that allow plug-ins or compound documents.

Avoiding Blooper 8

Menubar menus should be stable. Users start learning applications by scanning the menubar, seeing what's where and how many commands there are. Dynamic menus thwart this strategy. Instead of thwarting this useful learning strategy, GUI designs should support it. Therefore, commands should not come and go from menubar menus. Deactivate (gray out) inapplicable commands rather than removing them (Figure 2.55).

Figure 2.55

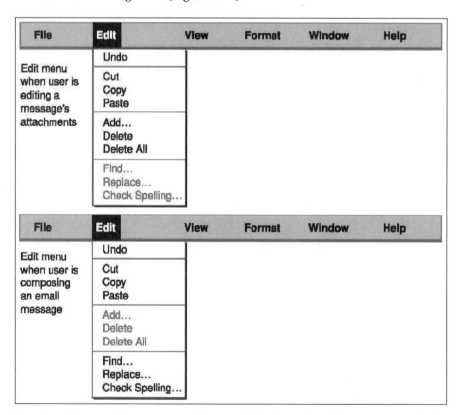

Non-dynamic menus: items on menu activate and deactivate depending on current selection.

Add and remove menus, not menu items

An application can add and remove entire menubar menus as the user changes the selection. Maybe a certain window or type of content has commands that apply only to it. When a user is working with that window or content, instead of adding commands to a menu, it can add its own menus to the menubar. When the window or content loses the focus, the menu disappears from the menubar (Figure 2.56).

Users can *see* the extra menus appear and disappear as the selection changes. In contrast, when items in menus appear and disappear, the changes are invisible, so users learn the dependencies slowly, if at all. Therefore, adding and deleting menus from the menubar is the preferred approach in applications that support plug-ins or compound documents. Microsoft uses this approach heavily in the Vista versions of its Office applications.

Adding and removing entire menus at a time requires you to think hard about what goes into what menu. You have to choose and design the menus carefully to avoid anomalies such as menus with the same name or menus of only one item.

If you don't want to add and remove menus, you can require plug-ins for "foreign" data types to use generic commands. This allows commands already in the application's regular menus (such as Create, Move, Copy, Delete) to apply to any object, with the precise meaning of a command depending on the object. When the selection changes from one data type to another, a Delete command on a menu could be changed to point to the new data type's Delete method. From the users' point of view, the menu is stable, but from the software's point of view, one type-specific command has been replaced by another.

Figure 2.56

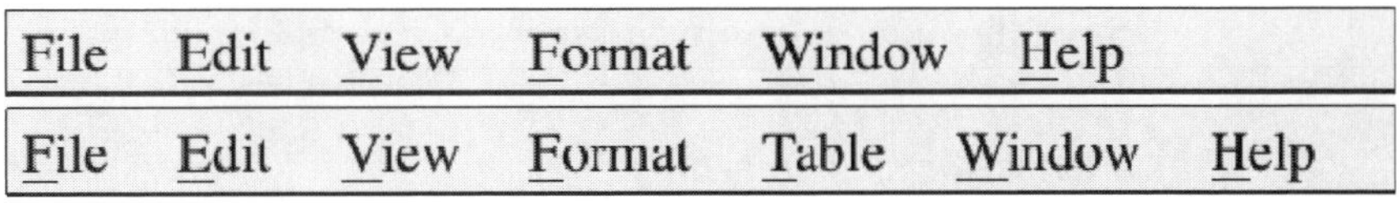

Table menu appears if a table is selected.

An exception: "quick-pick" lists

Many GUI applications have menus that show recently edited files, currently opened windows, and bookmarked documents. These quick-pick lists change over time. As long as changes in menubar menus are restricted to quick-pick lists, you have not violated the design rule.

DILBERT © Scott Adams/Dist. by United Feature Syndicate, Inc.

Blooper 9: Intolerant data fields

If your application or Web site contains text or number type-in fields, it must of course check what people type to make sure it is valid. To be friendly and helpful, you should tolerate reasonable variations in what people type. Unfortunately, text fields in many applications and Web sites are intolerant.

Easy to code, hard to enter

United.com rejects Frequent Flier numbers entered with spaces—the format United uses on Frequent Flier cards and mileage statements (Figure 2.57). This no doubt made the code that checks the numbers easier to write, but it makes life difficult for their customers.

Similarly, StuffIt.com rejects credit card numbers typed with spaces (Figure 2.58). Finally, desktop software installers and registration functions sometimes require registration codes to be entered differently than the codes appear on product packaging and download receipts.

Spaces are in those numbers for a *reason*. They make it easier to scan and check the numbers. Software should let users include them.

Must we be so intolerant?

Why are these Web sites so intolerant and uncooperative? Why are they so particular about what people type? Why can't they even accept data in common formats—even just one—or in formats that the companies themselves use elsewhere?

A common excuse is that it is hard to write software to interpret and accept data typed in multiple formats. Perhaps, but consider how many user-hours are wasted for each programmer-hour saved. Then consider the revenue lost due to intolerant, annoying forms. Consider the impression you give your customers when your Web site or application rejects numbers typed *exactly* as they appear in your own packaging and literature.

Figure 2.57

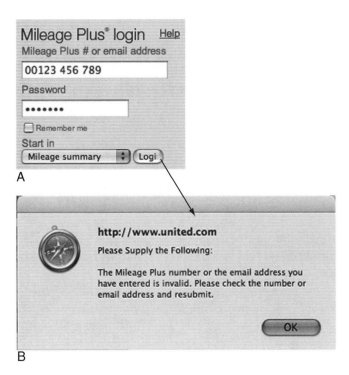

A

B

United.com: rejects Frequent Flier numbers with spaces, the format United uses elsewhere.

Figure 2.58

Stufflt.com: rejects credit card numbers with spaces.

Avoiding Blooper 9

Providing user-friendly, tolerant type-in fields is not hard:

■ *Match field length to data:* The visible length of a field should suggest the length of the data to be typed. It needn't be exact, because that would create ragged looking forms and isn't feasible anyway because of variable-width typefaces. What is important is that fields be: (a) long enough to hold their data and (b) not a lot longer than that.

Figure 2.59

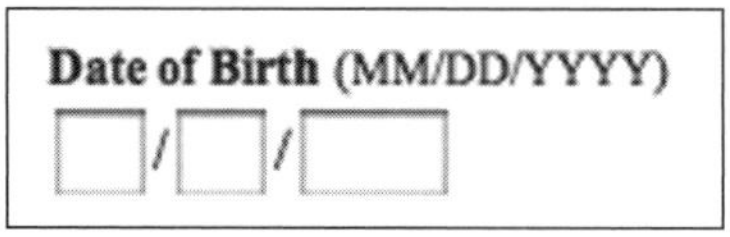

Date of Birth (MM/DD/YYYY)

□ / □ / □

REI.com: provides pattern; segments date into subfields.

- *Accept common formats:* If the data has a common, accepted format, allow it. If there are several, common formats, allow as many as is feasible. A Time field could accept times in any of the following formats: 12:30 am, 12:30 AM, 12:30 a, 00:30, 00:30 h.

- *Accept your own formats:* Accept data in the formats you use elsewhere. If your software license codes look like "ZX-4563-33-QR," then all license-code fields in your software and on your Web site should accept license codes in that exact same format.

- *Beware of rejecting legitimate data:* Think hard about who might be using your form. Customers from Canada or the United Kingdom, where postal codes include letters, would be greatly annoyed at an order form that required a "Zip Code" but rejected letters.

- *Make letter case irrelevant:* If you expect users to type codes that include letters, and if letter case is not significant for the data, allow users to type either upper- or lowercase into the field.

- *Provide a pattern:* Give an example of a valid format, e.g., "DD/MM/YYYY" or "Sample Serial #: QP-00275-5559." Put it near the field: above, below, on the side, or inside (grayed). REI.com provides an example of a data field labeled with a pattern (Figure 2.59).

- *Structure text fields:* Unless you must accept different—perhaps international—formats, build the format you want into the form by structuring the fields. For example, if you are certain that only U.S. phone numbers will be entered into the form, you can structure it into fields for area code and number, as at REI.com (Figure 2.59). If you segment a text field into subfields, you *must* make it easy for users to move between fields. The Tab key should always move the insertion point from one field to the next. A form can automatically move the insertion point to the next field when the required number of characters has been typed.

Blooper 10: Input fields and controls with no default

As explained in Chapter 1, the less users must specify to get what they want, the better (Basic Principle 4, page 32). Therefore, where possible, data fields and choices should have defaults. The defaults should be the most likely values. This lets users simply scan the settings, change a few, and proceed.

Unfortunately, this important design principle is not widely followed. Many applications and Web sites have settings without defaults. At best, this forces users to make explicit decisions and choices, consuming their time. Worse, users may not notice the settings, try to proceed, and either get scolded for omitting required information or end up with undesired results.

Reasons for omitting default

Of course, some settings cannot offer a default value. There are two reasons for this:

- *No reasonable default:* For example, a Web site's registration form might have a menu for applicants to indicate their gender (male or female). Few organizations would have a basis for setting a default gender. Similarly, people joining an organization may be asked for their home state. If the organization is nationwide, such as the American Civil Liberties Union, there is no basis for making any of the 50 United States the default. However, if the organization is ACLU's San Francisco chapter, the State field should default to California.

- *Social, political, or legal requirement:* In some situations, UI designers must avoid offending anyone by being presumptuous. Imagine the trouble a Canadian government Web site would be in if, offering visitors a choice of English vs. French, it defaulted to English. *C'est un faux pas, n'est ce pas?*

Nonetheless, most settings should have defaults. Let's examine the controls that should have defaults but often do not.

Text and number fields with no default

Filling in a text or number field usually requires multiple clicks and keystrokes: one to put the insertion focus into the field and more to enter the data. Sometimes you can save users keystrokes by providing defaults: likely or recently entered values.

Multiply a few saved keystrokes by several thousand—or million—users and that's a lot of saved keystrokes and time. In forms containing many fields, the saved effort can even be significant for one user. To order items from a catalogue, a person should not have to fill in quantity zero (0) for all the items one does *not* want. Instead, the quantity for all items should be initialized to zero—or at least a blank response should be taken as zero.

A recent Northwest Airlines customer survey asked how many trips one had taken to various parts of the world but required customers to enter zero for all places they have *never* visited (Figure 2.60). This no doubt diminished the number of surveys completed.

Figure 2.60

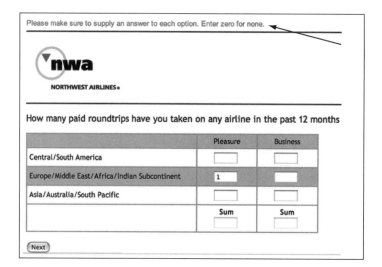

NWA.com: survey requires users to enter zeros manually for all places they haven't traveled.

Radio buttons with no initial value

Sometimes radio button choices start with none of the buttons selected. Programmers may design radio buttons this way intentionally, to:

- avoid any presumptions about what users will choose,
- force users to choose explicitly, or
- allow users *not* to choose (this reason is much rarer than the first two).

Radio buttons with no default may sometimes be justifiable, but they do have usability costs, of which you should at least be aware:

1. They violate users' expectations about how radio buttons work.
2. They cannot be returned to their initial unset state after a choice has been made.
3. They violate the UI design guideline that, in cases in which no default makes sense, menus are preferable to radio buttons (see below).
4. They violate the UI design principle of letting users do as little as possible to get what they want.

Therefore, designers should have a compelling reason for presenting radio buttons without a default value.

Agilent.com has a form for visitors to submit comments about the Web site (Figure 2.61A). In most cases no response is necessary or expected. Nonetheless, the form not only provides no default for this choice, it *requires* the choice. Users cannot submit a comment without specifying whether they want a response. Similarly, the

Figure 2.61

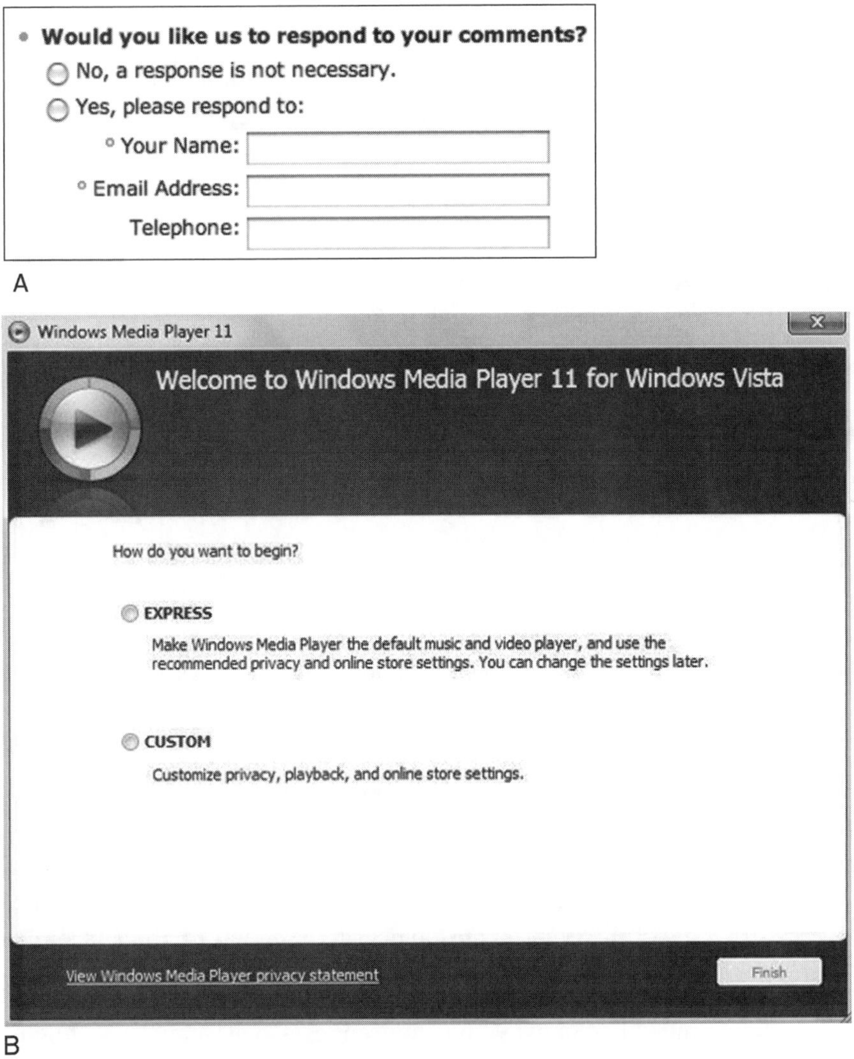

- **Would you like us to respond to your comments?**
  ◯ No, a response is not necessary.
  ◯ Yes, please respond to:
  ◦ Your Name: _____
  ◦ Email Address: _____
  Telephone: _____

A

Radio buttons with no default, even though one option is much more likely. (A) Agilent. com. (B) Windows Medial Player Installer.

Installer Wizard for Windows Media Player presents radio buttons for choosing an "Express" installation or a "Custom" installation, but does not default the choice to "Express," which is by far the more common choice (Figure 2.61B).

Dropdown menus with no default

Dropdown menus with no default are more common than radio buttons with no default. This is usually OK, for two reasons:

Figure 2.62

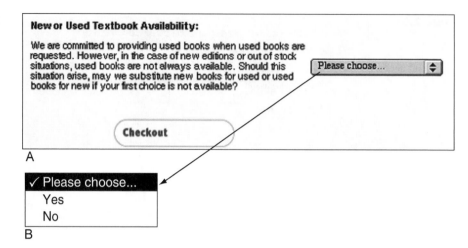

A

B

StanfordBookstore.com: dropdown menu with no default value and poor labeling.

1. A menu with no value is more natural than a radio-button choice with no value. "No value" on radio buttons means it is set to *none* of its possible values. In contrast, "no value" on a menu is an item on the menu: either a temporary prompt to users (e.g., "Choose a topping") or an explicit "none" option.

2. Menus can present more options than radio buttons can. Radio buttons are best for two to eight options. Menus can present dozens of options, making it less likely that one of them is a suitable default.

Nonetheless, dropdown menus should have useful defaults when possible. If it isn't possible, the label and prompt must make the choice clear. Otherwise, users have to pull the menu open just to see what the choice is.

Until recently, customers at the Stanford University Bookstore Web site, after clicking a link to go to the checkout page, were confronted with a menu with a paragraph-long label initialized to "Please choose" (Figure 2.62). The menu had only two possible values—"Yes" and "No"—but to discover that you had to open it. Furthermore, even *knowing* the menu options didn't clarify the choice; you had to read the paragraph-long label to Figure out what "Yes" and "No" meant. Of course few people read the long label initially. Worse, making a choice was *required:* you could not check out until you had answered it. The Stanford Bookstore recently fixed this blooper.

Avoiding Blooper 10

A UI designer's job is to make it as easy as possible for users to accomplish their goals. One way to do that is to provide defaults for as many data-entry fields and choices as possible, so users can focus on just those they need to change.

Figure 2.63

Google.com: Search input field provides menu of recent entries matching what user types.

Text and number fields

When there is a likely value for a text or number field, use it. Otherwise, design the field to remember what has been typed into it, so it can use the first characters a user types to pop up a menu of matching recent entries, as Google's search input field does (Figure 2.63).

Radio buttons

Radio buttons with no initial value should be avoided. Use only if you have strong justification.

A connected set of radio buttons is, from the users' point of view, a single setting that presents a one-from-N choice. It represents a discrete variable with N possible values. It is unnatural for it to have no value. Therefore, most radio buttons should have a default value (Figure 2.64).

If an application must allow users to indicate that they don't want any cheese on their pizza, then the radio button set should include an explicit value: "None" (Figure 2.65).

Figure 2.64

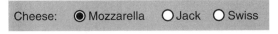

Radio buttons with default value.

Figure 2.65

Radio buttons with extra "none" value as default.

Figure 2.66

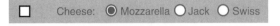

Radio buttons with associated ON/OFF checkbox.

Figure 2.67

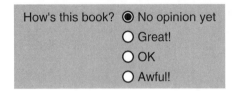

Radio buttons in survey with unbiased default value.

Alternatively, the entire setting could have a checkbox that activates and deactivates the radio button choice (Figure 2.66). If you do this, do it consistently throughout your application, so users will learn what it means.

Similarly, if you are designing an online questionnaire and don't want to bias users' answers by providing a default, add an explicit "no opinion" option and make it the default (Figure 2.67).

Dropdown menus

Menus, like radio buttons, should have defaults when possible. If one option is much more likely than the others, initialize the menu to that option (Figure 2.68). If a menu can remember the user's last choice, make that the default.

When no default can be assumed, menus are better than radio buttons

Sometimes you can't provide a default value for a choice, as when asking the user's gender. In such cases, use a menu rather than a radio button, because menus with no default are more natural than radio buttons with no default, even when the choice has only two options.

Figure 2.68

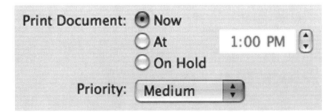

Microsoft Office: Print dialog box has radio button and menu choices, both with defaults.

Blooper 11: Poor defaults

A default value that is unlikely to be what users want is more harmful than no default. A user who overlooks a control that has *no* default often gets an error message, but overlooking a *bad* default can produce unwanted results.

One "reason" for poor defaults is that choice controls sometimes default to the first of their possible values if developers don't initialize them. An example comes from the Stanford University Bookstore Web site. Ordering a book requires indicating your home state. The State menu defaults to Alabama (Figure 2.69)—alphabetically first—even though most customers of this site are in California. Therefore, most customers have to change the State setting.

A similar poor default occurs at 1stSeattleHotels.com, a Web site for finding hotels in Seattle. Users specify the dates for which they need a hotel, but the menus for specifying the year default to 2004, even in late 2006 (Figure 2.70). The "reason" is that the page was created in 2004, so the menus list years starting then and default

Figure 2.69

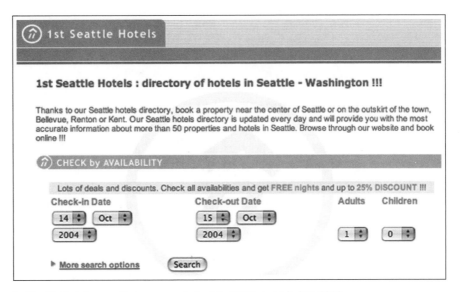

StanfordBookstore.com: State menu defaults to Alabama, for a customer of the Stanford University Bookstore, which is in California.

Figure 2.70

1stSeattleHotels.com: Year menus default to 2004, even in late 2006.

Figure 2.71

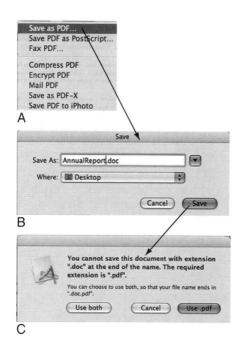

Microsoft Office: printing to PDF file doesn't default output file extension to the required .pdf.

to the first year in the list. Users now must change the year—assuming they notice it is wrong. Searching for hotel bookings in the past produces an error message.

Poor defaults also occur in desktop software. An example comes from Microsoft Office (for Macintosh OS X). "Printing" a document to a PDF file prompts users to name the PDF file, for which the extension must be .pdf. Unfortunately, Office does not automatically set the PDF file's extension to .pdf; it uses the document's original extension. If the user does not change the extension to .pdf, an error message results (Figure 2.71).

Avoiding Blooper 11

Choose default values by drawing on these sources of information:

- *Common sense:* Often, simple common sense works. On a form to write to a California senator, chances are good that the sender is from California, so that is a sensible default for a State setting (Figure 2.72).

- *Business logic:* If factory defaults don't match what your users usually need, change them to save work for users.

- *Experience and site data:* If common sense doesn't suggest a default, customer observations or Web logs will show commonly chosen options.

- *Individual users' data:* If no single default is suitable for all users, use different defaults based on whatever you know about a particular user.

Figure 2.72

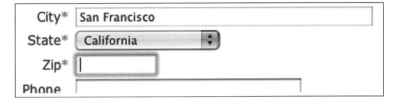

Boxer.Senate.gov: in form to contact Senator Boxer, State defaults to California, the state Boxer represents.

- *Arbitrary choice:* Finally, if no particular option seems any more likely than any other, there is sometimes no harm in arbitrarily declaring one to be the default.

Blooper 12: Negative checkboxes

Negative checkboxes are those that turn a feature or attribute OFF when checked and turn it ON when unchecked. They are "backward" from what users expect. If users don't read labels carefully, they may set a checkbox opposite from what they want. At the very least, checkboxes that "work backward" make users stop and think about how to set them, violating the design principle "don't distract users from their goals" (Basic Principle 5, page 35).

SmartDraw, a drawing program, includes a "negative" checkbox in its Shape Properties dialog box (Figure 2.73).

ExactTarget.com, an opt-in e-mail service, allows e-mail administrators to set access permissions of new administrative users, but uses "negative" checkboxes as well as positive ones (Figure 2.74).

Figure 2.73

SmartDraw: negative checkbox—checking it turns spell-checking OFF.

Figure 2.74

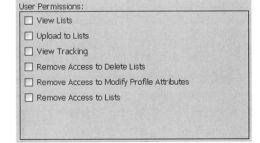

ExactTarget.com: user-permission settings include checkboxes that "remove" permissions.

Avoiding Blooper 12

Checkboxes should function in a positive fashion: they should turn things ON when checked and turn them OFF when unchecked. That is what users expect.

Examples of positive checkboxes are provided by Apple's Preview Print dialog box and MacOS X's Preferences dialog box (Figure 2.75).

Figure 2.75

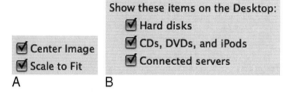

A   B

Positive checkboxes. (A) Apple Preview Print dialog. (B) MacOS X Preferences.

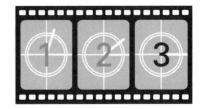

Navigation Bloopers

Introduction

The most pervasive problem software users encounter is navigation: finding their way to what they are seeking. This is due mainly to inadequate navigation cues—the equivalent of poor signage on hiking trails, city streets, or building hallways.

According to usability analyst Jakob Nielsen [1999d], successful navigation cues let people know:

- where they are,
- where they've been,
- where they can go.

To those I'll add:

- whether the goal is near or far.

Unfortunately, many software products and Web sites do a poor job of providing these cues, so people often don't find what they seek. Sometimes they even get lost.

This chapter describes the most common flaws that hinder, divert, and block software users from finding the content they seek and explains how to avoid those flaws.

Not showing users where they are

People use environmental cues to see where they are. If you see a stove, a toaster, pots, and pans, you know you're in the kitchen, while a couch, coffee table, and stereo suggest that you're in the living room.

Have you ever tried to get around in an unfamiliar town or building, but found yourself stymied by a lack of signs or signs that are hard to read? When it's difficult to see where you are, it's easy to get lost. Even if you aren't actually lost, you may *feel* lost, decreasing your confidence that you are progressing toward your goal.

The first three navigation bloopers are cases of not having accurate cues, hindering users' ability to see where they are and whether they are on track to their goal.

Blooper 13: Window or page not identified

Some applications or Web sites fail to provide any sign of where the user is.

Desktop applications: No window title

Application windows identify themselves with a title in their titlebar. The window body may also identify the application. Some applications don't title their windows.

The file-transfer application Fetch displays no title on several dialog boxes, for example, Delete File (Figure 3.1). This requires Fetch users to remember what function they invoked, aided a bit by the prompt in the window body.

A subtler example of the blooper occurs in Mozilla Firefox. The Preferences window has a title, but the title does not name the window. Instead, it shows which preference category is being shown (Figure 3.2). That is not what window titlebars are for.

Figure 3.1

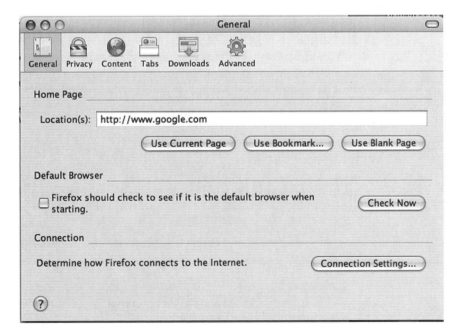

Fetch: Delete File dialog box has no window title in titlebar.

Figure 3.2

Firefox: Preferences window titlebar identifies current preference category, not window.

Figure 3.3

Flashlight.com: current page not indicated. This is the "About KBS" page.

On the Web: Page not identified

Web software can identify the current page by either marking the current item in the navigation bar or displaying a page title prominently on the page. Many do neither, forcing visitors to guess what page they are on.

One example is Flashlight.com, the Web site of Koehler-BrightStar (Figure 3.3). The navigation bar at the top of each page does not highlight the current page and the page does not include a title.

Some Web sites try to indicate the current page by using the HTML < TITLE > tag to display a page title in the *browser's* titlebar. This doesn't work: people rarely notice what is in the browser's titlebar, especially after they are already in a Web site. Sites *should* set titles for the browser, but that is mainly so the window identifies itself when it is minimized to the taskbar at the bottom of the screen.

Avoiding Blooper 13

Desktop applications should title all windows, including dialog boxes. Use this format:

< Application name > :   < window title >   (e.g., PageDesigner: Import Image)

Apple's Preview identifies its Preference window well, even though it doesn't follow the recommended format exactly (Figure 3.4).

Web software can indicate the current page in two ways. Well-designed sites use one or both of these on every page.

Figure 3.4

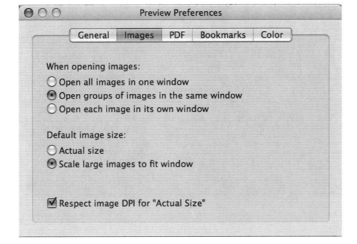

Apple Preview: application window well identified.

- *Navigation bar:* marking the current page's item in the site's navigation bar
- *Page title:* placing a page title prominently, near the top of the page content

IBM's Web site displays two page titles on each page (Figure 3.5). The site does not mark the current page in the navigation bar, but that is OK because the page title is displayed clearly.

AndePhotos.com highlights the current page on its navigation bar but does not display a separate page title (Figure 3.6). This works also.

If marking the navigation bar helps and showing page titles helps, doing both at once should be absolutely clear. Saba.com (Figure 3.7) does this.

Figure 3.5

IBM.com: current page indicated by page title separate from navigation bar.

Figure 3.6

AndePhotos.com: current page highlighted in navigation column; no separate page title.

Figure 3.7

Saba.com: current page indicated both on navigation bar and by title.

Blooper 14: Same title on different windows

Sometimes different windows or Web pages have the exact same title. This can mislead users about where they are. Such errors have four common causes.

Variation A: Window titles name application only

In the first variation, all windows of an application have the same name: that of the application (Figure 3.8). This can happen if the programmer assumes users will automatically recognize the function of each window or remember which function displayed it. Unfortunately, they won't.

The Windows XP Paint application has this problem: its Help window is labeled "Paint" (Figure 3.9).

Figure 3.8

Window titles identify application only, not specific window.

Figure 3.9

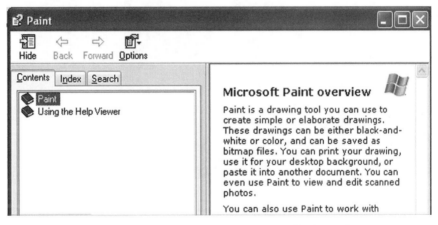

Microsoft Windows XP Paint: Help window title names application only.

Variation B: Programmer copied code but forgot to edit title

Programmers often add new windows to an application by copying the code from an existing similar window and editing it appropriately. New Web pages are often cloned from old ones. It is easy to forget to change the details in the copy, so the software ends up with multiple pages or windows with the same name. These are really bugs, not design flaws, but they're still bad.

This may be the cause of a duplicate page title at Canterbury.ac.nz: the "Search" page is labeled as the "Help and Accessibility" page (Figure 3.10).

Figure 3.10

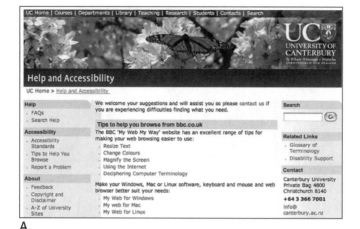

A

B

Canterbury.ac.nz: "Help and Accessibility" page title also appears on "Search" page.

Variation C: Programmer didn't know title was in use elsewhere

Development teams often assign different parts of an application or Web site to different programmers. When the programmers don't communicate, duplicate window titles can result.

Even one programmer working alone can forget that a particular title was already used. Window titles, unlike program variable or procedure names, are not checked by the compiler for uniqueness, so ensuring uniqueness is completely up to developers.

Variation D: Programmer thought title fit both

Programmers may assign two windows the same title because they think the name fits both windows' functions and can't think of a better title for either window. In most cases, one or both of the titles aren't precise enough. For example, the following are excerpts from reviews of applications for two client companies:

> *Company 1:* The "Network…" button in the Main window displays a dialog box named Control Network, and the "Select…" button displays a different dialog box also named Control Network. *Recommendation:* There shouldn't be two different windows with the same name. Rename one.

> *Company 2:* The Execution Monitor window that can be displayed from the My Investments window is a *different* Execution Monitor window from the one available from the Main window. *Recommendation:* These two windows should be combined. If that isn't feasible, they should have different names.

Figure 3.11 shows two identically titled windows from a hypothetical genealogy application. While the title "Show Family" is reasonable for each of these windows, two different windows with the same title will confuse users.

When duplicate window titles are noticed they are often regarded as a low-priority problem that is tedious to correct. Therefore, duplicate window titles in a software product sometimes survive all the way to the marketplace.

Figure 3.11

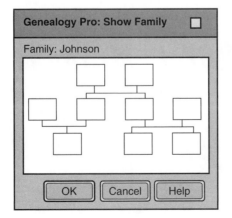

Blooper: different windows with the same functional title.

Avoiding Blooper 14

By following these rules, software developers can avoid duplicate window or page titles.

Every window or Web page should have a unique title

Each window or Web page corresponding to a distinct function of an application should have a unique title. The titlebars of the two hypothetical dialog boxes in Figure 3.12 clearly distinguish the two windows.

Message files can help

Place all text displayed by the software, including window titles, in a message file, rather than scattering them through the program code (Blooper 22, page 153). This reduces the likelihood of duplicate window names.

However, if the titles of two different windows point to the same text in the message file, the duplication won't be apparent. That type of duplication would have to be spotted by programmers in a code or UI review.

Special cases

Two special cases of duplicate window titles deserve mention:

- *Multiple windows represent same function applied to different data.* This can occur in text editor windows viewing different files or stock market monitors showing activity for different stocks. This duplication can be prevented by including the data name in the titlebar, e.g., "StockWatcher: Show Activity—Google (GOOG)."

- *Multiple windows represent same function or data with different user options.* Some application programs allow users to bring up several instances of the

Figure 3.12

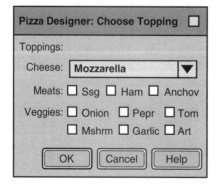
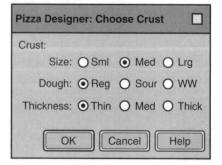

Avoiding the blooper: different windows with different titles.

"same" window to allow users to set different options in each one. A factory monitor tool might let users display multiple windows monitoring the factory's output, each polling the factory telemetry instruments at a different rate. In such cases, the convention is for the window title to end in an integer (separated from the title by a colon) indicating which instance of the window each one is. For example: "Factory Monitor," "Factory Monitor: 2," "Factory Monitor: 3."

Blooper 15: Window title doesn't match command or link

As people move around in an application or Web site, they need reassurance that they got what—or where—they were trying to get. A very common blooper in both desktop and Web software is a haphazard mapping between commands or links and the windows or pages they display.

The blooper in desktop software

Microsoft Windows XP has this problem (Figure 3.13). Clicking the "Change…" button in the System Proper ties Control Panel displays a dialog box titled Computer Name Changes, which not only doesn't match the invoking command very well, it is also grammatically ambiguous.

This mismatch is not minor or trivial. Computer users are very literal—often astoundingly so—in their interpretation of labels and other navigation aids on the screen. If two phrases differ, even if only slightly, users usually assume they mean something different. When someone chooses a Change… command

Figure 3.13

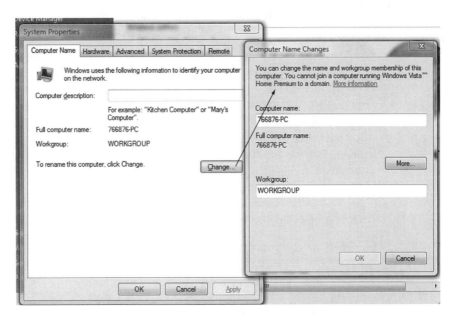

Windows XP: "Change…" button displays Computer Name Change dialog box.

Figure 3.14

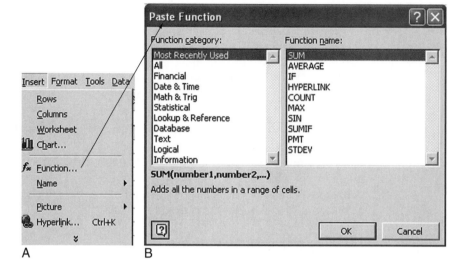

Microsoft Excel: Insert => Function... command displays Paste Function dialog box.

and the window that appears is labeled "Computer Name Changes," their first impression is that they didn't get what they wanted. This is especially true of nonnative speakers of the language displayed by software.

A somewhat more serious example comes from Excel. In the Insert menu, the (Insert) Function... command displays a window named "Paste Function" (Figure 3.14). "Paste" implies a prior "Cut," whereas "Insert" does not, so this mismatch will cause misunderstandings.

A common cause of the blooper

This blooper occurs when New < object >... or Create < object >... commands display dialog boxes titled Edit < object > or < object > Properties. The attributes users specify to create a new object are usually the same as those edited in existing objects, so GUI programmers often use one dialog box for both functions. That makes sense to a developer, but not to users. If the dialog box has a static title, the title won't match one of the two commands that display the dialog box. For example, Adobe Reader's "New Group..." button displays an Edit Group dialog box (Figure 3.15).

The blooper on the Web

Similar labeling mismatches occur on the Web. The WebMail application at Apple's ".mac" service has a link to add an e-mail folder, but it displays a Manage Folders window (Figure 3.16).

A more serious mismatch occurs at Dr. Dobb's Portal, DDJ.com. The navigation bar's "Subscribe" link displays a page titled "Dr. Dobb's Journal Print Subscription Services" (Figure 3.17A). Not good, but not terrible. However, a different link on the navigation bar—"Newsletters"—displays a page titled "Subscribe" (Figure 3.17B). *That* will confuse people.

Figure 3.15

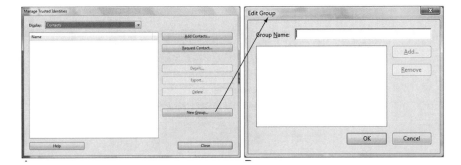

Adobe Reader: "New Group..." button displays Edit Group dialog box.

Figure 3.16

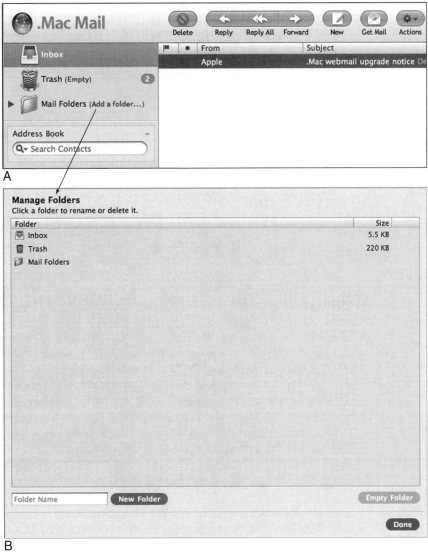

mac.com WebMail: clicking "Add a folder" displays a window titled "Manage Folders."

Figure 3.17

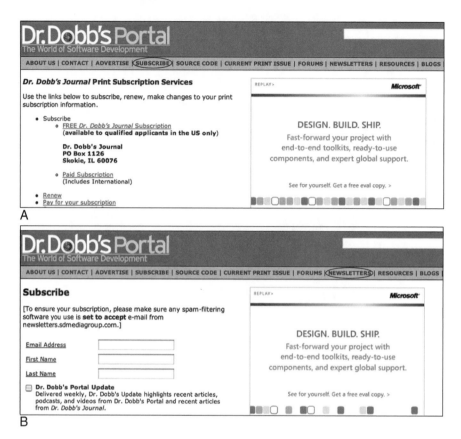

DDJ.com: Navigation bar links don't match their page titles. (A) "Subscribe."
(B) "Newsletters" link.

Avoiding Blooper 15

The title of a window or Web page should reflect the command that displayed it. This shows users that they hit the button or menu item they meant to hit.

You can do this by making window or page titles identical to the names of the commands that invoke them. Since command labels should be verb phrases, the titles of the windows will, for the most part, also be verb phrases.

Although Microsoft Excel's "Insert" menu provided an example of the blooper, it also provides an example of an exact match. The (Insert) Hyperlink command displays a dialog box with exactly the same words as its title (Figure 3.18).

Inexact matches are OK if they work for users

As long as users see the connection, commands and titles need not be identical. The difference between "Show Order Status" and "Status of Order 6823"

Figure 3.18

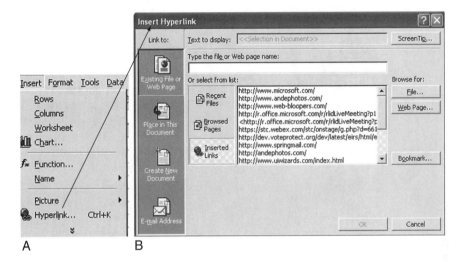

A   B

Microsoft Excel: Insert => Hyperlink... command displays Insert Hyperlink dialog box.

is probably minor enough that it wouldn't confuse anyone. However, the *users* are the judges of whether commands and the resulting window titles are similar enough, not the developers. Any command and resulting window that are named differently is a potential usability problem and should be avoided if possible and tested on users if unavoidable. Most differences—even minor ones—will cause users to wonder at least briefly about whether they hit the right button or link.

A *useful solution*: *Allow commands to set window titles*

A common reason for a difference between a command's name and the title of the resulting window is that different commands display the same window. Three cases are typical:

1. Open..., Save As..., Import..., and Export... commands all bring up a dialog box titled File Chooser.
2. Create Account and Edit Account commands both bring up a window titled Edit Account.
3. View Graph and Edit Graph commands both bring up a window titled Graph.

In all three cases, command-label mismatches can be eliminated by allowing commands and links to set the titles of windows or pages they display. In case 1, that is usually done: file chooser components allow the calling code to set the dialog box's title, so programmers normally give file choosers command-specific names like "Save As." Therefore, case 1 of the blooper is fairly rare. Cases 2 and 3 are not rare, even though the same solution would work for them.

By Bunny Hoest and John Reiner

"Our ancestors were hunter-gatherers, but we've evolved into browser-purchasers."

Leading users astray and not showing the way

Pirolli and Card [1999] showed that people follow an information "scent" to their goals. This scent comes from cues in the user interface that suggest what actions do or where they go. If someone is using photo-editing software and wants to lighten a dark photo, the word "lighten" or "brightness" on any command or link "smells" like the user's goal. Users go in the direction that emits the strongest scent of their goal.

Therefore, software should not only show users where they are, it should also provide cues—scents—that guide users toward their goal. At the very least, cues should not divert users *away* from their goals. This section examines bloopers that fail to lead users to the goal or even lead them *away* from it.

Blooper 16: Distracting off-path buttons and links

A software application or Web site is designed to support certain user goals. The software's user interface should guide users toward those goals. Unfortunately, many applications and Web sites throw up distractions that *divert* users from accomplishing their goals.

The Web site of the Institute of Electrical and Electronics Engineers (IEEE. org) has a "Renew Membership" page. At the top center of the page is a link "Begin Membership Renewal" (Figure 3.19). IEEE members arrive here with the goal of renewing, so this link seems clear. However, elsewhere on the page are links that may seem applicable as well. If users carefully read the page, they would know that they should click "Begin Membership Renewal" to renew, but few users will read carefully. Most will quickly scan the page and click any link that seems relevant.

A quick scan suggests that students might have to follow different renewal instructions. Only a careful reading makes it clear that students use the same link as everyone else. The link "Using a secure connection" (just below "Begin Membership Renewal") could be misinterpreted as an alternative starting point for renewing using a *secure* connection, as if the main renewal link were *not* secure. However, the "secure connection" link just skips down the page to an explanation of "secure vs. non-secure." In sum, this page will at least cause many users to hesitate, unsure what the right first step is, and may lure some users off track when they click other links and have to find their way back here.

Figure 3.19

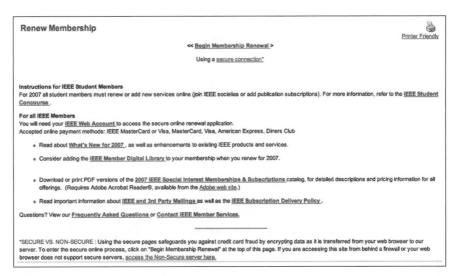

IEEE.org: "Renew Membership" page has many distracting links.

Lured off track. Can't get back. Ack!

When a customer searches for flights on Southwest Airlines's Web site, it lists flights matching the customer's criteria (Figure 3.20). The list has links to explanations of Southwest's various fare categories. By itself, this is OK; most customers would understand that these links are just explanations, not on the path toward booking a flight.

The problem is what happens if a customer follows one of these explanatory links. The list of flights *disappears* and is replaced by a page titled "Southwest Airlines Fare Information," which provides information about many things, including Southwest's refund policy. How does the customer then return to the list of flights? No return link is provided. Customers must click the "Back" button to return to the list of flights. Some customers, seeing the navigation bar at the top of the fare-information page, will click the "Reservations" link, believing that would take them back to making their flight reservation. But of course that link won't take them back to the list of flights. It puts them back at the start of the reservation process. Potential sale delayed, perhaps even lost if the user is frustrated enough.

Poorly positioned promotion lures customers off track

Computer users don't read screens carefully; they scan quickly looking for anything matching their goal. In Western societies, people usually scan from top left to bottom right. After entering data into a form, a user quickly scans to the

Figure 3.20

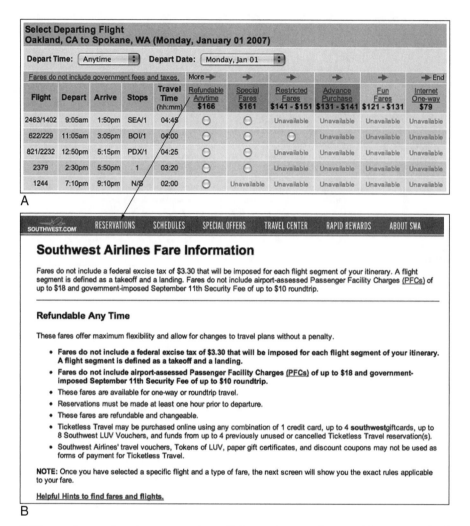

A

B

SWA.com: fare-explanation page replaces flight-results page, but provides no route back.

bottom right for a button or link to submit the form. At REI.com, many users who have filled out the new customer registration form will do that and spot what they are looking for: a link labeled "Continue" (Figure 3.21). They'll click it and find themselves staring at an unrelated—probably unwanted—form to subscribe to product promotion e-mails. Oops, wrong link.

Worse, when people realize they somehow ended up in the wrong place, they'll hit BACK, but will find that the registration form is now blank. They must register again. Or (grrrr) not.

Figure 3.21

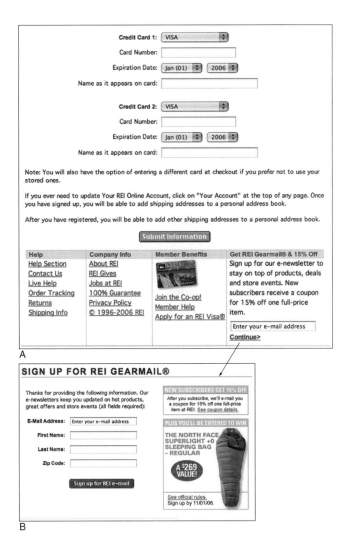

REI.com: registration form—users may not see "Submit Information" button and click "Continue" for different form.

Avoiding Blooper 16

Don't distract customers from their tasks. Help people finish the primary tasks your application or Web site is designed to support.

Once people have started down a task path, don't distract them from completing it. Create a "process funnel" that guides users toward their goal and keeps them on the path toward achieving it [Van Duyne et al., 2002]. Attractive buttons and links that lead off path decrease the likelihood that users will finish a task, especially if it is hard for users to return to the task path.

Figure 3.22

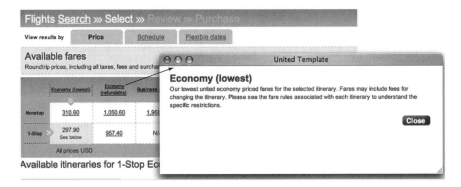

United.com: fare explanations appear in separate windows to preserve task context.

Make sure off-path button or link labels don't trick users into thinking they are on the task path. Links that explain details, terms, and conditions should appear in separate windows so they don't cause users to lose where they are. For example, flight search results at United.com, like those at SWA.com, include links to explanations of United's fare categories. However, at United, the explanations appear in separate small windows, with "Close" buttons to help customers get back to booking their flight (Figure 3.22).

However, even links that pop up explanations can slow users down, annoy them, and waste their time, so you should use them sparingly.

Blooper 17: Self-links

An extremely common navigation blooper is for a Web page to include an active link to itself. Clicking on such a link merely reloads the page. This not only wastes people's time as the page reloads, it can be disorienting: users may not recognize the redisplayed page as the one they were on. How? Like this:

- The user clicks a self-link while scrolling down the page, but it redisplays at the top. The user may never have even *seen* the top of the page due to arriving from elsewhere via a direct link to an anchor point partway down the page.

- The page has images that change each time it is displayed.

- The page contains animations, applets, or other dynamic content that takes time to start, so users cannot immediately see what page it is.

Disguised self-links can also cause users to lose data that they entered into forms on the page. This blooper has several variations, depending on where the active self-links are positioned on the page.

Variation A: Self-links in navigation bar

This variation happens when all links in a site's navigation bar are active on all pages. FannieMae.com has a navigation column (on the left) in which links are active on their own page (Figure 3.23). The page shown is the home page, on which the "Home" link on the navigation column is active.

This variation is very common because the HTML code for the navigation bar is often copied onto every page of the site, so every navigation bar link is active on every page. It takes more work to alter the code for each page so that a page's own navigation bar item is not active.

How harmful is this? It depends on how obvious it is to users that the link is a self-link. If the current page is strongly identified and matches the link label, users probably know that the link is a self-link. If the current page is not clearly identified or the link doesn't match the page title, users may not realize that the link is a self-link and may click it.

FannieMae's home page doesn't indicate that this *is* the home page. Visitors might think the home page is a *different* page, click "Home" to go there, and discover that they were already there.

Variation B: Which home page?

On large sites that have multiple subsites (e.g., for different countries or regions in which they do business) and hence multiple home pages, site visitors can easily lose track of which site they are in. Subsites of course provide links to the parent site and to other subsites. However, when subsites

Figure 3.23

FannieMae.com: links in left navigation column stay active, even on their own page.

Figure 3.24

PWC.com: United States home page has active self-link "United States" at upper left.

have active links to themselves, that can confuse visitors. The U.S. home page of PriceWaterhouseCoopers's Web site (PWC.com) provides an example: the "United States" link (upper left) redisplays this same page (Figure 3.24).

Variation C: Self-links in navigation breadcrumb

A navigation aid often used in Web software is a "breadcrumb" or "breadcrumb path." It shows the current page's position in the page hierarchy by listing the pages on the most direct path from the home page to the current page. The name comes from the idea of dropping breadcrumbs on the ground while traversing a landscape, to show the way back. An example of a breadcrumb is:

> Home > About Us > People

This would indicate that the "People" page is currently displayed and is reached from "About Us," which is reached from the home page.

A common blooper is for a breadcrumb to show the current page as an active link, for example:

> Home > About Us > People

Figure 3.25

A

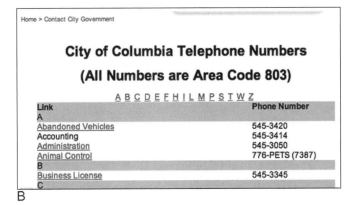

B

Last item in breadcrumb path is active (self) link. (A) KFC.com. (B) ColumbiaSC.net.

KFC.com and ColumbiaSC.net both have this blooper (Figure 3.25): all items in both breadcrumb paths are active links, including the last one. The ColumbiaSC.net breadcrumb is more likely to confuse users because the page title doesn't match the last breadcrumb item.

Variation D: *Self-links elsewhere*

Self-links that are *not* in the formal navigation links tend to be more trouble than those in navigation bars. Site users often can't tell whether such links come back to the current page. Users who click on such a link may not at first realize that the same page has been redisplayed.

In Sun Microsystem's online product documentation, any reference to a Sun online product document is a link—even references to the one the user is reading (Figure 3.26). Users may not recognize these as self-links and may click them and find themselves—after a reload delay—back at the start of the document they were reading.

Figure 3.26

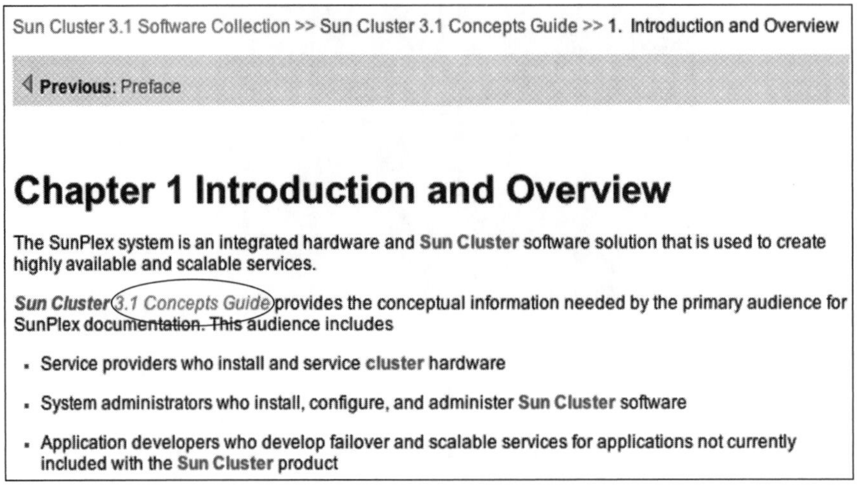

> Sun Cluster 3.1 Software Collection >> Sun Cluster 3.1 Concepts Guide >> 1. Introduction and Overview
>
> ◄ **Previous**: Preface
>
> # Chapter 1 Introduction and Overview
>
> The SunPlex system is an integrated hardware and **Sun Cluster** software solution that is used to create highly available and scalable services.
>
> *Sun Cluster 3.1 Concepts Guide* provides the conceptual information needed by the primary audience for SunPlex documentation. This audience includes
>
> - Service providers who install and service **cluster** hardware
>
> - System administrators who install, configure, and administer **Sun Cluster** software
>
> - Application developers who develop failover and scalable services for applications not currently included with the **Sun Cluster** product

Sun.com: in online documents, references to all documents are links, even to same one.

Avoiding Blooper 17

Nielsen and Tahir [2001] give the following design rule:

> Don't include an active link to the home page on the home page.

This rule can be generalized to any page:

> Don't include an active link to the current page on the current page.

Self-links in navigation bar: Hard to avoid?

Self-links in navigation bars are common because it is easier to use the exact same navigation bar code on every page than it is to alter the code for each page. Web developers sometimes argue that it is difficult to implement navigation bars in which the current page's item is not an active link. It is not hard. It just requires editing the code for each page and removing the link code for the current page's item on the navigation bar. Google.com and NWA.com avoid self-links in the navigation bar (Figure 3.27).

If the navigation bar code is generated dynamically, then just make sure the software that generates it suppresses links on navigation bar items for the current page.

Avoiding breadcrumbs to "here"

Self-links in breadcrumbs are easily avoided: the item for the current page should not be a link. This "best practice" design can be seen at United.com (Figure 3.28).

Figure 3.27

A

B

Navigation bar avoids link to current page. (A) Google.com. (B) NWA.com.

Figure 3.28

Home > Mileage Plus > Purchase Miles > Personal Miles

Personal Miles

Perfect if you are just a few thousand miles short of your next award trip. You can apply these miles toward award travel on United or any Mileage Plus airline partner, or toward upgrades on United.

United.com: last item (for current page) in breadcrumb path is not a link.

Blooper 18: Too many levels of dialog boxes

Developers often are so focused on designing windows or Web pages that they don't step back to look at the larger picture. How many windows or pages are there, and how easy is it for users to find their way around? Many software products and Web sites have too many windows or pages, or they have window/page hierarchies in which users get lost easily. "Where am I? How did I get here? How do I get back to where I was? Where is that Line Width setting? What was I doing before the phone rang?"

Constructing a representation of the software's entire window or page structure can show developers the "big picture." The best representation is a chart (Figure 3.29).

Some applications and Web sites have so many windows or pages that a chart is impractical because it would cover an entire wall or it would be a tangled mess of boxes and lines that would not be helpful. In such cases, use an outline instead (Figure 3.30).

Constructing a chart or outline that lays out the entire window or page structure of an application or Web site shows where the structure may be too deep.

A real example of the blooper

In Apple's Final Cut Pro, exporting an image from a video, optimized for streaming, requires navigating through *five* levels of dialog boxes:

1. Save As displays the Save dialog box (Figure 3.31A). Enter the file name, set the format to "Still Image" and, because there is no setting on this dialog box to optimize the image for streaming, click "Options...."

Figure 3.29   Checkbook window hierarchy

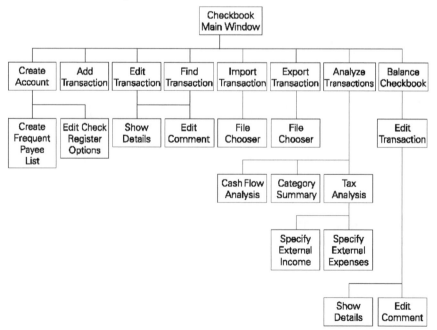

Window hierarchy graph for checkbook management application.

Figure 3.30

Checkbook window hierarchy

- Checkbook MainWindow
  - Create Account
    - Create Frequent Payee List
    - Edit CheckRegister Options
  - Add Transaction
    - Show Details
    - Edit Comment
  - Edit Transaction
    - Show Details
    - Edit Comment
  - Find Transaction
  - Import Transactions
    - Filechooser
  - Export Transactions
    - Filechooser
  - Analyze Transactions
    - Cash Flow Analysis
    - Category Summary
    - Tax Analysis
      - Specify External Income
      - Specify External Expenses
  - Balance Checkbook
    - Edit Transaction
      - Show Details
      - Edit Comment

Window hierarchy outline for checkbook management application.

2. The Export Image Sequence Settings dialog box appears (Figure 3.31B). (The window title doesn't mention "Options"; Blooper 15, page 117.) There is still no setting here to optimize the image for streaming, so click "Options...."

3. The QuickTime Image Options dialog box appears (Figure 3.31C). As this dialog box still has no direct setting to optimize the image for streaming, again click "Options...."

4. The Compression Settings dialog box appears (Figure 3.31D). (Note again the mismatch between the button label and the window title.) Yet again click "Options...."

5. The Photo JPEG Options dialog box appears (Figure 3.31E). Finally, a setting to optimize the image for streaming. Click it, then click OK on this dialog box, then OK on the fourth, then OK on the third, then OK on the second, then OK on the first.

Now, what were we doing?

Deep hierarchies of dialog boxes are bad for two reasons: (1) they divert users from their original goals and (2) users lose track of exactly which "OK" and "Cancel" buttons are the current ones. People don't handle deep hierarchical information structures well; when they have followed a hierarchy down more than a few levels, they tend to lose track of where they are, what they were doing, and how to get back.

Figure 3.31

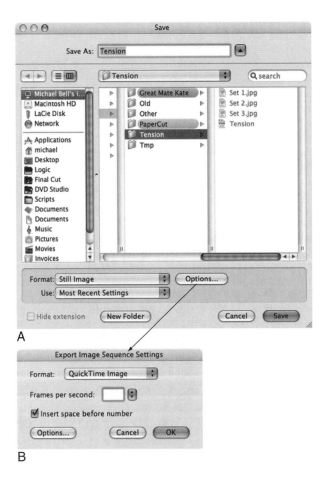

Apple FinalCut Pro: exporting image from video, optimized for streaming, requires (A), (B), (C), (D), and (E).

(Continued)

Figure 3.31

(Continued)

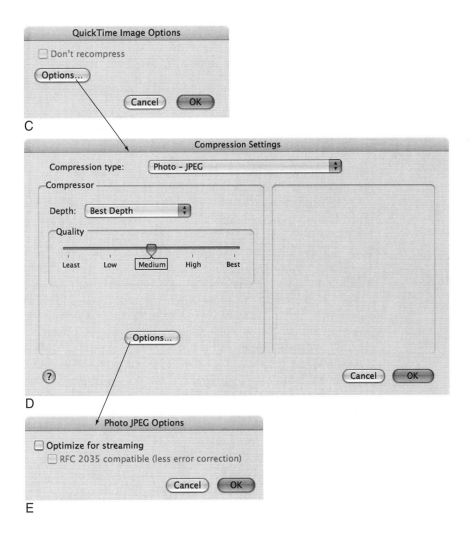

Other examples

Excerpts from two software reviews show other situations in which the blooper occurs:

- The hierarchy outline shows that certain areas of StockUp's window hierarchy are too deep, for example, the hierarchy below the various Monitor windows (five levels) and that below the Analysis window (six levels). Simplifying StockUp requires flattening these deep areas of the hierarchy.

- The chart shows that the designers' concern that the hierarchy is too deep is mostly unwarranted. The only area where the hierarchy seems too deep is in the networking monitoring and maintenance functions, which most users will not use.

Avoiding Blooper 18

The general rule is: Avoid more than two levels of dialog boxes. A dialog box can bring up another one, but beyond that, users may lose their way.

However, this rule is oversimplified and easy to misinterpret. It needs to be clarified and qualified.

Qualification 1: *It applies only to dialog boxes*

Dialog boxes are transient windows that allow users to specify arguments for a function, set attributes for a data object, or acknowledge having seen a message.

Most software applications display a main window, various dialog boxes, and a few additional primary windows. Primary windows function like outpost bases of operation and navigation; they serve as a temporary "home away from home." Therefore, they aren't counted against the depth limit of two levels.

Primary windows should come only from other primary windows. Dialog boxes should not display primary windows.[1] It would be unclear what would happen to a primary window when the user closed the dialog box that displayed it. In an application's window hierarchy, no branch should ever have a primary window below a dialog box. Any single line traced down the hierarchy should have some number of primary windows, ending with at most *two* dialog boxes. In practice, the number of levels of primary windows should also be kept low to avoid disorienting users, but there is no widely used design rule.

The same qualification applies to Web sites and Web applications, but is a bit more complicated due to ambiguity about what qualifies as a dialog box in the Web environment. There are three different ways to display a "dialog box" on the Web:

- *True dialog boxes:* Web browsers can display dialog boxes that are separate from the browser window. Such dialog boxes are exactly like the ones in desktop software. Web browsers provide several types of dialog boxes, each for a specific purpose, such as error, warning, information, and file chooser.

- *Separate browser windows:* Web applications sometimes display information or controls in pop-up (small) browser windows. Some pop-up browser windows function as dialog boxes: they display messages or settings with "OK" and "Cancel" (or similar) buttons at the bottom.

- *Dialog-box-like pages:* Some Web applications contain normal pages that function as dialog boxes even though they do not open separate windows. They show messages or settings with navigation buttons at the bottom. They are transient; users view them briefly, perhaps edit some settings, click OK or Cancel, and return to a previous page.

Web "dialog boxes," regardless of how they are displayed, are all subject to the two-level limit. On the other hand, they are also subject to Qualification 2.

---

1. With the exception of the Help document browser.

Qualification 2: Some types of dialog boxes don't count

Some dialog boxes provide functions that are so simple, idiomatic, and familiar that their presence won't distract or disorient users. Therefore, they are exempt from the two-level limit.

For example, many applications contain functions that require users to specify a file name. They display a file chooser dialog box, and users either type a file name or browse through the file hierarchy to choose a file. File choosers are so common that most users know what to do with them. Users don't regard them as a "place" in the application, but rather just as a choice mechanism. Paraphrasing Gertrude Stein, "there is no *there*" in a file chooser. File choosers add no noticeable complexity to an application. Therefore, even if a file chooser were a third-level dialog box, it would not violate the two-level maximum. This exception includes other simple and common "chooser" dialog boxes as well, such as color and date choosers.

Another type of dialog box that should be excluded when counting dialog box levels is error messages that accept only one response: "OK, I saw the message." As with choosers, the reason for exempting simple error dialog boxes is that they do not really add navigational "places" to the application and so do not noticeably increase the complexity of navigating in it.

The dialog boxes that are excluded from the two-level limit display no dialog boxes of their own. In other words, they are end points in the hierarchy. This is very important. Any dialog box that can display another dialog box, regardless of its type, should count against the two-level limit.

Chart or outline the window hierarchy

Developers cannot know whether their software violates or conforms to the two-level rule unless they know the software's window structure, which usually requires representing it as a chart or outline. Many developers don't do this and end up with overly deep hierarchies. You should create and maintain a representation of the window structure as part of your design process. These can also be used in user documentation.

When constructing a representation of the window hierarchy, omit choosers and error dialog boxes. Including them makes the chart or outline too unwieldy.

Ways to cut excess levels

If the window or page hierarchy for an application is too deep in some places, what can you do? That depends on *why* you have settings on separate windows.

- Some GUIs use additional windows to provide progressive disclosure—hide details until users ask to see them. In that case, you can use a "Details" panel instead of a separate window.

Figure 3.32

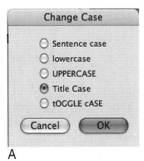

A

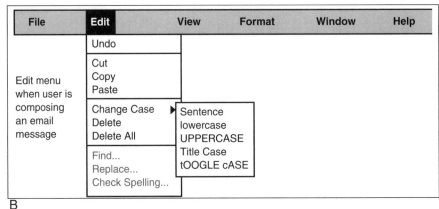

B

(A) Word Change Case dialog box. (B) Case options in cascading menu instead of dialog box.

- Some dialog boxes provide options on commands. For example, Microsoft Word's Change Case function displays a dialog box offering several ways to change the case of the selected text (Figure 3.32A). This dialog box is not embedded in excessive levels, but if it were, a designer could eliminate it by putting the choices in a cascading menu (Figure 3.32B).

Poor search navigation

One way for users of interactive systems to find their way to their goals is by using Search functions. However, not all Search functions are created equal. Some make searching easy, while others make it difficult. Some Search functions complicate the search-input stage by providing too many ways to search without enough guidance about when to use which one. Other Search functions complicate the search-output stage by returning results that make it hard to find the truly relevant items. This chapter's last section examines common ways in which Search functions complicate navigating toward users' goals.

More Search-related bloopers are described in *Web Bloopers* [Johnson, 2003].

Blooper 19: Competing search boxes

When users are faced with multiple search boxes, they often wonder: "Which one should I use?" "Are they different?" "Do they search the same data?" It's a poor design that distracts users from their own goals and makes them think about the software [Krug, 2005].

Variation A: Oops! Wrong search!

Sometimes different search boxes on a page search different things, but users may not know that. The New Zealand University of Canterbury's Web site (canterbury.ac.nz) provides an example. The site's "Courses, Subjects, and Qualifications" page has two search boxes (Figure 3.33). Many assume that both boxes can search the Course catalogue for specific courses. In fact, only the box on the left does. The box on the right is for searching the site itself—either the whole site or just the Courses section. Given a course code, it won't find course listings; only articles and pages that mention the course. However, most users notice the search box on the right first because that is the site's standard position for the search box. This causes many students to try at first to search for course information using the *wrong* search box.

Variation B: Two identical search boxes. How to choose?

A second variation of the blooper is when a site or application has two identical or very similar-looking search boxes on the same page. Users may assume that if there are two, they must differ somehow. Even if users know that the search

Figure 3.33

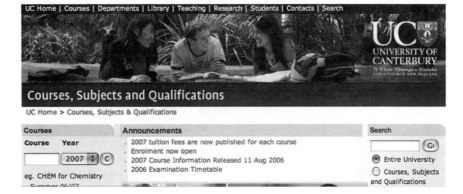

Canterbury.ac.nz: two search boxes on page. Which one searches for courses?

Figure 3.34

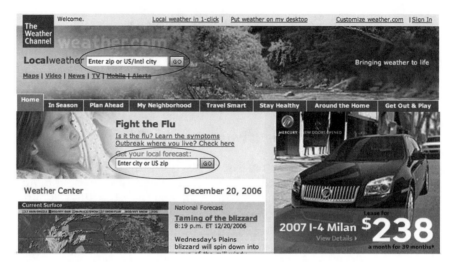

Weather.com: two identical search boxes on page. Users must choose one arbitrarily.

boxes are the same, they have to choose one… arbitrarily. An example occurs at Weather.com (Figure 3.34).

Variation C: Hmm. Which one's best?

Canterbury.ac.nz, already cited above for committing Variation A, also commits the third variation. The site's search page offers three search boxes—four if we count the main search box on the upper right of the page (Figure 3.35). This page has three problems:

- Site users may not realize that the ubiquitous upper-right search box and "UC Search" are the same. They have to learn this. Even once they do, we have Variation B.

- "Advanced Search" uses the same search engine as "UC Search" but provides more controls. The difference in controls is minor, unlike some sites, in which an advanced search has many extra controls. For this minor difference, a separate "Advanced Search" box seems unwarranted. Also, some users may assume that "Advanced Search" uses a different search engine.

- The "Google Search" uses the Google search engine and advises that "this is best for multi-word searches." This makes users think: "Should I use the other search boxes for single-word searches? Is Google worse for single-word searches? Why should I use 'UC Search' and 'Advanced Search' at all?"

Figure 3.35

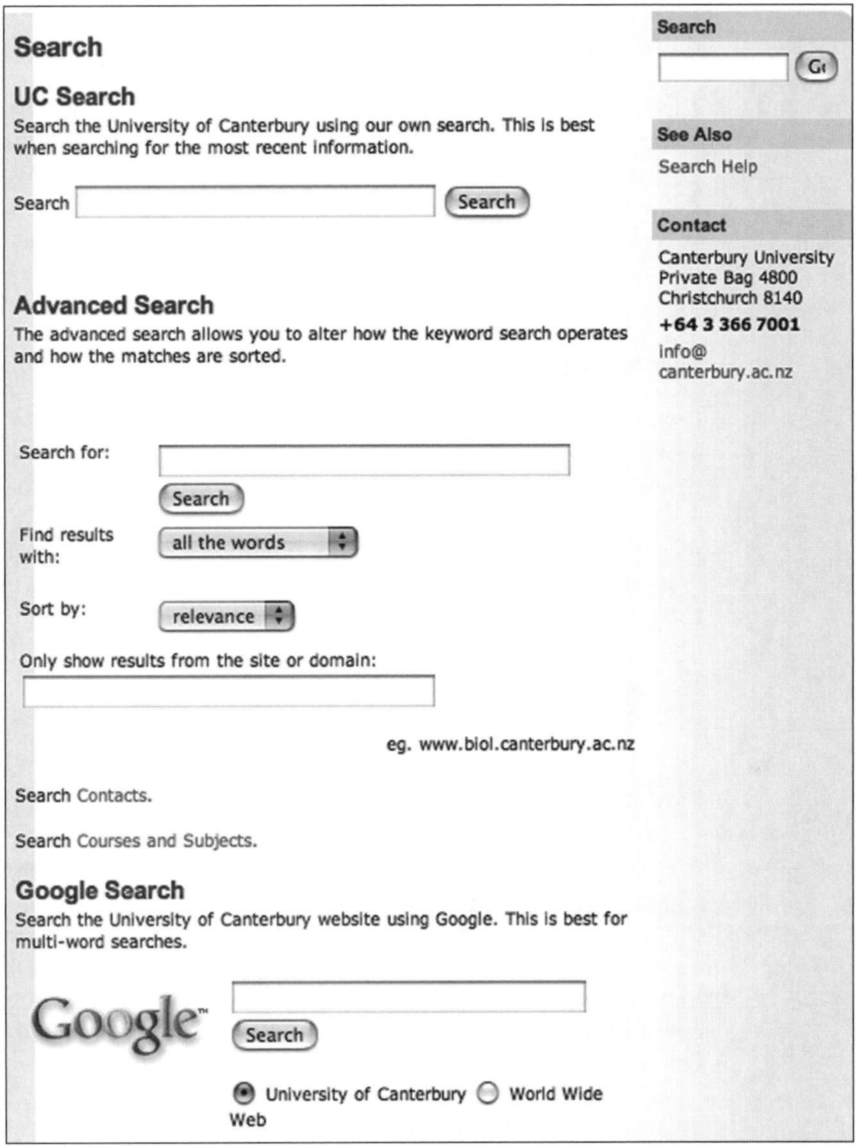

Search

UC Search

Search the University of Canterbury using our own search. This is best when searching for the most recent information.

Search [_____] (Search)

Advanced Search

The advanced search allows you to alter how the keyword search operates and how the matches are sorted.

Search for: [_____]

(Search)

Find results with: [all the words ⬍]

Sort by: [relevance ⬍]

Only show results from the site or domain:

[_____]

eg. www.biol.canterbury.ac.nz

Search Contacts.

Search Courses and Subjects.

Google Search

Search the University of Canterbury website using Google. This is best for multi-word searches.

Google™ [_____]

(Search)

◉ University of Canterbury ◯ World Wide Web

Search

[_____] (G⟩

See Also

Search Help

Contact

Canterbury University
Private Bag 4800
Christchurch 8140
+64 3 366 7001
info@
canterbury.ac.nz

Canterbury.ac.nz: four search boxes on page, but it's unclear how users choose one.

Avoiding Blooper 19

GUI designers may have reasons for providing multiple competing search boxes on a page. However, doing that has *costs* that must be weighed against the benefits. The costs boil down to this: the search boxes compete for attention.

If competing search boxes represent *different* Search functions, as in the examples from Canterbury.ac.nz, one cost is that people might use the wrong one. They might notice the wrong one first and use it, overlooking the correct one. Even if they see both, they might not know how they differ—or even that they differ—and choose the wrong one for their intended search.

If search boxes are for the *same* Search function, as at Weather.com, users must *decide* which one to use. According to Raskin [2000], providing multiple ways in a UI to do the same thing costs users time and distracts them from their main tasks.

Less is more

For Search functions, as for user interfaces in general, less is more. In fact, for search boxes on a page, the best number is 1. More than one causes confusion, delay, and error.

If you are considering putting two or three copies of the same search box on a page because you aren't sure where visitors will look, don't do it. Place just one search box prominently, in one of the standard places: top left under the logo, top right, or lower left under the navigation column. Make sure users recognize it as a search box.

If you plan to include a box for searching the entire Web, heed this advice from Nielsen and Tahir [2001]:

> Don't offer a feature to "Search the Web" … Users will use their favorite search engine to do that, and this option makes search more complex and error-prone.

If you want to provide different Search functions for searching different data sources, such as general site content vs. news articles vs. stock prices, design them to look *completely* different. Design each search box to look specific to its own search domain. None of the special-purpose search boxes should look like a general search box (Figure 3.36A). A function for looking up stock quotes could be sized to fit only stock symbols, and its button could be labeled "Get Quote" instead of "Search" (Figure 3.36B).

The home pages of BarnesAndNoble.com and IEEE.org have well-distinguished Search functions on the same page (Figure 3.37).

Finally, if a page has two search boxes to let users choose between search engines having different characteristics, ask if that is the real reason. If the *real*

Figure 3.36

| | Search | Symbol: | Get Quote |

A   B

Search boxes for different purposes look different. (A) Main site search. (B) Stock quote lookup.

Figure 3.37

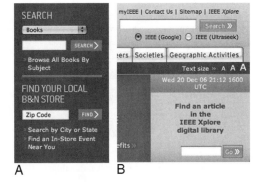

Search boxes for different purposes look different. (A) BarnesAndNoble.com. (B) IEEE.org.

reason is that the *developers* can't decide between the search engines, choose one and consider the other one "exploratory development." If the intent to give users a choice is sincere, ask whether users really care. Even if they do, don't offer the choice on your home page. The home page should have one general search box, period. Options should be confined to the "Advanced Search" page. Even there, the choice should be an option affecting a single search box, rather than multiple competing ones.

Blooper 20: Poor search results browsing

Imagine that you've just used a Web site's Search function. You are now looking at the results. Browsing search results often includes looking through several results pages for relevant items. Many search result displays don't provide an easy way for users to navigate through pages of hits. Many list the hits in batches of however many fit on a screen and make users click "Next" repeatedly to get to pages beyond the first.

At IBM.com, searching for "tablet computers" yields 138,039 hits, listing 10 per page (Figure 3.38). The results page provides only one way to move through the results pages: page by page using "Next" and "Back" links at the bottom of the page (Figure 3.38), waiting for a page load each time. There is no easy way to get to the last page, or the sixth.

The product Search function at BuyReliant.com, an online electronics store, commits a worse form of this blooper. It lists products 20 at a time with only "Next" and "Back" to move between pages, but also doesn't indicate the total number of products found. If it found more than 20, the first page of hits has a "Next" button (Figure 3.39). If it found more than 40, the second page has a "Next" button, and so on. Only by tediously "NEXTing" to the last page can users learn how many products were found.

Figure 3.38

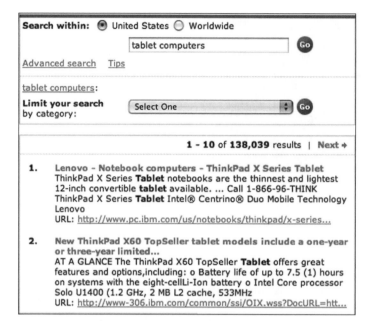

IBM.com: search results are difficult to browse because only "Next" and "Back" are provided.

Figure 3.39

Code	Name	Price		
29740	GE Cordless Answerer	$65.00	Add to Cart	Buy Now
MPR650	Coby MP3 Encoder Player	$159.00	Add to Cart	Buy Now
FF665	Southwestern Bell Cordless Telephone	$47.50	Add to Cart	Buy Now
29880	GE Caller ID*/Answerer Telephone	$29.99	Add to Cart	Buy Now
29096	GE Caller ID	$18.00	Add to Cart	Buy Now
CTP820IV	Coby Speaker Telephone	$12.90	Add to Cart	Buy Now
27993GE3	GE Cordless Telephone Answwerer	$42.50	Add to Cart	Buy Now
29257GE1	GE Single Line Corded Telephone	$8.99	Add to Cart	Buy Now
CTP30	Coby Caller ID/Call Waiting	$12.90	Add to Cart	Buy Now
CTP920	Coby Digital Telephone Answering System	$19.90	Add to Cart	Buy Now
CTP650	Coby Caller ID Desktop Telephone	$16.90	Add to Cart	Buy Now
CTP730IV	Coby 13 Memory Speakerphone	$11.99	Add to Cart	Buy Now
SMP115	Jensen MP3 Player	$77.90	Add to Cart	Buy Now
DXI7286-2	Uniden 2.4 GHz Extended Range	$39.90	Add to Cart	Buy Now
SMP215	Digital Audio Player with Back-Lit Display	$92.90	Add to Cart	Buy Now
SS210	Telephone with Caller ID	$27.90	Add to Cart	Buy Now
DCT646-2	Uniden 2.4Ghz with Extra Handset and Base	$64.90	Add to Cart	Buy Now
CTP8600BK	Coby 2 Line Cordless Caller ID Speakerphone	$39.90	Add to Cart	Buy Now
PSR295	Yamaha Music Making Fun Keyboard	$179.90	Add to Cart	Buy Now
DGX205	Yamaha Portable Grand	$268.50	Add to Cart	Buy Now

Search For The Following Word(s): flash memory   [Search]

Next >

BuyReliant.com: search results don't give hit count and provide only "Next" and "Back."

Figure 3.40

CompUSA.com: links for all pages of hits support easy search results browsing.

Avoiding Blooper 20

Search results should not only remind users what the search terms were and indicate the number of hits [Johnson, 2003], they should also make it easy for users to browse through the hits. If a large number of hits is displayed in a series of pages, it should be clear how many results pages there are, and it should be possible to get to any results page in one or two clicks.

CompUSA.com makes it easy for users to browse pages of search results (Figure 3.40).

Blooper 21: Noisy search results

Even if search results allow users to navigate through pages of hits, there is still the issue of how easy it is to spot the truly relevant hits amid all the others. Consider how you do it. Do you carefully read each hit, scrutinizing every detail? Do you click on each hit one by one? Of course not! You quickly scan the list for a few hits that look promising.

Now imagine you are an evil Web designer. You want to make it hard for people to spot promising items in the search results. How could you do that? Simple:

1. *Bury differences in noise.* Include superfluous gobbledygook in each item so items are hard to distinguish. Force people to carefully examine each one to see what it's about and how it differs from other items. You could load each hit with marketing hype, navigation links, or database output that is the same for every hit. That'll slow them down!

2. *Force users to click on hits*. Even better, make the hits look *exactly* alike. Then the only way to check one's relevance is to actually click on it, consuming the user's valuable time while the browser loads the page.

Many Web Search functions use these "techniques" so well, they seem to have been designed by evil designers *trying* to make searching difficult for visitors.

An example of burying differences in noise comes from a Search function on the Web site of the Federal Reserve Bank of Minneapolis. Each hit in the search results includes three pieces of repeated content (Figure 3.41):

- The top link on every item starts with the text "Federal Reserve Bank of Minneapolis."

- The text excerpted from the page usually starts with "I'm at > > > > Articles Publications Articles Toolbox ( )"—probably navigation links common to most pages.

- A URL is displayed prominently for each hit, including the part indicating that the item was found at http://www.MinneapolisFed.org, which is obvious, since that is the site searched.

Figure 3.41

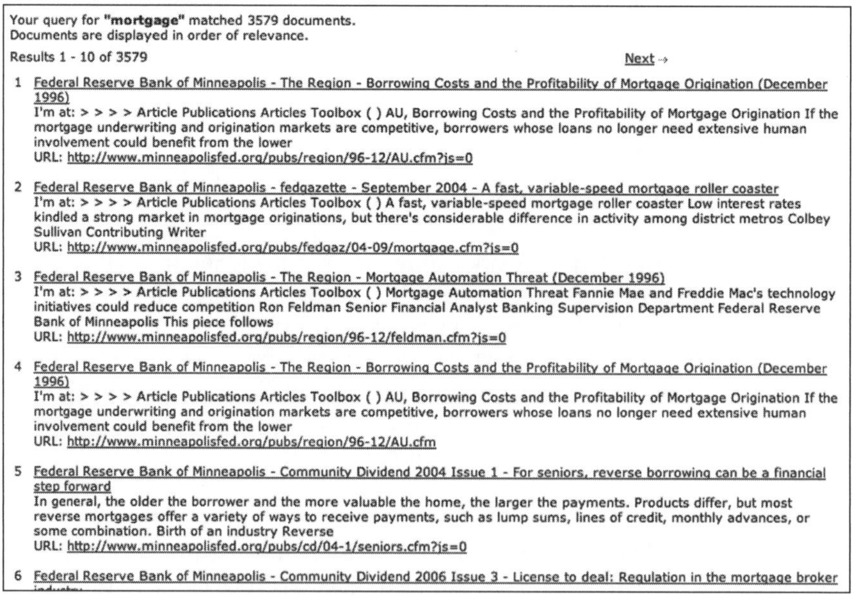

Your query for **"mortgage"** matched 3579 documents.
Documents are displayed in order of relevance.

Results 1 - 10 of 3579   Next →

1 Federal Reserve Bank of Minneapolis - The Region - Borrowing Costs and the Profitability of Mortgage Origination (December 1996)
   I'm at: > > > > Article Publications Articles Toolbox ( ) AU, Borrowing Costs and the Profitability of Mortgage Origination If the mortgage underwriting and origination markets are competitive, borrowers whose loans no longer need extensive human involvement could benefit from the lower
   URL: http://www.minneapolisfed.org/pubs/region/96-12/AU.cfm?js=0

2 Federal Reserve Bank of Minneapolis - fedgazette - September 2004 - A fast, variable-speed mortgage roller coaster
   I'm at: > > > > Article Publications Articles Toolbox ( ) A fast, variable-speed mortgage roller coaster Low interest rates kindled a strong market in mortgage originations, but there's considerable difference in activity among district metros Colbey Sullivan Contributing Writer
   URL: http://www.minneapolisfed.org/pubs/fedgaz/04-09/mortgage.cfm?js=0

3 Federal Reserve Bank of Minneapolis - The Region - Mortgage Automation Threat (December 1996)
   I'm at: > > > > Article Publications Articles Toolbox ( ) Mortgage Automation Threat Fannie Mae and Freddie Mac's technology initiatives could reduce competition Ron Feldman Senior Financial Analyst Banking Supervision Department Federal Reserve Bank of Minneapolis This piece follows
   URL: http://www.minneapolisfed.org/pubs/region/96-12/feldman.cfm?js=0

4 Federal Reserve Bank of Minneapolis - The Region - Borrowing Costs and the Profitability of Mortgage Origination (December 1996)
   I'm at: > > > > Article Publications Articles Toolbox ( ) AU, Borrowing Costs and the Profitability of Mortgage Origination If the mortgage underwriting and origination markets are competitive, borrowers whose loans no longer need extensive human involvement could benefit from the lower
   URL: http://www.minneapolisfed.org/pubs/region/96-12/AU.cfm

5 Federal Reserve Bank of Minneapolis - Community Dividend 2004 Issue 1 - For seniors, reverse borrowing can be a financial step forward
   In general, the older the borrower and the more valuable the home, the larger the payments. Products differ, but most reverse mortgages offer a variety of ways to receive payments, such as lump sums, lines of credit, monthly advances, or some combination. Birth of an industry Reverse
   URL: http://www.minneapolisfed.org/pubs/cd/04-1/seniors.cfm?js=0

6 Federal Reserve Bank of Minneapolis - Community Dividend 2006 Issue 3 - License to deal: Regulation in the mortgage broker industry

MinneapolisFed.org: content repeated in hits makes results "noisy" and hard to scan.

This repetition contributes no value to the results list; it adds only visual noise, thereby making the results hard to scan quickly.

What about the second evil technique: having hits look so alike that the only way to check their relevance is to click on them? In early 2006, the U.S. Department of State's Web site (state.gov) had a Search function that displayed the same title for several successive hits, as is shown by the results for a search for "Colin Powell" (Figure 3.42). It also prominently displayed the location of each hit in the site's page hierarchy. The location is highly likely to be the same or very similar for successive hits, so it is not very useful for evaluating and distinguishing hits.

By late 2006, the State Department had redesigned their search results to be much easier to scan and evaluate, as the results of a recent search for "Colin Powell" show (Figure 3.43).

Another example comes from AYA.Yale.edu, the Web site of the Yale University Alumni Association (Figure 3.44). Every hit shows navigation links that are the same for all hits.

Given results like these, a user might assume that a faulty search engine returned several links to the same item. There are differences between the hits, but they are hard to spot and not useful for deciding which hits are relevant.

Figure 3.42

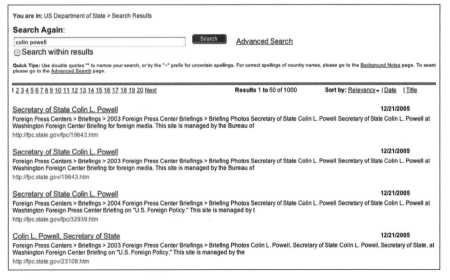

state.gov (Jan 2006): data displayed for each hit is mostly useless for distinguishing them.

Figure 3.43

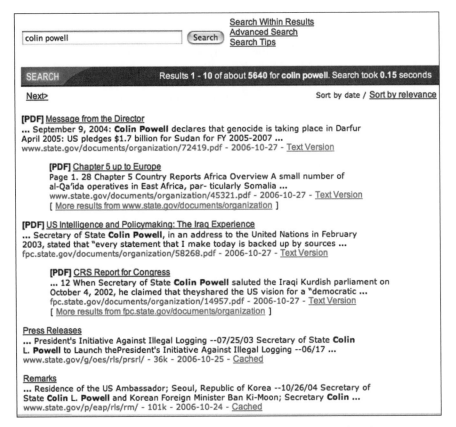

state.gov (Oct 2006): data displayed for each hit is easier to scan and evaluate.

Avoiding Blooper 21

Any designer wants users of their software to be able to scan search results quickly and find the relevant items. How can you avoid letting the evil designer within you compromise your good intentions? Easy: invert the evil designer's rules:

1. *Show and stress important data.* Minimize repetition between hits. Most of each item should be information that lets people *distinguish* items from one another. The distinguishing data for each item should be emphasized. Repetitive information should be cut or deemphasized. Cut the visual *noise* and focus users' attention on the *information* in each item.

2. *Minimize the need to click.* People should have to click on hits *only* to actually get the item (purchase, read). They should not have to follow links just to see which ones are relevant.

Contrast the poor search results displayed by the Yale Alumni Web site (Figure 3.44) with the much more usable results displayed by Yale's main site (Figure 3.45). In both examples, the search was for "chemistry." Note how the main site minimizes repetition between hits and visually deemphasizes the hit URLs, which of course are similar.

Figure 3.44

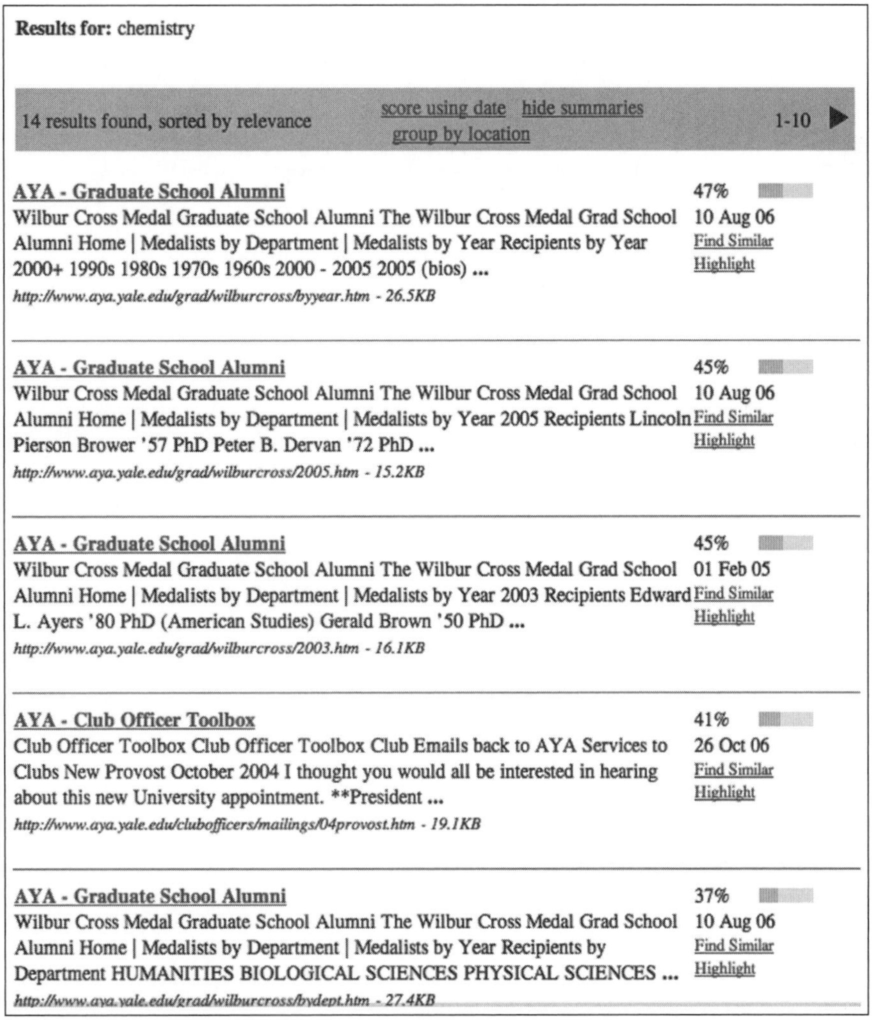

Results for: chemistry

14 results found, sorted by relevance   score using date   hide summaries   group by location   1-10 ▶

AYA - Graduate School Alumni   47%
Wilbur Cross Medal Graduate School Alumni The Wilbur Cross Medal Grad School   10 Aug 06
Alumni Home | Medalists by Department | Medalists by Year Recipients by Year   Find Similar
2000+ 1990s 1980s 1970s 1960s 2000 - 2005 2005 (bios) ...   Highlight
http://www.aya.yale.edu/grad/wilburcross/byyear.htm - 26.5KB

AYA - Graduate School Alumni   45%
Wilbur Cross Medal Graduate School Alumni The Wilbur Cross Medal Grad School   10 Aug 06
Alumni Home | Medalists by Department | Medalists by Year 2005 Recipients Lincoln   Find Similar
Pierson Brower '57 PhD Peter B. Dervan '72 PhD ...   Highlight
http://www.aya.yale.edu/grad/wilburcross/2005.htm - 15.2KB

AYA - Graduate School Alumni   45%
Wilbur Cross Medal Graduate School Alumni The Wilbur Cross Medal Grad School   01 Feb 05
Alumni Home | Medalists by Department | Medalists by Year 2003 Recipients Edward   Find Similar
L. Ayers '80 PhD (American Studies) Gerald Brown '50 PhD ...   Highlight
http://www.aya.yale.edu/grad/wilburcross/2003.htm - 16.1KB

AYA - Club Officer Toolbox   41%
Club Officer Toolbox Club Officer Toolbox Club Emails back to AYA Services to   26 Oct 06
Clubs New Provost October 2004 I thought you would all be interested in hearing   Find Similar
about this new University appointment. **President ...   Highlight
http://www.aya.yale.edu/clubofficers/mailings/04provost.htm - 19.1KB

AYA - Graduate School Alumni   37%
Wilbur Cross Medal Graduate School Alumni The Wilbur Cross Medal Grad School   10 Aug 06
Alumni Home | Medalists by Department | Medalists by Year Recipients by   Find Similar
Department HUMANITIES BIOLOGICAL SCIENCES PHYSICAL SCIENCES ...   Highlight
http://www.aya.yale.edu/grad/wilburcross/bydept.htm - 27.4KB

AYA.Yale.edu: many hits look almost identical.

Figure 3.45

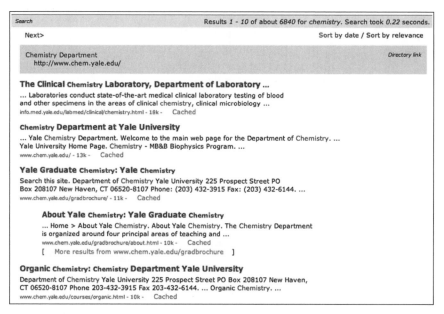

Yale.edu: search results are easy to scan and evaluate.

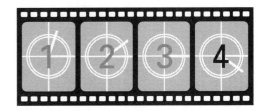

Textual Bloopers

Introduction

One irony of graphical user interfaces is that most aren't very graphical. The typical GUI contains a lot of text:

- The labels for commands in menus or on buttons are mostly text.
- Instructions are almost always text.
- Most user input consists of typing or selecting words and numbers.
- The labels on most controls and form fields are text.
- The names users assign to data files and other data objects are always textual.
- Error and warning messages are mainly textual, even if highlighted with a color or a symbol.

Therefore, do not underestimate the importance of text in GUIs.

Software designers may try to minimize the use of text in software, but many concepts simply cannot be expressed without text. The saying "A picture is worth a thousand words" is an oversimplification: sometimes a few words are worth more than any number of pictures.

For example, the designers of an interactive movie game wanted the game's navigation controls to be purely graphical, but found it necessary to augment many symbols with text to clarify their meaning [Johnson, 1998].

Even in the most graphical of user interfaces, text usually plays a role. Creative's Surround Mixer application is more graphical than most (Figure 4.1). Nonetheless, it makes use of text: the company logo, the application title, the menus, and the tooltips for controls.

Textual usability problems are usually easy and cheap to correct. On the other hand, they often have root causes in the development process or organization. Correcting those is, of course, not easy or cheap.

Because text plays an important role in user interfaces, there are many ways to use it badly. These are textual bloopers. This chapter describes three categories of textual bloopers, explains why developers sometimes commit them, and provides advice on how to avoid them.

Uncommunicative text

The first four textual bloopers are caused by poor writing. They often result from assigning the writing of text in a GUI to people who are not skilled at that.

Blooper 22: Inconsistent terminology

One of the most common textual bloopers is to be haphazard and inconsistent about which terms are used for what concepts. This makes software much harder to learn.

Many development teams aren't aware that inconsistent terminology is bad, so they make no effort to ensure that their terminology is consistent. What begins as a flaw in their development *process* turns into a flaw in their *products*: many-to-one and one-to-many mappings between terms and concepts.

Eye-opener: List all the terms

It is useful to construct a table showing the terms used in an application and its manuals for each concept user to see. The results are usually eye-opening to development managers: "I had no idea! No *wonder* users are having trouble learning to use our product!" Unfortunately, the typical reaction from programmers is "So what? We have more important problems to worry about than whether we use the exact same term from one screen to the next."

There are two different ways for terminology to be inconsistent.

Variation A: Different terms for the same concept

The more common variation is for software to use multiple terms for a single concept. It might refer to "results" in one window and "output" in another, even though the same thing is meant. If you were trying to confuse users, this would be one of the best ways.

Figure 4.1

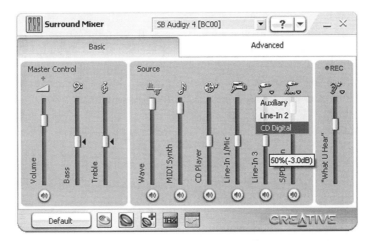

Creative's Surround Mixer: highly graphical, but like most GUIs, includes text.

The following are samples of terms used interchangeably in real applications:

- Properties, attributes, parameters, settings, resources
- Welcome window, Introduction window
- Version, revision
- FAQ (frequently asked questions), QNA (questions and answers)
- Find, search, query, inquiry
- Server, service
- Exit, quit
- Order size, order quantity
- Stock symbol, instrument ID, instrument, instr ID
- Task, step
- Specify goal, define goal

Inconsistent terminology can result from name changes during development that were not corrected everywhere in the software and documentation. It can also result from not creating and using a product lexicon during development. Sometimes inconsistent terms are caused by a lack of communication or a lack of agreement between programmers. Programmers also may not have considered using consistent names important, given the time pressure they were under. All of these causes come from Blooper 67: Anarchic development (page 348).

A very common case of multiple terms for a concept is when error messages use a form field's *internal* name rather than its label on the form. Examples come from CityCarShare.org, Evite.com, and UBS.com (Figure 4.2).

When different words are used to describe the same thing, users may not realize that. Users think mainly about the goal they are trying to achieve and the data they are creating and manipulating (Basic Principle 5, page 35). They think hardly at all about the user interface, such as whether a "User ID" is the same thing as an "Alias." Inconsistent terminology causes users to either make errors or spend mental effort figuring out how terms relate.

Variation B: *The same term for different concepts*

The opposite error is almost as common: using a single term for more than one concept, also known as *overloading* a word. For example, here are the many things "View" meant in one application:

- The data-display windows, e.g., Understanding View, Evaluation View, Fields Ranking View

Figure 4.2

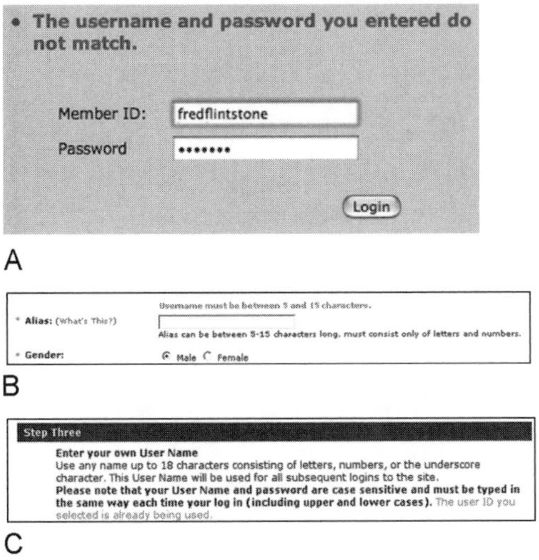

- **The username and password you entered do not match.**

Member ID: fredflintstone
Password   •••••••

(Login)

A

* **Alias:** (What's This?)   Username must be between 5 and 15 characters.

Alias can be between 5-15 characters long, must consist only of letters and numbers.

* **Gender:**   ⦿ Male ○ Female

B

Step Three

Enter your own User Name
Use any name up to 18 characters consisting of letters, numbers, or the underscore character. This User Name will be used for all subsequent logins to the site.
Please note that your User Name and password are case sensitive and must be typed in the same way each time your log in (including upper and lower cases). The user ID you selected is already being used.

C

User ID named differently in error messages. (A) CityCarShare.org. (B) Evite.com. (C) UBS.com.

- Different ways of filtering the Understanding View, e.g., Required View, Specific View
- Actions that affect the data-flow diagram, e.g., Shrink View, Enlarge View
- The View menu, which controls display of other parts of the application
- Some items in the View menu treated "View" as a verb (e.g., "View → Results") while others treated it as a noun (e.g., "View → Enlarge").

Using the same term for different things is usually not intentional; it happens because developers don't think about it. In normal conversation, people use words that have multiple meanings, and listeners resolve ambiguity either from the context in which the word is used or by asking the speaker to clarify. Human–computer communication is less forgiving of ambiguity. It doesn't provide much conversational context. Requests for clarification are one-way only: software can ask its user to clarify an input, but the user cannot ask software to clarify the meaning of a word. Therefore, overloaded words are less acceptable in user interfaces than in communication between people.

Microsoft Word has overloaded terms. Word's Insert menu includes both an Insert Object… command and an Insert Picture… command (Figure 4.3). Insert Object inserts many different types of objects, including Equations, Excel worksheets, Word documents, and Word pictures. Users might expect Insert Object with Word Picture as the object type to do the same thing as Insert Picture. Wrong! Inserting a Word Picture using Insert Object inserts a graphics frame for creating line drawings. In contrast, Insert Picture displays a file chooser that lets users import an externally created image file.

Figure 4.3

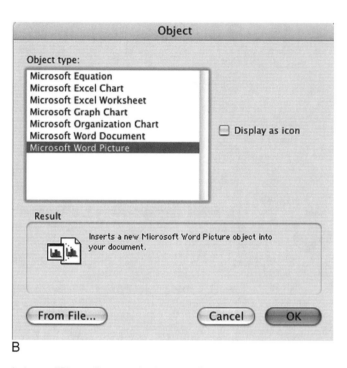

Microsoft Word: overloaded term "Picture" means both image file and line-drawing area.

Often the same term means both an object and a part of the object. In an e-mail program, the word "message" might sometimes mean the entire file received from another user, including headers, message body, and attachments. Other times, the word "message" might mean just the text content. The ambiguity would confuse new users, slowing their learning.

A commonly overloaded term is "select." It often is used to mean both: (a) clicking on an object to highlight it and (b) adding an object to a list. Consider, for example, the Available Updates dialog box from Adobe Reader (Figure 4.4). The list on the right is labeled "Selected." The "Add" button adds an item from the left list to the right list. The item it adds is the highlighted item in the left list. What do we call that item? The *selected* item, of course.

When you assign extra meanings to "select," you open the door to confusing instructions such as:

> To select the updates you want to install, first select them in the Available list and click the "Add" button, which adds them to the Selected list.

The Print & Fax Preferences window in MacOS X also misuses "select" (Figure 4.5). The first of two settings refers to the "selected" printer, meaning the *default* printer. (We will save for later the blooper of exposing the GUI toolkit term "dialog" to users.)

Figure 4.4

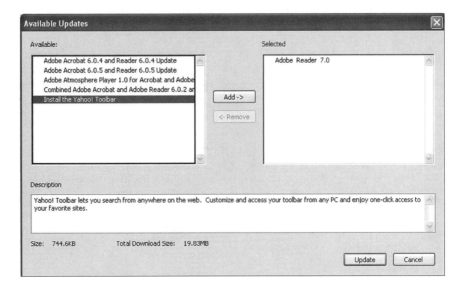

Adobe Reader: uses the reserved term "selected" incorrectly.

Figure 4.5

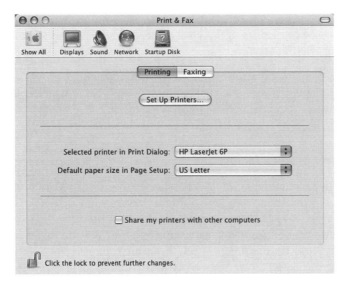

MacOS X: "selected" misused for *default*.

Confusion between the terms "cursor," "text insertion point," and "screen pointer" is another source of ambiguity. Before GUIs, there was no such thing as a screen pointer, and the text insertion point and the cursor were the same thing. Nowadays these are distinct concepts, but "cursor" sometimes means the text insertion point and sometimes means the screen pointer.

Avoiding Blooper 22

Software users are trying to find their way in an unfamiliar application. They don't know that the programmer of the main window calls searching a database "making a query" while the programmer of most of the dialog boxes calls it "specifying an inquiry." They don't know that an "employee" and a "record" are the same thing or even that "record" is a noun in this program.

Furthermore, computer users don't *want* to know these things. They just want to do their work. They are not interested in the computer and its software per se. They don't care how developers view the software. They are often so focused on their work that if they are looking for a Search function but it's labeled "Query" here, they may miss it. Therefore, design the terminology in a UI as if the users will interpret it extremely literally.

One name per concept

Caroline Jarrett, an authority on GUI and forms design, states this rule for terminology in software and Web sites:

> Same name, same thing; different name, different thing—Caroline Jarrett, www. formsthatwork.com

Terms in software should map strictly 1:1 to concepts. Even terms that are ambiguous in the real world should mean only one thing *in the software*. Otherwise, the software's usability will suffer.

Create a product lexicon

Early in development, you should specify the concepts the software will expose to users. This is called developing a "conceptual model" (Basic Principle 2, page 18). From that your team should develop a product "lexicon."[1] It lists a name and definition for each concept that will be exposed to users in the product and its documentation. It should map terms 1:1 onto concepts. It should not assign different terms to a single concept or a single term to different concepts.

Terms in the lexicon should come from the software's supported *tasks,* not its implementation. Terms should fit well into the users' normal task vocabulary, even if they are new. Typically, UI designers, developers, technical writers, managers, and users all help create the lexicon.

---

1. Also called "nomenclature," "vocabulary," "dictionary," "terminology standard."

Use industry-standard terms for common concepts

Certain concepts in GUIs have industry-standard names. These are the GUI equivalents of "reserved words" in programming languages. If you rename such concepts or assign new meanings to the standard names, you will confuse users.

One reserved term is "select." It means clicking on an object to highlight it, marking it as the object for future actions. The word "select" should not be used for any other purpose in a GUI, e.g., adding an item to a list or a collection. Adobe Reader could avoid the blooper by using the label "To Be Installed" instead of misusing the word "select" (Figure 4.6).

Standard terms and their definitions are given in platform style guides, such as the ones for Windows [Microsoft Corp., 2006], Macintosh [Apple Computer, 2006], and Java [Sun Microsystems, 2001]. You should use the industry-standard GUI vocabulary for your target platform.

Enforce the lexicon

The product lexicon should be followed consistently throughout the software, user manuals, and marketing literature. To ensure this, someone has to enforce the lexicon. This can be either the project's information architect or the head technical writer. The enforcer reminds developers to either use the agreed-upon term for a concept or petition to *change the lexicon*.

Figure 4.6

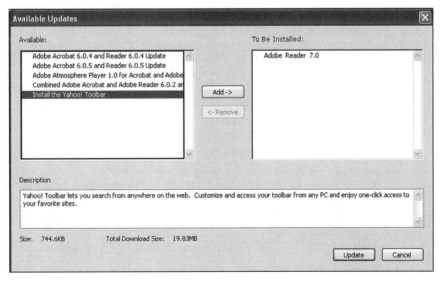

Adobe Reader could avoid misusing "selected" by relabeling the right list "To Be Installed."

"Enforcer" conjures up images of burly men carrying violin cases, but it is better if the enforcer is friendly. Here's one side of a phone conversation between the lexicon enforcer and a programmer:

> "Hey, Anoop, it's Sergei. Got a minute? On your pages in our customer service Web site, you use the term "bug report" for when customers submit a problem. But our agreed-upon term is "action request," remember? That's what's in the lexicon. Where's the lexicon? At the project's Intranet Web site. Can you please change "bug report" to "action request" on all your pages? We're running usability tests on Thursday, so I'm hoping you can make these changes by Wednesday. You will? Great, thanks!"

The lexicon should be treated as a living document: it changes as the product evolves based on new design insights, changes in functionality, usability test results, and market feedback.

Test the lexicon on users

As the lexicon is developed, it should be tested on people who are typical of the software's intended users to see if it matches the users' vocabulary. If it doesn't, change it.

Terminology can be tested before the software is implemented or even fully designed. Users can be shown terms and asked to explain what each term means to them. They can also be asked to match terms with descriptions by arranging 3 × 5 cards or by drawing lines between terms and descriptions printed on paper. Finally, the terminology can be tested in early mock-ups.

Use message files

Before release, a systematic review of all text can uncover both variations of this blooper: different terms for the same concept and the same term for different concepts. However, if the only way to review a program's messages, labels, and instructions is by operating the program or searching through its source code, oversights are likely.

If the text displayed by a program is in a message file,[2] reviewing it and checking it for conflicts and inconsistencies are much easier. That is only one of the many advantages of using message files.

When different parts of the software need to refer to the same concept or present the same message, they should simply reference the same text string in the message file. That reduces the chances of committing Variation A of the blooper: different terms for the same concept.

---

2. Often called a "resource file."

Message files also make it easier to avoid Variation B of the blooper: the same term for different concepts. When the message file is reviewed, duplicate text strings in it are one of two possibilities:

1. *Redundant text strings that should be one:* These are errors. Leaving them separate makes it possible that someone will change one and neglect to change the other, causing the software to manifest Variation A of the blooper. All but one instance of the string should be deleted, and all references to that string should point to that one instance.

2. *Text strings for different situations that are the same:* These are probably errors, giving rise to Variation B of the blooper. They should be reworded so that they differ (while staying true to the product lexicon). A few such duplications might be legitimate homonyms or heteronyms, e.g., a program might use both the verb "refuse," meaning "decline," and the noun "refuse," meaning "garbage." In such a case, consider changing one of the terms, for example, using the word "garbage" instead of the noun "refuse." When translated to other languages, the words that are spelled alike would probably be translated to different words anyway; for example, the verb "refuse" translated to German becomes "ablehnen," whereas the noun "refuse" translates to "Abfall."

Using message files not only enhances textual consistency, it also provides a single place for technical writers to check the text and greatly simplifies translation to other languages.

Blooper 23: Unclear terminology

Even when software uses terms consistently, the terminology can still be unclear and prone to misinterpretation. This can happen in three different ways.

Variation A: Ambiguous terms

Terms that mean only one thing in the software can still be ambiguous. A term may have other meanings *outside* of the software. Users then have to ignore what they know about the term and learn what it means *in the software*.

"Enter" is often used in computer software to mean typing data into the computer. However, "enter" also means "to go into." In computer software and especially in Web sites, that meaning of "enter" may make just as much sense to users as the "type data" meaning. Designers are often so focused on their own intended meaning of a term that they fail to realize that the term has other equally appropriate meanings.

One application had a splash screen with a graphically labeled button that on mouse-over displayed this tooltip text:

Click here to enter application.

Clicking the button displayed the application's main window. However, novice users could misinterpret the tooltip as meaning that clicking the button would display a text box in which they could enter the name of a software application.

Textual ambiguity can be worse when verbs are used as nouns. A software company developed an application development tool for C++ programmers. The main menubar included the command Build Window. The developers intended this to be a noun phrase: the window for *building* a program—compiling and linking the various modules of the program together—the *Build* Window. Unfortunately, users—hard-core C++ programmers—persisted in reading the command as a verb phrase: Build *Window*. This alternative interpretation—building a window—made at least as much sense in the application development tool as the intended interpretation did. It was a surprise to the designers that anyone would interpret the command that way.

Problems caused by turning verbs into nouns are discussed more fully in Blooper 26 (page 173).

Variation B: Terms for different concepts overlap in meaning

Programmers sometimes use synonyms to name distinct concepts: for example, "delete" for deleting text and "remove" for deleting files. When two different functions have names that are usually synonyms, users have to learn which synonym means which concept.

Apple's MacOS uses the word "copy" for copying document content while using "duplicate" for copying document files. Users have to learn this arbitrary distinction.

The e-mail program Eudora (Figure 4.7) provides another example. The "Special" menu (a vague, catch-all name) contains a Find cascading menu with commands for searching stored e-mail messages. The Find menu has the two commands Find and Search, which do different things. Find searches the headers of messages in the currently open e-mail folder and highlights the first matching message. Search searches one or more e-mail folders for messages containing the specified text in any part and lists *all* matching messages.

Here are two more real-world examples:

■ An Intranet Web search facility provided two different functions for finding information related to one's previous search. One was Find Related

Figure 4.7

Eudora for Mac: users must learn arbitrary distinction between Find and Search.

Concepts; the other was Find Related Terms. Many users did not understand the difference between these two functions, and some did not even realize that they were different.

- A company developed a Web site for people seeking to buy a home in the United States. Logged-in users could keep two types of notes for future use: (1) preferences for a home, such as price range, size, number of rooms, and (2) an annotated list of homes they were considering. These two types of notes were separate, but had similar names: notes on home-buying goals were in a "Personal Planner," while notes on appealing homes were in a "Personal Journal." Not surprisingly, testing found that users confused these two.

Variation C: Concepts too similar

In Variation B, it is hard to say whether the *terms* were too similar, the *concepts* were too similar, or both. Sometimes, concepts in an application are so similar that users confuse them no matter what they are called. This is not a naming problem, but rather a deeper, conceptual design problem. Therefore, it is discussed fully in Chapter 6, Interaction Bloopers (Blooper 42, page 246). For now, it is enough to say that overlapping concepts make an application hard to learn.

Avoiding Blooper 23

This blooper results from perceiving a UI from the designers' perspective—which is biased by knowing what everything in the UI means—rather than from the users' perspective (Basic Principle 3, page 26). The terminology for a software product should reflect the users' perspective and should be designed to be easy to learn and remember (Basic Principle 6, page 37). Three rules will help you achieve that.

Avoid synonyms

Don't use words that are normally synonyms to mean different things in the software. Make sure the software's terms for its various concepts are clearly distinguishable from one another. Google's GMail application, in contrast with Eudora, uses only one term for searching: "search" (Figure 4.8).

Avoid ambiguous terms

Avoid using terms that are ambiguous in the real world or that have real-world meanings that could be confused with their meanings in the software. Don't assume that just because you've defined a word to have a certain meaning, users will interpret it the same way. Consider how *users* will interpret the words you've chosen.

Test the terminology on users

Software developers sometime say: "That term isn't confusing. It's obvious what it means!" Whether a term is confusing is not for software developers to judge on their own; it must be determined by observing and asking users. Therefore, it is not enough to produce a conceptual model and product lexicon. The lexicon must be tested on representative users, as was explained under how to avoid Blooper 22. If testing identifies terms that users confuse with one another, change them.

Figure 4.8

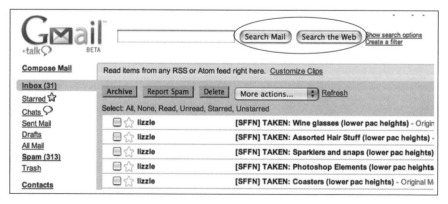

Gmail: one term for searching: "search."

If users misinterpret the terminology used in your software, it's not their problem; it's *your* problem. They'll use something else that doesn't mislead or confuse them. Therefore, try hard to find terminology that does not mislead or confuse your users.

Blooper 24: Bad writing

Even if software uses terms consistently, doesn't redefine common words, and avoids programmer jargon, code terms, and ambiguous words, the writing can still be inadequate for the commercial marketplace. It can vary in style from one label to another. It can use bad spelling and grammar. It can be incorrectly capitalized. In short, it can be bad writing.

Even if it doesn't hurt usability, poor writing tells customers: "We are amateurs! We don't know how to produce polished products!" This blooper occurs in two variations.

Variation A: Inconsistent writing style

Many applications exhibit stylistic inconsistencies in the text of built-in instructions, command names (in menus and on buttons), setting labels, window titles, and so on. Common inconsistencies include:

- naming some commands after actions (verbs) but others after objects (nouns), e.g., Show Details vs. Properties;
- using terse, "telegraphic" language for some setting labels or messages (e.g., "Enter send date") but wordy language for others (e.g., "Please specify the date on which the message is to be sent");
- using title capitalization (e.g., Database Security) for some headings but sentence capitalization (e.g., Database security) for others;
- ending some but not all sentences (e.g., in instructions or error messages) with periods.

Here are some examples from software I've reviewed:

- In the Startup dialogue box, two choices were labeled "Create New Study" and "Open An Existing Study." Only the second includes the article "An."
- Some fields for entering names were labeled "X Name" while others were labeled "X", e.g., "Table Name:" vs. "File:". Both should include the word "Name" or neither should.
- The Graph menu on the menubar contained the inconsistently capitalized commands: "Add Meter ...," "Print meter ...," "Add Graph ...," and "Print graph ...." Probably different programmers implemented the Add and Print functions, and no manager or technical writer checked their command labels for consistency.

The "Search" page of the Web site of the Association for Computing Machinery (ACM.org) has an example of inconsistent writing style. It offers five different searches. Three say they search "now" (Figure 4.9). Users may wonder if this means the other two search *later*. Three of the links mention ACM. Users could assume this means the others are for other organizations. In fact, all five links are for ACM, and all five search now. The options are labeled inconsistently. This conveys a lack of standards and therefore amateurishness. It can also cause confusion.

Variation B: Poor diction, grammar, spelling, and punctuation

Many software applications suffer from poor spelling and writing. Although user documentation is usually written by technical writers, text that appears in the software is usually written by programmers. Programmers are trained to write code, not prose text, and it shows in the quality of the writing in many programs.

Two costly examples of poor writing in software are provided by two medium-sized Silicon Valley software companies that shall remain nameless. Each had a team developing a large desktop application for the Microsoft Windows operating system. On both projects, the engineers were responsible

Figure 4.9

- Search the ACM Digital Library Now
  Bibliographical references and
  full-text articles from ACM.

- Search the Guide to Computing Literature Now
  A substantive bibliographic database
  from the key publishers in computing
  including books, journals, proceedings
  and theses.

- Search the ACM Portal Now
  Comprised of the ACM Guide and the
  ACM Digital Library woven together
  with a set of internal and external
  reference and citation links, affording
  access to current research and an
  extensive archive.

- Search the Calendar of Events
  to find computer science and
  industry events.

- Search ACM's LISTSERV Archives

ACM.org: inconsistent language. Some links include ACM, others don't. Some end with "now"; others don't.

for all text displayed by the software, none of which was reviewed by technical writers. In fact, one of the two teams didn't even have any technical writers.

Although the software was intended for English-speaking customers, none of the developers on either team were native speakers of English. Both of these companies hired most of their programmers from overseas, mainly India, Taiwan, and Russia. While the engineers on both teams were highly competent programmers, their attempts to write command names, setting labels, error messages, and instructions bordered on amusing. However, potential customers were not amused. Management at each of these two companies probably thought that their hiring practices provided skilled programmers at a discount, but they failed to anticipate that those practices would also either add reviewing and rewriting costs or reduce the sales of the product.

Recent examples of poorly written text are provided by Adobe Reader and UBS.com (Figure 4.10). Odds are that neither error message was written by a trained writer of English or even by someone *fluent* in English.

Not all examples of poor writing are serious enough to impair understanding. Sometimes they are just simple typographical errors that were not caught. Typographical errors in software give users an impression of careless workmanship and amateurishness. An example of such an error occurs in the Web site of B&H Photo/Video/Audio. The order form (Figure 4.11) has a typographical error. Can you spot it? It should have been caught before release.

Figure 4.10

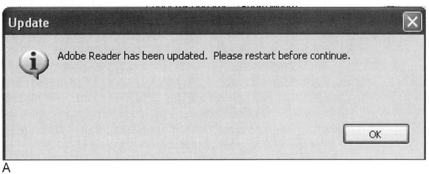

A

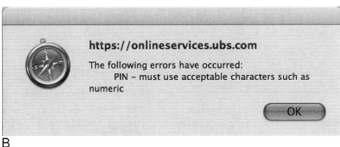

B

Poor English. (A) Adobe Reader. (B) UBS.com.

Figure 4.11

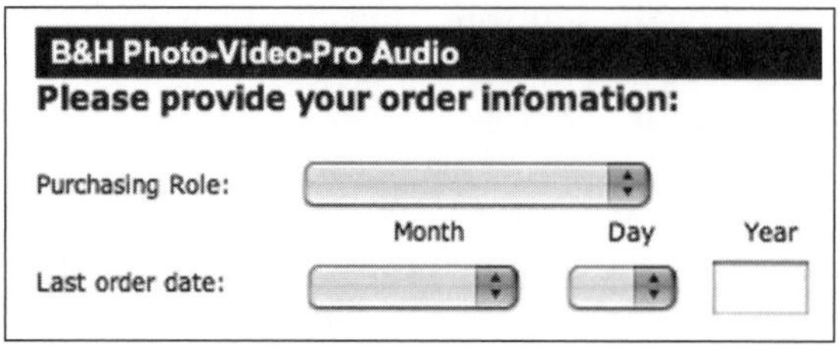

> **B&H Photo-Video-Pro Audio**
> **Please provide your order infomation:**
>
> Purchasing Role: [▲▼]
>
>   Month   Day   Year
>
> Last order date: [▲▼] [▲▼] [   ]

BandHPhotoVideo.com: typographical error in e-commerce Web site.

Avoiding Blooper 24

By following these rules, software developers can ensure that the text displayed by their software conveys an impression of professionalism and care.

Use people who are skilled at writing

If software developers want their products and services to be professional, they need to get professionals for *all* of the jobs involved with software development. Programmers are professionals at writing code. They are amateurs at writing prose. Programmers should not write the text that appears in software. Information architects and technical writers are the right professionals for that job.

All text in an application—instructions, warnings, error messages, setting labels, button labels—should be reviewed by the information architect, technical editors, and technical writers. Not only does this improve the quality of text displayed by software, it helps ensure consistency with user manuals.

Until recently, the Web site FinancialEngines.com provided a example of inconsistent writing style. The site's customer registration form asked for three pieces of information—name, postal zip code, and e-mail address—using three different label forms: question, one-word label, and command (Figure 4.12A). Recently, the page was revised to correct the inconsistency (Figure 4.12B) and so now conveys a more professional impression.

Figure 4.12

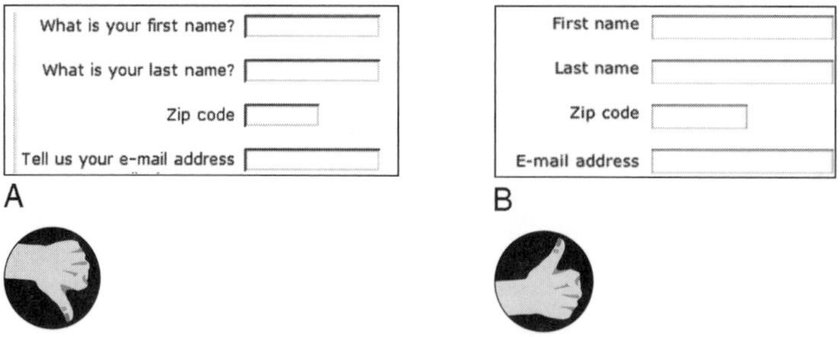

A

What is your first name? [   ]
What is your last name? [   ]
Zip code [   ]
Tell us your e-mail address [   ]

B

First name [   ]
Last name [   ]
Zip code [   ]
E-mail address [   ]

FinancialEngines.com. (A) Inconsistent form labels. (B) Consistent.

Spell-check all text

All text appearing in an application should be spell-checked. The first pass would be with spell-checking software. Ingenuity may be required to get spell-check software to check message files. The text should also be checked by human technical editors or writers.

Blooper 25: Too much text

An important type of bad writing is too much text. Needless text is bad anytime [Strunk and White, 1999], but especially bad in software. When navigating to what they want, software users don't read; they scan for anything that matches their goals [Krug, 2005]. Unfortunately, unnecessary text is very common on the Web and fairly common in desktop applications.

Verbose instructions and labels

Verbose labels and instructions, when not ignored, "bury" important information and slow users down. Imagine yourself trying to set the drawing application SmartDraw's Text Entry Properties (Figure 4.13).

Figure 4.13

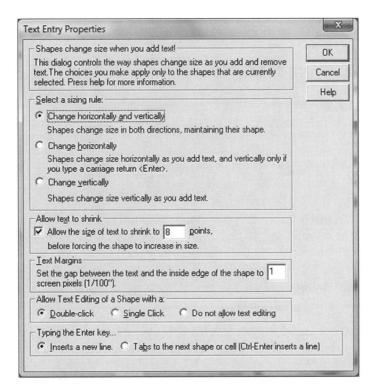

SmartDraw: overly wordy instructions and labels.

Figure 4.14

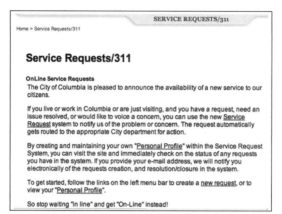

A

B

ColumbiaSC.net: wordy instructions. (A) "Service Requests" page. (B) Login/registration page.

Similarly, unneeded "welcome" text and overly wordy instructions just get in the way of users of the Columbia, South Carolina, city government Web site (Figure 4.14).

Lengthy links

Textual links in Web sites, when too long and especially when in lists, are hard to scan. If text is repeated between links, scannability and legibility suffer even more. A long list of links from the California Department of Motor Vehicles' Web site shows this (Figure 4.15). Headings are also too wordy, e.g., the first duplicates "Driver License Information" from the title just above it.

Figure 4.15

> **Driver License Information**
>
> **Driver License Information for Persons Over 18**
>
> - How to apply for a driver license if you are over 18
> - How to apply for a commercial driver license (CDL)
> - How to change my name and/or birth date with the Social Security Administration (pdf)
> - How to replace or obtain my birth date/legal presence document at the U. S. Citizenship and Immigration Services' local office.
> - How to apply for a motorcycle or moped driver license if you are over 18
>
> **Provisional Driver Permit and License Information for Persons Under 18**
>
> - How to apply for a provisional permit if you are under 18
> - Cumulative credit on a provisional instruction permit
> - Parents' or guardians' signatures - Accepting liability for a minor
> - Driver Education and Driver Training Information
> - Provisional driver license restrictions during the first year
> - How to apply for a motorcycle or moped driver license if you are under 18
>
> **Renewals, Duplicates, and Information Changes for Driver Licenses and/or ID Cards**
>
> - How to renew your driver license in person
> - How to renew your driver license by mail
> - How to renew your driver license by Internet
> - How to renew your instruction permit
> - How to apply for a duplicate driver license or identification (ID) card
> - How to change your name on your driver license and/or identification (ID) card
> - How to notify DMV of my change of address
> - How to register for the organ donor gift of life program

DMV.ca.gov: wordy and repetitious text links are hard to scan.

Avoiding Blooper 25

Use no more text than is necessary to convey the intended information.

- Avoid long prose paragraphs.
- Use headings, short phrases, bullet points.
- Keep links short, one to three words; explain with nonlink text.
- Avoid repetition in link lists; cut repeated text or move it into headings.

Usability authors Jakob Nielsen [1999d], Steve Krug [2005], and Ginny Redish [2007] all advocate brevity. Krug warns that long prose passages won't be read and suggests:

> Get rid of half of the words on each page, then get rid of half of what's left.

Example of cutting needless text

Jeep.com shows how text can be cut. In late 2002, they simplified their verbose "Find A Dealer" page (Figure 4.16A): a long paragraph was cut to one sentence and three bulleted steps (Figure 4.16B). They also realized they didn't need both zip code *and* state. More recently, they simplified it further, to six words, including the labels (Figure 4.16C).

Figure 4.16

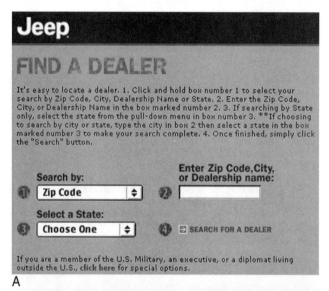

A

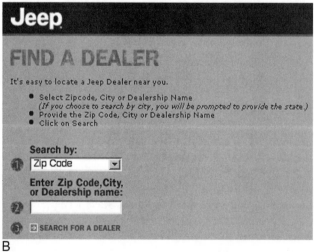

B

C

Jeep.com: wordy instructions cut to a few bullets, then to six words. (A) Early 2002. (B) Late 2002. (C) 2007.

The goals: scannability, clarity, simplicity

Brevity is only a means to the true goal: ease of comprehension and navigation, scannability, clarity, simplicity. Users don't read; they scan. Brevity helps them comprehend and navigate by scanning.

If you forget this and strive for brevity for its own sake, usability can suffer [Raskin, 2000]. Needlessly limiting button or link labels to one word can seem to users like cryptic codes they must learn.

Developer-centric text

The next three bloopers are cases of text using computer jargon and presenting the developers' point of view.

Blooper 26: Speaking Geek

Suppose you installed some new software on your computer, but when you tried to use it, you discovered that you had somehow obtained a foreign-language version of the software. You would discard it and try to get the version that was in your own language.

For many people, the "foreign" language their software displays is technobabble, also known as Geek. However, people whose software speaks Geek are *worse* off than those whose software uses a foreign language because they can't get replacement versions in a language they understand. There are several different ways to speak Geek.

BEETLE BAILEY *Mort Walker*

BEETLE BAILEY © KING FEATURES SYNDICATE

Variation A: Using programmer jargon

Most professions and hobbies have a jargon—a specialized vocabulary that allows practitioners to communicate more precisely and efficiently. Using specialized jargon is good when you are communicating with others who share your specialty: it enhances efficiency and clarity. However, using specialized jargon when communicating with people who do *not* share the specialty is bad: it *hinders* efficiency and clarity. When communicating with people outside of your area of expertise, you should switch off the jargon.

Many software developers don't switch off their jargon when writing text that appears in software intended for nonprogrammers. Why?

- A lack of awareness that they are using jargon
- An inability to switch the jargon off even though they are aware that they use it
- A belief that if people want to use a computer, they need to understand computer jargon
- A tight deadline and insufficient writer support, coupled with an assumption that someone will check and improve the wording later
- A design that exposes technical concepts and implementation details that are irrelevant to users' tasks (Blooper 40, page 241)

For these reasons, a lot of software uses acronyms such as "USB" and "PDF," pure computerese such as "device drivers" and "flash memory," words that are rarely used in standard English such as "mode" and "buffer," phrases that turn verbs into nouns such as "do a compare" and "finish an edit," and terms that reflect the developer's point of view rather than the user's such as "user defaults." The effect on users is reduced understanding and slowed learning.

Many error messages displayed by the e-mail program Eudora are in Geek. When a user logs in with an invalid password, Eudora pops up an error message that describes the communications protocol between Eudora and the e-mail server (Figure 4.17A). Blooper! Maybe Eudora's developers and network administrators care about the client–server communication, but most Eudora users do not.

Eudora displays an even more geeky error message when an attempt to fetch new mail fails because the domain-name server did not respond (Figure 4.17B). This message is cryptic even for Eudora users who know what a domain-name server is.

Figure 4.17

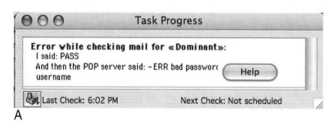

A

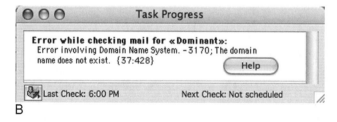

B

Eudora: technobabble error messages. (A) Invalid password. (B) Server didn't respond.

Examples of software speaking Geek

- *Example 1:* A Web application required users to login, but called it "authenticating." The login page was labeled "User Authentication." This was bad because: (1) users don't know what "authentication" means and (2) the word "user" is software developer jargon; users don't identify with that term. Worse, if a user left the application unused for more than 15 minutes, the application's back-end logged the user off, but the application in the user's Web browser continued to appear as the user left it. Users who had interrupted their use of the application to do something else would often return to the application, find it as they expected, try to do something, and suddenly get the following message:

  Your session has expired.

  Please reauthenticate.

  [OK]

  When users clicked "OK," they were taken to the "User Authentication" page. I suggested getting rid of the word "user," replacing "authenticate" with "login," and increasing the auto-logoff timeout (since they couldn't eliminate it).

- *Example 2:* A company developed an e-commerce application for networked PCs. The application let users create and save templates for common transactions. It gave users the option of saving templates either on their own PC or on a network server. Templates stored on the server were accessible by other users; templates stored on the PC were private. The problem was that the software referred to the two storage options as "database" and "local." The developers used "database" for templates on the server because the they were kept in a database. The developers used "local" for templates on the users' own PC because that's what "local" meant to them. I recommended that they use "shared" or "public" instead of "database" and "private" instead of "local."

Some software applications and Web sites include the GUI toolkit name of a control in its label or instructions. Two examples come from the Web sites of the State of California's Employment Development Department and Northwest Airlines (Figure 4.18).

One business application displayed the structure of the application's data using a Windows tree control. The problem was that the application called it a "tree control." Not surprisingly, testing showed that many users didn't know what the term meant. Some probably wondered what the software had to do with trees.

Also common are error messages that contain actual bits of software code. Most computer users have seen error messages like one displayed by Intuit.com (Figure 4.19), which mixes code excerpts with information users can understand: "There was an error in processing your request." The code excerpts may have been useful to programmers while the site was being debugged, but should have been removed before the site went live.

Figure 4.18

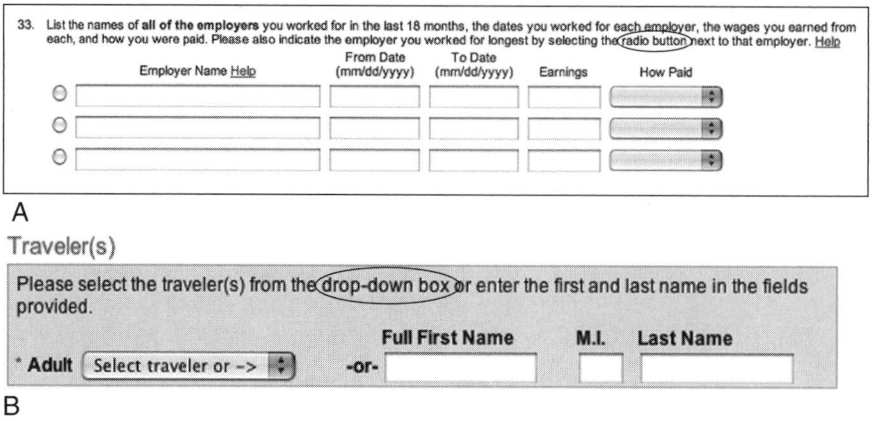
33. List the names of **all of the employers** you worked for in the last 18 months, the dates you worked for each employer, the wages you earned from each, and how you were paid. Please also indicate the employer you worked for longest by selecting the radio button next to that employer. Help
Employer Name Help
From Date (mm/dd/yyyy)
To Date (mm/dd/yyyy)
Earnings
How Paid
A
Traveler(s)
Please select the traveler(s) from the drop-down box or enter the first and last name in the fields provided.
Full First Name
M.I.
Last Name
* Adult
Select traveler or ->
-or-
B

Exposing GUI toolkit control names. (A) EDD.ca.gov. (B) NWA.com.

Figure 4.19

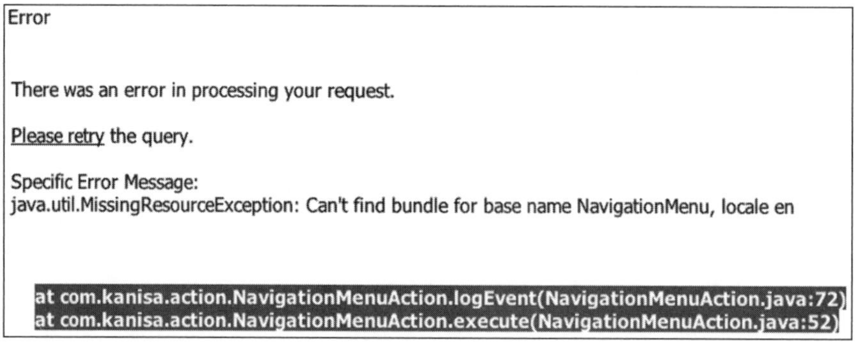
Error
There was an error in processing your request.
Please retry the query.
Specific Error Message:
java.util.MissingResourceException: Can't find bundle for base name NavigationMenu, locale en
at com.kanisa.action.NavigationMenuAction.logEvent(NavigationMenuAction.java:72)
at com.kanisa.action.NavigationMenuAction.execute(NavigationMenuAction.java:52)

Intuit.com: exposes code in error message.

Sometimes users are exposed to implementation terms because the operating system displays error messages on its own instead of passing them to the application. For a more complete discussion of such situations, see Blooper 28 (page 184).

Variation B: Turning common words into programmer jargon

Programmers often redefine common words to have specific meanings in software. If you redefine common words and expect the users to adapt to them, you are putting an extra load onto the users and committing a blooper.

In common English "dialog" means a conversation, but in GUI-programmer jargon it is shorthand for "dialog box." Programmers and UI designers forget that "dialog" has a common meaning and that, even in GUI jargon, it is shorthand. When software exposes the jargon meaning to users, as in Adobe InDesign (Figure 4.20), it's a blooper.

To programmers, the word "string" means textual data in software. To nonprogrammers, string is for tying things together. Examples of exposing the software jargon meaning to users come from the desktop software Clock and Track and the publisher Web site Elsevier.com (Figure 4.21). This use of "string" should *never* appear in a UI intended for nonprogrammers.

To most English speakers, an argument is a verbal dispute. To programmers, arguments are input to software functions. Some of CorporateExpress.com's users might like to have an argument with the designers of the site's Search function (Figure 4.22).

Figure 4.20

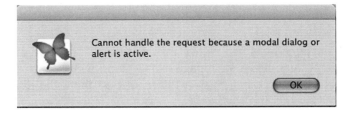

Adobe InDesign: exposes the GUI jargon term "dialog."

Figure 4.21

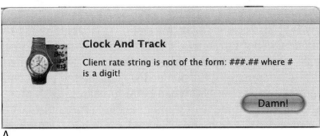

A

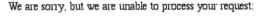

B

Error messages expose the software term "string." (A) Clock and Track application. (B) Elsevier.com.

Figure 4.22

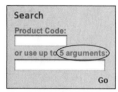

CorporateExpress.com: exposes the software jargon word "arguments" in instructions.

 She did what it said

> A secretary called the Compuserve customer support hotline to say that even though she did what the software told her to do, it didn't seem to work. Compuserve's software had displayed an error dialog box containing the message:
>
> *Type mismatch*
>
> The secretary said that when she saw this message, she typed "mismatch" several times, but it didn't help. [From Interface Hall of Shame, http://homepage.mac.com/bradster/iarchitect/shame.htm]

Other often-redefined words are "resources," "object," and "client." One Web application had a login page titled "Thin-Client Login." Some users were probably surprised and pleased that it offered them the login page for *thin* clients instead of the alternative.

Variation C: Turning verbs into nouns

Another sort of jargon is verbs used as nouns. This is not restricted to computer software; it happens in many fields. Stockbrokers use "buys" and "sells" as nouns when discussing stock transactions, airplane pilots refer to "takeoffs," fishermen talk about the day's "catch," and book reviewers describe books they like as "a worthwhile read." Programmers say "the compile failed," "start the build," "do a compare," "finish an edit." This is fine when communicating with other programmers, but bad when communicating with nonprogrammers.

National Geographic Trip Planner includes a guidebook with information about routes and destinations. The guidebook has a Find function so users can search it. Users can set preferences for how Find works. The command to do that is Find Preferences (Figure 4.23).

Figure 4.23

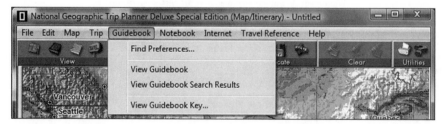

National Geographic Trip Planner: Find Preferences command is a noun phrase.

Verbs to nouns

> Here are two more examples of programmers turning verbs into nouns:
>
> - In a data-mining application, one function was called "Explore Data." The programmers called using that function "doing an Explore." An auxiliary function predicted the time and resources needed to "do an Explore." It was named "Explore Prediction," a noun phrase. Another function compared two data files. Using it was called "doing a Compare." An auxiliary function defined comparisons that could be run repeatedly on different data. It was called "Compare Definition," another noun phrase.
>
> - An application provided a "wizard" (multistep dialog box) for creating data objects. The button that started this wizard was labeled "Create Object Wizard." The developers meant for this label to mean "start the (Create Object) wizard." However, users read it as a verb phrase, "create the (Object) wizard," and wondered what an "Object" wizard was and why they would want to create one.

Avoiding Blooper 26

Geek-speak must go.

When commercial automobiles were first introduced and for about 40 years afterward, operating one required mastering a lot of automotive technical jargon: choke, RPMs, oil pressure, generator voltage. Now most of that jargon is gone. Computer applications began to appear in the late 1970s. Thirty years have passed since then. In 10 more years, will your software's users still have to be aware of modems, startup files, device drivers, and RAM? Hopefully not. Let's not wait 10 more years; let's achieve that goal now.

How can developers avoid Geek-speak? By following these steps.

Know thy users

Learn about your users. Visit them, observe them, interview them, invite them to focus groups. Ask them to describe how they work, what they like and don't like about their current tools, and what their most serious problems are. Get their ideas about how their work might be improved. Compile a list of all the concepts the intended users mentioned in their descriptions of their work. Pay special attention to the objects (nouns), actions on objects (verbs), and attributes of objects (adjectives) they mention.

Develop a product lexicon based on users' task vocabulary

Use the information gathered from intended users to develop a conceptual model for the planned software product or service (Basic Principle 2, page 18).

The conceptual model will include an object/action analysis and a lexicon. The lexicon should list all the concepts (objects, actions, attributes) that the software exposes to users and indicate the name for each concept. When possible, use industry-standard names.

The goal is that the user interface and documentation use a vocabulary that is consistent, both internally to the software and with industry standards for the platform, and also grounded firmly in the tasks and vocabulary of the intended users (Basic Principle 3, page 26). Toward that end, develop and maintain a product lexicon and enforce adherence to it. All text displayed in the software should be written or at least reviewed by a technical writer, and any Geek-speak should be filtered out. Labels and messages should be in message files, separated from the program code, to facilitate review and translation.

Some have argued that the UI and the terms it uses should match the implementation, so the UI does not mislead users about how the application works. Yes, but the right way to accomplish that is to design the UI first and then match the implementation—structure, concepts, and terminology—to that.

Leave GUI component names out of the GUI

Don't include the GUI toolkit name of controls in the title or label for a control. Figure 4.24A shows examples of geeky labels: they include GUI toolkit jargon. Figure 4.24B shows good labels for the same settings. The good labels eliminate needless words as well as Geek-speak.

Figure 4.24

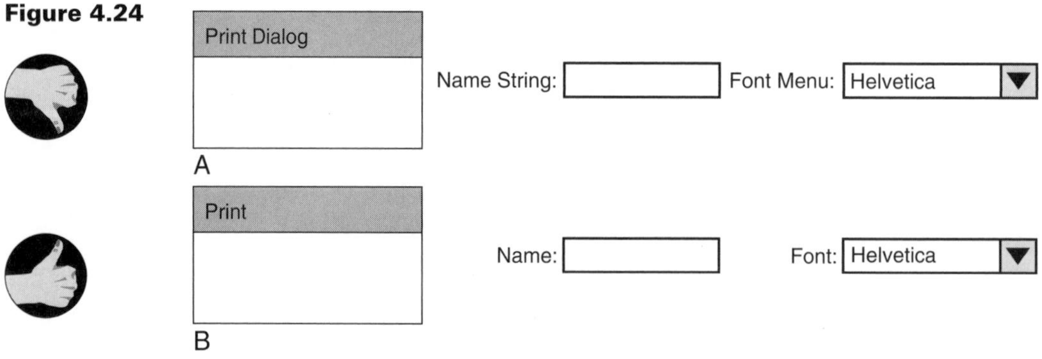

(A) Labels that include GUI toolkit jargon. (B) Improved labels.

Blooper 27: Calling users "user" to their face

Related to speaking Geek is the blooper of callin g your users "user" in the UI.

"Users" is what we—software and Web *developers*—call people who use our systems. It's a *fine* term to use when we are talking with other designers and developers. It's part of our professional jargon—our way of communicating succinctly with peers. But "users" is *not* what people who use computer-based products and services call themselves.

Only two industries call their customers "users." One such industry is ours: computer software. Do you know what the other industry is?[3]

Software applications, Web sites, and electronic devices should be designed from the point of view of the people who *use* them, not the point of view of the system's designers or developers. The people who use computer-based products and services see themselves as customers, site visitors, members, guests, etc.—not "users." Therefore, interactive systems that call users "user" to their face are committing a blooper.

National Geographic Trip Planner allows users to annotate and highlight locations on the program's maps that interest them, but uses the terms "User Label" and "User Highlight" (Figure 4.25A). Microsoft Windows XP's "Accessibility" control panel exhibits two points of view simultaneously: it calls a user-specified style sheet "User style sheet" in one label and "my style sheet" in another (Figure 4.25B).

FinancialEngines.com and LinkedIn.com not only call users "user"; they make users call *themselves* that (Figure 4.26).

Figure 4.25

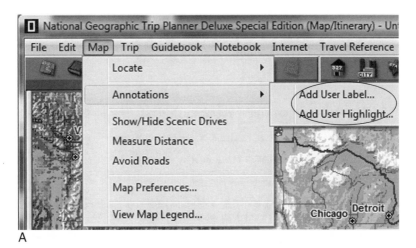

A

Microsoft calling users "user." (A) National Geographic Trip Planner. (B) Windows XP.

(Continued)

---

3. Hint: heroin, cocaine, methamphetamines.

Figure 4.25
(Continued)

Accessibility
Formatting
Ignore colors specified on webpages
Ignore font styles specified on webpages
Ignore font sizes specified on webpages
User style sheet
Format documents using my style sheet
Style sheet:
Browse...
OK
Cancel

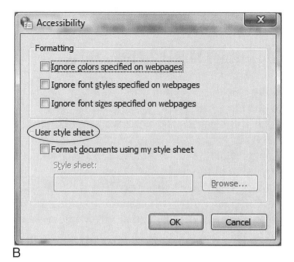

B

Figure 4.26

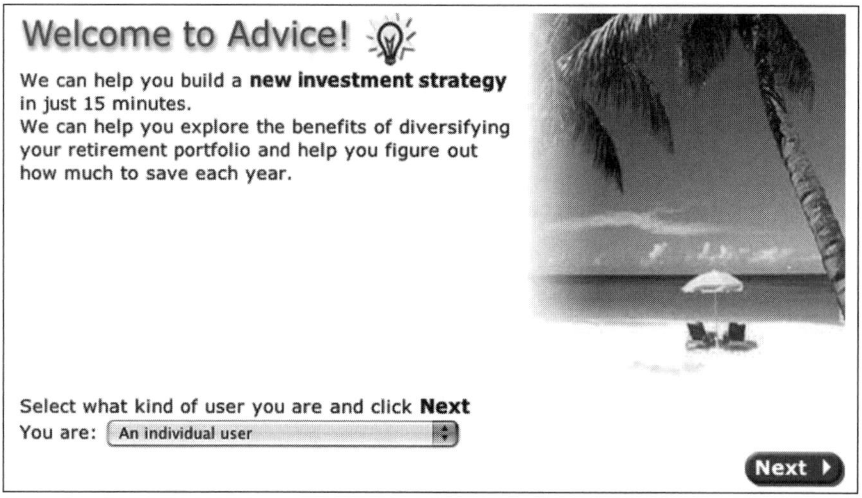

Welcome to Advice!
We can help you build a **new investment strategy** in just 15 minutes.
We can help you explore the benefits of diversifying your retirement portfolio and help you figure out how much to save each year.
Select what kind of user you are and click **Next**
You are: An individual user
Next

A

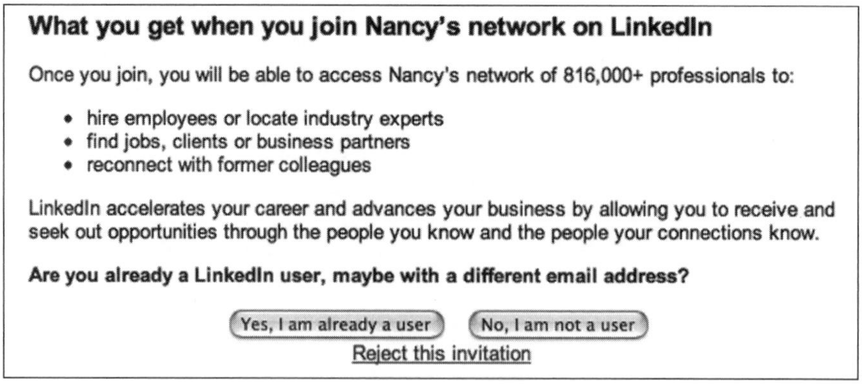

What you get when you join Nancy's network on LinkedIn
Once you join, you will be able to access Nancy's network of 816,000+ professionals to:
hire employees or locate industry experts
find jobs, clients or business partners
reconnect with former colleagues
LinkedIn accelerates your career and advances your business by allowing you to receive and seek out opportunities through the people you know and the people your connections know.
Are you already a LinkedIn user, maybe with a different email address?
Yes, I am already a user
No, I am not a user
Reject this invitation

B

Making users call themselves "user." (A) FinancialEngines.com. (B) LinkedIn.com.

Figure 4.27

PAMF.org: buttons on "Accept/Reject Link" page force users to call themselves "user."

A potentially ambiguous case occurs at PAMF.org (Figure 4.27), a medical clinic. In that context, "user" could be interpreted to mean "drug user."

Calling users "user" to their face is an easy mistake to make: "user" is developers' jargon for people who use the Web site. If a development team doesn't explicitly *think* about this and choose a more appropriate word, "user" is the word that will be used. That's why this blooper is so common.

Avoiding Blooper 27

As easy as it is to make this blooper, it's just as easy to avoid it. Using a non-developer-centric term like "visitor," "customer," or "member" instead of "user" costs next to nothing. It just takes awareness and a few moments' thought. Three Web sites that show evidence of such awareness and thought are Yale AlumniConnections.org, Fedex.com, and Apple Mac.com (Figure 4.28).

Figure 4.28

Not calling users "user." (A) Yale AlumniConnections.org. (B) Fedex.com. (C) Apple Mac.com.

Blooper 28: Vague error messages

A blooper related to speaking Geek is displaying error messages that announce a vague, generic error condition instead of giving users helpful, task-oriented information about what happened and what to do about it. This happens for three reasons.

Variation A: *Message displayed by low-level code*

Sometimes low-level service functions detect errors and display error messages themselves. Task-level functions the user explicitly executes—e.g., Save—can express errors in task-related terms, but low-level service functions—e.g., file. Open()—cannot.

In Apple's Safari Web browser, suppose a user tries to visit a florist's Web page. If the page has buggy JavaScript code that tries to assign a null value to a variable, Safari's JavaScript interpreter displays an error: "TypeError—Null value" (Figure 4.29).

The user's reaction would probably be something like: "Huh? I just want to send some flowers to my mom. What's this about JavaScript, type errors, and null values?" If the user is more computer savvy, she might say: "You stupid browser—I didn't write the faulty JavaScript code. Show the error to the site's *developers,* not to its *users!*"

 Error message displayed by low-level code

A top-notch programmer had emigrated to the United States. His poor English was not a problem because he wrote low-level device-driver code that had no UI. He was asked to write a driver for a new display. No one checked his work because the driver was supposedly invisible to users. And it was ... almost. It had a bug that occasionally caused it to hit a memory limit and display this message:

Nesting level too dip.

This error message and the code that displayed it had already been burned onto ROM and shipped with thousands of consoles worldwide. The main problem with the error message was *not* the misspelling of the word "deep," but that it was displayed by the display's firmware. Users of the display would have no idea what the message was about or what to do about it.

Figure 4.29

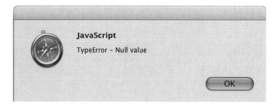

Apple Safari browser: error message from JavaScript interpreter.

This variation of Blooper 27 is often difficult to correct. The low-level code that detects the error and displays an unhelpful error message may not be in the application itself, but in the operating system on which the application is running. If your application calls an operating system utility function and the function sometimes displays a poor error message, you probably won't be able to fix the message because it isn't from your code. Nonetheless, your users will see the message as coming from your application. If the message is seriously misleading, you have no choice other than changing the code so that it does not use the operating system utility function.

Variation B: Reason for error not given to higher level code

Sometimes applications display vague error messages because of poor communication between low-level service functions and the task-level function the user executed. For example, when a user tries to open a PowerPoint presentation but PowerPoint can't open it, an error message pops up listing three possible reasons for the failure (Figure 4.30). The service functions PowerPoint calls to open and load the presentation apparently don't give PowerPoint enough detail about why they failed to allow it to identify the exact cause of the failure.

Users are left not knowing what to do, because the remedies for these three possible causes are quite different.

One application displayed this error message when a user tried to load a nonexistent data file:

> Error parsing datafile. Data not parsed.

The message was true—no data was parsed—but it was misleading. The real problem was that the data file was not found. After trying to load the file, the code did not check whether the load operation succeeded; it just passed an empty data buffer to the parsing procedure, which duly reported that it couldn't parse the data.

Variation C: Generic message components

Another common cause of vague error messages is generic error message components. To save development effort, developers sometimes create generic messages to cover whole categories of errors and use them even when the software could give users more specific feedback.

Figure 4.30

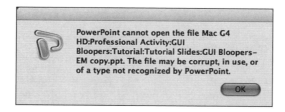

Microsoft PowerPoint: error message lists three possible problems.

Figure 4.31

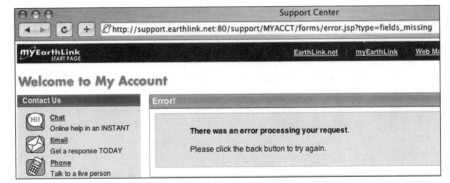

Earthlink.net: vague error message. Specifics in URL, where few users will look.

Earthlink.net displays a vague error message when a user updates his/her contact information but omits a phone number (Figure 4.31). It actually "knows" that the problem is a missing phone number; you can see that in the URL—but normal consumer users won't look there. Yet the error message it displays is generic.

One stock investment application allows investors to buy or sell stocks. Users often get this error message when they place orders:

Order size not multiple of trading unit.

The number of shares bought or sold must be a multiple of the "trading unit." The trading unit differs for each stock, but the error message does not say what the trading unit is. The trading unit is also not shown anywhere on the ordering screen. Users just have to know, or guess, what the trading unit is for the stock they want to buy or sell. Users not only waste time trying to find the trading unit for a stock, they sometimes start transactions they don't want.

Examples of generic error messages

The following are examples of software that displayed generic, uninformative error messages.

- *Example 1:* User tried to give a data object a name containing characters not allowed in names:

    Name contains invalid characters.

    Wonderful. Pray tell, which characters might those be? The software knows, but won't say.

- *Example 2:* Error message displayed when user tried to import a data file:

    File missing or you don't have access.

    This message is vague: it doesn't say which of two quite different problems has occurred. The message doesn't name the file it is talking about.

Figure 4.32

Windows Media Player (for Mac): vague error message.

And the winner is ...

The mother of all generic, uninformative error messages—the message that, if there were a prize for vagueness, would be the winner—has to be the error message displayed by Windows Media Player for Mac (Figure 4.32). What are users supposed to do with this?

Avoiding Blooper 28

Express the error in terms of the task

A good error message describes the problem in terms related to the task the user was trying to do. If the user has just given the command to paste an image into a document and the software encounters an error, the message should be expressed in terms of pasting images, not in terms of operating system functions, implementation data types, program exception codes, or irrelevant application concepts.

Don't just identify the problem; suggest a solution

A good error message also provides enough information that the user can see how to correct the error. That means providing enough detail that a user can determine what he or she did to cause the problem or, if the problem wasn't the user's fault, what did cause it and why. A programmer friend of mine put it this way:

> "Error messages should focus on the solution. Geeks love to describe the problem."

To counter that tendency, error messages should always contain the following:

Error symbol; Problem: Solution

An example of software that follows this guideline is SWA.com, the Web site of Southwest Airlines (Figure 4.33).

Table 4.1 shows suggested improvements for poor error messages discussed above.

Figure 4.33

SWA.com (Southwest Airlines): excellent error message.

Table 4.1   Poor and improved error messages

Poor error message	Improved error message
File.Move() failed. [*User tried to save e-mail message, but specified Sent folder as destination by mistake.*]	Messages cannot be saved into the Sent folder. Please try Saving to a different folder.
JavaScript TypeError: Null value	Warning: Page contains coding errors. Content may not display as intended [*or no message*].
Nesting level too dip.	[*No message. Console just restarts if necessary.*]
Name contains invalid characters.	< *Object-type* > names may not contain '-', '/', '@', '#', or '&' characters.
File missing or you don't have access.	[*Separate messages for the two error types:*] File < *filename* > not found. You don't have access to file < *filename* >.
Order size not multiple of trading unit.	Sorry: < *stockname* > stock must be traded in multiples of < *trading unit* > shares.

Pass errors up to code that can translate them for users

Low-level service routines and application software platforms should *never* display error messages directly. They should always pass errors to the application so that it can handle them in an appropriate way.

When an application receives an error notification from a lower level procedure, it should pass the error up the call stack to code that can handle the error in a task-relevant way. That code should either:

■ translate the error into terms that are meaningful to users and display the translation with advice on how to correct the problem or

■ assume that the cause of the error was temporary and try the operation again.

Design messages and message-bearing components to accept details at runtime

Error messages and error dialog box components that cover many situations should be designed to allow details—object names, constraints, data field names, etc.—to be inserted into them. This would, for example, allow an error message to say *which* file could not be read, show *which* characters are not allowed, or indicate *which* required data was not given.

Different types of messages have different audiences

Finally, recognize that error messages displayed by software have three possible functions, each having a different audience:

■ Indicating user errors: for end users

■ Logging activity: for system administrators at users' site

■ Facilitating debugging and tracing: for developers

By the time software is ready to ship, developers should make sure that each type of message is seen only by its intended audience.

Misleading text

The last three textual bloopers concern error messages and labels that mislead users.

Blooper 29: Erroneous messages

Nothing confuses and angers software users more than instructions and error messages that are wrong. They waste time and effort by leading users down wrong paths, perhaps leading to costly mistakes.

United Airline customers, when reviewing their frequent-flier mileage account on United.com, can ask the site to list account activity that occurred between specified dates. If a user specifies a date that is in the future, the site *could* gently say that, or just overlook the error and use *today* as the upper date limit. Instead, United.com harshly informs users that they have made an "Invalid Date Entry" and tells them to check whether they entered nonexistent dates, such as June 31 (Figure 4.34). The suggested remedy is unrelated to the user's actual error.

Worse are false error messages when a user hasn't even made an error. If an Earthlink Web-mail customer tries to login at a time when the company's domain-name servers are down, Earthlink Web mail displays an error message telling the user that the specified domain name is "invalid" (Figure 4.35). The domain name is not invalid; the server just cannot authenticate *any* domain names at the moment. This message will cause Earthlink customers to waste time checking and retyping their e-mail address in vain.

Figure 4.34

United.com: incorrect error message. User entered future date, but message misleads.

Figure 4.35

Earthlink.net: incorrect error message. Domain name is valid, but name server is down.

Even worse are error messages that scare users needlessly by announcing something awful when nothing is wrong. Microsoft Windows for the Pocket PC sometimes inexplicably displays a truly frightening system error message (Figure 4.36). The error dialog box commits another blooper as well, trapping users by presenting unclear options (Blooper 50, page 281), but this message's main fault is that it is wrong. Regardless of whether the user clicks Yes or No, the Pocket PC continues operating normally and nothing is erased.

Finally, we have text that is wrong due to carelessness. This problem can often be seen in Web sites in which prices, events, or product catalogues are not kept up to date or in other ways don't match reality.

Erroneous text can also be found in desktop software. The Web-based e-mail program TrueDesk allows its users to create lists of "Safe Senders"—e-mail addresses from which e-mail is trusted—and "Blocked Senders"—e-mail addresses from which e-mail is blocked. However, the "Blocked Senders" description says that blocked e-mail will go exactly where trusted e-mail goes: into the users' Inbox (Figure 4.37). This must be wrong. Whoever created this page apparently copied the text from the "Safe Senders" description to that of the "Blocked Senders" and failed to edit it. But users may not figure this out right away.

Figure 4.36

Microsoft Pocket PC Windows: false error message. Nothing is wrong.

Figure 4.37

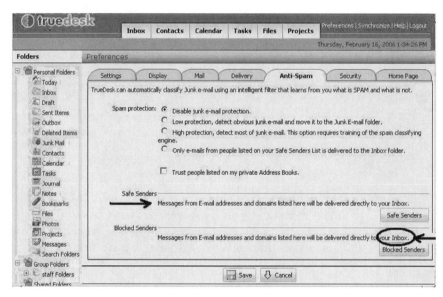

TrueDesk: Anti-Spam tab has labels that are wrong.

Avoiding Blooper 29

It is very bad for software to lie to its users. It can waste users' valuable time and effort as well as cause them to make unrecoverable errors.

Error messages that scold users for the wrong error or for errors they did not commit, and instructions that are false, are software flaws—bugs. They should be checked for during software quality-assurance testing and reported and tracked with bug management mechanisms. They should have a high priority for correction, because their impact on users is high: they divert users from achieving their goals, they sometimes cause data loss (or, in the case of mission-critical systems, other types of loss), and they really decrease customer satisfaction.

Blooper 30: Text makes sense in isolation but is misleading in the GUI

Jakob Nielsen has pointed out (at UseIt.com) that software and Web developers often write labels, headings, descriptions, and instructions without considering how users might interpret the text in the context of all the other information the system displays. This often results in text that may make sense in isolation but isn't as clear in the GUI.

Most Web shoppers have been stymied by e-commerce Web sites that display similar descriptions for different items. Imagine a printer vendor Web site on which four different printers are described as "perfect for your small business" or an online catalogue of PhotoShop plug-in filters that all promise to "help you create professional-looking images." The marketing manager in charge of each product naturally wants to make it sound as appealing as possible, but that can make it difficult for customers to choose.

Just as unplanned *similarity* between item labels can sow confusion, so can unintended *differences*. One company's customer support Web site included a page of software patches that customers could download and install to correct known bugs in the company's software. A section of the "Patch" page highlighted patches that the company was strongly recommending that customers install. That section was labeled:

Recommended Patches

These patches have been tested and will keep your Company X workstation running smoothly.

This might suggest to some customers that the other patches had *not* been tested and were *not* recommended. The person who wrote the section label had considered only how the label fit its own section, not what it implied about the rest of the page on which it appeared.

Avoiding Blooper 30

When writing text describing an item, consider how people who aren't intimately familiar with the item will interpret it. Also, don't simply consider each piece of text in isolation. Look at it in all contexts where it will appear, and make sure it conveys its intended meaning in each such place. When in doubt, test it on users.

Blooper 31: Misuse (or nonuse) of "…" on command labels

In the early 1980s, the designers of Apple's Lisa computer (a predecessor of the Macintosh) devised a way to distinguish commands that execute immediately from ones that first prompt for more information. Commands that need more information had "…" (ellipsis) on the end of the command label, for example, "Save As…" Commands that execute immediately don't end with "…". This convention is for command labels, whether they appear in menus or on buttons.

The ellipsis became a standard

It is helpful for users to know in advance whether a command executes immediately or prompts for more information. It is safer to click on unfamiliar commands if users know they just bring up a dialog box.

Over time, the convention spread beyond the Macintosh to other computer platforms, such as Microsoft Windows and various Unix-based desktop operating systems. Today, it is so pervasive that software not following this convention risks misleading users.

Some developers don't know the standard

Alas, violations of this convention are becoming *more* common. Some developers are just unaware of it. Others know there is a convention but misunderstand it.

Variation A: Omitting "…"

The most common error is to omit the "…" on commands that need it: no commands have "…". Users guess or learn from experience which commands need more input and which don't. Microsoft Outlook's "Change Password" button displays a dialog box to check the user's current password and get a new one (Figure 4.38). The button's label should end with "…", but does not.

Figure 4.38

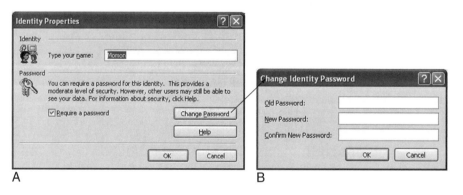

A   B

Microsoft Outlook: missing "…" on "Change Password" button.

Figure 4.39

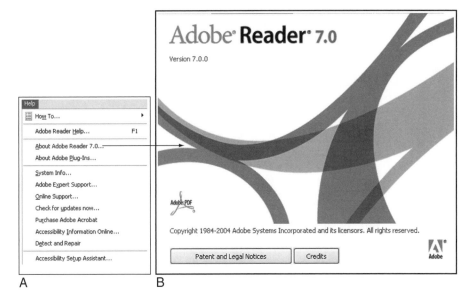

A   B

Adobe Reader: About Adobe Reader 7.0... command wrongly includes "...".

Variation B: Overusing "..."

The next most common error is to append the ellipsis to command labels that should not have it. Designers who commit this variation of the blooper have overgeneralized the convention. They think "..." is for any command that opens a new window. If a Show Graph... command just displays a graph and doesn't need more information before it does that, the command label should not end with "...".

In Adobe Reader's Help menu, the About Adobe Reader 7.0... command displays a splash screen showing the program version and other information (Figure 4.39). It needs no additional input from the user. The "..." is misleading.

Avoiding Blooper 31

The ellipsis shows that the command brings up a dialog box before executing. It shows that there will be an opportunity to cancel.

Not for any command that opens a window

The "..." is not for commands that just open a window. For example, Show Network might open a window to display the status of a computer network. Such a command should not have "..." at the end of its label.

Mozilla Firefox uses "..." correctly in its Help menu and elsewhere. The Help and Release Notes commands open windows that display information

Figure 4.40

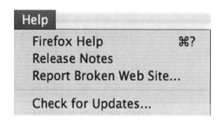

Mozilla Firefox: correct use—and nonuse—of "...".

and so do not end with "...". The Report Broken Web Site... and Check for Updates... commands open dialog boxes that prompt for user input needed to complete the command and so do end with "..." (Figure 4.40).

Standard across all platforms

All the major GUI platform style guides state the same rule:

- Java Look and Feel Guidelines [Sun Microsystems, 2001]
- Windows Vista User Experience Guidelines [Microsoft Corp., 2006]
- Apple Human Interface Guidelines [Apple Computer, 2006]

What about graphical button labels?

Many buttons are labeled graphically rather than textually. The ellipsis mark doesn't work for graphical labels. A solution is to include the ellipsis on the button's tooltip text, which appears when the screen pointer is held over the button.

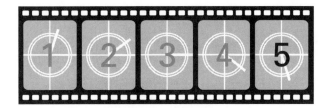

Graphic Design and Layout Bloopers

Introduction

Bad layout and window placement

Troublesome typography

Introduction

Once you have GUI controls that are appropriate for your software and you've labeled them well and written any required instructions, you have to decide on presentation details: layout, colors, and text fonts. The basic principles that should guide graphic design and layout decisions in GUIs were covered in Chapter 1 (Basic Principle 7, page 41). Not following those principles usually results in certain common mistakes: "graphic design and layout" bloopers.

Graphic design and layout bloopers definitely diminish software's perceived quality. It only takes a few to make a product look amateurish and untrustworthy. Poor graphic design and layout can also decrease users' ability and motivation to absorb whatever information or content the software offers.

Software developers come mainly from engineering and don't see how similar their industry has become to the one that produces magazines, newspapers, books, TV shows, and movies. Most software developers haven't yet learned to develop and follow strict standards for layout and graphic design and to pay as much attention to detail as traditional publishers and media studios do. As a result, graphic design and layout bloopers often get a "Who cares? It looks OK to me!" reaction from developers.

Fortunately, graphic design and layout bloopers are easy to spot once you know what to look for and fairly easy to avoid or correct. Showing you how is the purpose of this chapter. Because this book was not printed in color, two bloopers about poor use of color could not be included. They are in a Web appendix at the book's Web site: www.gui-bloopers.com.

Bad layout and window placement

Most of the common graphic design and layout bloopers concern the layout of information and controls on windows, forms, and Web pages and the placement of windows on the display.

Blooper 32: Easily missed information

Software developers often assume that if information is displayed, users will see it. Not so!

People filter information

People miss information constantly. Our perceptual system filters out more than it lets in. That isn't a bug; it's a feature! If we didn't work this way, we couldn't function in this booming, buzzing, rapidly changing world. We'd be overloaded.

Millions of years of evolution designed us to ignore most of what is going on around us and to focus our attention on what is important. When our prehistoric ancestors were hunting in the East African veldt, what was important was what was *moving* and what looked *different* from the grassy background. It might be animals they regarded as food ... or animals that regarded them as food.

In modern times, when a pilot scans cockpit displays, what is important is what is *abnormal,* what is *changing,* and *how* it is changing. When a business executive prepares a presentation, what is important is the presentation *content* and anything that seems like it will help her prepare her presentation on time. Everything else is irrelevant and is ignored.

A *common design flaw: not focusing users' attention*

Good design focuses users' attention on what's important by taking advantage of how human perception works. Unfortunately, many applications and Web sites achieve the opposite: unimportant details draw users' attention away from the important information.

Throughout history, poor design has caused people to miss important information and make errors—sometimes serious ones [Norman, 1983]. This includes the position of safety catches on guns, the position of gearshifts in vehicles, warning lights on nuclear power plant control panels, teletype printouts from network monitoring systems, fuel gauges and oil lights in vehicles and airplanes, and status lines in software.

The types of information often missed are:

BIZARRO (NEW) © DAN PIRARO. KING FEATURES SYNDICATE.

- *Status indicators:* for example, whether a DVD player's power is on and a disk is in it, the page currently displayed in a Web browser, or the number of files a file-transfer function has left to copy

- *Mode indicators:* for example, Caps Lock mode in a document editor (Blooper 48, page 269)
- *Prompts for input:* for example,

Password: [   ]   or   Delete All?   (Cancel)   (OK)

- *Results:* for example,

Estimated Payment: $1530.34   or   Cabin Pressure:

- *Error and status messages:* For example,

Could not import 'godzilla.doc': unknown file format

- *Controls:* For example, buttons, sliders, menus, and data fields

Users often miss these important items because of several different common design mistakes.

Variation A: Too small or plain

Some software displays important information in such a small size that it might as well not be there. If an indicator is a 16 × 16-pixel image on a 1200 × 900-pixel display, it will be easy to miss unless it is very bright or moves. This is especially true if the indicator is surrounded by other data or is at the edge of the users' field of vision.

Some software applications and Web sites display important information in the same (small) text font as everything else. In many office applications, data input fields and results fields look almost the same: the result fields have no special formatting or highlighting to attract users' attention.

Variation B: Not where the user is looking

Status indicators and other important information often appear in out-of-the-way locations, where many users won't notice them. Human visual acuity is best in a small area in the center of the field of vision, called the "fovea." Our ability to discriminate colors also is limited mainly to the fovea. Outside of the fovea, we have poor visual acuity and color vision. Stationary objects that are not right where we are looking are easily missed or misrecognized.

For example, consider the "Login" page of a Web application a company developed a few years ago. If a user typed an invalid ID or PIN, the page

Figure 5.1

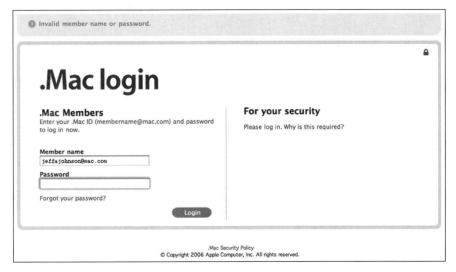

Client Web application: error message is easy to miss. See it?

Figure 5.2

Mac login: error message is easy to miss, even though it is displayed in orange.

reappeared showing an error message (Figure 5.1). The message's placement (upper left corner), size, and color made it easy to miss. After entering their ID and PIN and clicking "Login," users were looking at the bottom center of the page. Users who mistyped their ID or PIN often wasted several seconds wondering why the "Login" screen had just redisplayed. Often they would try again, only to return here again, until they finally saw the error message.

In Apple Computer's ".Mac" online service, entering invalid login information causes an error message to appear in the upper left corner (Figure 5.2). Even though the message is orange, its small size and out-of-the-way location make it possible to miss.

Variation C: Buried in "noise"

Important information is sometimes buried in a sea of sameness or visual "noise." Computers are great at producing repetition. Computers are great at producing repetition. Computers are great at producing repetition. See? Sometimes this is good, but when you are trying to make sure users receive important information, it's bad. Repetition and visual noise put our perceptual systems to sleep, causing us to miss important things when they come along.

Consider these two prompts:

Enter filename and press ENTER

Enter username and press ENTER

The only difference is the second word. That's the only information; the rest is noise. The capitalized word draws our attention, but is just noise. If software displayed these two prompts, users would sometimes confuse the two prompts and type an inappropriate response. Here are two prompts that are easier to tell apart:

Filename:

Username:

Status displays are another common trouble spot. Consider these:

Containing tank: normal   **Pressure valves: normal**

Fuel rods: abnormal   **Discharge pump: normal**

In these messages, the important information is buried by repetition and poor presentation.

The drivers' license information page at the California Department of Motor Vehicles Web site has lists of wordy, repetitive links (Figure 5.3). It is hard to scan the list quickly to find the link you need.

Results displays are another situation in which information is often buried in a sea of noise. Software often spews out repetitive, uninformative chaff, through which users must sift to find the few grains of wheat. As stated in Chapter 1, "Computers promise a fountain of information, but deliver a glut of data."

The important results of searches are often buried in repetition and visual noise. The issue here is *not* how good or bad a search engine is at finding relevant items; it is how the results are displayed.

In 1999, the Web search service Lycos.com displayed search results poorly (Figure 5.4). The first line for each item was its position in Lycos's category hierarchy. In search results, successive items are likely to be in similar categories, so this design produces repetition. In these results, the first four words in each found item are the same and so are noise, not information. The information is in the *differences* between items, but Lycos's 1999 results emphasize the similarities between items more than the differences.

Figure 5.3

- How to renew your driver license in person
- How to renew your driver license by mail
- How to renew your driver license by Internet
- How to renew your instruction permit
- How to apply for a duplicate driver license or identification (ID) card
- How to change your name on your driver license and/or identification (ID) card
- How to notify DMV of my change of address
- How to register for the organ donor gift of life program

DMV.ca.gov: wordy links with repeated text make list hard to scan quickly.

Figure 5.4

- **Arts > Music > Instruments > Guitar > Acoustic > Magazines**

    Acoustic Guitar Central - The home page of **Acoustic Guitar** magazine

- **Arts > Music > Instruments > Guitar > Luthiers**

    James Goodall Guitars: Acoustic Guitar Excellence - James Goodall manufactures some of the world's finest accoustic steel string **guitars**. Superb craftsmanship, an exacting finesse for detail and wood choice, combined with robust, three dimensional sound character — these are qualities which embody every James Goodall **guitar**.

- **Arts > Music > Instruments > Guitar > Fingerstyle**

    Acoustic Guitarists' Annotated Guide to the Internet - A broad overview of the **acoustic guitar** spectrum.

- **Arts > Music > Instruments > Guitar > Magazines**

    Flatpicking Guitar Magazine Online - specializes in all aspects of flatpicking the **acoustic guitar** - online articles (news & reviews) - info on contributors - US instructors list

Lycos.com (1999): search results for "acoustic guitar." Noisy, hard to scan for relevant items.

Figure 5.5

Web Results provided by ASK 1 thru 10 of 6,822,000 (Info)

1. **Acoustic Guitar** Central: Home for all **Acoustic Music**
   Acoustic Guitar Central offers free lessons, giveaways, gear reviews, beginner tips, discussion forums, and the latest from **Acoustic Guitar** magazine.
   http://www.acousticguitar.com/

2. **Guitar Noise**
   Guitar education site featuring free online lessons, musician columns, and theory pointers.
   http://www.guitarnoise.com/

3. **Guitar Notes**
   Everything about **guitar** - mp3, **guitar** tab, lessons, luthiers, music shops, your favorite guitarists, and much more! Add your own **guitar** links ...
   http://www.guitarnotes.com/

4. **Guitar Man Acoustic Guitar** Care and Playing Tips
   ... **acoustic guitar** tips, care, preservation, playing, maintenance, guitarists, clubs, wallpaper, Real Audio, tuners, jokes, music and ...
   http://www.nb.net/~alanb

5. History of the **Guitar**
   Are you doing a research paper on the history of the **guitar**. Here's an article that will help you learn about the history of the **Guitar**.
   http://guitar.about.com/library/weekly/aa042199.htm

6. **Acoustic-Electric Guitar** Buying Guide
   12 questions you should ask before buying an **acoustic guitar**. ... The type and quality of wood used to construct the **acoustic guitar** is the ...
   http://www.guitarimports.com/acoustic-guitars.htm

Lycos.com (2007): search results for "acoustic guitar." Less noisy, easier to scan for relevant items.

Compare that to how Lycos.com displayed results in early 2007: much less noisy and much easier for users to scan quickly (Figure 5.5).

Despite improvements in Web search results, many site-specific search functions still display results poorly. Blooper 21 (page 145) shows several Web sites that produce unusable search results.

Messages that won't die

One way to make users miss important messages is to display new messages over similar old ones.

Microsoft Office lets you search its Clip Gallery to find art to add to a document. You enter keywords; it searches for clip art tagged with those keywords. If you search for "dial," you get a message saying it found nothing (Figure 5.6A). If you change the keyword to "gauge" and search again, the message remains (Figure 5.6B). Did it also find nothing for "gauge" or is it still searching? You can't tell. Clearing previous search results or messages when the user enters a new search term would fix this.

Figure 5.6

 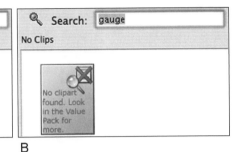

A   B

Microsoft Office Clip Gallery Search leaves old error messages up and displays new ones over them.

Avoiding Blooper 32

Here are guidelines for making information hard for users to miss.

Construct a visual hierarchy

Organize information displays into chunks, subchunks, subsubchunks, etc., so users can quickly spot the right chunk, then the right subchunk in that chunk, etc. That lets users ignore irrelevant chunks and find what they want *much faster* than if they had to scan—or worse, read—through everything on the screen. The windows on computers provide high-level chunking, but it is up to you to chunk the information in your software's windows or pages.

Make important information bigger

The rear brake lights and turn signals on today's automobiles are larger than they were in 1980. This is not just fashion; it makes the lights more noticeable. Size matters, especially for indicators that must be noticed even though they are not in the center of the viewer's visual field.

The same applies to on-screen information, whether it is controls, symbols, text, or areas of color. The larger the indicator, the more retinal cells its image covers and the more difficult it is to miss.

However, if everything in a display is big, nothing stands out. *Relative* size is what really matters.

Put important information where the user is looking

Placing information closer to the center of the viewer's visual field improves its visibility and legibility. Peripheral vision is poor and gets poorer with age.

Putting an indicator on the cursor is a good strategy for small, critical indicators because that is where users are usually looking. Displaying important messages in message lines at the bottom of application windows only works if you do something special to draw users' attention to the message.

Use color to highlight

Contrasting colors can draw attention to information. In Western societies, red traditionally indicates something is wrong, and so it is a good color for error messages. Use an orangeish red rather than a pure red for maximum visibility.

In mission-critical systems (e.g., air traffic control systems, intensive-care medical monitoring systems, and power plant control panels), emergency messages are displayed in red. Yellow is often used to warn or indicate caution.

AOL.com's e-mail account registration form uses red to get attention. If someone tries to register but omits required data, a red error message appears at the top and all incomplete required fields are labeled in red (Figure 5.7).

To really grab users' attention, you can change color in real time. For example, an error message can alternate *once* between red and yellow and then stay red.

One application displayed error messages on a message line at the bottom of the application's window. To be noticed, messages appeared briefly in red, then changed to black after a second. That not only drew users' attention, it also indicated whether a message was new or left over from a previous error.

Other ways to make information stand out

In addition to size, position, and color, you can also use:

- *Boldness, density, color, saturation:* **Boldface** text stands out. Graphics can have thicker or darker lines and fill shades. Color images can be made more saturated. However, boldness, density, and saturation should be used with restraint. **It does little** or no **good** to **make text bold** if **most** of the **text around it** is **bold.**

- *Graphics and symbols:* Graphics, icons, and symbols can attract users' attention, especially if most of a display is text. The red error message at AOL.com (Figure 5.7) would be even more noticeable if it started with a big red X, stop sign, or large exclamation point. As the page is, the most eye-catching object is the symbol of a person.

The heavy artillery: use sparingly and with caution

If information or prompts are absolutely critical (e.g., a potentially disastrous problem in a nuclear power plant), there are three techniques that can make messages or prompts nearly impossible to ignore:

1. *Dialog boxes and pop ups:* Error messages, warnings, and prompts can be displayed in dialog boxes, which pop out of the browser and get "in the users' face." Dialog boxes can be modal, blocking users from doing anything else with the application (or in some cases, with their computer) until they acknowledge or dismiss the dialog box, or they can be nonmodal. REI.com, unlike AOL.com, uses a dialog box to tell users that required data is missing from a form (Figure 5.8).

Figure 5.7

Red

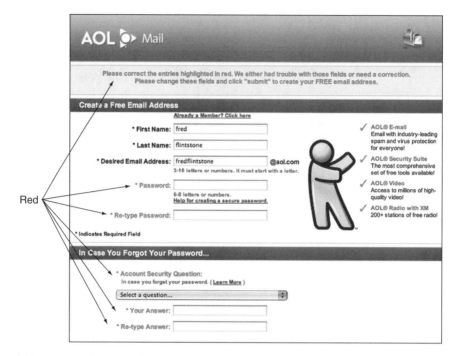

AOL.com: e-mail account form highlights error messages and labels of incomplete data fields in red.

Figure 5.8

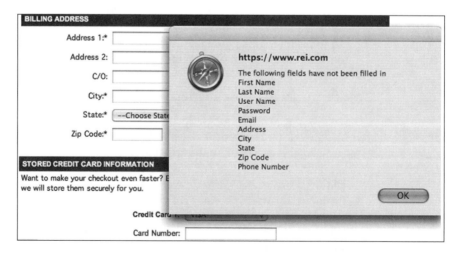

REI.com: new customer application form indicates incomplete data fields in an error dialog box.

2. *Sound:* A new message, a limit exceeded, or an error detected can be announced with sound. Simple beeps are usually sufficient if it is clear where to look for details. Some new cars play an artificial "barump, barump, barump" sound when a car starts to drift out of its lane. Like boldface, sound can easily be overused. People can't distinguish more than a few arbitrary sounds. It also won't work where there is a lot of ambient noise or where people work in close quarters.

3. *Vibration and animation:* Peripheral vision for stationery objects is poor, but it is very good at noticing movement or changes. We quickly look at whatever draws our attention, so flashing or movement can draw attention to important data. However, they are distracting and annoying if continuous, and Web designers have abused them to get people to notice advertisements. Many designers, such as Flanders and Willis [1998], now discourage their use. If you use animation or flashing, make sure it stops quickly. If you can't stop it, *don't use it*. Unfortunately, many Web sites violate this rule. The home page of PondMarket.com, a fish pond supply store, has several animations that run constantly (Figure 5.9).

Don't bury the wheat in chaff

Software should deliver information, not just data (Basic Principle 7, page 41). Therefore, avoid displaying data that carries no useful information, especially noninformative, repetitive data. Emphasize important information using the methods given above.

Instead of displaying computed results as prose text descriptions, display them in tables, charts, and graphs [Tufte, 1990, 2001]. Many Web search results would be better presented in tables.

If nontabular text is unavoidable, minimize the verbiage. Users are searching for the wheat, and non-information-bearing text is useless chaff. Format text to focus users' attention on the useful information.

Figure 5.9

PondMarket.com: pointless, constant animations that distract from important content.

Displaying information graphically instead of textually

The RhythmTutor music instruction program helps people learn to read music by providing practice in reading rhythm notation—note durations and rests. RhythmTutor poses exercises by showing music notation and sounding a metronome tone. You "play" the music by pressing the Space bar for every note at the metronome's tempo. At the end of each exercise, RhythmTutor rates your performance, showing how many notes you missed, how many extra notes you played, and whether notes started and ended late, early, or on time.

RhythmTutor's beta-release presented all feedback numerically, embedded in prose text (Figure 5.10A). In the released product, the user feedback was much easier to understand (Figure 5.10B).

Figure 5.10

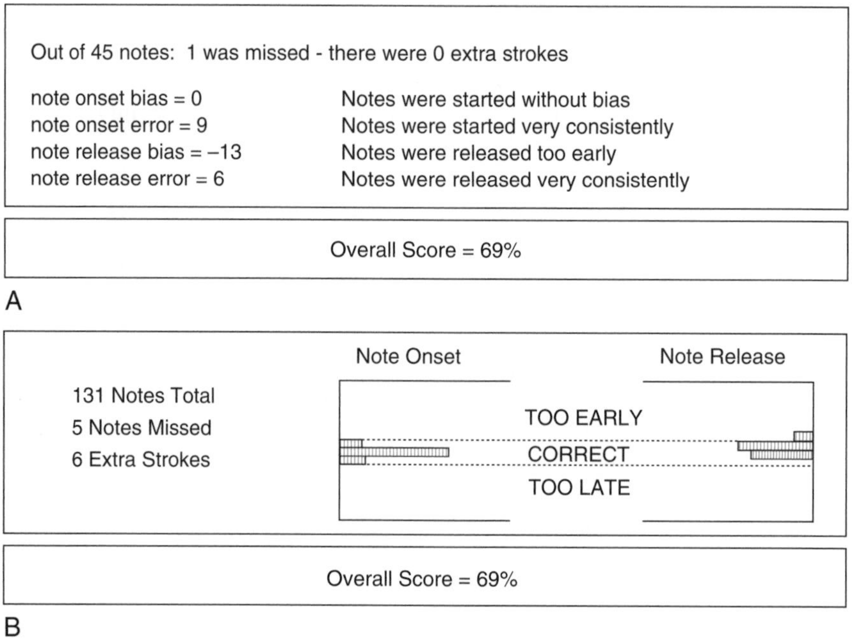

Out of 45 notes: 1 was missed - there were 0 extra strokes

note onset bias = 0	Notes were started without bias
note onset error = 9	Notes were started very consistently
note release bias = −13	Notes were released too early
note release error = 6	Notes were released very consistently

Overall Score = 69%

A

	Note Onset	Note Release
131 Notes Total		TOO EARLY
5 Notes Missed		CORRECT
6 Extra Strokes		TOO LATE

Overall Score = 69%

B

RhythmTutor score display. (A) Before redesign: textual. (B) After: more graphical.

Blooper 33: Mixing dialog box control buttons with content control buttons

Many dialog boxes put the standard buttons "OK," "Apply," "Close," "Cancel," and "Help" in the same place as buttons that control specific data or settings. Imagine you were creating an application for tracking stock prices. In the dialog box for adding stocks to be tracked, "Add" and "Delete" buttons would let users manage the "Tracking" list. You might put "Add" and "Delete" at the bottom of the dialog box, next to "OK," "Cancel," and "Help" (Figure 5.11), because the bottom is a convenient place to put all the buttons.

Figure 5.11

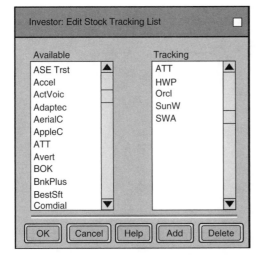

Window control buttons not separated from content control buttons.

That would be a design error for two reasons:

1. Placing data-specific buttons far from the data they control makes it hard to see the connection between button and data.
2. There is no visual distinction between buttons that control the whole dialog box and those that control specific data in it.

In PhotoShop's Levels dialog box, "OK" and "Cancel" close the window; the other four buttons affect or save the brightness histogram (Figure 5.12A). In Outlook's Move Items dialog box, the "New…" button creates a new folder, while "OK" and "Cancel" close the dialog box (Figure 5.12B). On both, it is good that the content control buttons are near the content, but bad that dialog box control buttons are there too.

Figure 5.12

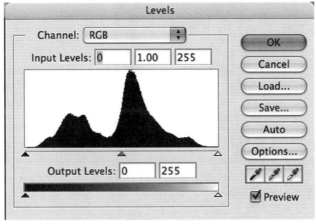

A

Mixing window control and content control buttons. (A) Adobe PhotoShop. (B) Microsoft Outlook.

(Continued)

Figure 5.12

(Continued)

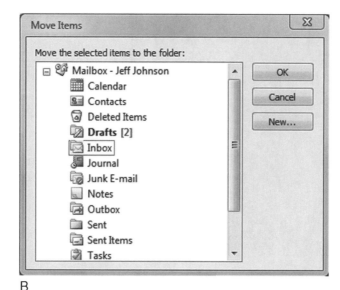

B

Avoiding Blooper 33

Buttons that affect the entire dialog box—"OK," "Apply," "Close," "Cancel," "Help"—should be separated from those that control specific data or settings. "Add" and "Delete" buttons should be between the scrolling lists they affect, making their function much clearer and reserving the bottom row of the dialog box for "OK," "Cancel," and "Help" (Figure 5.13). A line helps separate content control buttons from the dialog box control buttons, but with adequate spacing it is not necessary.

Figure 5.13

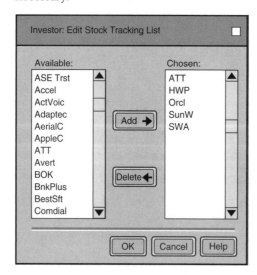

Content control buttons separated from window control buttons.

Two examples of good button layout come from dialog boxes of two e-mail programs: Mozilla Thunderbird and Microsoft Outlook (Figure 5.14). The Outlook dialog box uses a separator to distinguish the dialog box control buttons from the rest, while the Mozilla dialog box does the same thing with just good positioning and spacing.

Figure 5.14

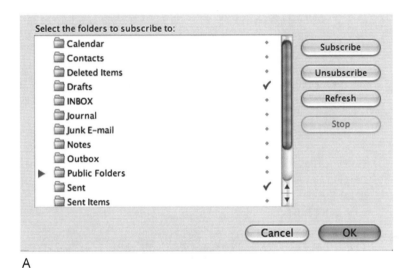

A

B

Separating window and content control buttons. (A) Mozilla Thunderbird. (B) Microsoft Outlook.

Blooper 34: Misusing group boxes

Most GUI toolkits provide group boxes[1] for putting a visible border around related controls. Group boxes have a slot for a label, usually on the top left edge. A classic good use of group boxes can be seen in Microsoft Internet Explorer's Accessibility dialog box (Figure 5.15).

Variation A: *Group box around one setting*

A common layout blooper is to place a group box around a single setting. Usually this is done to use the group box's built-in label to label the setting. For example, one company regularly put group boxes around scrolling text areas and tabbed panels in order to label them (Figure 5.16).

Using group boxes merely as holders for labels ignores their true purpose—grouping things—and clutters the display needlessly. It also often is redundant: many GUI controls, e.g., tables, scrolling lists, option menus, and text fields, have their own borders.

Microsoft Window's Custom Game Controller dialog box and the Guidebook window of National Geographic Trip Planner have the blooper. The Custom Game Controller dialog box has three group boxes, two of which are around single items (Figure 5.17A). In Trip Planner, the group box surrounds the upper scrolling list of Guidebook Topics (Figure 5.17B). In both, the group boxes are just label holders.

Figure 5.15

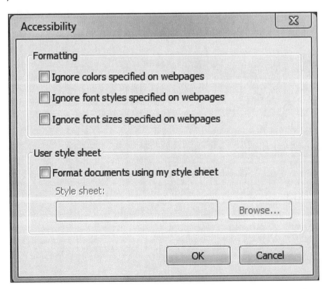

Microsoft Internet Explorer: classic use of group boxes to organize settings.

---

1.   In some GUI toolkits, this is called a "border."

Figure 5.16

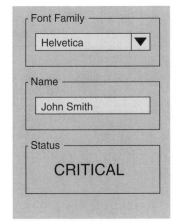

Group boxes around one control, misused as place for label.

Figure 5.17

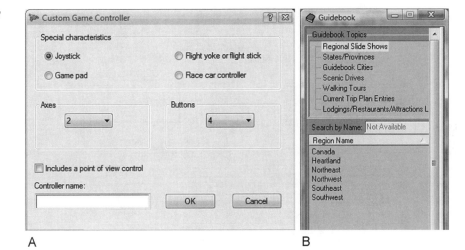

A   B

Group boxes around one item. (A) Microsoft Windows. (B) National Geographic Trip Planner.

Variation B: Group boxes within group boxes

A second variation of this blooper is to nest group boxes within group boxes. This makes for a needlessly cluttered display (Figure 5.18).

Showing that real life can be stranger than fiction, SmartDraw has a dialog box with group boxes nested *three* deep (Figure 5.19). It also has group boxes around single items, serving as label holders.

Figure 5.18

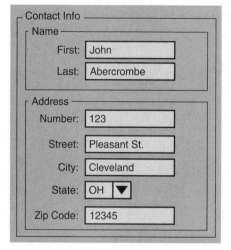

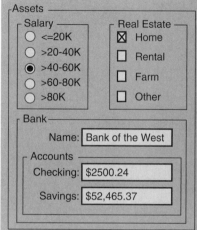

Group boxes within group boxes, causing needless clutter.

Figure 5.19

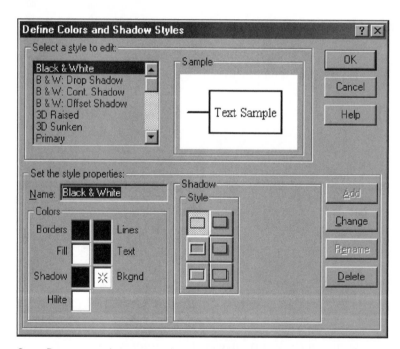

SmartDraw: group boxes nested two and three deep. Some are merely label-holders.

Variation C: One group box in a window

A third misuse of group boxes is to put one around everything in a window. The box may group multiple settings, but it doesn't separate those settings from any others. Thus, the group box is unnecessary.

A developer may do this to hold the window title (Figure 5.20). However, the title *should* be in the window's titlebar, e.g., "Investor: Edit Stock Tracking List." Alternatively, a developer might use a group box to separate the bottom row of control buttons from everything else. However, there are better ways to do that, as described under how to avoid Blooper 33.

Dialog boxes in SoundBlaster Wave Studio and Windows Media Player exhibit this variation of group box misuse (Figure 5.21). In both, the outer group box only adds clutter.

Figure 5.20

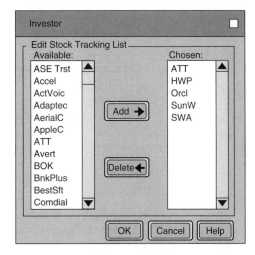

Group box around everything, causing needless clutter.

Figure 5.21

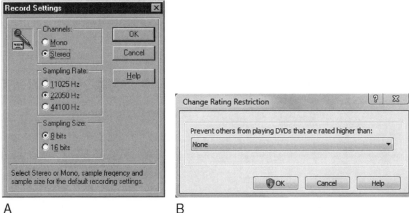

A   B

Unlabeled group box around everything. (A) SoundBlaster Wave Studio. (B) Windows Media Player.

Avoiding Blooper 34

Group boxes are for what their name suggests: boxing related *groups* of settings. Container controls such as tables, scrolling lists, and editable text fields provide their own built-in borders and don't need extra borders.

Label a single setting without putting a group box around it, using a Label or Static Text control. Labels should be above or to the left of the item—whichever is better for overall layout. The Microsoft Windows Mouse Properties dialog box makes good use of group boxes (Figure 5.22). There is no need for a group box around the Customize list: it has its own border.

Group boxes should be used sparingly. Placing group boxes within group boxes clutters the display. Careful spacing and labeling can clarify the organization of a control panel while minimizing clutter. Windows Media Player's Change Rip Music Location dialog box uses no group boxes at all (Figure 5.23). When spacing alone isn't enough, separators can help provide visual order.

Sets of radio buttons are a special case: even though they are one setting, it sometimes helps to put group boxes around them to separate them from other nearby radio-button settings, as in SoundBlaster Wave Studio (Figure 5.21A). However, radio-button settings can be separated using lines or blank space, as in dialog boxes from Microsoft Word and Apple Preview (Figure 5.24).

Figure 5.22

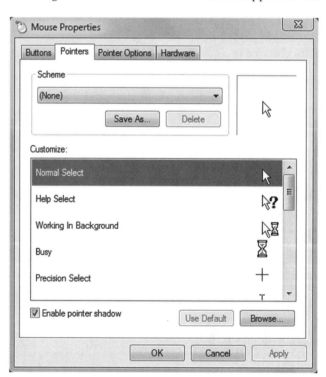

Microsoft Windows Mouse Properties window: good use of group boxes.

Figure 5.23

Microsoft Windows Media Player: Change Rip Music Location dialog box has no group boxes.

Figure 5.24

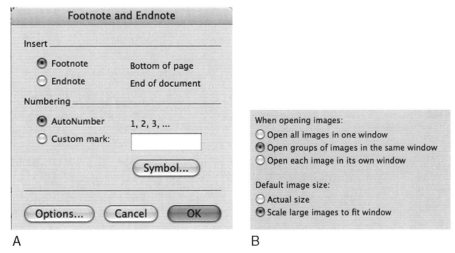

A   B

Radio buttons labeled without group boxes around them. (A) Microsoft Word. (B) Apple Preview.

Blooper 35: Radio buttons too far apart

Sometimes radio buttons are so far apart that they don't look like a single setting (Figure 5.25).

The problem in the hypothetical example is excessive horizontal spacing. A form on the IEEE.org Web site shows that excessive *vertical* spacing can make radio buttons look disconnected (Figure 5.26) as well.

Figure 5.25

| Display: | ⦿ Summary | ◯ Details |

Radio buttons spaced too far apart to be seen as related.

Figure 5.26

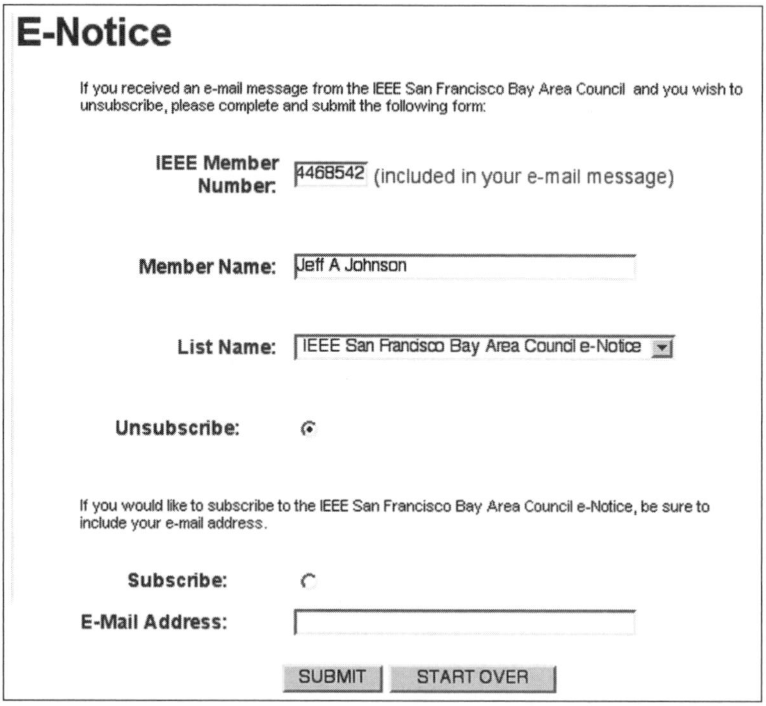

E-Notice

If you received an e-mail message from the IEEE San Francisco Bay Area Council and you wish to unsubscribe, please complete and submit the following form:

IEEE Member Number: `4468542` (included in your e-mail message)

Member Name: `Jeff A Johnson`

List Name: `IEEE San Francisco Bay Area Council e-Notice ▾`

Unsubscribe: ⦿

If you would like to subscribe to the IEEE San Francisco Bay Area Council e-Notice, be sure to include your e-mail address.

Subscribe: ◯
E-Mail Address: `_____`

[SUBMIT]   [START OVER]

IEEE.org: radio buttons spaced too far apart to be seen as related.

If different radio-button groups are next to each other, users may misunderstand how they are grouped. This can happen if radio-button groups are laid out horizontally, with the buttons in each group closer to buttons in *other* groups than to buttons in their *own* group (Figure 5.27). The buttons are in rows, yet appear to group by columns.

Users might be able to figure out from the labeling how the buttons are grouped, but users should not have to stop and think about how a UI is organized. Also sometimes the labels don't help (Figure 5.28).

Figure 5.27

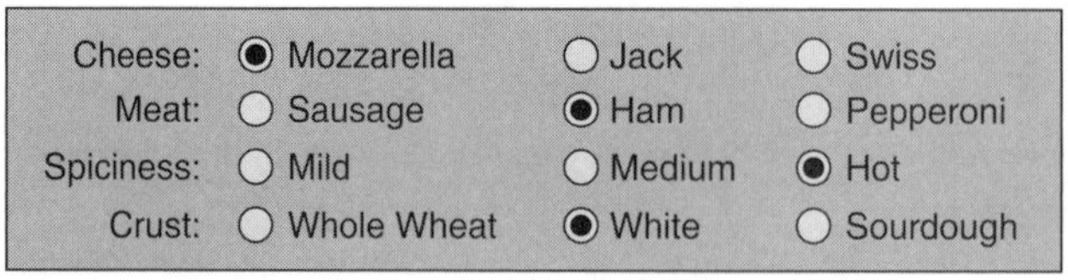

Cheese:	⦿ Mozzarella	◯ Jack	◯ Swiss
Meat:	◯ Sausage	⦿ Ham	◯ Pepperoni
Spiciness:	◯ Mild	◯ Medium	⦿ Hot
Crust:	◯ Whole Wheat	⦿ White	◯ Sourdough

Radio buttons in each intended group are farther from one another than from those in adjacent groups.

Figure 5.28

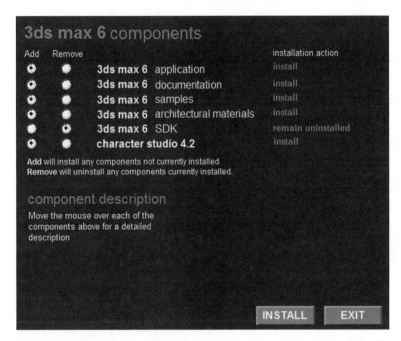

Radio buttons appear grouped in columns rather than the intended rows.

Figure 5.29

Discreet installer wizard: radio buttons appear grouped in columns rather than in the intended rows.

A real example occurs on the component selector page of Discreet Software's wizard for installing the company's products from a CD (Figure 5.29).

Avoiding Blooper 35

Radio-button settings should be laid out so users can see at a glance how they are grouped. One way to do this is with group boxes or separators (Figure 5.30).

Another approach is to use blank space. If the space between groups is greater than the average space between buttons within a group (including their labels), users will perceive the intended groupings (Figure 5.31).

In Figure 5.32, the radio buttons are arranged in a neat matrix. If the number of options varies from group to group or if option labels in different groups vary greatly in length, it is better to space each group tightly, even though that

Figure 5.30

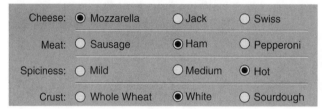

A

B

Radio-button groups separated so users see intended groupings. (A) Group boxes. (B) Separators.

Figure 5.31

Radio-button groups spaced so users see intended groupings.

Figure 5.32

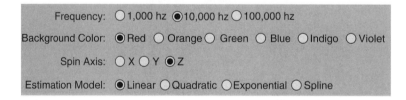

Radio-button sets spaced tightly and irregularly so users perceive correct groupings.

destroys the neat matrix arrangement (Figure 5.32). An irregular layout may bother your aesthetic sensibilities, but your job is to avoid confusing users.

Blooper 36: Labels too far from data fields

GUI developers are usually under pressure to produce a UI quickly. They often toss in controls and labels as fast as they can without worrying about their exact placement and assume that the placement can be refined sometime in the future when there is more time. Unfortunately, that time rarely comes.

This yields GUIs in which labels are too far from the controls they label, making it hard for users to see at a glance which label goes with which control. This blooper has two common variations.

Variation A: Labels on extreme left; data fields on extreme right

The most common label spacing flaw occurs in online forms. An easy way to lay out a form is to place field labels in a column attached to the left edge and data fields in a column attached to the right edge. This often puts labels so far from their data fields that users cannot easily see the connection. A classic example occurs at the Web site of the International Online Booksellers Association (Figure 5.33).

Figure 5.33

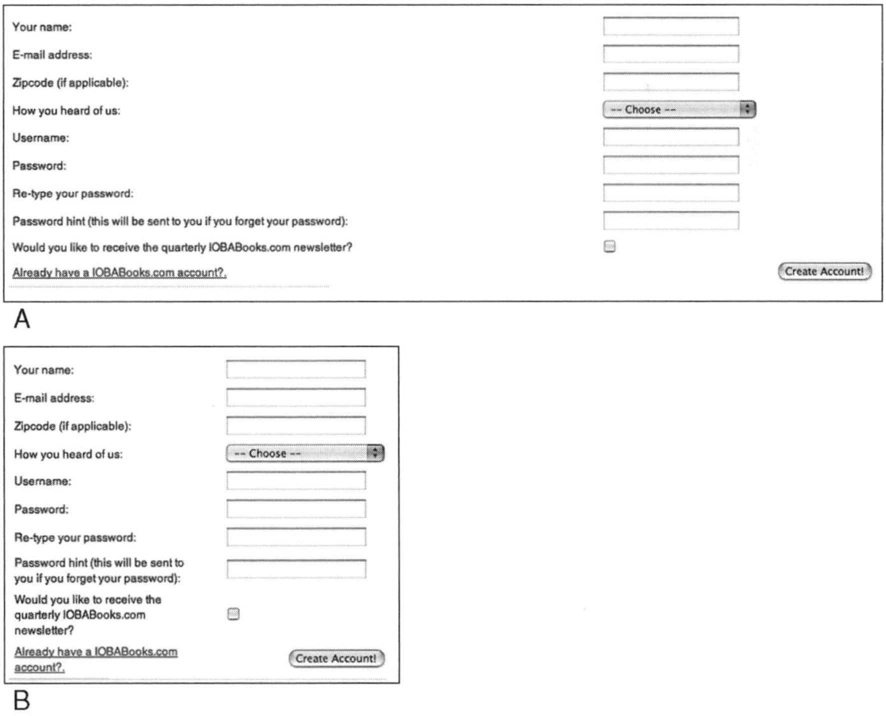

Your name:

E-mail address:

Zipcode (if applicable):

How you heard of us: -- Choose --

Username:

Password:

Re-type your password:

Password hint (this will be sent to you if you forget your password):

Would you like to receive the quarterly IOBABooks.com newsletter?

Already have a IOBABooks.com account?.   Create Account!

A

Your name:

E-mail address:

Zipcode (if applicable):

How you heard of us: -- Choose --

Username:

Password:

Re-type your password:

Password hint (this will be sent to you if you forget your password):

Would you like to receive the quarterly IOBABooks.com newsletter?

Already have a IOBABooks.com account?.   Create Account!

B

IOBA.org registration form: labels too far from their data fields. (A) Wide browser. (B) Narrow browser.

Figure 5.34

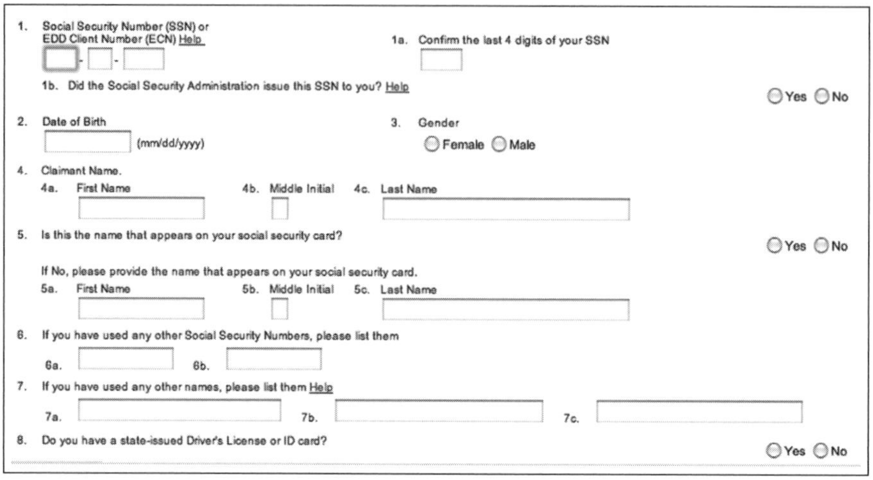

1. Social Security Number (SSN) or EDD Client Number (ECN) Help

1a. Confirm the last 4 digits of your SSN

1b. Did the Social Security Administration issue this SSN to you? Help

○ Yes ○ No

2. Date of Birth

(mm/dd/yyyy)

3. Gender

○ Female ○ Male

4. Claimant Name.

4a. First Name   4b. Middle Initial   4c. Last Name

5. Is this the name that appears on your social security card?

○ Yes ○ No

If No, please provide the name that appears on your social security card.

5a. First Name   5b. Middle Initial   5c. Last Name

6. If you have used any other Social Security Numbers, please list them

6a.   6b.

7. If you have used any other names, please list them Help

7a.   7b.   7c.

8. Do you have a state-issued Driver's License or ID card?

○ Yes ○ No

CA.gov unemployment insurance form: "Yes"/"No" radio buttons are too far from their labels.

A more subtle example occurs in an unemployment insurance form at the State of California's Web site, CA.gov. Yes/No choices are radio buttons attached to the right edge, far from their question (Figure 5.34).

This blooper is made worse by variable-width layout in which the distance between labels and data fields depends on how wide users make the window.

Variation B: Labels closer to other settings than to their own

The second most common label placement flaw is for property labels to be closer to another data field than to the field they label. A perfect example occurs at LLBean.com (Figure 5.35).

How close objects are to each other determines our perception of how they are grouped. Therefore, poor label placement is not just an aesthetic issue; it can diminish software's usability.

Why would anyone position labels as at LLBean.com? Designers and developers are usually under great time pressure. They also may not know how strongly label placement affects the usability of forms.

A third reason is that from the developer's perspective, the labels may not *be* far from the data fields. Assume that a form has two text fields and a menu. A developer might make the labels wider than their text requires, perhaps to fit translations into other languages. In Figure 5.36, the hypothetical label components are inverted to show their boundaries. From the developer's point of view, the labels are next to their settings; from the user's point of view, they aren't.

Figure 5.35

LLBean.com: State and ZIP labels closer to previous data field than to their own.

Figure 5.36

LLBean.com: hypothetical label components inverted to show their full width.

Avoiding Blooper 36

Users should not have to scrutinize a form or control panel carefully to figure out how controls and data fields are labeled. A quick scan should be enough. Therefore, put labels close to their object. Follow these four simple rules.

Rule 1: Don't attach labels and data fields to opposite edges of a form or control panel

If columns of an invisible table are used to lay out labels and data fields on a form or dialog box, the two columns should be adjacent. They should be attached to each other, not to opposite edges of the form. Alternatively, labels can be attached directly to their data fields in rows, with spacing calibrated so that labels and fields align.

In MacOS, Linux/Unix, Web, you can right-align labels to put them near their fields. On some platforms—such as Microsoft Windows—the convention is left-aligned labels. With left-aligned labels, it is very important to minimize the gap between labels and data fields [Penzo, 2006].

Rule 2: Don't allow a few long labels to dictate the alignment of the entire form

Sometimes a form has one field with a label that is much longer than the others. Aligning *all* the labels and their fields to the long label and its field wastes a lot of space (Figure 5.37). With left alignment, it also puts the shorter labels too far away from their fields.

One solution is to wrap the long label to multiple lines, as is shown by a form at uBid.com (Figure 5.38). Another solution is to abbreviate long labels, as long as that doesn't hurt comprehension or ease of translation.

If it is impossible to wrap or abbreviate long labels in a way that makes sense to users, you can simply lay out the fields that have long labels separately from the others (Figure 5.39).

Figure 5.37

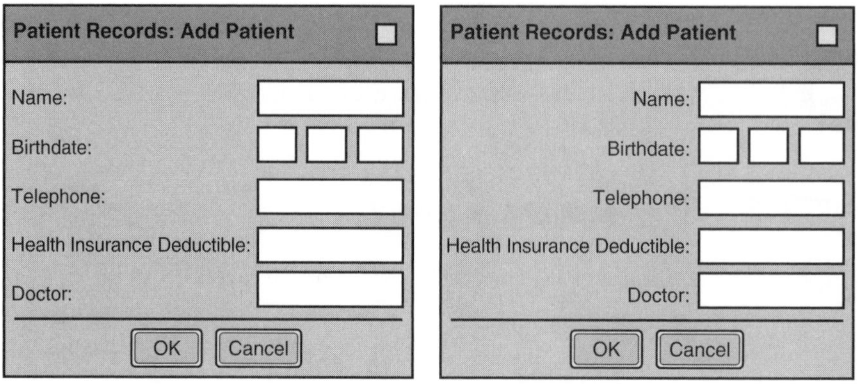

Patient Records: Add Patient ☐
Name: [   ]
Birthdate: [ ] [ ] [ ]
Telephone: [   ]
Health Insurance Deductible: [   ]
Doctor: [   ]
[OK] [Cancel]

Patient Records: Add Patient ☐
Name: [   ]
Birthdate: [ ] [ ] [ ]
Telephone: [   ]
Health Insurance Deductible: [   ]
Doctor: [   ]
[OK] [Cancel]

Long label problem: with either left or right alignment, very long labels are a problem.

Figure 5.38

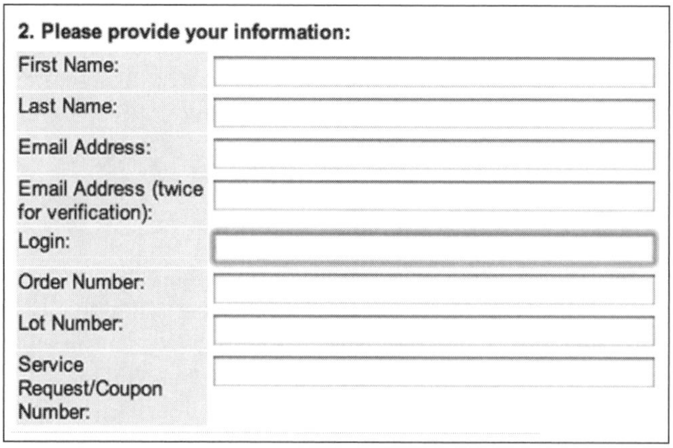

2. Please provide your information:
First Name: [   ]
Last Name: [   ]
Email Address: [   ]
Email Address (twice for verification): [   ]
Login: [   ]
Order Number: [   ]
Lot Number: [   ]
Service Request/Coupon Number: [   ]

uBid.com: long labels can be wrapped so shorter labels are not too far from their fields.

Figure 5.39

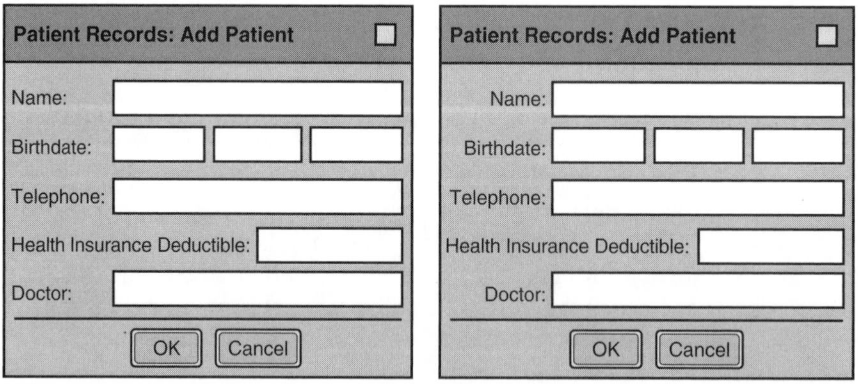

Patient Records: Add Patient ☐
Name: [   ]
Birthdate: [   ] [   ] [   ]
Telephone: [   ]
Health Insurance Deductible: [   ]
Doctor: [   ]
[OK] [Cancel]

Patient Records: Add Patient ☐
Name: [   ]
Birthdate: [   ] [   ] [   ]
Telephone: [   ]
Health Insurance Deductible: [   ]
Doctor: [   ]
[OK] [Cancel]

Long label solution: align the shorter labels and fields, and place the long label separately.

Figure 5.40

Labels closer to their own data field than to others.

Rule 3: Labels should be closer to their own field than to other fields

When several labeled fields are positioned horizontally, their proximity should show the intended pairing of labels with fields. The distance between labels and their associated data fields should be less than the distance between different settings (Figure 5.40). There are two ways this can be done:

- Right-align setting labels. This is feasible only on platforms for which right-aligned labels are acceptable (e.g., MacOS or Web). It isn't feasible under Microsoft Windows, in which the convention is to left-align setting labels.
- Adjust label width to length of text. If the label doesn't change, determine its width during design. If the label can change—e.g., when the software is localized for a different language—the label's position can be determined automatically at installation or runtime.

Rule 4: Put labels above fields

Placing labels directly above fields is a good way to keep labels next to their fields. This approach is becoming increasingly popular, partly because it works well for forms that are provided in several languages. United Airlines's Web site provides an example (Figure 5.41).

Figure 5.41

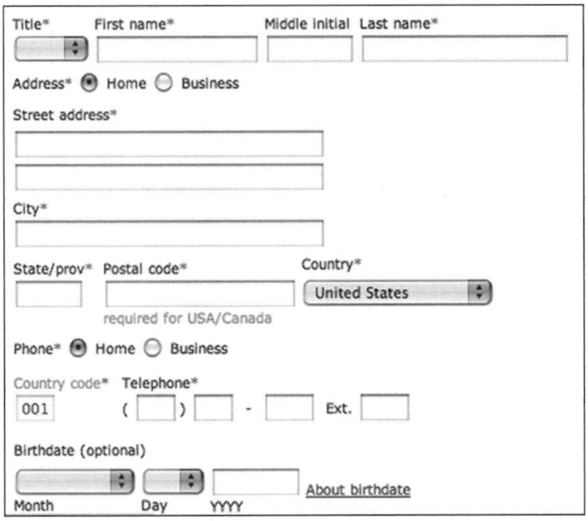

United.com: labels above fields.

Blooper 37: Inconsistent label alignment

When labels are placed to the left of their data fields, they can be either left-aligned or right-aligned. A very common blooper is to align the labels of controls or data fields inconsistently: left alignment in some places, right alignment in others. An example can be seen in two dialog boxes from a WebMail application at the University of Canterbury (Figure 5.42).

This blooper is even more common in Web sites than in applications. It occurs in online forms at uBid.com (Figure 5.43).

Figure 5.42

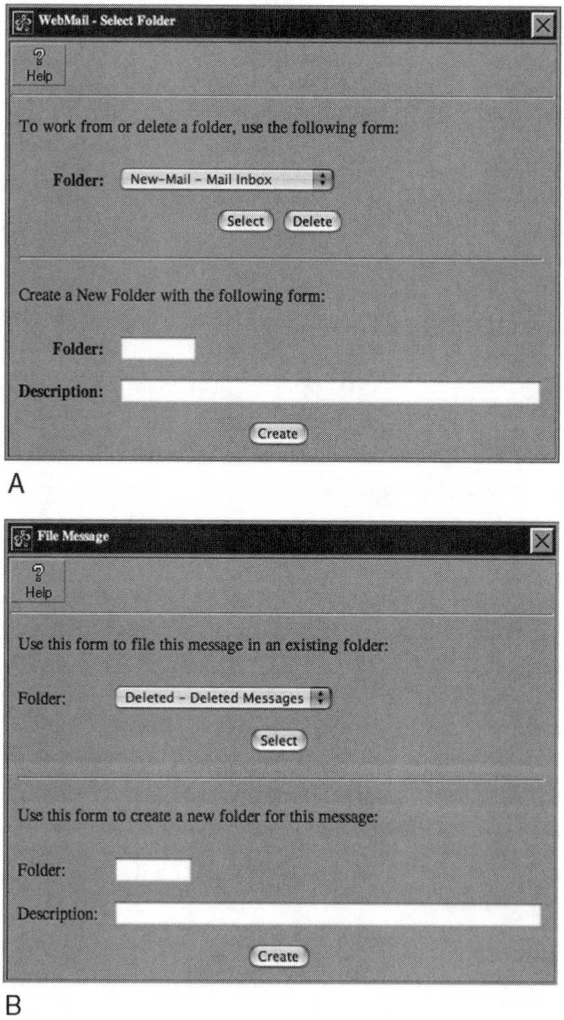

A

B

University of Canterbury WebMail: left- and right-aligned labels in same application.

Figure 5.43

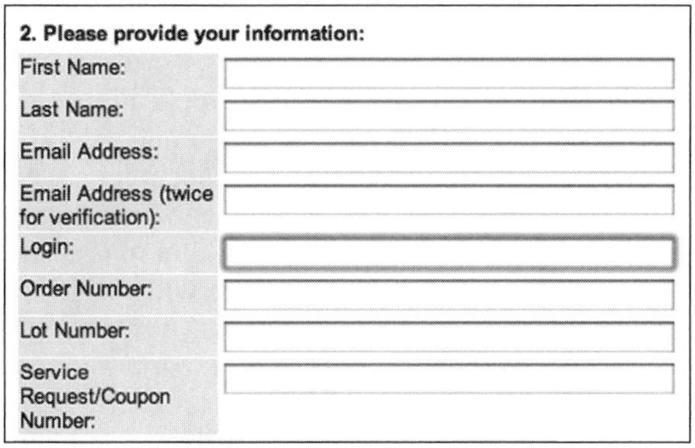

2. Please provide your information:

First Name:

Last Name:

Email Address:

Email Address (twice for verification):

Login:

Order Number:

Lot Number:

Service Request/Coupon Number:

A

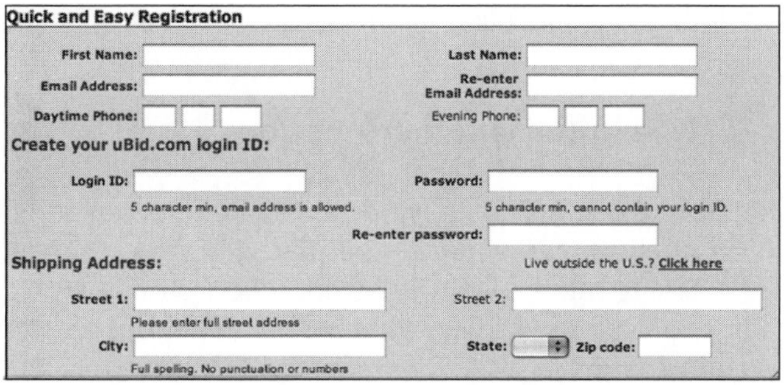

Quick and Easy Registration

First Name: Last Name:

Email Address: Re-enter Email Address:

Daytime Phone: Evening Phone:

Create your uBid.com login ID:

Login ID:

5 character min, email address is allowed.   Password:

5 character min, cannot contain your login ID.

Re-enter password:

Shipping Address: Live outside the U.S.? Click here

Street 1:   Street 2:

Please enter full street address

City: State: Zip code:

Full spelling. No punctuation or numbers

B

uBid.com: left- and right-aligned form labels on the same Web site.

Sometimes you find inconsistent label alignment in a single window or Web page. In the Print dialog box of Microsoft Office for Mac (Figure 5.44), the top two data fields are supplied by MacOS, while the other fields come from Office. That explains the inconsistency, but does not excuse it. This is the MacOS version of Office, so the entire dialog box should use the MacOS convention: right alignment.

Figure 5.44

Printer: 206Laser

Presets: Standard

Copies & Pages

Copies: 1   ☑ Collated

Pages: ◉ All

Microsoft Office for MacOS: inconsistent label alignment in a single dialog box.

Avoiding Blooper 37

Within an application or a suite of related applications, alignment of labels should be consistent. Some UI designers recommend right alignment because it puts labels close to settings, making the connection between labels and their settings easy to see. Other designers recommend left alignment, arguing that right-aligned labels create a ragged left margin that makes a form hard to scan.

It really is not important whom you agree with. It is important to choose a standard—preferably the dominant practice for your target platform—and use it consistently throughout your application, suite of applications, or product line. On the Microsoft Windows platform, the dominant standard is to left-align labels. On MacOS, the dominant practice is to right-align them. On Linux- and Unix-based platforms, there is no standard: applications are free to determine their own. The Web similarly has no standard for label alignment; each site creates its own.

Blooper 38: Bad initial window location

Most applications have a main window and a number of other windows. Where should an application's windows be placed? Once a window appears, users should be able to move it anywhere, but where should it *first* appear?

Many applications display windows in unhelpful locations. This blooper has several variations.

Variation A: Displaying all windows at the same coordinates

A common form of the blooper is for an application to display all or most of its windows at the same screen position. The position of a window is specified by the screen coordinate of its upper left corner, so positioning windows at the same location means their upper left corners coincide. This is easy for programmers: they don't have to figure out where each window should go. However, it forces users to move windows to keep important data visible.

A special case is when GUI programs open all new windows in screen position [0, 0], the upper left corner of the screen (Figure 5.45). That is usually the window manager's default location if no location is specified. Taking the default is easy from a programming standpoint, but it gives users an impression of a shoddy implementation.

Until recently, Microsoft PowerPoint displayed the Hyperlink to Slide dialog box over the top of its parent Action Settings dialog box (Figure 5.46). This, plus the dialog box layout, caused confusion about which "OK"/"Cancel" buttons to click, as a colleague explained:

> I **always** click the wrong OK button. Even when I do this frequently, say 30 times within 3 minutes, I don't get trained until the 25th time or so. And if I do it again after a lapse of 5–10 minutes, I forget and go right back to clicking the wrong button.

Figure 5.45

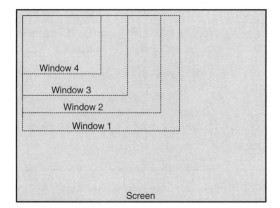

Blooper: all of an application's windows open at position [0, 0].

Figure 5.46

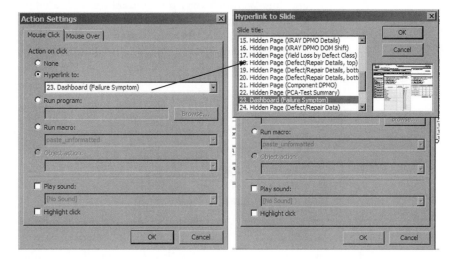

PowerPoint: Hyperlink Action Settings dialog box opens Hyperlink to Slide dialog box at the same top position, confusing users about which "OK"/"Cancel" buttons to click when done with the second dialog box.

Variation B: Displaying subordinate windows in middle of parent

Another strategy is to center each child window over its parent window. Centering one window over another requires only a little more calculation than does placing the upper left corners at the same place.[2]

---

2. The formulae for calculating the coordinates of a window to be centered (NewWindow) are:

NewWindow.x = ParentWindow.x + (ParentWindow.width − NewWindow.width)/2,

NewWindow.y = ParentWindow.y + (ParentWindow.height − NewWindow.height)/2.

Figure 5.47

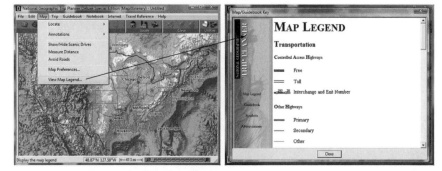

National Geographic Trip Planner: map legend opens over map, making users move it.

Centering child windows over their parent has the same problem as opening all windows at [0, 0]: they all appear over each other. However, most applications have a hierarchy of windows: *multiple* windows can display child windows. Distributing the initial locations of child windows across multiple parent windows alleviates the "all on top of each other" problem a bit, but several problems remain:

1. All child windows of a particular parent window still open over each other. For parent windows with many child windows, we're back to the "all on top of each other" problem.

2. A child window that opens over its parent may cover important content in the parent. National Geographic Trip Planner does this: its Map Legend window covers the map (Figure 5.47).

3. Sometimes child windows are larger than their parents. In such a case, the parent is completely hidden when the child appears. Users may forget it is there.

4. On most GUI platforms, applications can display subordinate windows either as "external" windows, which are outside of the parent, or as "internal" windows, which are inside their parent window. When a child window is centered directly over its parent and smaller than its parent, users cannot tell (without trying to move it) whether it is external or internal.

Because of these problems, applications that display all subordinate windows centered over their parents are committing a variation of Blooper 35.

Variation C: Displaying subordinate windows off-screen

The most user-hostile initial window location would be off-screen, so users won't even know they are there. Some applications actually do this!

One company had a stock-investment tool that displayed a Trade Monitor Summary dialog box immediately above the main window. If the main window was maximized or placed at the top of the screen, the dialog box opened just off the top of the screen—out of view. New users often complained that the Trade Monitor Summary dialog box was not displaying. In response, developers pulled the main window down to show that the Trade Monitor Summary dialog box *was right there* ... off-screen. Those stupid users ... always complaining!

Another company's application sometimes displayed windows partly off-screen, as is described in this excerpt from a UI review of the product:

> Dialog boxes that open from the main window appear with their upper left corner centered on it. Since the main window is small, if it is at the edge of the screen, large dialog boxes appear partly off-screen.

Avoiding Blooper 38

The following guidelines will help you avoid stacking windows on top of each other.

Decide where each window appears

Someone must decide where each new window should appear initially. Don't abdicate this responsibility by using simplistic placement rules, such as opening all windows at screen position [0, 0].

Optimal position depends on the type of window

Most software applications display many different types of windows: main windows, subordinate primary windows, object property dialog boxes, command dialog boxes, error dialog boxes, warning dialog boxes, confirmation dialog boxes, and so on. The best initial position of a window depends at least partly on what type of window it is.

Error, warning, and confirmation dialog boxes should appear in prominent locations, to get the users' attention. The best position for that is to center the window at the cursor position. Almost as good is displaying the dialog box near the command that gave rise to the message. Otherwise, use the center of the screen. Object property dialog boxes should appear near the object they represent.

Main windows and subordinate primary windows can appear just about anywhere on the screen initially, as long as they don't all appear in the same place. When a user moves a window to a new location, the software should remember that location and display that window in the same place the next time.

General heuristics

Beyond the placement design rules that depend on the type of window, here are rules for all windows:

- Windows should always open entirely on-screen. As necessary, adjust window positions that are relative to the location of other objects, such as the cursor or the corresponding command or data.
- Stagger position of successive windows of the same type. Each one appears a little further rightward and downward from the last one.
- External child windows should only partly overlap their parent so users can see that they are not internal to the parent.
- Make sure child windows don't cover important information in their parent. For example, Microsoft Word's Find/Replace dialog box is always placed so that the found text in the document is visible.
- Don't place windows directly on top of each other. Even random window placement is better than always using location [0, 0].

Troublesome typography

The last graphic design and layout blooper concerns typography.

Blooper 39: Tiny fonts

Many software applications and Web sites display text in font sizes that are too small. The main problem with text in small fonts is that people who have impaired vision can't read it. That includes almost everyone over the age of 45.

Think of startup companies full of twenty-something developers with excellent vision churning out investment Web sites for people approaching retirement, and you'll begin to understand the problem.

The navigation bar on the Web site of the Federal Reserve Bank of Minneapolis is labeled with very small fonts—perhaps 8 point[3] (Figure 5.48). Furthermore, this is displayed as an image, so users cannot adjust its font size in their browser. Many users will have trouble reading the bar.

Even tinier fonts are used on Frontier Airlines's online route map (Figure 5.49). Again, this map is an image, so users can't adjust the font size. If they can't read the city names or the text below the map, they're out of luck ... or maybe Frontier Airlines is.

---

3. The screen images in this section are shown at full size; they have not been shrunk for this book.

Figure 5.48   MinneapolisFed.org: tiny, nonadjustable fonts in navigation bar.

Figure 5.49

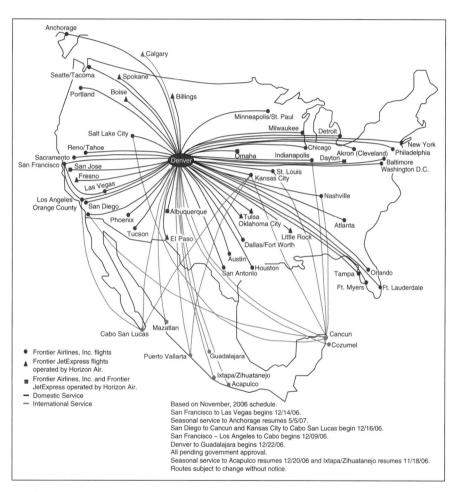

FrontierAirlines.com: tiny, nonadjustable fonts.

It's not just a Web problem

Excerpts from usability reviews show that tiny fonts occur in desktop applications as well as Web sites:

- Most of the fonts in the application are too small and not adjustable (even smaller than those in the current product, which already border on being too small). You made the fonts smaller to fit more in, but fitting more in isn't useful if people cannot read the text.

- The software's default text fonts are too small for users over 45 years old to be able to read comfortably. Consider changing to a larger default font, and definitely make it easy for users to increase the font size.

- The labels on the keys of the number pad are too small. Many users will not be able to read these labels comfortably. There is plenty of room on the keys for larger labels.

Common excuses for tiny fonts

Developers have many excuses for using tiny fonts. Here is a sampling, with suitable responses:

- "I can read it. What's the problem?"—The problem is that users can't read it.

- "We need all this information on here."—If the users can't read it, it isn't there, is it?

- "I just used the toolkit's default font size." Don't use the default, or change the default to a larger font.

- "It's not my fault: the text is in an image."—Send the image back to the artists and ask them to make the text in the image larger. Better: ask them to send you the text separately rather than embedding it in the image. Display the text over the image and allow users to adjust its size.

- "It's big enough in low resolution."—What percent of customers use low-resolution monitors? Without knowing that, the excuse is baseless.

 Memo from the Big Boss

Memo
From: The Big Boss
To: All employees
Subject: Font sizes
Date: 1 April 2009

Effective immediately, all employees are asked to use the smallest text fonts available in all documents. The MIS department has informed me that our file servers are getting full. They asked me to allocate funds to purchase more disk drives, but the request comes at a time when we need to conserve expenses. It occurred to me that by using smaller fonts, we could save a lot of disk space, reducing the need for additional disk drives.

With all of your cooperation, we will have a successful 2nd Quarter.
Thanks.

Avoiding Blooper 39

You want your software's users to be able to read the text. The following guidelines will help you ensure that they can.

Factors affecting text size

Two factors affect the absolute size of text displayed on a computer screen:

- *Screen resolution:* both the maximum resolution a display is capable of and the resolution setting in the user's operating system, e.g., 800 × 600, 1024 × 768, 1280 × 854. The *higher* the resolution, the *smaller* the text of a given font size appears.
- *Display size:* if a 15-inch display and a 24-inch display are set to the same resolution (e.g., 1024 × 768), 12-point text will appear larger on the larger display.

In addition, text's apparent size depends on the user's viewing distance. Text that is large enough for someone working at an office PC may be too small for users looking at a wall-mounted status display.

The key point is that designers do not have total control over how big or small text looks to users. The challenge is to ensure that everyone you want to read the text can.

The minimum font point size is 10; 12 is better

Never use a screen font smaller than 10 point. Ever. Ten point should be the minimum. Even 10 point is borderline. At high screen resolutions (above 1000 × 700), 10 point may be too small. To be on the safe side, use 12-point fonts.

Choose font sizes suitable for high-resolution displays

If designers make the fonts in their application or Web site large enough to be legible by the intended users when at the highest screen resolution, there will be no problem at lower resolutions.

Let users adjust font size

Font sizes should be adjustable by users. This applies both to content text and to text that is part of the GUI.

Providing adjustable font sizes in desktop applications usually requires work. However, there are users, probably in your target market, who cannot see text that is smaller than 24 point. You can either make *all* the text 24 point, or you can have the text default to 12 point for most users and let those who need larger text adjust it. If you don't do either, you're losing customers.

Font control on the Web: leave it to users

User-adjustable font size is much easier to accomplish on the Web than in desktop software. All Web developers have to do is *not* specify any font size or specify it in relative units (e.g., 1.5 em) rather than absolute units (e.g., 18 pt). On the Web, you have to do *more* work to *commit* the blooper than to do the right thing. On the Web, there is no excuse for nonadjustable fonts.

In the book *Web Pages That Suck* [Flanders and Willis, 1998], co-author Vincent Flanders rants about Web developers who hard code font sizes into pages, preventing users from adjusting the size:

> There are a lot of things I don't understand: atomic theory, Existentialism, … and why Web designers use the < FONT > tag and FACE argument to create unreadable pages.… Granted, I'm 49 years old and have bad eyesight, but still folks … if the text is too hard for the average person to read, they're going to hit the Back button faster than Larry King gets married.

Flanders's rant is even more appropriate now than it was when he wrote it, because cascading style sheets (CSS) have replaced presentational HTML as the best way to style text in Web sites and browser-based applications. CSS makes it easy for Web developers to specify font sizes in relative, rather than absolute, units.

Design to accommodate larger fonts

It does little good to allow users to adjust an application or Web site's font sizes if the layout breaks down when users actually *do* enlarge the font. Flight search results at FrontierAirlines.com are displayed in small fonts, but if users increase the font size, the tabular layout falls apart (Figure 5.50).

Test it on users

Whether you're developing software for the Web, PCs, or consumer appliances, test your font sizes! On real users, not just on the twenty-something developer in the next cubicle. Preferably *before* release.

Figure 5.50

Los Angeles CA (LAX) to Detroit MI (DTW) OCT 31, 2006						
Flight Numbers	Depart	Arrive	Via	Travel Time	Stops	Aircraft
F9144/623	6:40 AM	3:20 PM	DEN	5h40m	1	319
F9144/625	6:40 AM	5:55 PM	DEN	8h15m	1	319
F9401/625	9:10 AM	5:55 PM	DEN	5h45m	1	319
F91913/108/629	12:30PM	11:40PM	SFO-DEN	8h10m	2	318/319
F9412/629	2:55 PM	11:40PM	DEN	5h45m	1	319

A

Los Angeles CA (LAX) to Detroit MI (DTW) OCT 31, 2006						
Flight Numbers	Depart	Arrive	Via	Travel Time	Stops	Aircraft
F9144/623	6:40 AM	3:20 PM	DEN	5h40m	1	319
F9144/625	6:40 AM	5:55 PM	DEN	8h15m	1	319
F9401/625	9:10 AM	5:55 PM	DEN	5h45m	1	319
F91913/108/629	12:30PM	11:40PM	SFO-DEN	8h10m	2	318/319
F9412/629	2:55 PM	11:40PM	DEN	5h45m	1	319

B

FrontierAirlines.com: flight search results. (A) At default font size. (B) At larger font size.

Courtesy of Jen Sorensen, www.slowpokecomics.com © 2004.

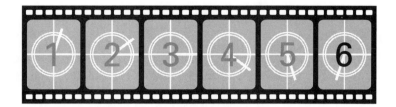

Interaction Bloopers

Introduction

The bloopers covered in the previous chapters—GUI control, navigation, textual, and graphic design and layout—are fairly easy to spot in usability reviews and tests.

However, it pays to dig deeper: more bloopers lie below the surface. Some concern how well an application supports *tasks,* not just how well particular windows or pages are designed. Others concern how a UI design interacts with human perception and cognition.

These are "interaction" bloopers. These deeper bloopers are not violations of look-and-feel guidelines, but rather violations of basic UI design principles. Those principles have emerged from research on human perception, reading, information processing, problem solving, and motivation, as well as from decades of experience with interactive computer applications.

Interaction bloopers are more important than GUI control, navigation, textual, and graphic design and layout bloopers because:

- *They are larger in scope.* Interaction bloopers are often generalizations of more specific look-and-feel bloopers. For example, Blooper 26 (Speaking Geek, page 173) is just one of the problems caused by Blooper 40, exposing the implementation to users (below). Therefore, recognizing and eliminating a single interaction blooper may result in the correction of dozens of GUI control, navigation, textual, and graphic design and layout bloopers.

- *They are harder to identify.* Interaction bloopers usually aren't directly visible in software displays. To spot them, you have to know the basic design rules. Less experienced observers tend to focus on concrete and visible usability problems, often missing deeper ones.

- *They are harder to avoid.* Interaction bloopers are often a result of decisions that were made deep in the product's implementation or even in its platform and environment: the GUI toolkit, operating system, or communication network. If a blooper was built into the GUI toolkit and an application programmer lacks the time or the expertise to code around it, the blooper will be in the application. Even when an interaction blooper is entirely local to the application, it may be the result of a design trade-off or a customer request.

- *They are harder to correct.* Correcting an interaction blooper can mean fixing all of the resulting more specific look-and-feel bloopers. If an interaction blooper results from deep implementation decisions, fixing it can require extensive reimplementation unless it is found very early in development.

Deviating from task focus

The first three interaction bloopers concern user interfaces that are poorly focused on the tasks the software is intended to support. Some UIs needlessly expose the implementation, impose unnecessary constraints, or present confusable concepts, distracting users from their goals and impeding their learning of the software.

Blooper 40: Exposing the implementation to users

Developers sometimes allow an application's implementation—its inner workings—to "leak out" into the user interface. Often the problem is just that the UI exposes implementation *terms* to users (Blooper 26, page 173). However, some applications expose not only terms, but internal structure and concepts that are unrelated to users' tasks and goals.

An example is provided by a graph from an application developed by a software company (Figure 6.1). The graph's horizontal axis had strange intervals—1.0, 105.4, 209.8, etc.—rather than more natural intervals that would make more sense to users—e.g., 0, 100, 200, 300, etc. The developers defended the design, arguing that it was easier for them to code the graph by dividing the length of the longest plot by 10 and letting the intervals fall wherever they did. They allowed the implementation to leak out into the GUI, damaging usability.

Figure 6.1

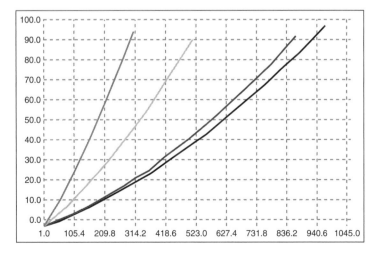

Graph's horizontal intervals designed for convenience of programmers, not users.

Forcing users to think like a programmer

> One prototype Web application had dialog boxes for each function. One drop-down menu setting appeared in several dialog boxes. Changing it in one dialog box changed it everywhere else as well. Users normally expect menus to stay as they were set the last time the user used that dialog box, but in certain situations a setting that changes everywhere might make sense to users.
>
> When asked to explain why the menu worked as it did, the programmer said he decided it was inefficient to put copies of the menu in every place it was needed, so he wrote the code so there was only one menu, which *appeared* in many dialog boxes. A *user*-centered answer would have explained that studies had shown that users expect the menu to change everywhere when they change it in one place.
>
> The programmer made a decision, based purely on implementation considerations, that resulted in behavior that probably didn't match users' expectations. The programmer exposed the implementation to the users.

Avoiding Blooper 40

Focus the user interface strictly on the tasks

Design your application's user interface according to a conceptual model that includes only objects, actions, and attributes from the application's target tasks (Basic Principle 2, page 18). Be wary of foreign concepts creeping into the UI. Create, maintain, and enforce a product lexicon to uncover discrepancies between the UI and the conceptual model.

Design for the convenience of users, not of developers

Make a strong commitment to design the user interface for the convenience of *users,* not of programmers. Developers tend to design for their own convenience. What separates exceptional UI designers and developers from most is a commitment to overcome that tendency—to put users' requirements first. Management can of course help.

Blooper 41: Needless restrictions

Software can violate users' sense of naturalness and intuitiveness by imposing arbitrary, needless restrictions. Needless restrictions, like unnatural actions, are hard to learn, easy to forget, and annoying (Basic Principle 3, page 26).

When my stereo broke, I took it to a repair shop. The shop technician filled out a repair order form, using a computer. After typing my contact information and the brand and model of the stereo, he asked me to describe the problem. As I spoke and he typed, a concerned expression came over his face. He interrupted me:

Technician: "Um … can you describe the problem … shorter?"

Me: "Let me guess: you have 64 characters in which to explain what's wrong with my stereo."

Technician (eyes widening noticeably): "Thirty-two, but how did you know?"

The repair shop's software limited descriptions to 32 characters. The limit was probably imposed by the database the application used. Whatever the reason for the limit, it made describing a stereo's problem more difficult.

Software applications, online services, and appliances are full of such restrictions: credit-card fields that don't allow spaces, login names restricted to eight characters, company-name fields that allow only letters or numbers ("AT&T" rejected), spreadsheets that can have only 256 columns, data identifiers that must be typed in UPPERCASE to be recognized. All of these examples are real.

Ever since its introduction in the mid-1980s, Microsoft Excel has limited spreadsheets to 256 columns. In the 1980s, the limit was imposed by the limited memory of personal computers. Today's PCs have about 500,000 times as much memory as those of the 1980s, so Excel's 256-column limit is artificial and unnecessary. To create a spreadsheet to record a stock price every day for a year, it would be natural to assign a column to each day. No can do with Excel: you run out of columns on September 13 (Figure 6.2).

Excel has a second annoying restriction: users cannot open two spreadsheet files that have the same name (Figure 6.3). If you have a backup of a spreadsheet in a different folder, you can't open it and the original simultaneously to compare them. Microsoft Word has no such restriction.

Our final example of a vexing restriction is from the Apple Macintosh's DVD player. DVDs are coded for the region of the world where they were made. To play a DVD, the Mac's DVD drive must be set to the same region code as the DVD. It's annoying that users have to set this; the player should just set itself. But that's minor compared to the problem that the DVD drive's region code

"What do you mean Rumpelstiltskin is too long for a password?!"

Reprinted by permission, Andrew Toos.

Figure 6.2

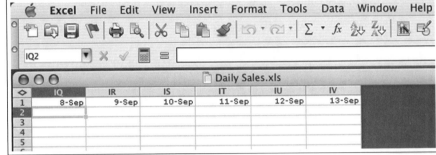

Microsoft Excel: 256-column limit is artificial and prevents creation of useful spreadsheets.

Figure 6.3

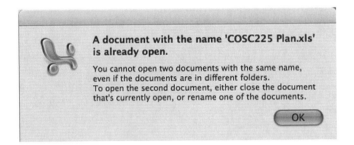

Microsoft Excel: blocks opening two files with same name.

can be changed only five times over the drive's lifetime (Figure 6.4). After five changes, the region setting becomes permanent. Huh? People who travel between regions can't play local DVDs?

Some limits are worse than others

The worst restrictions are ones that users constantly bump into, such as descriptions that must be shorter than 32 characters. Such limits force users—repeatedly—to waste time figuring out how to express what they need to express within the limit.

Limits that users hit only occasionally might seem less troublesome. In fact, they are almost as bad as limits that users hit often, but for a different reason: users who encounter such limits won't have much experience figuring out how to work around them.

Imposing limits that are powers of 2: Geeky

Numerical restrictions imposed by computer software are often powers of 2: numbers like 8, 16, 32, 64, ... , 1024. Computers represent numbers and

Figure 6.4

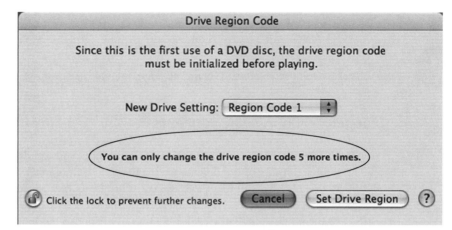

Macintosh DVD player (OS X): region code can be changed only five times.

memory addresses in binary (base 2) numerals, so programmers are used to binary numbers and regard them as "normal."

Most software users don't see powers of 2 as "normal." They learned to do arithmetic in base 10 and so are used to powers of 10. To them, binary numbers are arbitrary and geeky.

Bottom line

A product with many arbitrary restrictions won't have satisfied users. Many software restrictions are due to faulty priorities of the developers (including management). Developers often don't realize how many user-hours can be saved by one extra programmer-hour spent overcoming an annoying restriction.

Consider the total time wasted worldwide between 1975 (when personal computers first hit the market) and 1995 (when Windows 95 was released) by millions of computer users trying to devise meaningful file names no longer than eight characters. That blooper wasted *millions* of user-hours.

Avoiding Blooper 41

Don't impose numerical limits, if possible. You can eliminate them by allocating data storage dynamically at runtime, as needed, rather than statically in the source code. If limits are unavoidable, make them so high that users will rarely or never encounter them.

When limits cannot be avoided and users will encounter them, use powers of 10, not powers of 2. Even where limits *are* powers of 2, you can tell users they are powers of 10, as MacOS does for the high-color options on its Colors menu (Figure 6.5).

Figure 6.5

MacOS X: higher "number of colors" options expressed as powers of 10.

Blooper 42: **Confusable concepts**

All software applications expose a conceptual model (Basic Principle 2, page 18). The model consists of the objects users create and manipulate, the actions users perform on objects, and the user-visible attributes of objects. From the conceptual model presented in an application's UI and manuals, users form a *mental* model of how the application works. Their mental model helps them operate it. Complex and confusing conceptual models give rise to confused mental models.

One way an application's conceptual model can be confusing is to include concepts that overlap in meaning or functionality.

One company's customer support Web site presented four concepts that the developers thought were quite different:

- *Membership:* whether a company had paid for the customer support service
- *Subscription:* whether a company had subscribed to a customer support newsletter
- *Access:* which areas of the customer support Web site users in a company could access
- *Entitlements:* services provided for each membership level

Users confused these four concepts. They needed to be merged into one concept or, at least, fewer than four.

Another company developed a Web site for people seeking to buy a home. There were two ways to look for a home: (a) name the state, county, or town or (b) point to a location on a map. Users had to choose whether they wanted to find a home "by location" or "by map." A usability test found the following:

> Many users did not distinguish between finding a home "by map" vs. "by location." Both are really by location; they differ only in how the location is specified.

The designers of this site created an artificial distinction, expecting users to understand and accept it. They didn't.

Apple Computer's .Mac online service confuses subscribers with two different "home" pages. The first is the portal page subscribers are taken to after logging into www.mac.com (Figure 6.6A). Its link on .Mac's navigation bar is a house icon. The second is the user's page for publishing documents, photos, and other files to the Internet (Figure 6.6B). Subscribers are taken

Figure 6.6

A

B

Apple .Mac.com online service: two different "home" pages.

there first if they login to homepage.mac.com. Its link on .Mac's navigation bar is "HomePage." The two pages contain some of the same elements, such as lists of published files. Some .Mac subscribers don't understand the difference.

If a new implementation of a function is introduced, but the old implementation is still present, users are faced with two competing implementations of the same function. This seems to be the reason for confusable concepts in Apple's MacOS X and Microsoft's Windows Vista.

MacOS X offers two Sticky Note implementations: a new Stickies *widget* for posting notes on the Dashboard and an older Stickies *application* for posting notes on the Desktop (Figure 6.7). I've observed Mac users struggling to post Dashboard sticky notes on their Desktop, because they did that with the Stickies application they used before. Mac users will confuse these two Sticky Note implementations until Apple decides which one to keep and removes the other.

Microsoft Windows has always provided a function for capturing screen images, using the Print Screen key (Figure 6.8A). Windows Vista introduced a

Figure 6.7

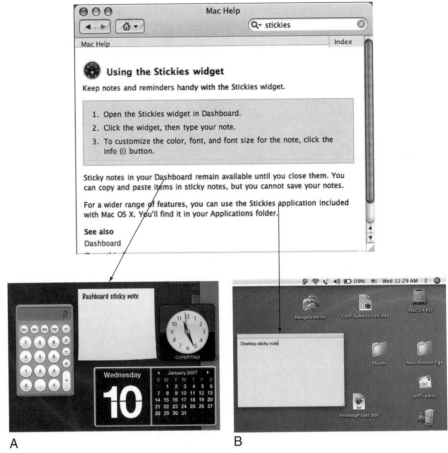

A   B

MacOS X: two different stickies implementations. (A) On Dashboard. (B) On Desktop.

new way to capture screen images: the Snipping Tool (Figure 6.8B). Confusion will result.

Both MacOS and Microsoft Windows are open platforms for which developers can develop a variety of applications, so occasional duplication of functionality is not surprising. But open platforms per se do not cause the blooper. Many computer users have more than one Web browser on their computer but are not confused by that. Each browser is well branded, so users are well aware of the difference, and it helps that many users installed the extra browsers themselves. In contrast, MacOS X's two Sticky Note implementations and Windows Vista's two screen-capture methods are packaged with their operating systems, with no branding or explanation—not even in the Help files—to distinguish them.

Figure 6.8

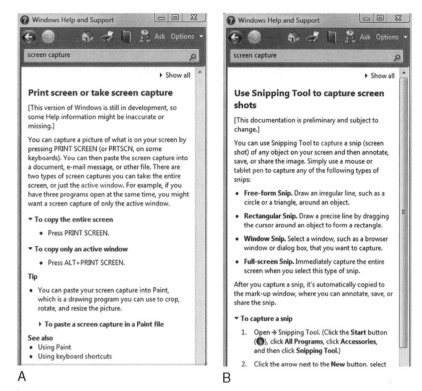

A   B

Windows Vista: two ways to snap screen. (A) Print Screen (old). (B) Snipping Tool (new).

Avoiding Blooper 42

Avoid overlapping concepts. Think carefully about the conceptual model pre-sented by your product. Are the concepts in it clearly distinct, or do they over-lap in meaning and/or function? Are users likely to confuse them? Remove any areas of overlap to make concepts more distinct. Better, combine the two concepts into one, simplifying the conceptual model.

When you introduce a new implementation of an existing function, think hard about whether your users really need the new one. Does it solve a problem they had with the old implementation or is it just something the developers created and want to try out? If you do provide the new version, remove the old one. If you think you need to retain both to gather market feedback, think again. Feedback from the market is difficult to interpret and ambiguous. If you need customer feedback to decide which implementation to keep, collect it *before* product release, using usability tests and customer focus groups. If you decide to provide two competing implementations of a concept, blend them by making them work together. Failing that, find a way to make the distinction clear.

Requiring unnecessary steps

A UI should be designed so that the most common tasks that the software is intended to support are quick and easy to do (Basic Principle 4, page 32). That means minimizing the steps required to do those tasks.

If users have to do unnecessary steps to accomplish their tasks, that is a blooper. This section describes three such bloopers.

Blooper 43: Asking users for unneeded data

One sure way for software to annoy its users is to ask them for data the software obviously doesn't need.

Variation A: We forgot. Tell us again.

The form of this blooper that annoys users the most is asking them to reenter data they already entered.

Registered Travelocity.com customers can have the site monitor airfares for specified trips and notify them when good fares are available. If a user, in specifying trip's origin and destination, names a city that has multiple airports, Travelocity lists the airports and asks the user to select one. This can be annoying: often it should be clear which airport was meant (Blooper 45, page 258). However, what is *really* annoying is that Travelocity requires users to reselect the intended airport(s) in multiairport cities *every time* they update *any* aspect of their fare monitor (Figure 6.9).

Variation B: Unnecessary questions

A second way to require unneeded data is to ask users for data that could be deduced from other input. The Web site of the U.S. House of Representatives has a "Write Your Representative" page. It requires citizens to enter both their *state* and their *zip code* to direct their e-mail to their Representative (Figure 6.10A), even though state can be deduced from zip code. In contrast, the home page's Find Your Representative box requires only a zip code (Figure 6.10B).

In California's online unemployment insurance form (Figure 6.11), one question asks applicants to list recent employers, including the dates of employment. The same question then asks which of those listed employers the applicant worked for the longest, even though that could be calculated from the employment dates. The next question asks how long the applicant worked for their longest listed employer, which could also be calculated from the employment dates.

Figure 6.9

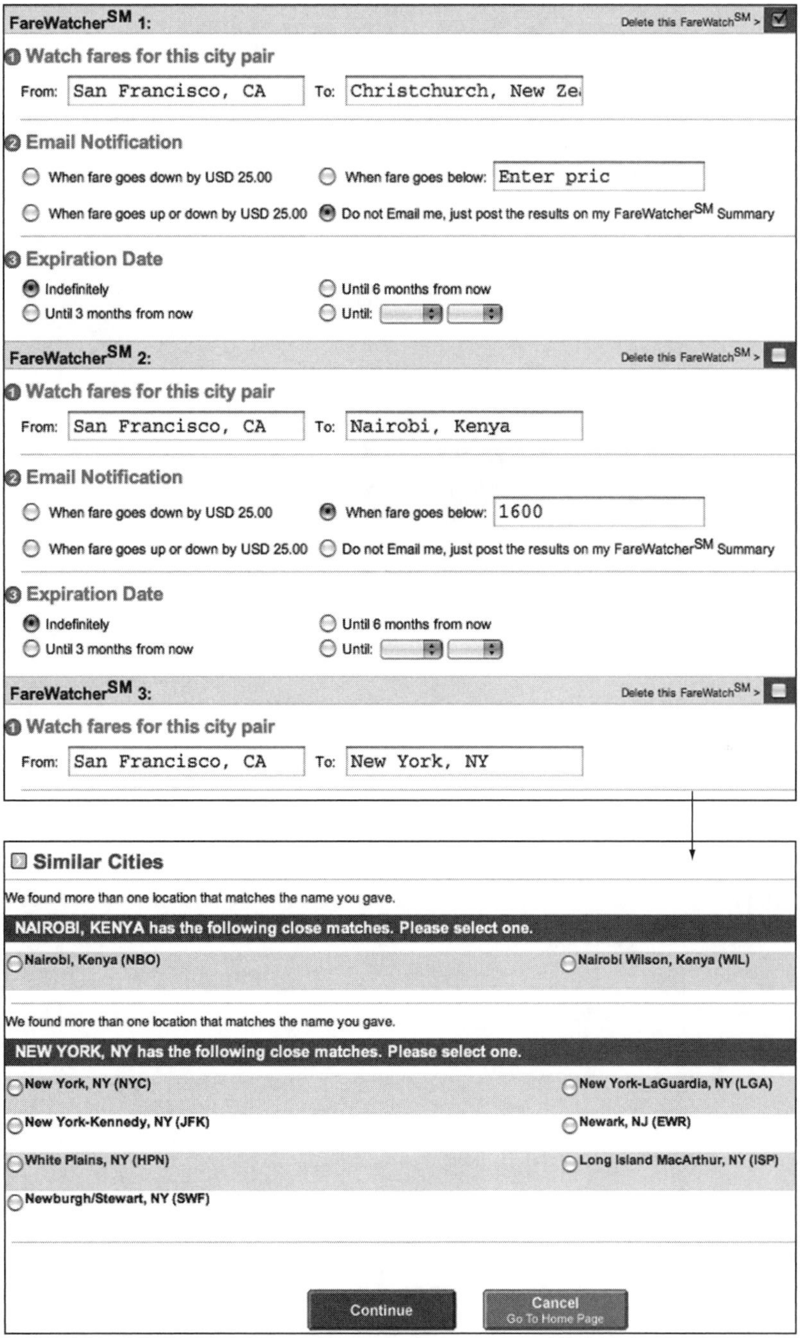

FareWatcher^{SM} 1:   Delete this FareWatch^{SM} > ☑

❶ **Watch fares for this city pair**

From: San Francisco, CA   To: Christchurch, New Ze

❷ **Email Notification**

○ When fare goes down by USD 25.00   ○ When fare goes below: Enter pric

○ When fare goes up or down by USD 25.00   ◉ Do not Email me, just post the results on my FareWatcher^{SM} Summary

❸ **Expiration Date**

◉ Indefinitely   ○ Until 6 months from now
○ Until 3 months from now   ○ Until: [▼][▼]

FareWatcher^{SM} 2:   Delete this FareWatch^{SM} > ☐

❶ **Watch fares for this city pair**

From: San Francisco, CA   To: Nairobi, Kenya

❷ **Email Notification**

○ When fare goes down by USD 25.00   ◉ When fare goes below: 1600

○ When fare goes up or down by USD 25.00   ○ Do not Email me, just post the results on my FareWatcher^{SM} Summary

❸ **Expiration Date**

◉ Indefinitely   ○ Until 6 months from now
○ Until 3 months from now   ○ Until: [▼][▼]

FareWatcher^{SM} 3:   Delete this FareWatch^{SM} > ☐

❶ **Watch fares for this city pair**

From: San Francisco, CA   To: New York, NY

☑ **Similar Cities**

We found more than one location that matches the name you gave.

NAIROBI, KENYA has the following close matches. Please select one.

○ Nairobi, Kenya (NBO)   ○ Nairobi Wilson, Kenya (WIL)

We found more than one location that matches the name you gave.

NEW YORK, NY has the following close matches. Please select one.

○ New York, NY (NYC)   ○ New York-LaGuardia, NY (LGA)

○ New York-Kennedy, NY (JFK)   ○ Newark, NJ (EWR)

○ White Plains, NY (HPN)   ○ Long Island MacArthur, NY (ISP)

○ Newburgh/Stewart, NY (SWF)

[Continue]   [Cancel
                        Go To Home Page]

Travelocity.com: requires user to disambiguate airports every time the FareWatcher is updated.

Figure 6.10

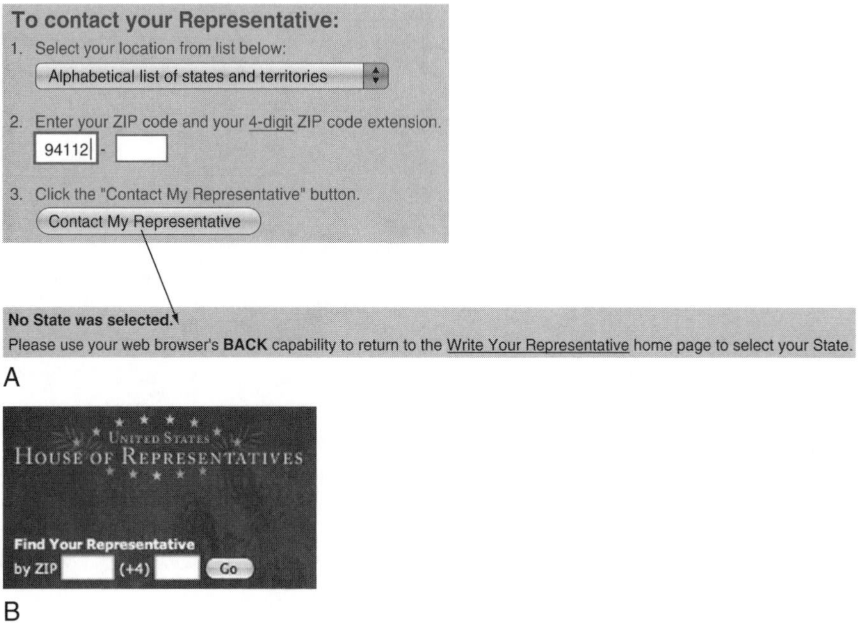

To contact your Representative:

1. Select your location from list below:

   [Alphabetical list of states and territories ▲▼]

2. Enter your ZIP code and your 4-digit ZIP code extension.

   [94112] - [   ]

3. Click the "Contact My Representative" button.

   (Contact My Representative)

No State was selected.
Please use your web browser's **BACK** capability to return to the Write Your Representative home page to select your State.

A

★ ★ ★ ★ ★
UNITED STATES
HOUSE OF REPRESENTATIVES
★ ★ ★ ★ ★

Find Your Representative
by ZIP [   ] (+4) [   ] [Go]

B

House.gov. (A) Write Representative page requires state and zip code. (B) Home page needs only zip code.

Figure 6.11

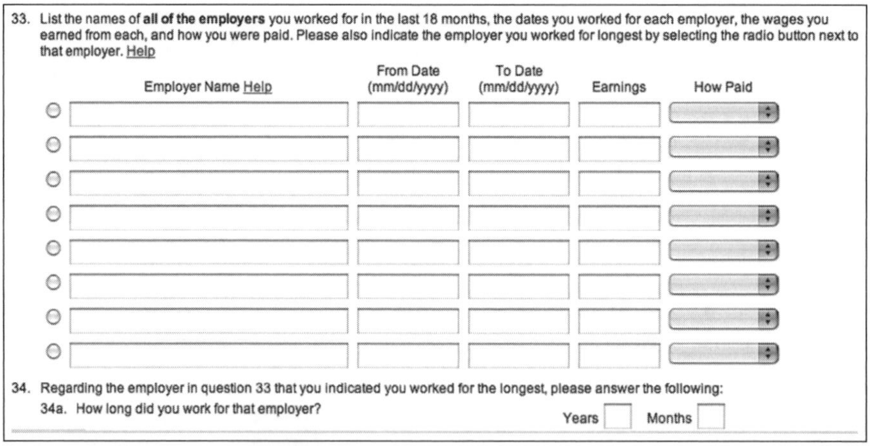

33. List the names of **all of the employers** you worked for in the last 18 months, the dates you worked for each employer, the wages you earned from each, and how you were paid. Please also indicate the employer you worked for longest by selecting the radio button next to that employer. Help

	Employer Name Help	From Date (mm/dd/yyyy)	To Date (mm/dd/yyyy)	Earnings	How Paid
○	[ ]	[ ]	[ ]	[ ]	[▼]
○	[ ]	[ ]	[ ]	[ ]	[▼]
○	[ ]	[ ]	[ ]	[ ]	[▼]
○	[ ]	[ ]	[ ]	[ ]	[▼]
○	[ ]	[ ]	[ ]	[ ]	[▼]
○	[ ]	[ ]	[ ]	[ ]	[▼]
○	[ ]	[ ]	[ ]	[ ]	[▼]
○	[ ]	[ ]	[ ]	[ ]	[▼]

34. Regarding the employer in question 33 that you indicated you worked for the longest, please answer the following:

   34a. How long did you work for that employer?   Years [   ] Months [   ]

EDD.CA.gov: form asks user for data that could be deduced.

Variation C: Requiring data that should be optional

Some online forms designate certain data fields as "required" for no good reason. For example, many Web site registration forms needlessly require a title (Mr., Mrs., Ms., Dr., etc.).

Agilent.com's form for submitting questions or comments about the site includes a Country setting and treats it as required (Figure 6.12). Why must users specify a country just to comment on the Web site? Maybe knowing a submitter's home country helps the Web master interpret their comment, but it shouldn't be *required*.

Variation D: Requiring repeated logins in a session

Many online systems require repeated logins. United.com provides an example. If United frequent flier customers are already logged in and ask to see a summary of activity on their mileage account, they are asked to log in again (Figure 6.13). United might argue that this is a security measure, but that would make sense only if the second login was required after a timeout (because the

Figure 6.12

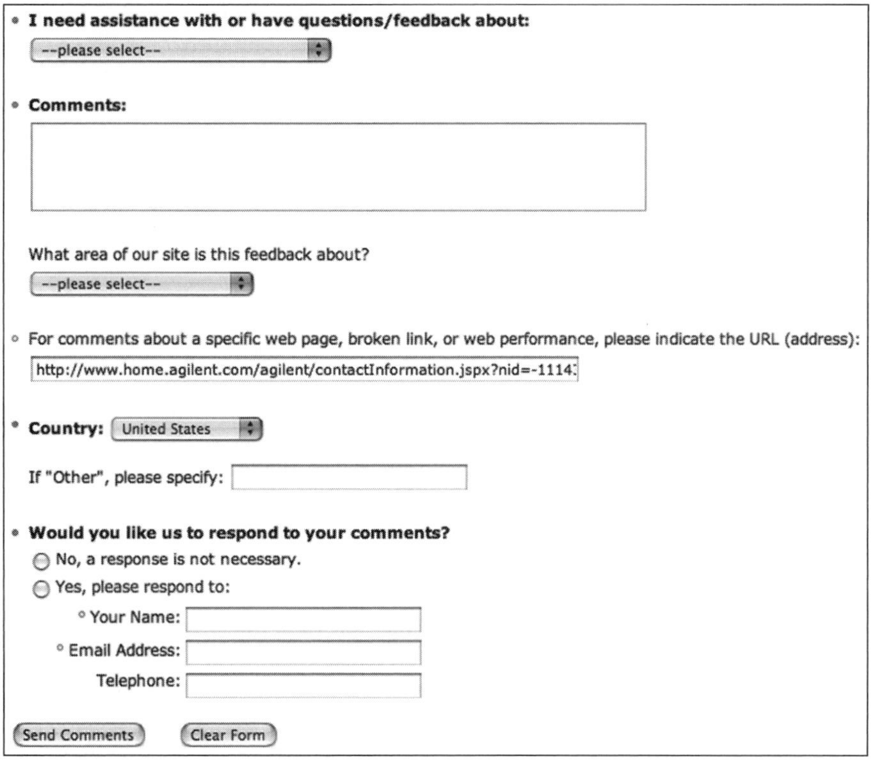

* **I need assistance with or have questions/feedback about:**

    [--please select-- ▾]

* **Comments:**

    [   ]

    What area of our site is this feedback about?

    [--please select-- ▾]

    ○ For comments about a specific web page, broken link, or web performance, please indicate the URL (address):

    [http://www.home.agilent.com/agilent/contactInformation.jspx?nid=-1114]

* **Country:** [United States ▾]

    If "Other", please specify: [   ]

* **Would you like us to respond to your comments?**
    ○ No, a response is not necessary.
    ○ Yes, please respond to:
        ° Your Name: [   ]
        ° Email Address: [   ]
        Telephone: [   ]

    [Send Comments]   [Clear Form]

Agilent.com: demanding more data than needed. Comment form requires country needlessly.

Figure 6.13

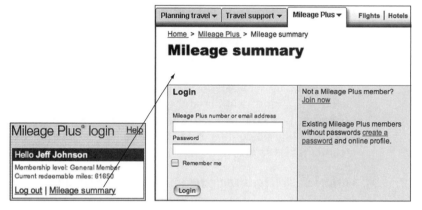

United.com: mileage summary page requires already logged-in user to login again.

customer might have walked away from a public terminal) or if the second login required a different login ID. Neither of those is the case.

The likely cause of the redundant login is that the "Mileage Summary" page is accessible from several places, some of which are behind a login and some of which are not. But that is a weak excuse for annoying tens of thousands of customers.

The Association of Computing Machinery's Digital Library (ACM.org) is another example. Every time you ask for a different article, you have to log in again. Why?

Avoiding Blooper 43

Make it a high priority *not* to require users to enter data repeatedly. Here are several ways:

- Ask only for data you really need. If you aren't sure what you will do with a piece of data, you don't need it.
- Stick to the current transaction. Data you would like for other purposes, such as marketing or establishing a relationship with the user, should be requested in separate and optional areas of software.
- Don't make any data "required" unless you really cannot proceed without it.
- Don't require data some customers won't have: you would just force them to make it up … or take their business elsewhere.
- When someone gives you information, deduce as much as you can from it. Use what you know to fill in other data fields.

Asking for data you don't need scares away customers who value their privacy, prevents customers from achieving their goals, frustrates those who don't *have* the information you require, and slows throughput.

In early 2006, Fedex.com required customers to enter their address, city, and zip code to search for a FedEx location near them (Figure 6.14A). By early 2007, customers could search by giving their zip code *or* their address and city (Figure 6.14B).

It can be hard to avoiding asking for the data repeatedly, but software developers can do better than they have.[1] Some applications and Web sites are better than others at remembering what users already input. If you downplay this issue to save development time or costs, you are making an important—possibly poor—business decision.

To avoid requiring repeated logins, applications and Web sites should make the user's login status accessible to all parts of the software. Don't assume that a user who arrives at a certain section either is already logged in or needs to be logged in. Instead, any section that needs the user to be logged in should check the user's login status and respond accordingly.

The American Cancer Society's Cancer Survivor Network site, ACSCSN.org, avoids repeated logins. Certain functions on the site are restricted to logged-in members, but no matter where members go on the site, they are never asked to log in more than once.

Some online services require multiple levels of security. A user may log in to access a low-security area, then log in again to access a higher security area. The higher security login should require *different* identifying information than the lower security one; otherwise it's not really higher security.

Figure 6.14

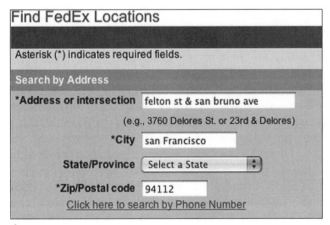

A

Fedex.com: FedEx Location Search form. (A) In early 2006, required address, city, and zip code. (B) By early 2007, required either zip code, or address and city, but not all three.

(Continued)

---

1. Methods for propagating data between forms in a Web site are described in *Web Bloopers* [Johnson, 2003].

Figure 6.14
(Continued)

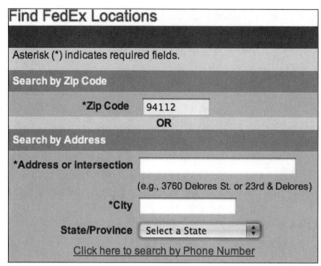

B

Blooper 44: Asking users for random seeds

A special case of asking users for unneeded data occurs in software that uses random numbers to sample data, run simulations, make characters move unpredictably, create unique file names, or generate unique keys. Random number generators must be "seeded" with a unique starting value; otherwise they generate the same "random" numbers every time.

Some applications get their seed value by asking users for a number—any number—or some text—any text. Asking users for random input is a double blooper: asking for unneeded data *and* exposing the implementation. Initializing a random-number generator is an internal software matter, meaningless to users. Users don't like entering meaningless values; it diverts them from their work.

People are also bad at being random. Ask several people for a "random number" between 1 and 100, and you'll get a set of numbers that isn't random. You'll get mostly *odd* numbers because *even* numbers don't seem "random." The number people usually give is 37.

One company was developing software for business statistical analysis. The software sampled data randomly from a database. To get different random samples for each analysis, the software asked users for a different "Sampler Seed" each time. Given the same seed twice, the software would extract the same "random" sample. However, users resented having to supply a seed. They couldn't remember what seed they used before.

Avoiding Blooper 44

Software should never ask users for random seeds. If your program needs one, it should get one for itself.

Base seeds on variable intervals

A traditional self-seeding method has been to get the time or date from the operating system and use it as a seed, but nowadays such seeds are considered not random enough. Modern applications seed themselves using variable time intervals between user-generated events, such as the time between keystrokes.

Give users only the control they need

If your users usually want the software to run differently each time, but sometimes want it to repeat a previous run, give them a way of specifying just that. Provide a button—labeled to match users' intent—that makes the software reseed itself (Figure 6.15A). Alternatively, give users a switch for turning automatic reseeding ON and OFF (Figure 6.15B), defaulted to ON.

Design the software to record with its results the seed it used to generate them. Then you can allow users to optionally specify a previous run to be matched.

However, make sure you understand the requirement. *Why* do users want to repeat past runs? If repeating a run just produces the same output, the only reason for doing it is that the user lost the previous output and needs to recreate it. Instead of providing a way to repeat past runs, it might be better to provide better ways of managing output files so users don't lose them.

Games don't ask users for random seeds

Many computer games provide built-in opponents whose movements must be unpredictable. Electronic gambling machines have to simulate tossing dice, pulling slot machine levers, dealing cards, and spinning roulette wheels. All of these must behave differently every time.

Figure 6.15

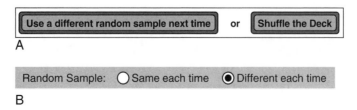

Task-focused ways to let users control seeding. (A) Commands. (B) ON/OFF switch.

Game software and electronic gambling machines *never* ask users for seed values. Game developers know that their market would not tolerate this blooper. Game software proves that requiring users to enter random numbers in *any* software is unnecessary.

Blooper 45: Pointless choice

A second special case of requiring users to enter unnecessary data is presenting users with unnecessary choices. There are four common variations of this blooper:

Variation A: No difference

Some Web sites confront users with choices in which the available options are all essentially the same. Choosing between them is a pointless, annoying waste of time.

Selection.co.nz is a bed-and-breakfast search Web site in New Zealand. If a user searches for the Rosecroft B&B in "Christchurch," the site returns no B&Bs but rather four New Zealand locations where a Rosecroft B&B was presumably found, forcing users to choose one before reaching the B&B listings (Figure 6.16). The first two locations are both the city of Christchurch, while the second two are nowhere near Christchurch. Why not just list B&Bs named "Rosecroft" in Christchurch?

Variation B: Users don't know

When the options are meaningless, users have no basis for choosing among them. If the software won't let users ignore the choice, they have to guess.

Figure 6.16

Selection.co.nz: search for "rosecroft" B&B in "christchurch" yields two locations that are both the city of Christchurch, plus two irrelevant locations.

Figure 6.17

Sibelius.com: users have no basis for choosing between download servers.

Sibelius.com allows customers to download software. However, the site makes customers choose which of three servers to download from (Figure 6.17). Any of these servers will work, so why should users choose one? Also the servers are labeled so cryptically that users will have no idea which one to choose. The options make sense only to Sibelius employees who manage the download servers.

Variation C: Obvious answer

Some applications and Web sites make users choose even though it is obvious which option is correct. The obvious choice can be based on frequency data, common sense, or previous user input in the current session. When software ignores the obvious, it forces users to choose needlessly.

Suppose you search United Airlines's Web site for flights from San Francisco (SFO) to Auckland, New Zealand, giving "Auckland" as your destination. The site replies "There are multiple airports in the city you entered. Please select …" (Figure 6.18). It lists Oakland, San Francisco, San Jose, and Auckland. Those are all airports in Auckland? The one you named, Auckland, is not even first or the default. Even odder, one listed destination is your *departure* airport.

A search at United.com for flights from SFO to Montreal yields similar results: a choice between Monterey Peninsula airport (default), Montrose County airport, Montreal's municipal airport (YMQ), Montreal's main airport (Pierre Trudeau Int'l, YUL), and Monterey airport. Only two of these are actually in Montreal, and of those two, only YUL is served by United. This choice is a complete waste of users' time.

That's nothing compared to the results United.com gives for a search for flights from SFO to Denver. The same "multiple airports" message appears, followed by a "list" of one airport: DEN (Figure 6.19). The site wastes users' time with this completely pointless "choice" step.

Figure 6.18

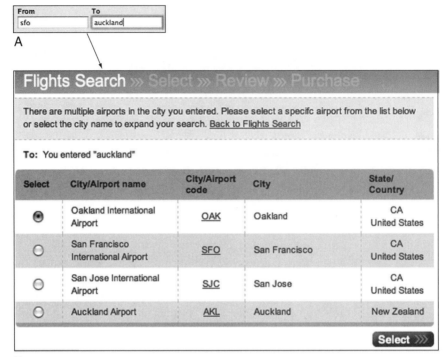

B

United.com: search for flights from SFO to Auckland results in needless choice.

Figure 6.19

B

United.com: search for flights from SFO to Denver results in needless "choice" of one.

Figure 6.20

A

B

HotelDiscount.com: search for hotels in "minneapolis, minn" results in "choice" of one.

HotelDiscount.com has the same blooper. If you search for hotels in "minneapolis, minn," the site responds "Your search for minneapolis, minn matched one or more of our cities. Please select …" and presents you with a menu containing exactly one city: Minneapolis, Minnesota (Figure 6.20).

Variation D: False choice

The most time-wasting variation of the blooper has unfortunately become very common in e-commerce Web sites. Companies are cutting costs by buying generic third-party back-end services instead of developing their own business-specific ones. Generic databases of airports or cities, for example, don't reflect any specific company's actual product or service offerings and may cause the company's Web site to offer nonexistent choices to customers.

A clear example of "false choice" comes from the bed and breakfast search Web site discussed under Variation A. Not only does Selection.co.nz present users with a needless choice, all four "locations" listed in the results turn out to contain nothing (Figure 6.21).

American Airlines's Web site, AA.com, has both the "obvious answer" and the "false choice" variants of "pointless choice." Searching for flights from SFO to Houston yields "We are unable to determine your desired airport(s) from your entry. Please select ..." with a list of five "airports," one of which is a bus station (Figure 6.22A). Selecting either of the two Houston listings in British Columbia (Canada) reveals that American Airlines does not provide service there—no flights, no buses—nothing (Figure 6.22B). They should not have been listed.

Figure 6.21

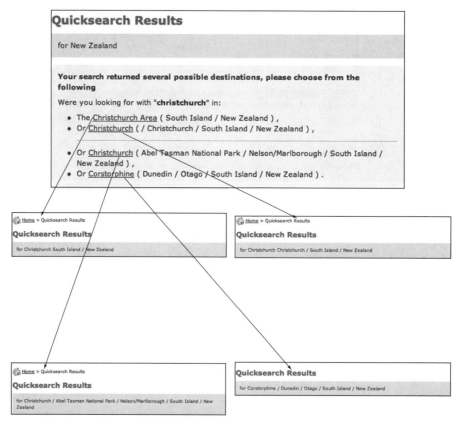

Selection.co.nz: search for "rosecroft" B&B in "christchurch" yields choice of four locations in which no B&Bs were found.

Figure 6.22

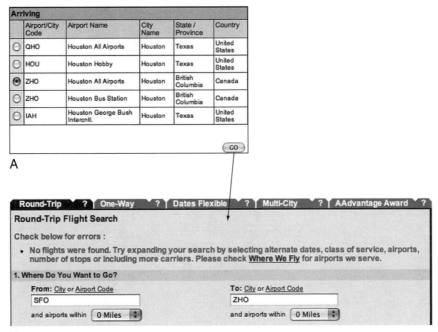

A

B

AA.com: search for flights from SFO to Houston displays pointless extra choice in which some options don't actually exist.

Avoiding Blooper 45

How to avoid presenting unnecessary choices depends on why the choice is unnecessary.

If the choice makes no difference, don't offer it

Asking users to choose between options that make no significant difference in what they get just wastes their time.

How do you discover that your site presents absurd, identical choices? Test it! You may be able to use members of your own team as subjects, but keep in mind that developers, when testing their own software, overlook many annoyances. Better would be to observe people who are like the site's intended users. Even if they don't explicitly complain about needless choices, you'll be more likely to spot the problem.

If users won't understand the question, don't ask

Consider whether the choice your software asks users to make makes sense. If they have no idea what the software is asking, you'll annoy them and won't get useful responses. If you haven't provided a default, users will just guess. If you *have* provided a default, as Sibelius.com does, users will probably just leave it as-is, whether or not it's right for their situation.

To find out if a choice presented by your software is meaningful to users, test it. Usability tests need not—and should not—wait until the software is about to be released. They can be conducted early and cheaply, using paper or HTML prototypes.

If there is an obvious option, choose it

Sometimes the correct option is obvious based on common sense, normal usage patterns, or previous user input. Software that doesn't make use of such "knowledge" waste users' time.

Don't offer false choices

If an employee of your company offered a customer choices that were not really available, the customer would consider the employee, and your company, to be either misinformed and incompetent or deliberately lying and untrustworthy. When your software lists "available" products or services, they must be available. You can list out-of-stock items or booked-up dates so customers can see them, but they should be *marked* as unavailable so customers won't go to the effort of ordering them only to discover several steps later that they wasted their time.

Burdening users' memory

Next are three interaction bloopers that place unnecessary burdens on people's memory, making it hard for people to remember what they are doing or plan to do.

Blooper 46: Hard to remember ID

The most obvious way to burden users' memory is to require authentication identification that they cannot remember.

Variation A: Assigned, nonchangeable passwords

Of all organizations, one would think that the Usability Professionals Association (UPA) would know better than to overtax peoples' memories. However, they do just that: they assign arbitrary account names and passwords to members and don't provide a way to change them.

UPA members receive a letter inviting them to use UPA's online services and assigning them a User ID and password. The User ID is a four-digit number, while the password is the member's family name. For example:

- User ID: 4567
- Password (case sensitive): Flintstone

UPA provides no way to change these to something easier to remember. Members who, despite this, want to use UPA's online services must either memorize their User ID and password or write them down, which is insecure. UPA's scheme also uses a number for the ID and text for the password, which is backward, uncommon, and easy to confuse.

Variation B: Unreasonable password restrictions

Some applications and Web sites allow users to create and change their user name and password, but impose such stringent requirements that nobody could remember their ID without writing it down and keeping it with them.

One application allowed users to change their personal identification number (PIN) "to a number that is easy ... to remember," but then imposed restrictions that made it impossible to do so (Figure 6.23). The last line of the instructions would be funny if it weren't so annoying.

Variation C: Security questions that don't work

Hard-to-remember ID occurs when Web sites ask users to select a security challenge question, but provide a limited selection and don't let users make up their own.

At Intuit.com, to purchase software, you must register. You can choose your own account name and password, and the restrictions are not bad. You can register a "password hint" so the site can remind you if you forget your password. This is all fine.

Figure 6.23

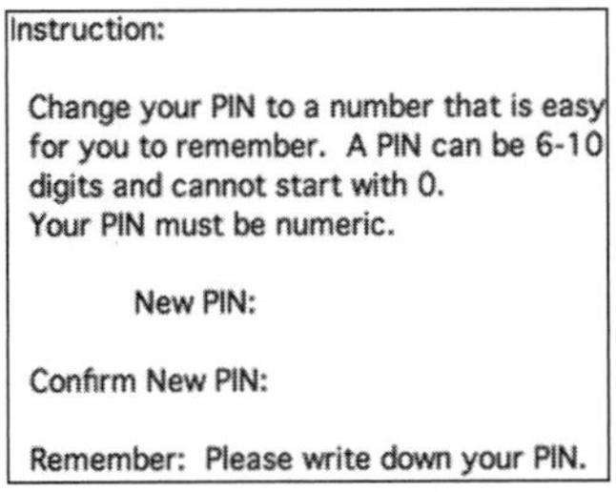

Instruction:

Change your PIN to a number that is easy for you to remember. A PIN can be 6-10 digits and cannot start with 0.
Your PIN must be numeric.

New PIN:

Confirm New PIN:

Remember: Please write down your PIN.

Client Web application: restrictions prevent users from devising easy-to-remember PIN.

Figure 6.24

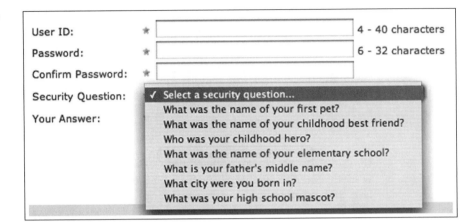

Intuit.com: limited security questions—user may have no unique, memorable answer for any.

The trouble occurs when the site asks you to "Select a security question …." You can't specify one; you choose from a menu (Figure 6.24). What if you can't answer *any* of the questions? Maybe your father has no middle name. Perhaps you had several childhood friends. Even one's birth city can be ambiguous for people born in rural areas. Some questions could have several possible answers. You have to pick a question and then *remember* which answer you gave to Intuit.

Avoiding Blooper 46

Here are guidelines on how to design security measures that don't overburden users' memory:

- Let users devise their own user names, passwords, and PINs. To avoid clashes in which many users want the same user name and have to use hard-to-remember ones like "Freddy54321," let people optionally use their e-mail address (including the domain, e.g., fred@bedrock.com) as a user name; those will be unique.

- Don't impose arbitrary and unnecessary restrictions on the password or PIN. Let users create ones that they can remember. Complex, "highly secure" passwords that people cannot remember are in fact not highly secure, because people just write them down and carry them around with them.

- Allow users to change their passwords and PINs.

- Include a way for users who forget their password or PIN to get or reset it. Sending the password, a password hint, or a reset-password link to the user account's registered e-mail address is a good way to do it if your users all have e-mail addresses.

- If you use challenge questions, provide a good selection, and provide an "Other" option so users can specify their own question.

Blooper 47: Long instructions that go away too soon

New UI designers sometimes create multistep instructions that vanish before all the steps are completed. This could be called the "helicopter door" blooper because some helicopters the U.S. Army used in the Vietnam War supposedly had a series of steps for evacuating printed on the inside of the door. The first step was to blow the door away. While trying to bail out of a falling 'copter, soldiers were supposed to read through *all* of the instructions, blow the door away, and remember enough of the instructions to complete the evacuation.

A classic software example comes from Microsoft Windows. As part of the process of connecting a computer to a wireless home network, Windows displays a dialog box giving multistep instructions for configuring the computer. The first step is to "click OK to dismiss this dialog" (Figure 6.25). And then … what were the rest of those instructions again?

A more subtle example of the "helicopter door" blooper comes from National Geographic Trip Planner. It has a Notebook in which users can keep notes about locations they have found. The first time a user opens the Notebook, a dialog box appears explaining three different methods for entering notes, each with multiple steps (Figure 6.26). The instructions don't say that the dialog box must be closed first, but it is modal, so it must be closed before a user can follow the instructions.

Often this blooper occurs because developers discover late in development that one function is too difficult to use, but it is too late or too costly to redesign the function. They stick instructions at the start of the function and hope users can remember them all the way through.

Figure 6.25

Microsoft Windows: long instructions are gone after first step.

Figure 6.26

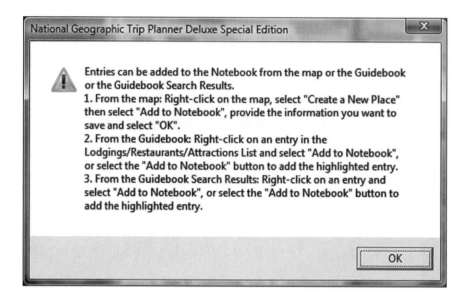

National Geographic Trip Planner: three options, each with several steps.

A related situation is when an application incorporates an external[2] function that cannot be changed. To help users use the external function, the application displays instructions just before the external function executes. That is OK, but when instructions go away before users execute all of the steps in them, it's a blooper.

Avoiding Blooper 47

Detailed instructions should remain displayed while the user is following them. Software designers—like helicopter designers—should not expect users to read multistep instructions and then remember them after the instructions are gone.

When users need assistance in traversing a multistep task, don't present all the steps at the start and expect users to remember them. Instead, do either of the following:

■ Provide a wizard. Display a multipage dialog box in which each page represents a step and presents any instructions for that step. This is the ideal design, but it isn't always feasible.

---

2. Developed previously (a.k.a. "legacy") or purchased from another company.

Figure 6.27

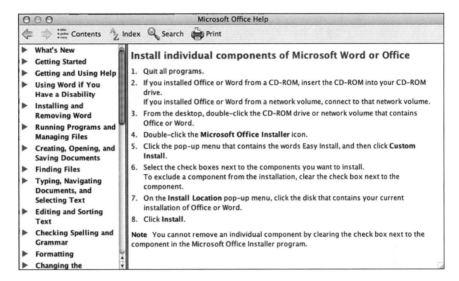

Microsoft Office: long instructions that remain displayed while being executed.

- Keep instructions up. Keep instructions displayed as long as a user is following them. Microsoft Office's Help window (Figure 6.27) does this.
- Wrap external functions. If you incorporate an external function into an application and cannot change it to match your application's UI, "wrap" it in new code that displays instructions and keeps them displayed while users work through the steps.

Blooper 48: Unnecessary or poorly marked modes

When software does something its user did not expect and did not want, the problem is often that the software was in a mode different from what the user thought it was in. Some examples follow:

- You are using a drawing program to edit an illustration. You want to move a rectangle to a new location. You try to drag the rectangle, but accidentally draw a new rectangle instead. Whoops! The program was in Draw Rectangle mode, not Select mode.
- You print a Web page, but the page prints in landscape format, cutting off the bottom. Oops! Forgot to set Page Orientation back to Portrait after printing a landscape page yesterday.

- On a stock investment Web site, you create a stock order and save it, intending to submit it later, but the order is immediately submitted. Argh! Forgot to turn off Auto-Submit mode after showing someone how it works.

What are modes, and why are they a problem?

Software has modes if user actions have different effects in different situations. To predict what effect a given action will have, users have to know what mode the application is in. For example, the effect of clicking a button on an application's window might depend on how a particular software option is set. The usability problems modes cause was recognized long ago:

> Each ... state in which a given operation by the user is interpreted differently by the program is called a command mode. The more modes in a command language, the more likely the user is to make mistakes by forgetting which mode he is in. [Newman and Sproull, 1979]

> My observations of secretaries learning to use ... text editors ... convinced me that my beloved computers were, in fact, unfriendly monsters, and that their sharpest fangs were the ever-present modes. [Tesler, 1981]

> Text editor users confuse modes, especially when the user spends a long time in a mode other than the "normal" one. [Thimbleby, 1982]

> Mode errors occur frequently in systems that do not provide clear feedback of their current state. [Norman, 1983]

Modes force users to keep track of what mode the software is in. They restrict users' actions to what is allowed in the current mode. They make it possible, sometimes even likely, that users will perform actions they did not intend or attempt actions that are not valid. Some mode errors are trivial and easy to correct, but others are serious.

A major airline crash was due entirely to a mode error. The pilot adjusted an autopilot dial to set a target altitude of 1700 meters, but the dial was in a Rate of Descent mode, so the airplane instead lost altitude at 1700 meters per minute, hitting a mountainside.

Most modes are unnecessary or inappropriate; a more careful design could eliminate them. Even software that needs modes often provides poor feedback about what mode it is in.

A moded GUI

Earthlink WebMail has a moded GUI in which it is easy to forget what mode it is in and make mode errors. The application has a Suspect e-mail folder that quarantines e-mail from unknown senders. You can look in it to see if any quarantined messages are ones you want. You can do four things to quarantined messages. You can move them to your Inbox with or without adding

Figure 6.28

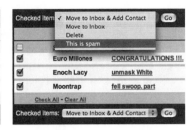

Earthlink WebMail: effect of "Go" button depends on action set by menu.

the sender to your Address Book. You can delete them or report them as spam (Figure 6.28).

Instead of providing four separate command buttons or a menu of four commands, WebMail provides only one "Go" button with a mode menu that sets which of the four actions "Go" will execute. WebMail users often select several quarantined messages and click "Go" without noticing that the mode menu isn't set as they want. Since the default mode is Move to Inbox and Add Contact and the most common action on quarantined messages is to report them as spam, the most common mode error is to select a bunch of spam messages and accidentally move them to your Inbox and add the spammer addresses to your Address Book. Oops!

Less harmful modes: Modal dialog boxes

All modes are not equal. Some are less harmful than others. In moderation and with good mode feedback, modes can even be helpful.

A common use of modes is to display modal dialog boxes, which block users from interacting with other windows in the application or on the whole display. They are called "modal" because they put the computer into a mode in which only input to the dialog box is accepted.

Dialog boxes can exhibit different degrees of modal-ness:

- *Parent modal:* Block interaction with its own parent window but allow interaction with other windows from the same application or from other applications.

- *Application modal:* Block interaction with all other parts of the same application, but allow users to interact with other applications.

- *Modal or system modal:* Block all interaction other than with the modal dialog box.

The purpose of modal dialog boxes is to force users to notice, read, and respond to them before doing anything else. This is necessary when:

- There is a serious problem that needs the user's attention. If an error dialog box is not modal, a user can miss it and click on another window, causing the error dialog box to vanish behind other windows.

- Other changes to the application are not allowed while the dialog box is displayed. If a dialog box is collecting input for an operation on a data object, the application may need to block users from deleting or altering the object until the operation is done.

Mode errors due to modal dialog boxes are pretty harmless: the user tries to click on something else but the computer only beeps. However, it can be frustrating to be blocked from doing anything else while a modal dialog box is displayed, especially if the dialog box says something horrible like:

Out of memory. All your data will be lost. [OK]

Mode settings can be harmless, especially if users never change them

Microsoft Word is teeming with modes. Here are just some (with the default modes in italics):

- View: *Normal*, Outline, Page Layout, Master Document
- Auto correct: *On*, Off
- Revision tracking: On, *Off*
- Background repagination: *On*, Off
- Auto save: *On*, Off
- Automatic word selection: *On*, Off
- Smart cut-and-paste: *On*, Off
- Drag-and-drop text editing: *On*, Off
- Inserted text overwrites: On, *Off*

Most of these modes do not cause mode errors. Why? The reason is *not* that the current values of these modes are prominently indicated so users cannot miss them. Most of them are hardly indicated at all. The reason is that the vast majority of Word users never change these settings from the defaults. Many Word users don't even know that these settings are in Word. If a mode setting is never changed, it effectively has only one value. As Larry Tesler [1981] said: "One mode is no modes at all."

One mode setting in Word that most users *do* change is View (Normal, Outline, Page Layout, Master Document). It therefore sometimes causes mode errors, such as accidentally editing a document in the Outline view and wondering why the formatting is odd.

Another View mode—a harmless one—is in Microsoft Windows file folders. Folders can be set to display files in five ways (Figure 6.29). The only explicit

Figure 6.29

Windows folder View mode: unlikely to cause mode errors.

indicator of the current View mode is in the folder's View menu, which is usually closed. That is OK because users can see the current view mode by how the folder lists files.

Badly named modes

Some mode settings include "mode" in their name; some don't. Names for mode settings are often idiosyncratic as well as inconsistent: whatever developers happened to think of at the moment they added the setting, without considering other settings and their names.

Sometimes mode settings are named simply "Mode," because nobody could think of a more descriptive name. CorelDraw's Options window provides an example (Figure 6.30).

 Toaster modes

Toasters have modes. The Darkness setting is one. Mode errors cause burned or "raw" toast.

The Darkness control supposedly lets you set the toaster for your preferences. If that were what it was really for, you would set it once and never change it unless you were making toast for someone else. Mode errors would be rare.

However, the Darkness control is misnamed: it sets toasting time, not toast darkness. For a given type of bread, longer toasting time means darker toast, but the same setting that turns French bread into smoking carbon barely warms German vollkornbrot. The Darkness control is really for different types of bread, not different users. Most mode errors occur when you forget to reset the toaster when toasting a type of bread different from last time.

To eliminate toaster mode errors, we can make the toaster modeless by requiring you to set the time each time. This sounds tedious until you realize that microwave ovens do exactly that. Toaster designers assume that users stick with one type of bread, while microwave oven designers assume that users heat a variety of foods in an unpredictable order.

Figure 6.30

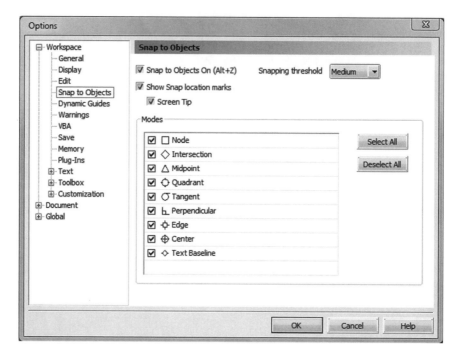

CorelDraw: drawing options collectively called "Modes."

Avoiding Blooper 48

Modes hurt software usability in three ways:

1. They require users to expend mental effort to keep track of the current mode.
2. They cause users to make mode errors.
3. They constrain users' actions to those valid in the current mode.

The first two are definitely problems. The third can be either a problem or a feature, depending on the designer's intentions and users' needs.

Eliminate modes by removing mode settings

Design your application's UI to minimize the number of mode settings—perhaps omit them completely. Devise modeless alternatives. You may have to add buttons or menus to do this, but it will pay off. The airline crash described above would not have happened if the autopilot had had two dials: one for rate of descent and another for target altitude.

One case illustrates how modes can be avoided or their impact diminished. A company was developing a browser for business data. The data was displayed at a high level, in tables. Users could scan the table, pick an interesting column, row, or cell, and "drill down" to see details.

The developers wanted drilling down to be easy, so they made double-clicking on a column or row drill down into it. They also wanted it to be easy for users to drill *up*—to return to a higher level view of the data. They made double-click do that, too, and included a drill direction mode to control whether double-clicking drilled down or up. A button on the browser's toolbar toggled the drill direction mode between "up" and "down."

The drill direction mode was awful. Users didn't remember which mode the browser was in, even though it was shown on the toolbar. They often drilled the wrong way: "Whoops! I wanted to go down, not up."

To eliminate users' mode errors, there were two alternatives:

1. Double-click always drills down. For drilling up, put a BACK button, a menu of levels above the current one, or a navigation breadcrumb path on the toolbar.
2. Double-click drills down, but Shift–double-click drills up. This makes the mode control tactile and spring-loaded, greatly reducing the chance of a mode error.

Minimize the use and impact of modal dialog boxes

Use modal dialog boxes sparingly. Don't restrict users' actions while a dialog box is displayed unless it is *crucial* that users not interact with other things on the display. Any restriction should be as narrow as possible; don't block users' access to data or controls that are irrelevant to the dialog box. Use the various types of modal-ness as follows:

- *Not modal:* most of the time
- *Parent modal:* as necessary
- *Application modal:* occasionally
- *Modal or system modal:* hardly ever

Avoid forced sequences or temporary restrictions on user actions

Avoid requiring users to do things in a predetermined order. Avoid temporarily limiting the actions that are valid.

A Move function can be moded or modeless. With a moded Move function, users indicate "Move *this* to *there*," with the software being in one mode while it is waiting for the *this* and another while it is waiting for the *there*. The "highlight, drag, and drop" form of Move is moded, but almost imperceptibly. A modeless Move capability uses separate Cut and Paste commands, with no intervening modes.

Modes are hard to avoid

Most software applications have modes of some kind. It is almost impossible to design software that is entirely modeless. Modes usually have advantages as well as disadvantages, so the decision of whether to have modes is often a design trade-off [Johnson, 1990].

Advantages of modes

Modes let users prespecify information. Using a command in an application requires (a) choosing the desired command and (b) setting the command's options. With no prespecification—without modes—choosing commands and setting the desired options can require verbose input, large command vocabularies, or lots of keys and controls. By letting users prespecify commands, options, or key interpretations, moded user interfaces allow for:

- *Terser control:* Options that users would otherwise have to specify repeatedly can be prespecified once in a mode, which applies to subsequent actions until the mode is changed.

- *Smaller command vocabularies and arrays of controls:* The same command or control can have different effects in different modes.

- *More guidance for users:* Software can lead users through a predetermined sequence in which only certain actions are possible at each step. Modal dialog boxes are a special case: there is only one step, but it is one the designers really want the user to take.

- *Safety:* Modes can be used to lock certain functions to prevent their accidental use. Trigger locks on guns and on nuclear missile launch panels are examples of safety mode controls.

- *Recognizing exceptional operations:* Many UIs are designed as if all functions they provide are equally important or likely. Modes can help make it clear in a UI that certain operations are exceptional.

Disadvantages of modes

Although modes have advantages, they also have costs, which are born by the users. When a software product or service has modes, its users must:

- *Preplan mode settings:* Before you need a mode, you have to think to set it.

- *Set modes:* Setting modes requires extra actions that are foreign to the software's supported tasks. It can be tedious and annoying if the software is often not in the mode you need.

- *Remember the current mode:* You have to keep track of what mode the software is in.

- *Recover from mode errors:* When you fail to do one of the first three items and make an error, you have to clean up afterward.

- *Yield to the software's control:* When software "drives" a task, constraining what you can do at each step, you must accept it, even though you may prefer to be the one in control.

Make mode indicators difficult to miss

If an application has modes, it should indicate the current mode prominently, as recommended in two classic and influential UI design handbooks:

> **Mode Designator.** DISPLAY MODE INDICATORS—When the system is operating in a special mode for which a different set of commands or syntax rules are in effect, provide users with an indicator that distinguishes this mode from other modes. Provide differences in headings, formats, or prompts, and use labels to remind the user of the mode that is in effect. [Brown, 1988]

> **Display of Operation Mode**—When context for sequence control is established in terms of a defined operational mode, remind users of the current mode .... [Smith and Mosier, 1986]

The best mode indicators are spring-loaded: as long as the user holds a key or pedal down, an alternative mode is in effect. When the user lets go, the mode reverts to "normal." Common spring-loaded modes are the Shift and Control keys on computer keyboards and the Sustain pedal on pianos. With spring-loaded modes, users *feel* what mode is in effect.

In contrast, the Caps Lock key on keyboards is not spring-loaded: it's a toggle-on toggle-off mode. When mode indicators are not spring-loaded, they must either be placed right where users are or be large and attention-grabbing. It doesn't work to put a little mode indicator in a corner of the display: no one will see it.

Taking control away from users

The final three interaction bloopers are ways software takes control away from users.

Blooper 49: Automatic rearrangement of display

Imagine a document editor that automatically scrolled your document so that the line you were editing was in the middle of the screen. If you put the cursor on a line near the bottom of the screen and began typing, the document would shift so the line you were typing was in the middle of the screen. Most people would find this annoying and disorienting. Two variations of this blooper are common.

Variation A: How to annoy users: rearrange their data

The document editor described above moves the users' data around on its own initiative. How long would you tolerate Windows, MacOS, or Linux frequently rearranging your desktop icons for you? Not long! When software does this, users lose track of where they are and what they have just done. It also annoys them.

Users are disoriented more when a display rearranges itself very quickly. When a big change occurs in the blink of an eye, users aren't sure what happened. On the other hand, if the display updates too slowly, they get frustrated at having to wait. When UI designers try to rearrange users' data for them, they are entering a user-interface mine field.

A lot of designers and developers go into this mine field and end up with this blooper. It is common in applications that manipulate complex, structured data. Here are some examples:

- A Java class browser displays a tree graph of the class hierarchy. When you rename a class, the entire tree is redisplayed, rearranged so the class branches are still in alphabetical order (Figure 6.31). Adding or deleting classes also rearranges the tree.

- Outline processors or file directory browsers can expand or contract items to show or hide subitems. Some expand and contract when you execute commands unrelated to expanding or contracting. For example, if you set the font style for level 3 items in an outline, the outline processor might automatically expand the entire outline down to level 3. If you drag an item from one folder into another in a file hierarchy, some file browsers automatically expand the destination folder to let you see what is in it.

- Drawing programs often allow graphic objects to be layered. In some drawing programs, simply changing a graphic object's attributes, such as color, line width, or fill pattern, causes it to be moved to the top layer. This is usually not what you want.

Figure 6.31

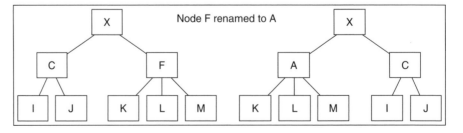

Class hierarchy, before and after class F renamed to A: subtrees swapped automatically.

Figure 6.32

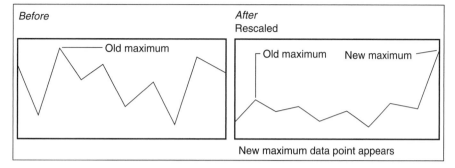

Graph rescales vertical axis automatically when data points arrive or depart.

- Data-graphing functions show how a value changes over time. Such graphs typically add new data points periodically on one end and scroll the graph slowly toward the other end. Some automatically scale the vertical axis to fill the height of the window (Figure 6.32). This may seem helpful, but it is disorienting if the graph automatically rescales when a new data point that represents a new maximum appears or when an existing maximum scrolls off-screen.

Applications move and rearrange users' data for two quite different reasons:

1. *Well-meaning but naïve developers:* Developers might believe that users would rearrange the data anyway, so rearranging it automatically saves them the trouble. Wrong!
2. *Overly simple implementation:* Developers may not have time to figure out how to limit updates to just what the user changed. They code the display to recompute, reformat, and redisplay completely when anything about it changes.

Variation B: Moving controls

A second variation of the blooper occurs when software automatically moves GUI *controls* around on the display. When controls move around on their own, users aren't sure where to find them. Moving controls also decrease users' feeling of being in control. Common types of automatically moving controls are:

- *Autonomous windows:* Windows are moved or resized by the software.
- *Warping cursor:* The cursor jumps suddenly to a new position.
- *Dancing tabs:* Tab rows swap places when the user clicks a tab in a back row.
- *Dynamic menus:* Commands in menus appear and disappear, often mysteriously.

Automatically moving controls is a GUI control blooper as well as an interaction blooper.

A related annoyance: Position of control varies across panels

Several years ago, Yahoo's message board put certain links in different places on different pages. Each message page had a banner advertisement at the top. The links to the next and previous posting in a topic were below the ad. The ads varied in height, so the navigation links moved up and down from one page to the next. You could not simply place the cursor over "Next" and click through messages to find an interesting one. You had to look to see where the links were on every page. Worse, the ads were randomly chosen when a page was displayed, so "Next" and "Previous" weren't even in the same place when you revisited a page (Figure 6.33).

Yahoo's "blooper" may have been intentional, to force users to look at each page and see the ad there before clicking to the next message. But if that were true, Yahoo would not have corrected the problem, as they did in later releases (Figure 6.34).

Information displays or controls should be in *exactly* the same place on each page, so users know where to find them.

Figure 6.33

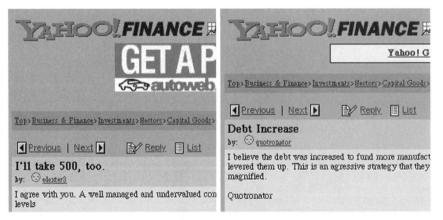

Messages.Yahoo.com (2000): position of "Previous" and "Next" links changes between pages.

Figure 6.34

Messages.Yahoo.com (2006): position of "Previous" and "Next" links is always the same.

Avoiding Blooper 49

This blooper violates two GUI principles: "the screen belongs to the user" and "preserve display inertia" (Basic Principle 7, page 41).

The screen belongs to the user

Users expect the display to be under their control. When software changes too much on its own, users become disoriented, frustrated, and annoyed. This is especially true for activities that require hand–eye coordination, such as moving the cursor or resizing windows. It also applies to arranging users' data, such as the layout of icons on the desktop, order of files or e-mail messages in folders, formatting of text or graphs, or expansion level of an outline.

Don't try to be too helpful: don't rearrange the display *for* users; let them manage the display. Provide explicit "rearrange" or "reformat" commands that users initiate. Examples of such commands are the MacOS Clean-up Desktop command and the Balance or Align functions of graphics editors. In contrast, Microsoft Word's automatic reformatting of text is so annoying that many users turn it off if they can figure out how.

Preserve display inertia

Preserving display inertia means that when a user changes something, most of the display should remain unchanged. Small, localized changes to the data should produce only small, localized changes on the display.

When large or nonlocal changes in the display are necessary (such as repaginating a document or swapping the positions of branches of a family tree), they should not be instantaneous. They should be announced clearly and be done so users:

- see and understand the changes and
- can continue working.

Animation can help. It provides visual continuity: users see a single object change rather than new objects replacing old ones. However, animating changes does not mean forcing users to wait for annoyingly slow ones to finish. People can perceive smooth motion even if it happens in a fraction of a second.

The default behavior when rescaling should be that graphs retain the same scale until the user asks the software to rescale. Automatic rescaling can be an option, but it should not be the default behavior.

Blooper 50: Dialog boxes that trap users

Dialog boxes sometimes provide no way out other than a direction that users don't want to go. This blooper comes in five common variations.

Variation A: No "Cancel"

Have you ever started an operation, but when you saw what was happening, you wanted to stop it? If the software gives you no way to cancel an operation, it exhibits the first variation of the "trapping users" blooper.

In Adobe PhotoShop, if you try to print an image but the selected printer doesn't match the print settings, a warning appears explaining the mismatch. A common response in this situation is: "Uh, oh! It's going to the wrong printer. I want the Postscript printer." Alas, the warning dialog box has no way to cancel the Print (Figure 6.35).

Variation B: All paths are wrong

Some dialog boxes provide more than one option, perhaps including a way to cancel, but omit one or more options that some users will want.

If a Macintosh user prints a document but the printer runs out of paper, MacOS displays a warning offering several options (Figure 6.36). All of them involve stopping or deleting the print job. The printer is already stopped; awaiting more paper. Why can't users just load more paper into the printer and continue?

Variation C: Required button is inactive

A dialog box can provide no paths the user wants because some of its options are inactive. When Apple's iPhoto encounters a problem that it wants to report to Apple, it displays a window and asks you to describe what you were doing when the problem occurred, then send the report to Apple. The "Send to Apple" button is initially inactive and is supposed to activate when you type a description, but it often remains inactive so you can't submit the report (Figure 6.37).

Variation D: Unclear choices

Some dialog boxes provide the required choices, but are so confusing that users feel trapped anyway or have to stop and think hard about which option they want.

Figure 6.35

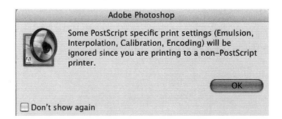

Adobe PhotoShop: Print setting warning provides no "Cancel."

Figure 6.36

Apple MacOS X: printer "Out of Paper" warning provides no way to load paper and continue.

Figure 6.37

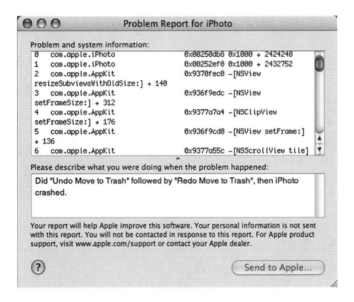

Apple iPhoto: Problem Report window's "Send to Apple" button stays inactive.

When you install a new version of the Skype client, Skype displays a confusing dialog box (Figure 6.38). Most users are stopped dead in their tracks by the lack of correspondence between the question and the response buttons. If we "allow the new version to access the same keychain," is that a change or not? Also, why is the change option labeled "Change All" instead of just "Change?"

Dialog boxes for canceling things—appointments, transactions, reservations—often are confusing. Which button cancels the cancellation and which button completes the cancellation?

Two classic examples are the "Cancel Appointment" page from Palo Alto Medical Foundation's online appointment system (Figure 6.39A) and the Cancel Payment dialog box from Wells Fargo's online banking system (Figure 6.39B). You tell it to cancel something—an appointment or a payment—and it displays a Cancellation dialog box. Instructions on the dialog box say that "Send" executes the cancellation and "Cancel" cancels the cancellation, but computer users don't read, they scan, so most won't see the instructions.

Figure 6.38

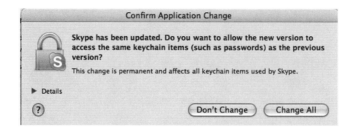

Skype: confusing dialog box—question and buttons use different terms.

Figure 6.39

A   B

Cancel dialog: "Send" cancels and "Cancel" cancels cancellation. (A) PAMF.org: cancel appointment. (B) Wells Fargo online: cancel payment.

A stock trading application had one of these confusing Cancel Cancellation dialog boxes. The developers argued that it was logical and consistent with other dialog boxes: "'OK' approves the current operation, which happens to be a Cancel operation, and 'Cancel' aborts it." Eventually, they conceded that users might be confused about which button to press. Since it was a stock trading application, it was important to eliminate any confusion about which button canceled and which one didn't. In the released version, the buttons were labeled "Cancel Order" and "Continue Order."

Variation E: No, not OK

There are dialog boxes that announce that something horrible has happened, or is about to happen, and ask you if that's OK (Figure 6.40). All you can do is sigh (or curse), OK the message, and start over. Even when such cases are actually unavoidable, labeling the acknowledgment button "OK" just throws salt on your wound. No, it is not OK.

Adobe InDesign (Figure 6.41) makes the same blooper, but at least you can recover lost work.

Figure 6.40

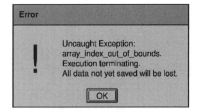

Error message traps user. No choice but to click "OK" and lose data.

Figure 6.41

Adobe InDesign: error message traps user. No choice but to click "OK."

A complex example, dissected

Some dialog boxes mix variations of the blooper. Here, we examine one in detail, to understand better this blooper and how it harms usability.

If you try to open a Microsoft Word document that is already open, a dialog box asks if you want to revert to the saved version of the document (Figure 6.42). Huh?

You could arrive here with any of three goals:

1. You didn't know the document was already open. Opening it twice was an accident. You would want to cancel the second opening. It isn't obvious, but to do that you click "No."
2. You knew the document was already open and want to replace the version you were editing with the last saved version. To do that, you click "Yes."
3. You knew the document was already open, but want to open the last saved version in a *separate* window to compare the two. You can't do that.

One problem with this dialog box is that it provides for only two of the three user goals. If you had the third goal, it commits the blooper of trapping you: none of the options is what you want.

A worse problem with the dialog box is its unclear labeling. It is clear that "Yes" corresponds to goal 2 (returning to the previous version), but it is not clear what "No" means. This is similar to Blooper 2 (page 62): it's hard to deduce the meaning of the "negative" response from that of the "positive" one.

If users arrive at this dialog box with goal 1 or 3, they will stare at the dialog box for a while, reading and rereading it until they have convinced themselves that

Figure 6.42

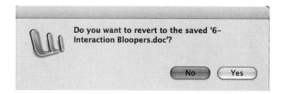

Microsoft Word: an attempt to open an already-open document displays a confusing dialog box.

Figure 6.43

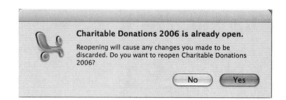

Excel's dialog box for reopening a file is only slightly better than Word's.

the opposite of "revert to saved" is what they want, and finally click "No." If they wanted to cancel the Open operation (goal 1), they will be in luck because that's what "No" does. They wasted time, but at least they got what they wanted.

Users who wanted to open the saved version of the document in a *new* window (goal 3) will be quite perplexed by what happens when they click "No": nothing. They may assume that a new window opened over the old one and move the window aside to see what is under it. They might try again on the assumption that something went wrong the first time. They might figure out that goal 3 isn't supported. In any case, they will have wasted time thinking about the software. Most users will encounter this dialog box rarely, so the next time it happens, they won't remember what "No" does, so they will go through the whole thing again.

The designer of this dialog box assumed that users know what the opposite of "revert to saved" is. It probably didn't occur to the designer that users might arrive at the dialog box with goal 3.

Microsoft Excel's "document already open" dialog box is only a little better. It's good that it begins by saying that the file you tried to open is already open (Figure 6.43). However, to know what "No" and "Yes" do, you must read the small print. Most users won't; they will skip to the buttons until they realize that they can't tell what the buttons do. Also, "Yes" (discard changes) as a default is wrong.

Avoiding Blooper 50

Provide users with sufficient alternatives so they won't feel trapped. Label the choices clearly so that it is clear what the options are.

Analyze it! Compare available options against users' likely goals

Do an analysis like the one above: list all the goals users could have when the dialog box appears. Knowing the possible goals helps you provide the right options and label them unambiguously. Excel's dialog box could be reworded to be crystal clear (Figure 6.44).

Even with perfectly clear instructions and labels, the dialog box still omits one possible goal: opening the document in a new window. Ideally, Word and Excel should provide that option, but they don't, so the dialog box can't offer it. Labeling should make clear what choices are offered, so users who want a missing option won't believe one of the offered ones is it.

Then test it!

Test dialog boxes to make sure users understand them and that all the required choices are provided. Dialog boxes can be tested informally long before they are implemented by showing hand-drawn sketches to users, explaining when the dialog box is displayed, and asking users to interpret what the message and the buttons mean. If they have to stop and think, redesign the box. When more of the software has been designed, dialog boxes can be tested in the context of the application using printed screen images or a working prototype. Finally, they can be tested in the running product before release.

Bad: "Your work will be lost. [OK?]"

Software developers should try hard to avoid situations in which only one unpleasant choice is available. Often, this is just a matter of making sure that the application catches all the error conditions that can arise, so that handling them is not delegated to the operating system.

When only one unpleasant choice is available, don't pretend that it is just a benign announcement. Technically, both "You have new mail" and "The program crashed and lost all your unsaved work" are announcements of fact, but users regard them differently. Label the acknowledgment button "OK" for the former, but something like "Acknowledged" or "Understood," or even "Sigh ... I hate computers!" for the latter.

Figure 6.44

Rewarded Excel dialog box: does not make users think.

Blooper 51: "Cancel" doesn't cancel

Dialog boxes let users view and set command options and object properties. They should have at least two buttons:

- Apply changes, close the dialog box, and proceed with the command (if any)
- Discard any changed settings and close dialog box

The first button is usually labeled "OK," but sometimes it is labeled with the command that displayed the dialog box, e.g., "Print." The second button is usually labeled "Cancel."

Users expect "Cancel" to "forget" all changes they made in the dialog box since they opened it or clicked the "Apply" button (if provided). But some "Cancel" buttons don't cancel. When "Cancel" doesn't cancel, the "OK" and "Cancel" buttons have the same meaning: close the dialog box and retain the changes. That's a blooper.

The blooper is not in the code that is executed when the user clicks "Cancel," which typically just closes the dialog box. The problem is in what happens *before* that, when the user edits settings in the dialog box.

Variation A: Dialog box directly edits application data

Sometimes the blooper is due to a simplistic implementation: the dialog box directly edits the application data, rather than a *copy* of it. Canceling such changes is impossible unless a sophisticated Undo mechanism has been built into the application, which is rare.

This error is especially common when a dialog box manipulates complex application data, like a table. Programmers often don't bother to copy a complex data structure into the dialog box, so changes in the dialog box affect the application data directly.

This blooper is also seen when actions in a dialog box have side effects outside the application, such as creating or deleting disk files.

Variation B: Changing between tabbed panels saves changes

"Cancel" buttons that don't cancel often occur in tabbed dialog boxes: merely changing from one tab to another applies changes you made in the first panel before switching to the new one, as if you clicked "Apply." By the time you click "Cancel," the changes have already been saved. Programmers often implement tabbed panels this way to avoid storing data for one panel while displaying another. Whatever the excuse, it is still a blooper.

Users regard tabs as a navigation mechanism (Blooper 4, page 67). They don't expect switching tabs to change application data. They won't understand why some changed settings were canceled and some weren't; they will assume that they encountered a bug.

Variation C: Wizards have side effects that "Cancel" doesn't cancel

A wizard is a multipage dialog box. Wizards lead users toward a goal, break the choices and decisions down into a sequence of simple steps, with instructions along the way.

Each page of a wizard should have a "Cancel" button in addition to "Next" and "Back." Clicking "Cancel" closes the wizard and aborts the operation. However, some wizards don't cancel everything the user did before clicking "Cancel."

Consider a wizard for creating Web sites. Each step offers options or collects content for the site, and when the wizard finishes, the site is created. If you cancel the wizard early, no site or partially built site should remain. If canceled wizards leave changes behind, that's a blooper.

Variation D: Multilevel dialog boxes

Some applications have multiple levels of dialog boxes. If dialog box A displays dialog box B and you edit dialog box B and click its "OK" button, then cancel dialog box A, what happens to the settings you changed in dialog box B?

Dialog box B acts as an extension of A. Its settings could, in a different design, have been put directly in dialog box A instead of a separate one. If it were designed that way, canceling the dialog box would cancel any changes. Why should the behavior be different for properties set in a separate dialog box? By this reasoning, canceling dialog box A should cancel any changes made in B. However, in many applications, the changes have already taken effect and cannot be canceled. That's a blooper.

Avoiding Blooper 51

Changes in dialog boxes should not be applied until the user clicks "OK" or "Apply." No other action should cause the application's data to be updated.

When a user clicks "Cancel," the application should be exactly as it was when the dialog box was opened or the user last clicked "Apply." If the dialog box changed anything in the application or the environment while it was open, "Cancel" must somehow undo those changes.

Dialog boxes display a copy of application settings

Dialog boxes should start with a *copy* of the application settings and let users edit that, so "Cancel" can just discard the copy. "OK" and "Apply" should update the application's data with the data from the dialog box. This should be true regardless of the complexity of the data manipulated by the dialog box (Figure 6.45). Even when dialog boxes open other dialog boxes, each level of dialog box should be cancelable without affecting the data in the parent dialog box or the application.

Figure 6.45

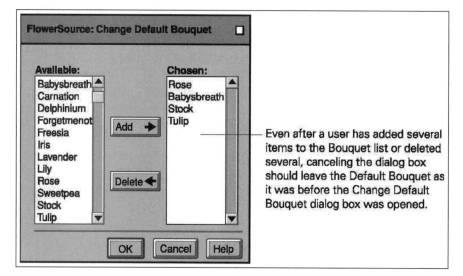

Even after a user has added several items to the Bouquet list or deleted several, canceling the dialog box should leave the Default Bouquet as it was before the Change Default Bouquet dialog box was opened.

"Cancel" cancels all changes made since dialog box opened.

Tabs, wizards, and multilevel dialog boxes are not excuses for the blooper

Switching between tabs is just navigation; it should not update application data. Each panel should retain its state until the dialog box is dismissed. No settings on any panel should be applied to the application until the user explicitly commands it.

Think of it this way: tabs organize settings into categories. If the settings were all on one panel, grouped with group boxes, it would clearly be wrong to apply changes in one group box when the user just moves the cursor to a different group of settings. If it is wrong for that case, it's also wrong to save changes when a user switches tabs.

Canceled wizards should leave nothing behind. If a wizard sets things up piece by piece as users go through the steps, "Cancel" must delete whatever was created and undo any other changes. It's better if a wizard simply collects user input until the end, saving any actual changes until it finishes. That way, "Cancel" can just close the wizard.

When an application has multiple levels of dialog boxes, canceling a parent dialog box should cancel changes that were made and applied in any of its child dialog boxes. As stated earlier, this makes sense because child dialog boxes are extensions of their parent.

Microsoft's Outlook Express has a dialog box for setting and changing a user's e-mail identity properties (Figure 6.46A). The identity password is set by clicking the "Change Password" button. The button opens a second-level dialog box to collect the new password (Figure 6.46B). After entering the new

Figure 6.46

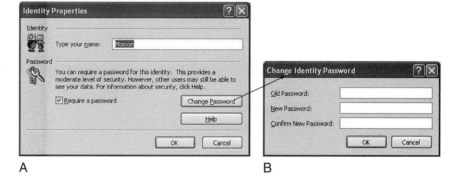

A   B

Microsoft Outlook: canceling dialog box (A) cancels changes OK'd in dialog box (B).

password, you click either "OK" or "Cancel." Suppose you OK the second dialog box, then cancel the first. Should the e-mail identity have a new password or not?

Outlook does the right thing: canceling the Identity Properties dialog box cancels any password change OK'd in the Change Identity Password dialog box.

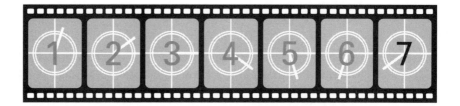

Responsiveness Bloopers

Introduction

Introduction

Responsiveness is very important in determining the usability of software (Basic Principle 8, page 45). That's "responsiveness," *not* "performance" or "speed." This chapter explains the difference and how to achieve responsiveness when performance is limited.

Highly responsive software:

- lets you know immediately that your keystrokes, pointing device movements, and clicks were received;
- estimates how long operations will take;
- frees you to do other things while waiting;
- manages queued events intelligently;
- performs housekeeping and low-priority tasks in the background;
- anticipates your requests.

Responsiveness differs from perform-ance. Performance is how quickly the software computes and displays *results*. High-performance software gives you results quickly; low-performance software is *slow* to produce results.

Software can be responsive even when its performance is slow. However, much of the software in today's market has both slow performance and low responsiveness, a bad combination.

Most responsiveness bloopers cannot be illustrated with software screen images because they concern what happens over time. This chapter illustrates them mainly with scenarios depicting dysfunctional human–human communication, along with a few visual examples and case studies.

Common responsiveness bloopers

Responsiveness bloopers are all closely related, so they are listed here and discussed together rather than one at a time. Examples of some of the bloopers follow the list.

- Blooper 52: Cursor doesn't keep up with you; it jumps around as the operating system processes mouse[1] movements and keeps moving after you have stopped the mouse
- Blooper 53: On-screen buttons acknowledge clicks too late or not at all
- Blooper 54: Menus, sliders, and scrollbars lag behind your actions, destroying the hand–eye coordination required for successful operation

---

1.   In this chapter, "mouse" means any pointing device: trackball, touchpad, joystick, etc.

- Blooper 55: Moving and sizing operations don't keep up with your actions and don't provide temporary "rubber-band" feedback
- Blooper 56: Application doesn't indicate that it is busy; it just ignores you
- Blooper 57: Application occasionally—and unpredictably—is unresponsive while it does internal housekeeping
- Blooper 58: Long operations don't display progress
- Blooper 59: Long operations provide no way to cancel
- Blooper 60: Application wastes idle time, and when you finally give a predictable command, it takes a long time to finish
- Blooper 61: Application gives no feedback when it hangs, with no indication of what is or is not happening
- Blooper 62: Web site has huge images and animations, so it is viewable only with a super-high-speed Internet connection
- Blooper 63: Web site always reloads whole pages in response to small edits

Examples: Poor responsiveness is poor communication

The lack of responsiveness of many applications would be considered dysfunctional, even intolerable, if it occurred in communication between people. Figure 7.1 gives three examples of poor computer responsiveness, depicted as poor person-to-person communication. Do any remind you of software you use?

Figure 7.1

A: *When the application is busy, the user gets no response at all.*
"Fred, what are our plans for this weekend?"
(Busy writing; no reply)
"Hey! Do you know if we have any plans for this weekend?"
(Still no reply)
"Earth to Fred! Earth to Fred! Do you read me?"
Finishes writing) "OK, that's done." (Looks up) "Did you say something?"

B: *Participants don't communicate time requirements and estimates.*
"I'd like to have this camera repaired." (Doesn't say that he needs it in two weeks for a wedding)
Sure. Once I get your information and a $25 deposit, I can put the job on our repair technician's queue." (Doesn't say that the technician is on vacation and won't be back for three weeks)

C: *Both participants are locked in a single serial process.*
"Hello. I'd like to fly from San Francisco to New York next Thursday, returning Sunday evening, as cheaply as possible."
"OK, I'll check flights and fares. I don't know how long it will take, but you must stay on the line, not doing anything else, until I find the answer. If you hang up, I'll forget about your request."

Poor responsiveness presented as dysfunctional person–person communication.

Figure 7.2

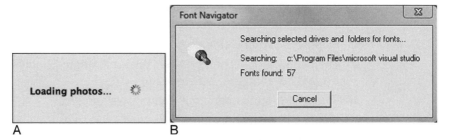

A   B

No progress bar for long operation. (A) Apple iPhoto. (B) Microsoft Font Navigator.

Examples: Long operations display no progress bars

When Apple iPhoto starts up, it loads its database of all the users' photos. If you have thousands of photos, loading can take many minutes. During that time, iPhoto displays no indication of its progress in loading the photos; only a "busy" indicator (Figure 7.2A). Similarly, Microsoft Windows Font Navigator can take minutes to search your hard disk for fonts, but during that time shows only where it is currently looking and how many fonts it has found (Figure 7.2B). Neither program tells you how long you have to wait.

Examples: Long operations display phony progress bars

Phony progress bars look deceptively like real progress bars: a bar with an animation indicating activity. However, in a phony progress bar, the fullness of the bar does not show the operation's progress. Some phony progress bars show the "progress" of the software for *each* item in a list of items; they fill up once for each item, starting over for the next item. Others simply fill up cyclically in correspondence to nothing in particular or display moving "barbershop pole" patterns. Phony progress bars are just fancy busy indicators.

Microsoft Windows XP Installer displays a phony progress bar when it installs applications (Figure 7.3A). The bar fills up, empties, fills again, empties, etc., for *each* of several steps in the installation. In MacOSX, burning a CD shows a fake progress bar: it fills up several times as a CD is burned—once per stage (Figure 7.3B). These displays are useless to users, who need to know how long the whole operation will take.

Examples: Long operations provide no way to cancel

Apple's iDisk online storage service displays a phony progress bar when you copy a large file to your iDisk (Figure 7.4). The bar fills up in less than a second,

Figure 7.3

A

B

False progress bars that fill up repeatedly. (A) Windows Installer. (B) MacOS CD utility.

Figure 7.4

Apple iDisk file copy: false progress bar, no time estimate, and cancel button is disabled.

then shows a barber-pole animation for 2–20 minutes, depending on the file's size. Worst of all, the dialog box provides no time estimate and the cancel button ("X") is disabled.

At least iDisk's dialog box has a cancel button. When MacOS converts a Postscript file to a PDF file, that can take several minutes, depending on the file's size. During that time, it displays a phony progress dialog box with no cancel button (Figure 7.5).

Figure 7.5

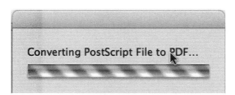

MacOS: phony progress bar with no cancel button.

Examples: Unresponsive buttons and no busy or progress indicators

Excerpts from UI reviews of three software products:

■ Product 1: When Generate Declarations is clicked, it can take up to five seconds for the window to appear, during which no feedback is provided that anything is happening. Many users will click again, and (eventually) get two Generate Declarations windows. Recommendation: When the button is clicked, the cursor should change immediately to a wait-cursor and the button should be disabled.

■ Product 2: After login, the main window appears and the program connects to its servers and downloads data. This can take 10–20 seconds. The main window's buttons appear immediately active and ready, but ignore all clicks until the initialization finishes. During initialization, the program displays "connecting to ..." and "loading ..." messages at the bottom of the window, but most users won't notice them. Recommendation: Best: Don't open the main window until the initialization is done; display a temporary "Loading—please wait" dialog box with a progress bar, so users can estimate how long loading will take. Alternative: Display the main window immediately, but deactivate its buttons and display a wait cursor until initialization is done.

■ Product 3: After Create Graph is clicked, it takes 10–60 seconds for the Create Graph dialog box to appear, with no feedback. The button doesn't even register a press. Users often click it multiple times, getting (and waiting for) several Create Graph windows. Recommendation: When clicked, the button should go inactive and display a wait cursor.

Reasons for poor responsiveness

Software applications and Web sites exhibit poor responsiveness for seven reasons.

Reason 1: The facts about responsiveness are not widely known

Although responsiveness has been repeatedly shown to be the most important factor in determining user satisfaction (Basic Principle 8, page 45), few developers know that.

Since most developers and development managers don't know how important responsiveness is, it is no surprise that they continue to churn out unresponsive software. Similarly, if customers don't fully understand the impact of responsiveness on usability, they won't demand it from software vendors.

Reason 2: UI designers rarely consider responsiveness during design

Many responsiveness bloopers are the fault of GUI designers, not of programmers. Designers rarely consider performance and responsiveness issues when designing software. They usually don't specify in their design documents what response times are desirable, acceptable, and unacceptable, but just assume that the specified functions will be fast enough. Most importantly, they don't consider how the best design might *depend* on what response times are achievable. If responses are long, a different design would be called for than if they were short or variable.

Consider scrollbars: they typically display an "elevator" to show what part of the entire document is visible, as illustrated by scrollbars from the Apple Macintosh and Microsoft Windows (Figure 7.6). Despite their superficial differences, both have an "elevator."

A responsiveness issue with scrollbars is how moving the elevator is linked to updating (i.e., scrolling) the window content. The issue is whether the scrollbar updates its appearance *while* or *after* the window content scrolls. There are two common designs:

- *While:* The elevator position is absolutely tied to that of the window content, so the elevator does not move until the content scrolls.

- *After:* The elevator follows the cursor to where the user drags it, then, when the user releases the elevator, the window content scrolls to its new position.

Figure 7.6

A   B

Scrollbars showing "elevators." (A) Macintosh OSX. (B) Windows Vista.

Which design is better depends on whether it is computationally expensive or cheap to scroll the document content to a new position. If scrolling the window content is easy and quick, the first method is better because it keeps the window content synchronized with the elevator and so provides more accurate feedback. If scrolling the window content is expensive and slow, the *second* method of operation is preferred because, with the first method, the elevator would often lag behind the user's cursor, making the elevator hard to position as desired.

If the UI designer has not specified what scrolling response times are acceptable or unacceptable, GUI programmers cannot be faulted for choosing the form of scrollbar operation that is easiest to code.

Poor responsiveness can render an otherwise nice feature useless. The software marketplace is full of nifty features that are useless because of poor responsiveness. Examples of such features were given in the list of common responsiveness bloopers.

Reason 3: Programmers equate responsiveness with performance

When a software product is not responsive enough, programmers tend to blame poor algorithms and inefficient implementation. They try to improve the algorithms and tune the performance of the application's functions. Their ideal is that all functions should execute as close to instantaneously as possible. This causes delays in release dates while programmers try to speed up unacceptably "slow" products. The software is often eventually released even though it is still slower than developers, managers, and customers had hoped.

Programmers also often blame poor responsiveness on slow computer hardware. According to this view, poor responsiveness is a trivial problem because higher performance computers will soon be available, and upgrading to those will solve the problem. This view ignores history: in the past 25 years, computer power and speed have increased by a factor of several hundred or more, yet responsiveness is still as much of a problem as ever.

Blaming poor responsiveness on a need to upgrade to faster hardware ignores the real world. Customers usually have less powerful computers and slower net connections than the software's developers have (Blooper 70, page 370). Computer companies release new, more powerful models every year, but customers don't upgrade that often. The programmers' faster computers and Internet connections may take years to appear in significant numbers in the marketplace. Furthermore, customers often run software under higher load than the developers anticipated (Responsiveness Principle 2, page 304).

Reason 4: Programmers treat user input like machine input

Programmers often assume that people control software in the same ways that software controls other software. Some applications don't distinguish being operated by a person from being driven by another program. Figure 7.7 presents an example, depicted as poor person-to-person communication. Do you recognize any applications you've used?

Equating human input with input from other software leads to naive design rules. One naive rule is that user input, like that from a machine, must be processed in the order received (Responsiveness Principle 5, page 307). Another naive rule is that all user input is important; none should be lost or ignored. Sometimes user input *should* be ignored (Responsiveness Principle 7, page 309).

One reason programmers often treat interaction with human users like interaction with other software is that they and their managers prefer simple, easy-to-code implementations (see Reason 5). Another is that programmers understand the behavioral characteristics of computers and software much better than the perceptual, motor, and cognitive characteristics of human users, so they pay more attention to the requirements of programmatic control.

Reason 5: Developers use simple implementations

Developers often use simple algorithms, data structures, architectures, and protocols to minimize schedule risk and maintenance costs. They favor implementations that are easy to program, e.g., single-threaded and synchronous. Their managers support them in this. This often hinders the goal of making software responsive. Figure 7.8 presents examples of simple implementations that harm responsiveness, disguised as poor person-to-person communication.

I once encountered a fax machine with a naïve implementation. I loaded a document, punched in a number, and told it to transmit. The fax flashed

Figure 7.7

> *Event queue is first-in-first-out. Human operators pay attention to external feedback, not the number of commands they've issued.*
> "OK, back' 'er up juuust a tad. A little more ...... more ...... more ...... more ......
> more ...... more ...... more ...... a little more ...... OK, stop. Stop! STOP!"
> (CRRRRUNNNNCH!!!)
> "Aw, man! Why didn't you stop when I said 'stop'?"
> "Because I got behind on the 'mores' and still had some to process before
> I got to your Stop command.

Human–human communication depicting software that treats human input like machine input.

Figure 7.8

> *A: Synchronous dialog; requests completely independent of each other; no anticipation of likely future requests.*
>
> "Hello, my '07 Toyota Prius needs new shock absorbers. Do you sell Acme shocks?"
> "Dunno. I'll check the warehouse. Please wait."
> (caller drums fingers on table for two minutes)
> (salesman returns to phone) "Yes."
> "How much do they cost?""Hang on. I'll check."
> (caller drums fingers for another minute)
> "They're $55 each installed.""What about Excelsior shocks?"
> "Dunno. I'll check the warehouse. Please wait..."
>
> *B: UI ignores weight of operation: provides no lightweight, quick feedback.*
>
> "Let's try putting the piano here."
> (mover moves piano to indicated location)
> "No, that doesn't work. How about over by the window?"
> (mover moves piano)
> "That's even worse. Let's try here..."
>
> *C: Event queue is first-in-first-out. No recognition that re-ordering tasks could save work.*
>
> (An apartment building custodian starts his day) "Let's see. What's first on my list for today? Sweep hallway floors. OK, let's do it!"
> (sweeps floors)
> "OK, that's done. What's next? Sand baseboards in hallway. OK..."

Poor responsiveness resulting from naïve, simplistic implementations.

"Add toner." I thought, "Huh? It shouldn't need toner to transmit." I waited. It insisted that I add toner. I didn't know how, so I asked someone for help, who explained that the fax wouldn't transmit when out of toner or paper, because it printed a confirmation when done. My task was blocked because the fax couldn't print a confirmation I didn't want. The developers chose a simple implementation to minimize their risk. The fax's users paid the cost of that choice.

Reason 6: GUI software tools, components, and platforms are inadequate

Because responsiveness is so important for user satisfaction, it may seem odd that software developers opt for overly simple implementations that hinder responsiveness. Don't they know that they are limiting demand for their products?

Often, they know, but their tools do not provide the support they need to create responsive software. Most GUI toolkits (for Windows, MacOS, Linux, and Java) make it hard to write software that meets real-time deadlines and prioritizes tasks at runtime.

Even responsiveness enhancements that should be easy are difficult. Displaying a busy cursor in Java or Windows requires writing multithreaded code, even if nothing else in the application requires multiple threads. This increases the level of programming complexity immensely. No wonder some developers don't bother displaying busy cursors.

Reason 7: Managers hire GUI programmers who lack the required skill

Contributing to a lack of responsiveness in GUI-based software is a lack of UI skill and experience among GUI programmers (Blooper 64, page 331). This almost guarantees that subtle aspects of GUI design and implementation, such as responsiveness, will be shortchanged.

This problem is exacerbated by the fact that writing responsive software often requires real-time and multithreaded programming. As described under Reason 6, GUI software tools, components, and platforms provide poor support for that, placing the burden on programmers. A software development manager and programmer explained:

> Multithreaded applications are hard. They require hiring expensive senior developers and often take a long time to debug and maintain.

Of course, some developers do manage to write real-time software. The software in fighter planes, missiles, factory robots, nuclear power plants, and space probes is heavily oriented toward satisfying real-time constraints. The problem is not that no one knows how to write real-time software. Rather, the problem is that the economics of the desktop and Web software industry, along with a lack of understanding among software developers of the importance of responsiveness, discourage development managers from hiring programmers who have the skill to write responsive applications.

Avoiding responsiveness bloopers: Design principles

This section describes and illustrates seven responsiveness design principles, which define what it means to be responsive and suggest how to achieve it.

Responsiveness Principle 1: Responsiveness is not the same as performance

Software can be responsive even if is slow. If you call someone to ask a question, he can be responsive even if he can't answer your question immediately:

he can acknowledge the question and promise to call back. He can be even more responsive by saying *when* he will call back.

Conversely, software can have poor responsiveness even if it is fast. Even if a watch repairman is very fast at fixing watches, he is unresponsive if you walk into his shop and he ignores you until he finishes working on another watch. He is unresponsive if you hand him your watch and he silently walks away without saying whether he is going to fix it now or go to lunch. Even if he starts working on your watch immediately, he is unresponsive if he doesn't tell you whether fixing it will take five minutes or five hours.

Personal computers are many times faster today than they were 20 years ago, but we users still wait a lot and wonder what is happening, so speed is obviously not the whole story. Nowadays most of our waiting is for network delays and massive data transfers.

Responsiveness Principle 2: Processing resources are always limited

The faster computers get, the more software people will load onto them: desk accessories, multiple applications, instant message client applications. Also, the faster computers get, the more users will try to have their computers do at once: playing music while editing a document, downloading data or software while browsing Web pages, printing long documents while doing other work. Peter Bickford put it this way in his book *Interface Design* [1997]:

> Macintosh II users rejoiced at a computer that effectively ran at four times the speed of the Macintosh Plus, and then willingly gave up much of the potential speed increase to run in color. As machines continued to get more powerful, users added 24-bit video, file-sharing, sound input and output, desktop movies, and so on. There's no real end to this trend in sight.

Also, as previously stated, customers probably have slower computers than the developers have. Even having the latest model computer doesn't mean that more computing resources will be available to a particular application.

Responsiveness Principle 3: The user interface is a real-time interface

Like software that controls aircraft, software that interacts with people needs to meet real-time constraints. Three time constants in human behavior set goals that software must meet in order to be perceived as responsive [Nielsen, 1993; Robertson et al., 1989, 1993]:

- *0.1 second:* This is the limit for perception of cause-and-effect between events. If software waits longer than 0.1 second to show a response to your action, cause-and-effect is broken: the software's reaction will not seem to be a result of your action. Therefore, on-screen buttons have 0.1 second to show they've been clicked; otherwise users will click again. If an object the user is "dragging" lags more than 0.1 second behind the cursor, users will have trouble placing it. This 0.1-second deadline is what HCI researcher Stuart Card calls the perceptual "moment." It is also close to the limit for perception of smooth animation: 0.063 second/frame (16 frames/second).

- *1 second:* This is the approximate normal length of gaps in a conversation. When gaps exceed 1 second, one participant will say something to keep the conversation going, even if only "uh" or "uh-huh." Similarly, software has about 1 second to either do what the user asked or indicate how long it will take; otherwise, users get impatient. One second is also the approximate minimum response time for reacting to unanticipated events, as when a child suddenly runs in front of a driver's car. In human–computer interaction, when information suddenly appears on the screen, users take at least a second to react to it.

- *10 seconds:* This is the approximate unit of time into which people usually break down their planning and execution of larger tasks. Card and his colleagues call this the "unit task" time constant. It is the approximate amount of time people can concentrate exclusively on one task. Every 10 seconds or so, people look up from their task, reassess their task status and their surroundings, relax, and so on. After 10 seconds, users want to mark a unit task complete and move on to the next one. This time constant has been observed across a range of tasks, such as completing a single edit in a text editor, entering a check into a checking account program, and executing a maneuver in an airplane dogfight. In human–computer interaction, 10 seconds is roughly the amount of time users are willing to spend setting up "heavyweight" operations like file transfers or searches—any longer and users start to lose patience. Computing the result can then take longer if progress feedback is given.

Each of these time constants is an approximation of several precise time constants observed in human perceptual, motor, and cognitive tasks.[2] The actual time constants are more precise than is needed for UI design. The three approximate time constants were set to make them easy to remember (Table 7.1).

---

2. The maximum interframe interval for smooth animation is less than 0.1 second: it is 0.063 second (16 frames/second). The average unprepared reaction time in driving is slightly less than 1 second: it is 0.7 second. The 10-second time constant is an approximation of several psychological time constants ranging from 5 to 30 seconds.

Table 7.1 The three time constants for human–computer interaction [from Robertson et al., 1989, 1993]

Time constant	Aspect of human behavior it applies to	Relevance in human–computer interaction
0.1 second	▪ Perception of successive events ▪ Perception of cause–effect ▪ Perceptual fusion, e.g., perception of smooth animation*	▪ Feedback for successful hand–eye coordination, e.g., pointer movement, window movement and sizing, drawing operations ▪ Feedback that a button has been clicked ▪ Displaying "busy" indicators ▪ Max interval between animation frames*
1 second	▪ Turn-taking in conversation, e.g., pause between utterances ▪ Minimum response time, for unexpected events	▪ Displaying progress indicators ▪ Finishing most user requested operations e.g., opening a dialog box ▪ Finishing unrequested operations, e.g., autosaving
10 seconds	▪ Unbroken concentration on a task ▪ Unit task: completing one "unit" task in a larger task	▪ Completing one step of a multistep task, e.g., a single edit in a text editor, entering a check into a checking account program ▪ Completing user input to an operation ▪ Completing one step in a wizard (a multipage dialog box)

*Actually 0.063 second.

Responsiveness Principle 4: All delays are not equal: software need not do everything immediately

Some events require immediate feedback; some don't. Software can therefore prioritize its handling of user events in order to give timely feedback where it is needed and delay other tasks.

As described above, for hand–eye coordination tasks, keystroke-level feedback must be immediate to be effective. Internal bookkeeping, updating areas of the screen where users aren't working, results of explicitly requested calculations or searches need not be immediate.

The classic UI design handbook *Human–Computer Interface Design Guidelines* [Brown, 1988] uses the concept of task "closure" to determine when software response delays are acceptable or unacceptable:

> A key factor determining acceptable response delays is level of closure.... A delay after completing a major unit of work may not bother a user or adversely affect performance. Delays between minor steps in a larger unit of work, however, may cause the user to forget the next planned steps. In general, actions with high levels of closure, such as saving a completed document to a file, are less sensitive to response time delays. Actions at the lowest levels of closure, such as typing a character and seeing it echoed on the display, are most sensitive to response time delays.

Trying to make all system responses equally fast cannot succeed. Everything can't happen at once and even if it could, users couldn't perceive it all.

Instant responses to certain user actions can even be *undesirable*. Faster is not always better. Users don't trust complex searches or computations that finish too quickly. A slight delay, blink, animation, or other feedback may be needed when a display changes to make users notice the change or believe that work was done. Many old computer games can't be played on today's computers because they were optimized for maximum speed on slow computers and run too fast on newer ones. Thus, the deadlines given for different types of feedback are not simply maximums, they are goals.

Responsiveness Principle 5: Software need not do tasks in the order in which they were requested

As with the janitor who first swept and then sanded (Figure 7.8C), performing tasks in a naïve, first-in–first-out order can create extra work, hurting responsiveness.

Intelligently reordering tasks in one's queue can save work and time, enhancing responsiveness. Tasks should be reordered so high-priority tasks are attended to first.

Responsiveness Principle 6: Software need not do everything it was asked to do

Sometimes an operation you request is unnecessary. Suppose you are editing a document and tell the software to save it. If you haven't changed anything since the last time you saved, there is no reason for the software to waste time resaving it. Instead, the software can just indicate that the file is saved. Many applications do that, but some save a document every time you tell them to. That can be annoying if you have the habit of hitting "Save" every few minutes to guard against software crashes, especially if the document takes a long time to save.

If a queued task becomes moot before the software has started on it, there is no reason to do it; it can simply be dropped. Figure 7.9 presents examples of people doing unnecessary work because they start a queued task without first

Figure 7.9

> *A: Tackling a large, difficult task based upon prior instructions, without rechecking their validity before starting.*
>
> "Here it is! I postponed my family's vacation and worked overtime all week to make sure I got the Smith proposal done on time."
>
> "Oh? Didn't someone tell you? We've decided not to go after the Smith contract."
>
> *B: Tackling a large, difficult task based upon default assumptions, not knowing until too late that the task is moot.*
>
> "Well, if it isn't the new owners! Come on in!"
>
> "We just stopped by to take some measurements."
>
> "Really? You're in luck. We just finished measuring the whole place. As you can see, we're putting in the new carpeting that we promised in the sale agreement. We'd intended to replace it before we put the house on the market, but didn't get around to it."
>
> "Oh? Well, don't bother. We like hardwood floors, so we're planning to rip out the carpet."

Poor responsiveness due to failure to check whether queued tasks were moot.

checking whether it is still wanted. If a task becomes moot *while* it is being executed, it can be aborted.

If it can be predicted before a task is started that it cannot be done on time, maybe there is no reason to do it. Figure 7.1B depicted two parties entering into a transaction without communicating time requirements and estimates, dooming themselves to failure.

Some requests are frivolous and evaporate completely when it is revealed that fulfilling them is not free. Fulfilling such requests at all is a waste of time and resources. Figure 7.10 presents an example of eliminating a request by explaining how much it would cost.

Apple's iMovie sometimes doesn't follow this principle. When you tell it to save a movie you've been editing, it displays a dialog box showing the progress of the save operation. That's good. It's also good that the dialog box provides a "Cancel" button. What is bad is that the "Cancel" button ignores you until the save is done. Apparently, the Cancel command can't get to the front of the queue while a save is in progress.

Figure 7.10

> Some requests are frivolous, and evaporate when it is revealed that fulfilling them is not free.
>
> "Can you print this document in color?"
>
> "Yes, but it will take an hour (or cost $100)."
>
> "Ack! Forget it! I don't want it that much."

Saving unnecessary work by communicating costs and unwillingness to pay them.

Responsiveness Principle 7: Human users are not computer programs

Users operate software differently than computer programs do. They cannot sustain high rates of input for very long. They may be able to keep the system busy for several seconds (about 10, maximum), but then they pause to think or rest.

People are not single-channel input/output devices. People can do several things in parallel:

- Read a book while humming a tune
- Tune to a station on a radio with one hand while steering a car with the other
- Play a melody on an organ keyboard with their hands while playing a bass line on the organ's pedals with their feet
- Walk and chew gum at the same time (well, some people, anyway)
- Type text or play music while reading ahead to the next text or music
- Talk on the telephone while making dinner

Software users perceive the results of their actions with their eyes and ears while they operate the software with their hands. As illustrated by the example about the vehicle backing up (Figure 7.7), users pay attention mainly to the feedback they receive from the software, rather than keeping track of the actions they have performed. They don't know how many times they've pressed Down or Next or how many inches they've moved the mouse. They watch the *display* and base their decision about whether to continue on what they see there. When the cursor or a scrollbar isn't yet at their goal, they keep moving. When buttons don't acknowledge a click immediately, users assume they missed and click again.

In contrast, software that is controlling an application cannot see the screen. All it knows is what commands it issued. Since the requirements of human and software control of applications differ so greatly, the same interface cannot serve both.

Avoiding responsiveness bloopers: Techniques

Understanding principles is not enough. To produce responsive software, you need implementation techniques and methods. This section describes several. They range from simple and static to complex and dynamic. They are grouped into four categories:

- Timely feedback
- Parallel problem solution
- Queue optimization
- Dynamic time management

Most of these techniques are ways to manage time and are applicable in domains other than software. People have said that they have found some of these techniques to be useful in managing their own time and professional and personal lives. This is not a self-help book, but if you find it useful, fine!

Timely feedback

The first responsiveness techniques are about meeting the real-time deadlines that determine whether a UI is perceived as responsive or not.

Acknowledge user input immediately

Even if the software can't act on user input immediately, it should at least acknowledge receiving it. This means giving feedback for mouse and keystroke-level actions within 0.1 second. Otherwise users' perceptions of cause and effect break down and they assume their action wasn't received. Delayed acknowledgment of user actions is almost as bad as no acknowledgment.

Figure 7.11 shows an example of this approach, expressed as human-to-human communication. Contrast this with the unresponsive Fred in Figure 7.1A.

A familiar software example is a button that immediately acknowledges being clicked by changing appearance or color or by making a sound. It does not matter that the button's command may take a long time to execute. When a button detects that it has been clicked, its highest priority is to acknowledge that. All other responsibilities of the button can be delayed.

Poor Responsiveness Reason 2 (page 299) describes another example of acknowledging user input immediately: if window content is slow to display, use a scrollbar that doesn't scroll the window content until the user stops moving the scrollbar. In such cases, it would be a mistake to use a "lock-step" scrollbar that first scrolls the window content and only updates the "elevator" position after the content has been updated. "Lock-step" scrollbars are fine if the content can scroll in 0.1 second, but if not, a loosely connected scrollbar is preferable. GUI toolkits should let programmers specify which protocol will be used.

Given the speed of today's computers, there is *no* excuse for GUI components that can't acknowledge user input within 0.1 second. Today's computers execute tens of millions of instructions in that amount of time. If an object cannot acknowledge a user action within 0.1 second, that means it—or the

Figure 7.11

> *Acknowledge input immediately*
>
> "Fred, what are our plans for this weekend?"
>
> "Just a minute. I'm trying to get this idea down on paper."
>
> "OK."
>
> (eventually finishes writing) "OK... done. Our plans for this weekend? Let's see..."

Acknowledging input immediately, even though producing the answer takes time.

application that displays it or the operating system that dispatches the action to the application—is wasting time executing millions of nonessential instructions at an inappropriate time. This suggests serious architectural flaws in the object, application, and/or operating system.

Developers need to make a strong commitment to responsiveness when an application is architected. Acknowledging user input should always be the software's highest priority.

Provide busy indicators

Provide busy indicators for functions that take longer than 0.1 second. If a busy indicator can be displayed within 0.1 second, it can double as the action acknowledgment. If not, the software's response should come in two parts: a quick acknowledgment within 0.1 second, followed by a busy or progress indicator within 1 second.

A common excuse for not displaying a busy cursor is that the function is supposed to execute quickly and so doesn't need to display one. But how quickly is "quickly"? What if the function doesn't always execute quickly? What if the user has a slower computer than the developer or one that is not optimally configured? What if the function tries to access data that is temporarily locked? What if the function uses network services and the network is hung or overloaded?

Software should display a busy indicator for *any* function that blocks further user actions while it is executing, even if the function normally executes quickly (e.g., in under 0.1 second). This can be very helpful if for some reason the function gets bogged down or hung. Furthermore, it harms nothing: when the function executes at the normal speed, the busy indicator appears and disappears so quickly that users barely see it.

Modern window-based operating systems, which are user-driven, multitasking, and multithreaded, make it difficult for application programmers to ensure that busy cursors are displayed at the appropriate times and screen locations. Sometimes, an application's failure to display a busy cursor is not the application programmer's fault. One GUI programmer wrote:

> I'm trying really hard to display a busy cursor, but something out of my control keeps switching it back to a normal cursor. There's probably a way around it if I programmed hard enough.

Complicating factors include the window manager, other processes and threads changing the cursor, and faulty exception handling causing the cursor to get out of synch. Debugging such problems can be very time consuming and can require great programming skill. As a result, the blooper is common. Whatever the reason for not showing a busy cursor at the appropriate times, the effect is the same: it leaves users clueless as to what is happening and so is a blooper.

Busy indicators range in sophistication. At the low end, we have simple, static "wait" cursors (e.g., hourglass). They provide very little information: only that the software is temporarily occupied and unavailable to the user for other operations.

Next, we have "wait" animations. Some of these are animated "wait" cursors, such as the MacOS rotating color wheel. Other animated "wait" cursors are a watch with moving hands, a human hand counting with its fingers, a swinging pendulum, and an hourglass with falling sand. Some "wait" animations are not cursors, but rather larger graphics elsewhere on the screen, such as the "downloading data" animations of Web browsers. "Wait" animations are more "friendly" to users than static "wait" cursors because they show that the system is working, not crashed or hung up waiting for a network connection or a data lock.

Display progress indicators for long operations

Better than busy indicators are progress indicators, which let users see how much time remains. The deadline for displaying a progress indicator is 1 second.

Progress indicators can be graphical (e.g., a progress bar), textual (e.g., a count of files remaining to be copied), or a combination. They greatly increase the perceived responsiveness of an application, even though they don't shorten the time to complete operations.

Progress indicators are more important the longer the operation. Many noncomputer devices provide progress indicators, so we often take them for granted. Elevators that don't show the elevator car's progress toward your floor are annoying. Most people wouldn't like a microwave oven that didn't show the remaining cooking time.

McInerney and Li [2002] list guidelines for designing effective progress indicators:

- Show work remaining, not work completed. Bad: 3 files copied. Good: 4 files left to copy.

- Show total progress, not progress on current step. Bad: 5 seconds left on this step. Good: 15 seconds left.

- For percentage complete, start at 1%, not 0%. Users worry if the bar stays at 0% for more than a second or two.

- Similarly, display 100% at the end only very briefly. If the bar stays at 100% for more than a second or two, users assume it's wrong.

- Show smooth, linear progress, not erratic bursts of progress.

- Use human-scale precision, not computer precision. Bad: 27 seconds. Good: Less than 1 minute.

Examples: Progress indicators

Progress bars from Apple Mac Software Update and Adobe Update Manager are fairly well designed (Figure 7.12). They show the progress of the *entire* installation. These are *much* more useful than those shown earlier in Figures 7.2–7.5. One minor deficiency of the Mac Software Update progress bar is that it doesn't estimate the remaining time. The Adobe progress bar also has a minor flaw: its time estimate is too precise.

Software developers often hesitate to provide progress indicators because it is hard to estimate the remaining time accurately. This is an unwarranted concern. Users aren't computers; they don't require much accuracy. A progress indicator can be off by a factor of 10 and still be helpful.

A multifile transfer operation can provide a useful progress indicator by showing how many files (or what percentage of files) remain to be transferred, even though some of the files may be 1 kilobyte in size while others are 12 megabytes. Any information is better than none. Users just want to know if they should wait, take a sip of coffee, check their voice mail, or go to lunch.

Apple MacOS X displays great progress bars for multifile transfers. The display includes an estimate of the total expected time (Figure 7.13). The time

Figure 7.12

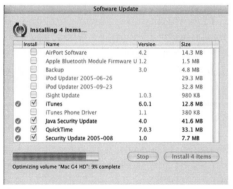

A

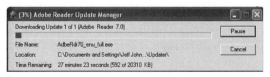

B

Acceptable progress bars show progress of whole operation. (A) MacOS software update. (B) Adobe Update Manager.

Figure 7.13

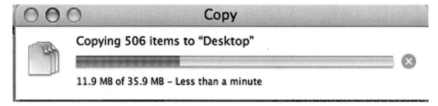

MacOS X file transfer: time estimate is only as precise as user needs.

estimate is very rough. It is often overestimated at first, but then adjusts to a more realistic value as the transfer proceeds. Apple's progress display tells users what they want to know.

Display important information first

Applications can appear faster than they are by displaying important information first, details and auxiliary information later. Don't wait until a display is fully rendered before letting users see it. Give users something to think about and act upon as soon as possible.

This has several benefits. It is a sleight-of-hand technique, like a magician who gestures flamboyantly with one hand to distract observers from what the other hand is doing. It distracts users from the fact that the rest of the information isn't there yet and fools them into believing that the computer did what they asked quickly. It lets users start planning what they are going to do next. Finally, because of the minimum response time for users to respond to what they see (see Table 7.1), it buys at least 1 more second for the software to catch up before the user tries to do anything. A second is a lot of time to a computer.

If it would take too much time to display everything the user asks to see, software can be designed to display certain information first. Here are some examples:

- Stock investment Web site: While you wait for your "Current Investments" page to load, the names of the stocks you own and their current market prices are displayed.
- Document-editing software: When you open a document, it shows the first screenful of information as soon as it has it, rather than waiting until it has loaded the entire document before displaying anything.
- Database or Web search facility: It lists some found items as soon as it has them, while continuing to search for more matching items.

If information is displayed in a time-consuming, complex format, the application can display the information in a simplified form quickly, replacing or elaborating it later. Images that appear at low resolution first and then are rerendered at full resolution are a good example.

Example of an early software program designed for responsiveness

In the early 1970s, many time-shared computer systems had a "time-of-day" utility program that displayed the current time. One displayed a graphical image of a clock. The clock showed the time with clock hands, rather than digits, and was very fancy and decorated. Computers and graphics displays were much slower then; the complete drawing, an elaborate Swiss cuckoo clock, took many minutes to display.

Whoever wrote the program realized that the clock displayed slowly and that people wouldn't want to wait long just to find out what time it was. The program was therefore designed so that the first thing it drew was two simple lines representing the clock's two hands (Figure 7.14). That took only a fraction of a second. It showed the approximate time immediately. Next came the numbers 3, 6, 9, and 12, giving a better idea of the time. The remaining numbers followed. Next, the program drew the clock's outline. Finally, the program began elaborating the clock's hands and numbers and adding decorations. At any point along the way, a user could stop the program by pressing Esc.

If users just wanted to know what time it was, they stopped the program after it drew the hands. Sometimes they waited until the numbers appeared to be sure they were reading the time correctly. If users were showing the "cool cuckoo clock" to a friend, they let it run to completion. That clock was an outstanding example of how software can be designed to be responsive even if its performance is slow.

Figure 7.14

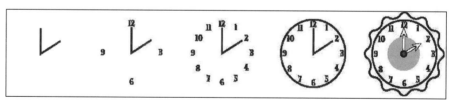

Clock displayed slowly, but put up the most important information first.

Fake heavyweight computations

In interactive software, some user actions require rapid successive adjustments until the goal is achieved. Examples include NEXTing through a set of postings, scrolling through a document, moving a game character through a landscape, resizing a window, or dragging an object to a new position. If feedback lags behind user actions, users will have trouble achieving their goal. When your software cannot update its data fast enough to keep up with users, provide lightweight simulated feedback until the goal is clear, then apply the real operation (Figure 7.15).

Figure 7.15

Provide feedback using a "lightweight" simulation until the adjustments cease

"Let's try putting the piano here."
"OK, but to save strain on my back, I brought a cardboard piano that we can move around until you know where you want it, then I'll bring the real piano in and put it there."

Avoiding unnecessary work by faking feedback while a user is still making adjustments.

Graphics editors fake feedback when they provide rubber-band outlines of objects that a user is trying to move or resize. Some document editors make quick-and-dirty changes to internal document data structures to represent the effect of user actions and straighten things out later.

Providing timely feedback on the Web

Readers who develop mainly Web software may have dismissed the time deadlines discussed in Responsiveness Principle 3 (page 304) as pure fantasy.

It is true that meeting those deadlines on the Web is difficult—usually even impossible. However, it is also true that those deadlines are psychological time constants, wired into us by millions of years of evolution, that govern our perception of responsiveness. They are not arbitrary targets that can be adjusted to match the limitations of the Web or of any technology platform. If your software does not meet those deadlines, users will consider its responsiveness to be poor, period. That means most Web software has poor responsiveness. The question is: what can you do to improve it? Here are some approaches:

- Minimize the size and number of images
- Provide quick-to-display thumbnail images or overviews, with ways to show details only as needed
- Break large amounts of data into smaller parts and provide ways to navigate through the parts
- Style and lay out pages using cascading style sheets instead of presentational HTML, frames, or tables
- Use built-in browser components where available instead of constructing them in HTML
- Download applets and scripts to the browser; use AJAX methods [Garrett, 2005]
- Use browser-side animation, e.g., Flash, in limited ways [Nielsen, 2002; Perfetti, 2005]

Parallel problem solution

A step upward in sophistication is to use one of two parallel processing methods: *delaying work* and *working ahead*.

Delay noncritical work

Non-time-critical work can be delegated to background processes, freeing the main process to respond to users. Delegate long tasks for which users don't require immediate feedback, such as the software's own internal housekeeping or requests that users expect to take a long time.

Figure 7.16 illustrates this approach. Unlike in Figure 7.1C, the caller here is freed to do other things while waiting for the answer.

Some office fax machines quickly scan document pages into their memory and transmit them later, allowing users to return to other activities. Fax machines that do this are more responsive.

When a delegated task isn't done by a separate computer, this technique gives the computer several tasks to juggle at once. It runs the risk of bogging the entire computer down, thereby failing to do what it is intended to do: free the main process to be responsive to users. To lower that risk, assign the main process a high priority relative to the background process, so the background process can be put on hold until there is more time.

What if there isn't more time? Don't worry. Users are not computers; they can't sustain high rates of input for very long. That ensures that the background task will eventually get done.

Consider Microsoft Word. Until the mid-1990s, repaginating a document was a foreground task. You had to invoke the Repaginate command and then wait many seconds—for long documents, minutes—for it to complete before you could return to editing the document. Now, repagination in Word is a background task, executed automatically as needed, allowing you to continue editing. Spell-checking has a similar history.

Figure 7.16

> *Interaction need not be synchronous. Delegate longish tasks to agents who operate in parallel with you.*
>
> "I'd like to fly from San Francisco to New York next Thursday, returning Sunday evening, as inexpensively as possible."
>
> "OK, I'll check the flights and fares and call you back."

Spawning parallel processes to perform long tasks.

Work ahead

Work ahead of users when possible. Software can use periods of low load to precompute responses to high-probability requests. There will be periods of low load because the users are human. Interactive software typically spends a lot of time waiting for input from the user. Don't waste that time! Use it to prepare something the user will probably want. If the user never wants it, so what? The software did it in "free" time; it didn't take time away from anything else.

Figure 7.17 provides examples of working ahead, expressed as human-to-human communication. One example (Figure 7.17A) shows "smart" work-ahead: with some knowledge of the tasks, the system can make educated guesses about what the user wants. The other example (Figure 7.17B) could be called "dumb" work-ahead: instead of task knowledge, it uses the simple fact that work can start before the instructions are complete. Dumb work-ahead is not bad; it can be just as helpful as smart work-ahead.

Working ahead should be done as a very low-priority background process, so it doesn't interfere with what the user is doing. Processes that are working ahead must check constantly whether the task they are working on is still relevant and abort if not.

Here are some examples of software using background processing to work ahead of users:

- A text search function looks for the next occurrence of the target word while you look at the current one. When you tell the function to find the next occurrence of the word, it already has it and so seems very fast.

- A document viewer renders the next page while you view the current page. When you ask to see the next page, it is already ready.

Figure 7.17

> *A: Anticipate what the user will want, and use spare time to prepare things before being asked.*
> "Here are the overheads for your talk. Also, I figured you'd want paper copies to hand out to the audience, so I made 20."
> "Thanks, Fred, you're a godsend!"
>
> *B: Even without task knowledge, it is possible to work ahead of users.*
> "And what would you like for the main course?"
> "Hmmm. We haven't decided yet. -There's so much to choose from!"
> "Well, while you decide, I'll go get your appetizer started and fetch your wine. -When I return, you can tell me what you want."

Work ahead of the user to make the software seem faster.

Queue optimization

The basic idea of queue optimization is to review the to-do list periodically to decide what tasks to do and in what order. Two different ways to optimize a task queue are:

- reordering it, also known as "nonsequential input processing," and
- flushing tasks from it that have become moot.

Nonsequential input processing

The order in which tasks are done often matters. Blindly doing tasks in the order in which they were requested may waste time and resources or even create extra work. Software should look for opportunities to reorder tasks in its queue. Sometimes reordering tasks can make completing the entire set more efficient, as is illustrated by Figure 7.18. Contrast this with the naïve approach illustrated in Figure 7.8C.

Airline personnel use nonsequential input processing when they walk up and down long check-in lines looking for people whose flights are leaving very soon so they can pull them out of line and get them checked in.

In Web browsers, clicking the Back or Stop buttons or on a displayed link *immediately* aborts any ongoing activity to load and display the current page. Given how long it can take to load and display a Web page, the ability to abort a page load is crucial to user acceptance.

Flush tasks that have become moot

Sometimes tasks on a to-do list become moot. Goals or requirements may change, deadlines for tasks may expire, recent requests may supersede earlier ones. Software can scan the queue so that moot tasks can be recognized and flushed from the queue or, if they have already been started, aborted. Doing

Figure 7.18

Pre-scan the queue and optimize its order.
(An apartment building custodian starts his day)
"Let's see. What's first on my list for today? Sweep hallway floors. Sand baseboards in hallway. Repaint stairway banisters."
"Well, let's see...... I won't bother sweeping until after I've sanded, because sanding will leave dust and grit everywhere. If I paint the banisters first, I'll have to wait a day or two for the paint to dry before I can sand the baseboards. So I'd better sand, then sweep, then paint."

Prescanning the task queue and reordering tasks.

Figure 7.19

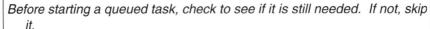

Before starting a queued task, check to see if it is still needed. If not, skip it.
"Well, if it isn't the new owners! Come on in!"
"We just stopped by to take some measurements."
"Really? We tried to call you but you must have been on your way over here. We promised in the sale-agreement to replace the old carpet. We ripped out the old carpet, but we wanted to double-check with you to make sure you want the new carpet."
"Well, you're in luck. We've decided to expose the hardwood floors, so we won't need the new carpet. But thanks for ripping out the old stuff!"

Checking the task queue to drop tasks that have become moot.

this can save a lot of wasted time and effort. This technique can be described as "faking speed by doing only what is necessary, not all that was requested." Figure 7.19 illustrates the technique, contrasting with Figure 7.9B.

A software example can be found in the EMACS text editor. EMACS provides both absolute-move commands (e.g., "move cursor to line 10") and relative-move commands (e.g., "move cursor 6 lines ahead"). Suppose EMACS is behind in processing your commands. It prescans its input queue and if it finds "move to line 26," it can skip any earlier queued "move down 3 lines" commands. A related technique used by some text editors is to combine eight up-arrow keypresses and three down-arrow keypresses found in the queue into five up-arrow keypresses.

Responsiveness Principle 7 (page 309) mentioned an important technique for maximizing the responsiveness of the mouse: delete or ignore any queued cursor movements. Users pay attention to the position of the cursor, not to the distance they've moved the pointing device. Moving the cursor is a hand–eye coordination task and so requires immediate feedback. Cursor-movement events are such a high priority that an operating system (OS) should process them as fast as the user generates them, but if it can't for some reason and falls behind, the OS should simply skip the queued cursor-movement events. Stated simply: queued cursor movements are moot by definition. Processing queued cursor-movement events is *always* wrong. The same is true for any relative-movement pointing device.

Dynamic time management

The most complex of the categories of responsiveness techniques is dynamic time management. The other techniques are static, design-time strategies for prioritizing and handling user input. Dynamic time management involves changing strategies at *runtime*, depending on what is happening at the moment. Dynamic time management is sometimes referred to as "real-time" programming, although that term usually refers to interfaces between computers and instruments, rather than between computers and users.

Four types of dynamic time management can help in implementing responsive UIs.

Monitor event queue; adjust strategy if not keeping up with user

Software can monitor its event queue and adjust its strategy if it isn't keeping up with the user. It can keep track of how many events are backlogged on the queue and switch to a faster strategy if the queue is too full. Banks, supermarkets, and highway toll plazas use exactly this strategy when they add tellers, checkout clerks, or toll takers when lines are long.

The WordStar document editor from the 1980s used dynamic queue processing to be responsive despite the severely limited performance of the 1-MHz 8080 and Z-80 processors on which it ran. Fast typists could easily cause document editors of that day, including WordStar, to lag behind in processing keystrokes. When lagging behind, most document editors in those days would queue up keystrokes and process them in the order received, so the display at any given time reflected not what the user had typed, but where the program was in processing its queue. In contrast, WordStar made sure that characters the user typed were visible immediately. When the user got ahead of it, WordStar changed its strategy: it concentrated on getting typed characters up onto the screen and stopped wrapping words, updating cursor position indicators, and tending to other niceties until the user slowed down.

Although today's computers are over 1000 times faster than the computers on which WordStar ran, many of today's applications are *less* responsive than WordStar. This is partly because today's applications do far more than their 1980s counterparts and partly because their designers didn't place a high priority on providing prompt feedback. High performance doesn't guarantee high responsiveness.

Monitor time compliance; decrease quality or quantity of work to keep up

Monitoring the length of the input queue is a fairly gross way for software to measure how well it is keeping up with users. A more precise way is to time itself: monitor its compliance with real-time deadlines. If the software isn't meeting its deadlines, it can decrease the quality or quantity of its work in order to catch up.

In this approach, the designer specifies—explicitly, in the code—maximum acceptable completion times for each operation, and the software continuously times itself to evaluate how well it is meeting its deadlines. If the software is missing deadlines or determines that it is at risk of missing a pending deadline, it adopts simpler, faster methods of doing its work, usually resulting in a temporary reduction in the quality or quantity of its output. This approach must be based on *real* time, not on processor cycles, so it yields the same responsiveness on different computers.

Some interactive animation software uses this technique. As described under Responsiveness Principle 3 (page 304), 16 frames/second is required for a succession of images to be perceived as smooth animation. Stuart Card and his associates developed a software "engine" for presenting interactive animations that treats the frame rate as the most important aspect of the animation [Robertson et al., 1989, 1993]. If the engine has trouble maintaining 16 frames/second because the images are complex or the user is moving them, it begins sacrificing other aspects of the images: text labels, three-dimensional effects, highlighting and shading, color, and so on. The idea is that it is better to reduce an animated 3D image of an airplane temporarily to a simple line drawing than it is to let the frame rate drop below 16/second.

The Cone Tree, developed at PARC, is an interactive display of a hierarchical data structure, such as file directories and subdirectories (Figure 7.20). Users can grab any part of the tree and rotate the tree. The rotation animates smoothly. While the tree rotates, the software might not have time to render all details of each frame while maintaining 16 frames/second. In that case, it might save time by rendering the file name labels on each folder as black blobs instead of as legible text. When the animation stops, the software displays the tree in full detail. Most users don't even notice a degradation of the image during the movement, because they attribute their inability to read the labels to motion blur.

A straightforward way to make software operate in a deadline-driven manner is to start with a gross approximation of the desired result and generate successively better approximations until time runs out. A clock-drawing function operating under a real-time deadline could use the strategy illustrated in Figure 7.14, rendering successively fancier clocks into a hidden display buffer, displaying the latest one when the deadline arrives.

Predict completion time; decide how to perform task

Even better than having software measure how well it *has been* doing is to have it predict how well it *will* do and decide based on those predictions how to proceed. This type of dynamic time management requires that software services and functions be able to estimate how long they will take.

When you click on a scrollbar and start dragging, the scrollbar could ask the window containing the to-be-scrolled content how long it would take to scroll the content a few pixels. If the window replies it would take 0.1 second or less, the scrollbar would do the scroll operation; otherwise, the scrollbar would move the scrollbar with the cursor and do the scroll operation after you release the elevator in its final position.

One use of time predictions is to avoid problems of simpler dynamic time management schemes. Simply tracking past compliance to real-time deadlines and adjusting the quality of work as necessary can cause undesirable oscillations. Consider an animation program that adjusts its rendering quality

Figure 7.20

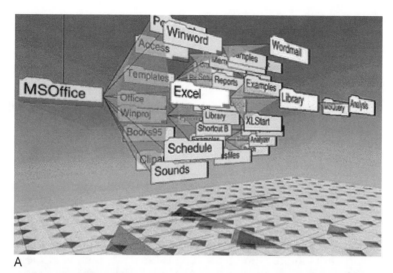

A

B

Cone Tree (A) renders folder labels as blobs while user rotates tree (B).

based on the average frame rate it has achieved over the last 10 frames. If the last 10 frames were rendered too slowly (i.e., at under 16 frames/second), it might decrease the image quality to a level that can be easily rendered in the required time. Soon, it is rendering frames too quickly or has free time available, so it increases the rendering quality, causing the frame rate to drop again, and so on, back and forth. Basing rendering quality on predicted time compliance as well as past time compliance can eliminate such oscillations.

Figure 7.21

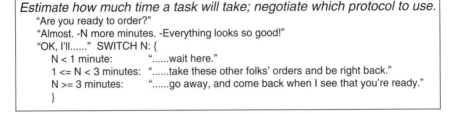

Spawning parallel processes to perform long tasks.

Software can also use time predictions to decide whether to do a task in the foreground or background. Software that is preparing to execute a function first asks the function for a time estimate. It then uses the estimate to decide whether to execute the function in the foreground (meaning that it will wait for the function to complete) or in a background process (which frees the calling process to do other work). Figure 7.21 illustrates this method, expressed as person-to-person communication.

In the dynamic approach, the decision about whether to execute the function as a foreground versus a background task is made at *runtime*, not design time. If a function always takes about the same amount of time, the decision about whether to run it in the foreground or background can be made when the software is written. Postponing the decision until runtime is necessary only if the time required by the function varies widely, e.g., if it depends on system load or availability of network resources.

Suppose you tell your e-mail program to fetch new e-mail. If the program sees that there isn't much mail, it could download the mail as a foreground task, tying up the UI briefly. If the program sees that there is a *lot* of e-mail, it could do it in a background task, letting you return to composing or reading e-mail (and telling you what it is doing).

Predict time compliance; negotiate quality or whether to do task at all

Finally, software can predict whether it will complete a task on time and, based on that prediction, negotiate the quality of its work or whether to do the task at all. This is the most sophisticated type of dynamic time management. The idea is that when an application prepares to invoke a function, it negotiates with the function about the quality and completion time. If the application and function can agree on the trade-off between quality and completion time, the function is executed; otherwise, it isn't. To be able to negotiate:

- The application must be able to state its deadlines. These can be hard-coded into it.

- The application must be able to state its quality requirements. These can be hard-coded.

- The function must at least be able to predict its completion time and indicate the quality of its work. Ideally, it should offer a range of quality levels with different completion times.

- A negotiation protocol must exist for finding the highest quality result that can be done within the deadline.

Most slide presentation applications—e.g., Microsoft Powerpoint—offer transitions between slides, such as fade, wipe, zoom, and page flip. Animated transitions are supposed to be smooth and quick, but can be shown on computers of varying speeds. When a presenter clicks to change slides, the application can negotiate with the transition function to find the best quality transition (image quality and number of frames) that can be shown in the required time on this particular computer. If the negotiation fails to find any acceptable version of the transition, the slide application simply switches the slides without animation.

Recall Figure 7.1C, in which the two people in a camera repair shop fail to mention their time requirements and so unintentionally blunder into a scheduling disaster. In contrast, Figure 7.22 presents situations in which the parties *do* communicate and negotiate their requirements, with better results.

Techniques involving runtime negotiation between software components may seem complicated. However, they are no more complicated than industry-standard protocols by which software components negotiate at runtime to find the best common format for a data transfer, e.g., ActiveX.

Figure 7.22

> **A**: *Some requests are time-dependent.*
> "Can you type this memo for me?"
> "I'm pretty busy. How soon do you need it? I can perhaps get to it tomorrow afternoon."
> "I need it in two hours. Never mind. I'll find someone else to do it or do it myself."
>
> **B**: *People will often accept something of lesser quality if more quality costs more.*
> "Can we get the documents for tomorrow's presentation copied in color?"
> "Yes, but I'll have to send it to Reprographics. They usually have a two day turnaround, so I'll have to submit it as a rush order, which raises the cost to 50 cents a page. Given the amount of stuff to copy, I figure it would cost us about $500."
> "Sigh. Just copy them on our own black-and-white copier."

Negotiating time and quality requirements to decide whether to do tasks.

Summary of responsiveness techniques

- Timely feedback
    - Acknowledge user input immediately (within 0.1 second).
    - Provide busy indicators or progress indicators for operations that take > 1 second.
    - Show important information first.
    - Fake heavyweight computations until final.
- Parallel problem solution
    - Delay work until there is time to do it.
    - Work ahead where possible.
- Queue optimization
    - Reorder the input queue for efficiency.
    - Flush tasks that have become moot.
- Dynamic time management
    - Monitor event queue; adjust strategy or resources if too far behind.
    - Monitor time compliance; decrease quality or quantity to keep up.
    - Predict response time; decide how to perform task.
    - Predict time compliance; negotiate quality, whether to do task at all.

Conclusion

Using the above techniques, you can create software that:

- lets users know instantly that their actions were received,
- lets users estimate how long lengthy operations will take,
- frees users to do other things while waiting for an operation to complete,
- manages queued events intelligently and efficiently,
- performs housekeeping and low-priority tasks in the background,
- makes use of idle time to anticipate (and precompute) users' likely future requests.

However, for responsive software to become common, the software industry must recognize that responsiveness is:

- of great importance to users,
- different from performance,

- not purely an implementation issue,
- not solvable merely by performance tuning or faster hardware.

Until these facts are widely recognized, software users will find themselves grinding their teeth, wondering what their computer is doing or whether it has crashed.

History shows that faster processors will not solve the problem. Even when personal computers and electronic appliances are as powerful as today's most powerful supercomputers, responsiveness will still be an issue because the software of that day will demand much more from the machines and the networks connecting them. For example, future software applications will probably be based on:

- deductive reasoning;
- image recognition;
- real-time speech generation;
- communication;
- data encryption, authentication, and compression techniques;
- downloading terabyte files;
- wireless communication between dozens of household appliances;
- collation of data from thousands of remote databases;
- complex searches through the entire Web.

The result will be applications that place a much heavier load on the computer than today's applications do. As computers grow more powerful, history shows that much of that power is eaten up by applications that demand ever more processing power.

Additionally, the growing use of cheap embedded computers means that not all computers of the future will have faster processors and more memory than today's desktop, laptop, and server computers. Thirty years from now, the 7th edition of this book could have figures consisting of flexible flat-panel touchscreens presenting interactive examples of bloopers. Each one might be driven by its own tiny embedded computer with only the power of today's top-of-the-line laptops. Performance and responsiveness would be as much of an issue in those displays as they are in today's computers.

It is time to start treating responsiveness as a usability issue and, more specifically, as a user-interface *design* issue. An important one.

Management
Bloopers

Introduction

The main cause of UI bloopers in software is not mistakes by the programmers. The programmers are usually doing the best they can under adverse circumstances. The adverse circumstances are created by their management. This chapter presents common ways that development organizations hinder the development of usable, useful software.

Lipstick on bulldogs

User interface consultants are often called in by companies to review, critique, and improve a product's bad UI shortly before release. In that role, we are often like a participant in a dysfunctional relationship with a self-destructive person. Our role is to smooth over the problem of the moment—the unusable product—with no mandate or resources to correct the flawed processes and attitudes that produced it. There are two problems with this.

First, "smoothing over" is a good way to describe what can be done late in development; only superficial improvements are possible. Deep, substantial improvements are ruled out due to insufficient time or will. A colleague called these last-minute attempts to rescue a bad UI "smearing lipstick on a bulldog" (Figure 8.1).

Figure 8.1

Trying to fix up a UI at the end of development is like putting lipstick on a bulldog.

Second, the limited role of UI consultants makes it difficult to leave companies better off than when we started. Clients hire us to identify their product's usability flaws and suggest how to fix them quickly and cheaply. They usually do not hire us to help them correct the development processes, organizational structure, or company culture that allowed an unusable product—or one that doesn't match any customer need—to be developed. Sometimes it seems that UI consultants help companies ignore, and therefore perpetuate, their real problem.

Breaking the cycle

To help the industry cease its dysfunctional behavior, this chapter describes management misconceptions and mistakes that normally are outside the purview of UI consultants, but that nonetheless lead to poor product usability. They fall into two categories: (1) counterproductive attitudes about usability and (2) counterproductive development processes. They are the most important bloopers in this book, as well as the hardest to correct. If software developers recognize these bloopers in their own companies, and take steps to correct them, the software industry and the public will benefit, and UI consultants can spend less time as bulldog cosmeticians.

Other authors have devoted whole books to management-level problems that hinder software usability and usefulness, e.g.:

- *The Trouble with Computers,* by Tom Landauer [1995];
- *The Inmates Are Running the Asylum,* by Alan Cooper [1999];
- *The Invisible Computer,* by Don Norman [1999].

Jakob Nielsen has also discussed management-level usability problems in his AlertBox blog [UseIt.com]. Scott Berkun describes how to manage development projects effectively in his book *The Art of Project Management* [2005].

Counterproductive attitude

First, we examine management misconceptions and faulty attitudes that ultimately cause many of the bloopers described elsewhere in this book.

Blooper 64: Treating UI as low priority

In many software development organizations, user interface and usability issues have low priority compared to other issues. This takes several forms.

Variation A: Assuming that usability has low impact on market success

Some software managers and developers believe that a product's usability has little impact on its market success. They are wrong.

Figure 8.2 shows cumulative expenses and revenue over time for a software development project. After the project starts, expenses accumulate. After the product is released, revenue begins to accrue. The time from start to release is the time to market. If the product is at all successful, at some point after release, total revenue exceeds total expenses. That is the break-even point. The time from start to break-even is the time to profitability.

Most managers are fixated on minimizing time to market. However, economic analysis suggests that shortening time to profitability is usually more important for a company's long-term health than shortening time to market. Considering usability early in a project may delay time to market and raise initial costs, but usually repays that investment by increasing revenue and reducing downstream expenses [Conklin, 1996].

Having a more usable product at release speeds market acceptance and increases the revenue curve's slope (Figure 8.3). The steepness of the revenue curve just after product release has a *much* greater impact on time to profitability and long-term revenue than does the exact date of release. Rushing a product to market without ensuring its usability decreases the slope of the revenue curve and increases customer support and training costs, pushing the break-even point out, thereby lengthening the time to profitability.

Figure 8.2

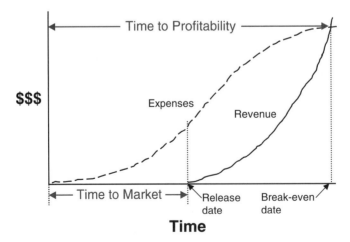

Total costs and revenue over time for a normal software development project.

Figure 8.3

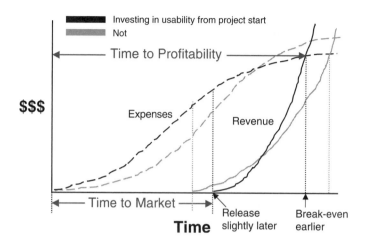

Total costs and revenue over time with and without early usability investment.

Furthermore, investing in usability early in a project does not always lengthen time to market. Often, it *shortens* it:

1. It gives programmers a clear implementation target, rather than letting them hack aimlessly. When you know where you are going, you can get there faster.

2. It simplifies implementation by providing a coherent, factorable design that provides exactly the functionality users require.

3. It localizes more of the design iteration in revisions of paper specifications, sketches, and low-fidelity prototypes, where it costs less than changing product code.

DILBERT © Scott Adams/Dist. by United Feature Syndicate, Inc.

More recent analyses of the business value of investing in usability can be found in the books *Cost-Justifying Usability* [Bias and Mayhew, 2005] and *Prioritizing Web Usability* [Nielsen and Loranger, 2006].

Since investing in usability early in development usually shortens time to profitability, increases total revenue, and shortens time to market, managers who don't do it are committing a blooper.

Variation B: Assuming that the UI is only "fonts and colors"

Some development managers have a narrow view of what "user interface" includes: a mistaken belief that it is only about the most superficial aspects of software and can therefore be put off until just before shipping. For example, one developer told me "UI design is often referred to by managers here as 'fonts and colors'."

User interface design is not only about fonts and colors. It isn't even *mainly* about fonts and colors (Blooper 65, page 337). It is more about *interaction:* how the software behaves, rather than what it looks like. It encompasses "deep" issues such as the ease with which users can learn the software, the fit of the software's functionality to users' goals, the directness of the mapping between concepts in the task domain and those presented by the software, and the efficiency with which common operations can be carried out. These issues cannot be put off until the end of development. If they aren't considered early in development and tested along the way, they won't be adequate in the released version.

Variation C: Assuming that users can adapt to anything

A common belief in the software industry is that UI doesn't matter: people will learn to use anything that provides the functionality they need. This is partially true. If a product has no competition or a captive market, having the required functionality may be enough. People are amazingly adaptable and can learn astounding things *if* sufficiently motivated and *if* given no other choice.

Those "ifs" are critical. Just because people *can* do something, doesn't mean they *will*. In a competitive market, it is risky to assume that prospective customers will overlook poor ease-of-use and buy a product for its feature list. Why should they? Maybe nobody is paying them to learn to use it. Maybe they have no time to struggle with it. A competitor's software may be easier to use while providing similar functionality. If potential customers don't like your software and don't buy or use it, they aren't the losers, you are.

Geeky shopping site goes nowhere

During the dot-com boom, a startup company was developing a Web application for comparison shopping. The idea was that consumers would download the application and use it to find the best price for whatever they wanted to buy. Users would type in a product's name and get back a table showing the price at different online stores. The application also had a shopping cart for buying items and a wish list for saving items for possible later purchase.

The company had no UI designers on staff and had done no user research. In a back room, H1-visa programmers churned out code based on scanty descriptions and a few sketches drawn by executives. The application's UI was horrible: full of the common bloopers described in this book as well as some unique flaws. When management began to suspect that their product was not user friendly, they decided to conduct usability tests to see exactly how bad it was.

Top management, including the CEO, Chairman, and VP of Engineering observed the test sessions from behind a one-way window. After sitting through three painful test sessions, in which none of the shoppers could complete *any* of the shopping tasks without help, the Chairman stood up, faced the others, and said sadly, "Gentlemen, our product is stillborn." The company folded a few months later.

Variation D: Rationalizing

For some software managers, considering usability to be low priority is just a rationalization: one way to perform triage in response to tight budgets, tight resources, and tight schedules.

The user interface is not a product feature that can be dropped to meet a deadline. It is how the functionality is presented and controlled. The quality of the UI determines each feature's value as well as the value of the overall product. A product without an effective UI is like a bookstore in which the books are in piles according to their size: the book you want may be there, but you can't find it.

Variation E: Assigning the GUI to junior programmers

Many development managers hold the UI in such low regard that they assign it to less experienced programmers. In some companies, the job of developing a GUI for a product is assigned to new hires or summer interns.

The flip side of assigning GUI development to inexperienced programmers is that engineers who design and develop GUIs tend to have lower status than those who develop system software. This was described more fully by Ellen Ullman in an insightful essay about working as a programmer [1995]:

> In regular life, "low" usually signifies something bad. In programming, "low" is good. Low is better.
>
> If the code creates programs that do useful work for regular human beings, it is called "higher." Higher-level programs are called "applications." Applications are things that people use. Although it would seem that usefulness by people would be a good thing, from a programmer's point of view, direct people-use is bad. If regular people, called "users," can understand the task accomplished by your program, you will be paid less and held in lower esteem. In the regular world, the term "higher" may be better, but, in programming, higher is worse. High is bad.
>
> If you want money and prestige, you need to write code that only machines or other programmers understand. Such code is "low."

Managers assign GUI development to less experienced programmers partly to minimize costs. Junior programmers are paid less. Experienced UI designers or programmers demand higher salaries (or consulting fees). Thus, hiring lots of junior programmers, but few highly experienced programmers, software architects, or designers, "saves" money.

However, you get what you pay for. Staffing in this way costs more than it saves. It results in poor usability, high customer support and training costs, unsatisfied customers, lackluster sales, and small, stagnant markets.

Avoiding Blooper 64

Management should make it a high priority to develop products that have high-quality user interfaces:

- Usability has a powerful impact on the success of products: it improves initial market acceptance and shortens time to profitability, thereby increasing total revenue.

- User interface is about "deep" issues, not just "fonts and colors." Deep usability issues discovered late in development will be difficult to correct because

DILBERT © Scott Adams/Dist. by United Feature Syndicate, Inc.

they require architectural changes. Test for and fix usability problems throughout development, starting early.

- Users can adapt to bad UIs, but banking on that is foolhardy because in an open, competitive marketplace, customers need not adapt: they can choose a competitor's product.

- The UI cannot be dropped to meet a schedule or budget constraint. It pervades and affects the entire product. If a product's UI is bad, the product is bad, because the UI is the aspect of the product that customers experience.

- Experience matters. Developing good GUIs not only requires sensitivity to users and their problems, it also requires an ability to make a GUI toolkit do everything short of backflips. It often requires real-time programming skills, including multithreaded programming. Make sure your GUI programmers have the skills to code the specified design on schedule.

Blooper 65: Misunderstanding what user interface professionals do

User interface and usability professionals have a problem: many others in the software industry don't understand what we do. The following conversation is unfortunately common:

> Development manager: "You're a user interface consultant? Are you a Windows toolkit hacker or a Java toolkit hacker?"
>
> Consultant: "Neither."
>
> DM: "Oh. Then you must be an XHTML hacker, or a PERL hacker, ... or a Visual BASIC hacker."
>
> C: "No. I design user interfaces and interactions. If I need a programmer to implement or prototype my designs, I hire one."
>
> DM: "Hmmm ... a designer. You draw the icons and make the Web links and buttons look cool."
>
> C: "Um, no. I'm not a graphic designer. I'm an interaction and UI designer. If I need a graphics designer to create realistic visuals for a design, I hire one."
>
> DM: "You're not a GUI programmer, and you're not a graphic designer. ... So what do you do?"

Many development managers are unclear on the distinction between user interface *designers* and user interface *programmers*. Others are unclear on the distinction between *graphic* designers and *user interface* designers. Let's examine the two misconceptions in turn.

Variation A: Assuming GUI programmers are GUI designers

Many software development managers mistakenly believe that all it takes to develop easy-to-use software is to hire skilled programmers who have experience using user interface development tools and component toolkits. According to this misconception, once you have good GUI programmers on board, you just have to tell them what software to write and give them the time and resources to write it. Managers often consider it wasteful to hire people who design GUIs or conduct usability tests but write little or no code.

This is a serious blooper. It reflects a profound misunderstanding of what GUI programmers versus GUI and interaction designers contribute to a development effort. It can also reflect a disregard for the value of well-designed UIs (Blooper 64, page 331).

Most development managers realize that programmers who are inexperienced in using a GUI toolkit often produce poor GUIs: they can't always make the toolkit do what they want. Fewer development managers realize that even experienced programmers who know a toolkit inside and out can produce poor UIs, even with plenty of time and resources. There are several reasons:

- *Lack of GUI design experience:* Programming experience is not the same as UI design experience, and experience programming GUIs is not necessarily experience designing them.

- *Designing GUI to fit toolkit:* If a programmer knows the toolkit very well but lacks an understanding of—or empathy for—how people think and work, programming convenience can win out.

- *Poor team-working skills:* Top-notch programmers are often strong-willed people who don't compromise or negotiate easily with others. When a development team contains several such members and their management does not assert authority, each will do things his or her own way, resulting in many inconsistencies (Blooper 67, page 348).

Other important reasons that good programmers produce bad GUIs are discussed by Gentner and Grudin [1990].

Variation B: Assuming graphic designers are GUI designers

Some development managers understand that to design easy-to-use software they need more than just good GUI programmers on their team, but are still unclear on exactly what other skills are needed. Many don't understand the difference between UI design and graphic design. They think the user interface is just the appearance of an application, so they hire appearance experts—graphic designers—to design it. The result of such a decision can be a product that demos well but supports user tasks poorly.

This misconception is becoming more common as Web sites and Web applications grow fancier, bringing aesthetic appeal, brand awareness, and entertainment value more to the forefront. With increasing frequency, prospective clients indicate that they are interviewing UI and graphic designers for the same job:

> Manager: "We're talking to another guy with an art degree who is a real hotshot with DreamWeaver, Visio, and PhotoShop and charges one-third of what you charge."

I take this as a warning that the hiring manager may not understand what UI and interaction design are. Sometimes I try to educate the manager right there on the spot; other times I just say: "OK. Call me when he's done."

Assigning jobs to amateurs yields amateur software

Imagine you're planning your dream house. You want state-of-the-art electrical wiring, so you hire a top-notch electrician. Your budget is limited, so you ask the electrician to also design the house's plumbing, heating, insulation, frame, roof, and foundation.

Ridiculous? This is exactly what many organizations do with properties far more valuable than any house: their software products and Web sites. People who are professionals at writing software are assigned additional tasks for which they are amateurs. This is at least partly due to management considering UI and usability to be low priority (Blooper 64, above) and thinking they can save money by asking programmers to design UIs too. The likely result will be some of the bloopers described elsewhere in this book. The fault for such bloopers lies not with the programmers who commit them, but rather with their *managers*.

Avoiding Blooper 65

To avoid committing this blooper, managers need to understand the difference between UI programmers and UI designers and the difference between UI designers and graphic designers. Then they need to make sure that all of those skills are present on—or at least available to—their development teams.

Don't confuse GUI programmers with GUI designers

Knowing carpentry doesn't make someone a designer of sought-after furniture or homes. Learning how to read and write music doesn't turn someone into a composer of enduring melodies. Similarly, knowing how to use GUI programming tools and components doesn't mean that someone will know what to do with them to create usable and useful software.

Having good GUI programmers on a team does not eliminate the need for a GUI designer. Management must make sure that products are designed by people who understand human–computer interaction and user requirements.

Don't confuse graphic designers with GUI designers

Designing GUIs and designing the graphic appearance of GUIs are different activities, requiring different skills. Both types of skill are needed to design good GUIs, but they are different.

UI designers are skilled at analyzing and understanding user task requirements and work context, at simplifying complexity, at determining what controls and information are required to support the target tasks, and at recognizing where users will have trouble learning or using an application. Some UI designers also know how to prepare, conduct, and analyze usability tests.

UI designers are less concerned with how the software *looks* and more concerned with how it *behaves,* how easy it is to learn, and whether it helps users accomplish their goals. For example, an application's buttons might look attractive, but its users still might not know which ones to click to achieve their goals. The problem could simply be unclear button labels, or it could be deeper: the button functions aren't related to users' goals. Perhaps some of the buttons could even be eliminated if the task-flow were simpler. Here are improvements a UI designer can help a company achieve:

- Reduce the number of commands from two hundred to two dozen
- Flatten a menu hierarchy from four levels to two
- Decrease the number of windows from 18 to 8
- Eliminate half of the clicks required to complete a common task
- Reduce the time to learn an application from two weeks to two hours
- Add links to a Web site's home page that take users in one click to popular content
- Reorganize an e-commerce Web site's categories to match how users categorize the products
- Change the UI from exposing convoluted implementation logic to presenting simple functionality that lets users accomplish their goals

In contrast, skilled graphic designers know how to provide a clear visual hierarchy, focus users' attention, design recognizable symbols, convey function graphically, present data effectively, use typography well, maximize production values, and devise consistent graphic styles for use throughout an application or product line (Basic Principle 6, page 37).

An area of overlap between the concerns of UI designers and those of graphic designers is the layout of controls and information in software displays.

Table 8.1   Comparing skills of GUI designers, graphic designers, and GUI programmers

Role	Skills
GUI designer	• Task analysis, conceptual design • Interaction design: context, high-level organization, task flow • UI design: input and output • Real-time responsiveness goals • Usability evaluation, usability testing • Assessing conformance to usability standards • Layout
Graphic designer	• Creating recognizable images, intuitive symbols • Production values, aesthetic appeal, brand awareness • Making best use of the available display medium • Conveying function graphically • Layout, visual hierarchy • Visual consistency
GUI programmer	• Dynamic prototypes • Implementing specified design: internal architecture, programming • Knowledge of GUI toolkit • Maximizing performance, meeting real-time goals • Assessing and explaining technical constraints, costs, and risks

The detailed appearance of each control is clearly the responsibility of a graphic designer. Exactly what controls are needed and how they operate is clearly the responsibility of the UI designer. Both sorts of designers will have ideas about how the controls are laid out on the display. This overlap in roles is one reason people sometimes confuse the two types of designers (see Table 8.1).

To avoid amateurish applications, appliances, and Web sites laden with bloopers, get the right professionals for each job.

Blooper 66: Discounting the value of testing and iterative design

Many development managers don't see a need for a development schedule to include usability testing or time for significant UI revisions. One would expect this decades-old attitude to disappear due to the rise of Agile development and Extreme programming (XP) methods, which call for frequent testing and design iteration, but it hasn't. The reasons vary.

Variation A: Agile/XP in name only

Some software development teams say they use Agile or XP methods, but actually do not. This is discussed more fully under Blooper 67 (page 348); for now suffice it to say that some teams label themselves "Agile/XP" to be stylish and to justify not using specification documents, but don't do most of what Agile/XP requires. In such teams, it is common to find old-fashioned attitudes still thriving, including the attitude that usability testing is unnecessary.

Variation B: *Good designers don't need iteration*

Some managers consider UI design a mysterious creative talent some people have. In this view, UI designers are artists who engage their right brain, invoke their muse, and conjure up excellent GUIs in blinding flashes of inspiration. The better the designer, the sooner the flash and the better the design.

There are advantages to being treated as a magician or an artist. UI designers can demand higher pay if our clients believe what we do is magical. Managers are less likely to try to micromanage creative artists.

However, the disadvantages outweigh the advantages. One disadvantage of considering UI designers to be artists is that it produces a "superstar" mentality: everyone wants their product designed by a few well-known UI design gurus who charge sky-high rates and are booked long into the future, while hundreds of competent UI designers have trouble finding contracts or permanent jobs. This is bad for the industry because many software products and services don't get the UI attention they need.

A more important disadvantage is that viewing UI designers as creative artists sets up faulty expectations about the need for testing and revision. UI design is a type of engineering, in which testing and revision are required. Treating it as a creative art leads one to discount or ignore a designer's need to generate and consider alternative designs and to test, evaluate, and revise a design. Considering alternative designs is, according to this view, wasteful and a sign of indecisiveness and inexperience. Revising a design is considered an admission of failure: if the new design is better, the old one must have been bad and therefore is a demerit for the designer. To managers who have this mind set, a UI designer who calls for usability testing is admitting incompetence. Managers have actually said:

> "Why are we wasting time considering design alternatives we won't use? Don't you know which design is better?"

> "Why do we need to test it? We hired you because you are supposed to be a good designer. Aren't you?"

> "We don't have time for testing and revising. We need you to make an effort to design it right the first time."

Code is constantly tested and revised. Agile/XP methods rely on iteration. Yet, when it comes to UI design, the need for iteration is less widely recognized.

Certainly, with an experienced UI designer on your team, you can have more confidence that the first design will be good than you can if the designer is a novice. However, using an experienced, skilled designer does not eliminate the need for usability testing and iterative design.

Let's say that GUIs range in quality from 1 to 10. A new UI designer might initially propose a design of quality 3–5. Usability testing and redesign might improve it to a quality of 6–8. An experienced designer's first design might have a quality of 5–7. However, testing and revision would still raise its quality, perhaps to 8–10. Regardless of which designer was hired, testing and revision would improve the product.

 ### How do UI designers get experience?

For UI designers, being "experienced" requires not just design experience, but also evaluation and testing experience. Designers may have designed hundreds of software products, but if they haven't received feedback on those designs from other UI professionals and from observing users, all those designs count for very little. Tracking the success or failure of products in the marketplace is insufficient, because many factors other than usability contribute to that. Experience is built up by receiving explicit feedback about usability problems in one's designs and using that feedback to revise the designs. Thus, usability testing and revision not only produce better designs, they also produce better *designers*. This is one reason entry-level jobs in the usability field tend to be in usability testing rather than UI design.

Testing and revising are also a way to reduce risk. Management would like the risk of market failure to be almost zero, but that is too costly. Instead, well-run software vendors reduce their risk in launching a new product to a "reasonable" level. Conducting usability testing and revising the UI are an excellent and relatively cheap way of reducing risk. This is true whether or not the designer is experienced. Even if a usability test showed that a product's UI was fine and no changes were needed, just *learning that* would reduce the risk of launching the product.

The most succinct argument for testing and iterative design comes from Fred Brooks's book *The Mythical Man-Month* [1995], even though Brooks wasn't referring only to UI design:

> Plan to throw one away. You will do that, anyway. Your only choice is whether to try to sell the throwaway to customers.

Warning: Brooks's statement does not give you license to create a shoddy, incoherent initial design and hope it can be revised into shape. Testing and revision cannot substitute for careful up-front design.[1] Brooks's statement means that managers should not fool themselves into believing that designers can get a design exactly "right" on the first attempt.

Variation C: "We don't have the luxury of usability testing"

A common variation of this blooper is for managers to try to shorten the development schedule by skipping usability testing. Some omit it when planning the schedule; others include it initially but squeeze it out when the schedule slips.

Usability testing is how you determine if your design is on course and what midcourse adjustments are needed. Without it, you are flying blind and may actually take longer to finish. Yet many managers treat usability testing as an expendable development-step that can be dropped to meet a looming deadline. This attitude is based on two myths:

Myth 1. *Testing is expensive.* Many developers think of usability testing as occurring in elaborate testing facilities with large banks of video equipment and rooms of observers behind half-silvered mirrors making notes as paid subjects use alpha-release software to do realistic tasks. Some usability testing is done that way, certainly. However, one can also conduct low-cost, quick tests devised on short notice and carried out using a paper or HTML prototype of the software and people recruited from the hallways (or employees' families) and paid in chocolate. Such tests can yield crucial information, such as which of two designs is best, whether users can find menu commands, or whether icons convey their intended meanings.

Myth 2. *Skipping testing will save money.* By avoiding usability testing, a manager may save some money but the company will not. The money saved by not doing a test-and-revise cycle before shipping will be spent many times over on postrelease revisions and increased support costs. Lost revenue due to a lack of customers will more than negate any savings from skipping usability testing.

DILBERT © Scott Adams/Dist. by United Feature Syndicate, Inc.

---

1. Even though some radical proponents of Agile/XP development dispute this.

Managers who skip testing are deluding themselves. They *will* do usability testing—it's unavoidable. By not conducting usability tests before release, they are deciding to conduct their tests in the marketplace, with paying customers as subjects.

A more serious problem with testing in the market is that the data obtained— customer complaints—is not very useful. Besides being too late, it is unsystematic, subjective, anecdotal, sketchy, self-selected, and mixed with bug reports and complaints about missing functionality. Imagine trying to decide how to improve a UI based on comments such as "three out of five stars" or "It SUCKS!" or "The commands make no sense" or "i use your software only because everyone else here does but i hate it because it's so different from my old software." Imagine basing UI changes exclusively on comments relayed through the sales staff.

Relying solely on marketplace feedback also makes you vulnerable to the "squeaky wheel" phenomenon. You have no way of knowing whether the feedback you receive is representative of the problems most users are having, so you will be biased toward addressing the complaints of your more vocal customers. There is simply no substitute for data obtained from explicit, closely monitored usability testing.

Variation D: Allowing no time to fix usability problems

The most perplexing variation of Blooper 3 is when managers conduct a review or test of a pending product's usability, but then allow no time to correct the problems that the review or test uncovers. Some managers hire a consultant to review or conduct a usability test, but when they get the results and recommendations, say: "We don't have time to change most of these things." Amazing! Why did they spend all that money? Here are four answers:

1. If managers believe that UI is only about presentation and graphic design, they will expect a UI review or usability test to find only superficial problems. Such problems, such as those concerning labeling, layout, and color, are easy to fix. When a usability review or test uncovers deep problems requiring conceptual redesign, architectural changes, or revisions to back-end services, many managers don't consider such issues as "user interface."

2. Developing a software product requires deciding which desirable features will "make the cut." Often, "user-friendly front end" is considered just a feature to rank against others, such as "ability to import Lotus 1-2-3 files" (Blooper 64, page 331). Developers sometimes refuse important usability improvements on the grounds that "there isn't time," while simultaneously wasting time adding bells and whistles that the developers consider "cool." Sometimes the release date slips continuously for months, yet the development manager resists usability improvements because at any given point "there isn't enough time."

3. Sometimes managers, developers, and even UI designers have so much ego invested in the design that they can't imagine a test finding problems.

When a test *does* find usability problems, it must be that the test was badly designed or that the wrong users were tested.

4. The manager may have ordered a usability test only because it is mandatory in the company's development process. The manager doesn't really care what the test finds, as long as the test can be marked as done. Fixing usability problems found by the test is not on the checklist.

Avoiding Blooper 66

UI design is not a mystical art based on innate talent and blinding flashes of creativity. It is a learned engineering discipline. It has many characteristics seen in other types of engineering:

- A scientific basis: human perception, learning, action, information processing, and motivation
- Industry standards and best practices
- A need for clear requirements
- Generation and consideration of design alternatives
- Working with constraints and trade-offs
- A need to test, evaluate, and revise

There are tests for every purpose, budget, and development stage

Usability testing is not something that you do only when software is about to ship, and it doesn't require elaborate testing facilities and equipment. During design and development, questions often arise that usability testing can answer. You can choose from a variety of testing methods that vary in cost, preparation required, rigor of results, and the point in development where they occur. For details and examples, see Appendix E (page 383).

When test participants are hard to get

What if you want to do a usability test, but representative users are scarce, busy, or prohibitively expensive? This is a difficult situation, but it does not rule out usability testing. Consider these solutions:

- Some aspects of a software product don't depend on the user having expertise in the software's target tasks. If an air traffic control system includes a mouse as a pointing device, you don't need air traffic controllers to test whether buttons on the screen are large enough to hit. If a Web-based medical reference for doctors uses tables that are meant to work like tables in Windows applications, you don't need doctors to test that.

- When task expertise is required, you can use less expensive, easier to recruit surrogates for the real users, for example, nurses or medical students instead of doctors, private pilots instead of airline pilots, middle managers instead of top executives, congressional staffers instead of congressional representatives. Questions may remain about how the real users would perform, but many important design questions will be answered and important flaws will be found.

- If true representative users are needed, it may be difficult or expensive to get them, but it isn't impossible. If the product is seen by users as a significant advance for them, it may be surprisingly easy to enlist their participation. For example, a team developing software for visualizing and preplanning brain operations managed to test their software on 50 neurosurgeons and an assortment of other surgeons. Surgeons volunteered their time because: (1) the project was cosponsored by a medical school neurosurgery department, (2) they saw the tool as a potential great advance for them, and (3) some of their colleagues had helped design the software [Hinckley et al., 1998]. Fifty neurosurgeons, free!

Use testing to improve products, not to grade designers

Create a culture in which usability testing is regarded as an indispensable tool for improving products and reducing the risk of market failure, not as a way to evaluate the performance of designers and developers. Empower team members to use quick-and-dirty tests whenever they feel the need. Before release, subject the software to comprehensive usability testing. Build the phrase "test early and often" into your organizational culture.

On projects that use Agile/XP development methods, frequent usability testing is mandatory. If you are developing software that has a UI, quality-assurance testing is not enough; you must test the software on users. If you don't conduct some kind of usability test on nearly every revision cycle, you aren't doing Agile/XP development.

Why test if you're going to ignore the results?

If usability tests are to have value, managers should foresee that developers will need time after a test to correct usability problems the test uncovers. Keep in mind that a test may find deep conceptual and architectural problems.

Usability testing: Just do it!

The bottom line: It is just plain stupid to develop and ship a software-based product without conducting some kind of usability testing before release.

Counterproductive process

The second category of management bloopers focuses on development *processes* that hinder the development of usable and useful software.

Blooper 67: Anarchic development

A rampant problem in the software industry is development processes that are anarchic: uncontrolled, nonrepeatable, and driven by individual whim and the crisis of-the-moment, rather than by proven, repeatable practices, company goals, and customer and user requirements. Alan Cooper's book *The Inmates Are Running the Asylum* [1999] explains why software development management has so little control over the products and services that their companies develop and why that is detrimental to product usability and hence company success.

Anarchic development → Inconsistency

One impact of anarchic development is easy to see: products or product suites that are fraught with inconsistencies because every development team or every programmer has done things differently. Some examples follow:

- A document editor requires users to name a document when they create it, but a graphics editor from the same company doesn't require a file name until the work is to be saved.
- In one dialog box, pressing the Tab key moves the input focus to the next data field, but in another dialog box, it doesn't.
- In one function, new data objects are created by clicking a "New ..." button and filling out the resulting dialog box, but in another function, they are created by filling out an always-visible form and clicking an Add textual link.
- In a drawing program, squares can be rotated and/or filled, but triangles cannot.
- One program preserves the previous version of a graph in a backup file, but a companion program does not.
- A command in the menubar menus is labeled "Database Search," but the same command on the toolbar has the tooltip label "Query Repository."

Unfortunately, such inconsistencies are endless. In some products, similar functions have very different UIs because the programmers who designed them didn't talk to each other or because each thought his design was better. Some corporate Web sites are cobbled together from pages produced and maintained by separate organizations within a company, and each organization's pages look and work differently from the others. Programmers sometimes even design one dialog box one way on one day and a similar one quite differently the next day simply because they didn't remember how they did it the day before and weren't motivated to check. Such discrepancies are a problem, but a more serious problem is that many development organizations are not set up to discover, resolve, and prevent them.

Users want to fall into unconscious habits as quickly as possible (Basic Principle 6, page 37). They want to be able to focus on their own goals. A consistent UI allows them to do that. Software that is riddled with inconsistencies forces users to keep thinking about the software itself, distracting them. Users have to learn how each application or each function within an application works. Inconsistent, incoherent UIs hinder learning, productivity, and, ultimately, sales revenue.

Herding cats

A colleague commented that organizing and managing software engineers "is like herding cats." Although it's difficult, maintaining control is necessary to produce coherent UIs and products that are aligned with company goals. Many software development organizations do a poor job of herding their cats.

Anarchic development → Fewer customers

Another result of anarchic development is products and services so full of programmerisms and design bloopers that customers reject them. Even if customers don't reject a product outright, they may just barely tolerate it. When customers use a product but curse it daily, they have no loyalty and will switch to a competitor without hesitation [Cooper, 1999].

Three varieties of anarchic development contribute to poor usability.

Variation A: No design

Many organizations start developing software applications without first designing them. Programmers hack based on back-of-the-envelope sketches or vague feature lists. Some companies are embarrassed that this is how they operate, but many aren't: "We don't do that here. In our market, we don't have time for UI specifications. We use Agile/XP development." As development schedules accelerate to so-called "Internet Time," and as Agile development and Extreme programming grow in popularity, the tendency to skip design and jump straight to coding is *increasing*.

Landauer discusses the consequences of this in his book *The Trouble with Computers* [1995]. Cooper also covers it in his book *The Inmates Are*

Running the Asylum [1999]. Unguided hackery is almost guaranteed to produce software that:

- reflects engineering considerations more than it reflects user requirements;
- has an incoherent, non-task-focused conceptual model that is hard for users to understand;
- is laden with UI inconsistencies and design bloopers;
- is not congruent with company goals.

Proponents of Agile/XP development may protest that those methods are not "anarchic development" or "unguided hackery"; they achieve the necessary guidance and control in ways other than specification documents. Some Agile/XP advocates also argue that creating a UI design first and telling developers to implement it is part of the discredited "waterfall" model of software development. A UI design, they say, should not be cast in stone, because it is impossible to determine all the requirements and the best design at the start. The design should evolve with the team's understanding of the requirements and possible solutions.

Indeed, Agile/XP development is supposed to be strongly driven by customer requirements based on frequent reviews and tests [Beck and Andres, 2004]. Teams—including users and other task-domain experts—should meet at least weekly in informal "scrums" to discuss design issues and devise solutions that will be implemented and tested in the next cycle.

In practice, however, many development organizations that claim to use Agile/XP methods don't do much of what the methods require: no domain experts on the team or nearby to provide feedback, no weekly scrums, no quick-and-dirty tests. They just avoid UI specs and call that "Agile/XP" development. In such cases, the label "Agile/XP" is just a cover for anarchic, unguided hackery.

Even if developers do follow Agile/XP recommended practices closely, skipping up-front design is still risky. It assumes that through testing and revision, a quick-and-dirty UI that users tolerate (or don't) will evolve into a coherent, task-focused, easy-to-learn one that users love. That assumption is extremely optimistic. More often than not, the result will be UIs that make users grimace, rather than smile.

Starting with no design can also often *cost* time rather than save it, as ad hoc UIs and software architectures are built, found to be inadequate, torn apart, and rebuilt many times. It results in a lot of aimless *commotion*, rather than purposeful *motion* toward a goal.

Variation B: No standards or guidelines

Many software companies have no standards for the software's operation or look and feel. They apparently don't understand that they are in the publishing business, like companies that create magazines, newspapers, books, TV programs, and movies.

Traditional publishers and broadcasters have strict standards for how information is presented (e.g., bar charts vs. pie charts), how words are spelled (e.g., "Khadafy" vs. "Gadhafi"), what typefaces are used (e.g., Times vs. Bookman), how text is formatted, whether articles begin with summaries, which direction people in photographs face, and so on. Publishers and broadcasters who don't follow standards and guidelines produce UIs that seem amateurish, even to users who cannot articulate exactly what is wrong, or that are hard to understand.

Software developers, as publishers, should have standards and guidelines that are appropriate for their products and customers, but few do. Developers often consider it anal-compulsive overkill to worry about inconsistencies in details such as the wording of commands and messages, the capitalization of setting labels, the spacing of controls, and the like. Management doesn't press the issue because that would add time to the schedule, not to mention that the work would have to be assigned to the programmers themselves because no one else is authorized to change the source code.

Some managers assume that the standards of their target platform(s)— Windows, Mac, Java, the Web—are sufficient. Not so. The standards for those platforms are insufficiently constrained. An application can conform to the Macintosh UI standards and still be full of design bloopers. Two software products can both be Windows compliant and yet look and feel so different that users would have trouble switching between them.

Variation C: No oversight

It is amazing how common it is for companies to hire programmers to develop interactive applications, give them very little guidance, and hope for the best. One software manager characterized this practice as:

> "Hire nerds, tell'em what you want, lock'em in their offices, and throw in pizza and T-shirts every few weeks."

The assumption that underlies this philosophy is based partly on the incorrect idea that GUI programmers are GUI designers (Blooper 65, page 337). Also contributing is the erroneous attitude that GUIs are low priority and can be assigned to less expensive junior programmers (Blooper 64, page 331).

The writing of text displayed by the software is often poorly supervised. Programmers often write the command labels, button labels, setting names, and error messages that their code displays, even though they are not trained to do that. When management fails to have technical writers and editors review software text, the software often goes to market with inconsistent terminology, programmer jargon, obscure error messages, spelling errors, grammatical mistakes, and generally poor writing (see Chapter 4).

A lack of oversight can be due to weak management as well as to misconceptions about what programmers are and are not good at. Many managers in software development organizations have weak people-management skills. Combine weak managers with programmers who lack UI design training and who don't cooperate or communicate well with each other, and you get anarchic development. Here is a typical scenario:

> The design and coding is divided among several programmers by program function, based on their interests and skills. The programmers either disagree about how the software should present controls and information or don't talk to each other about it. Each programmer designs the UI differently in the part of the software for which he or she is responsible. Their manager or team-leader is aware of the design inconsistencies and would like to correct them, but can't convince the programmers to confer and reach agreement and is too weak or indecisive to force his or her own decision on the team.

In situations such as this, some managers have a hidden agenda when they bring in a UI consultant. UI consultants are supposedly hired to find usability problems and recommend solutions, but often discover that they were actually hired to solve a management problem: the manager needs an outside "authority" to recommend what the manager already knows the programmers should do.

Managers may believe that programmers make only technical decisions, but in fact programmers often make decisions that strongly influence *business* outcomes, such as:

- who the product's customers will be and how much they will value the product;
- which functions of the software will be heavily used and which will be so rarely used they might as well not be there;
- what the company's reputation as a software developer will be;
- how fast the company's revenue from the product will rise, when it will exceed costs, when it will peak, and how long it will last;
- what the demand for customer support services will be.

Unfortunately, it is usually not until the product has been shipped to beta-customers—or even later—that all the business consequences of the programmers' decisions become apparent.

Example of programmers making business decisions by default

A company needed help redesigning the GUI of a network management product. The product manager explained that the product had been under development for over a year with no UI designer on the team (Blooper 68, page 357) and—surprise!—prospective customers were calling the product unusable. Checking my understanding, I used the metaphor of their product as a camera:

> Me: "If I understand correctly, your customers want an automatic point-and-shoot camera, but your programmers built a manually controlled professional camera."

> Manager: "No; it's worse than that. They built a kit for building cameras. You can build any camera you want with it. But our customers don't want to build a camera. They want a camera."

The programmers developed the software that they would want if they had the job of managing a network. But other people have that job, and the software they want is not what the programmers designed.

By developing a product that could not be sold directly to the intended customers, but rather would have to be sold through third-party system integrators and value-added resellers, the programmers made an important business decision for the company—a decision that management had not intended. Management at this company allowed development to proceed for over a year when what the programmers were developing was a gross mismatch with what customers wanted. Was no one paying attention?

Avoiding Blooper 67

Applications that have a GUI—or any significant user interface—should be designed according to user-centered design (UCD) principles and best practices.

Before you begin writing code, you should have an initial UI design to work from. If you carefully design what you're going to build before you start building it, the building will go faster and you're more likely to build a product that customers like [Cooper, 1999]. Whether the design is recorded in a text document, storyboards, or a prototype is up to you, but it should be recorded somewhere other than in people's minds. The design will undoubtedly change, and as it does, the record of it should be updated. Without a design, you are asking for trouble, both during development and after release.

UCD and Agile/XP are compatible

User-centered design, like Agile/XP development, places high value on:

- understanding customer and user requirements,
- enlisting the help of users and other task-domain experts,
- devising a task-focused conceptual model (called "object model" in Agile/XP),
- frequent testing,
- iterative design.

Also like Agile/XP development, user-centered design rejects the waterfall model. It recognizes that customer requirements are understood better over time and change even after they are understood. UCD acknowledges that designs evolve, but advises against starting to code until you have performed a task analysis, created use cases and user profiles, designed a task-focused conceptual model, and created a preliminary UI design (see Chapter 1). The purpose is not to carve these things in stone. Quite the opposite, it is to let you test them on users so you can revise and improve them *before* investing time, money, and egos on code. After implementation starts, the testing and revision continue, and the design evolves. There is no inherent conflict between user-centered design and Agile/XP development.[2]

Agile and XP methods were initially developed by software engineering experts, not UI design experts, so early writings on Agile/XP had blind spots concerning UIs, usability, user-centered design, and how they fit into the methods. According to Bankston [2001]:

> XP tends to promote a very tight focus; don't worry about what's coming, just code the card you're holding. … Unfortunately, … this approach can lead to disjointed, awkward or unnecessarily complicated interfaces designed around back-end functionality rather than the user's end goals. Designing an efficient and elegant user interface requires some conception of what steps comprise a given task, and how tasks interrelate to create an application's flow.

More recently, UI experts and Agile/XP experts have attempted to "marry" their methods. Most acknowledge the need for some up-front design:

- Scott Ambler, an Agile/XP guru, says that the overall architecture of an application should be modeled in a "phase 0" before the normal code–test–revise cycles start [2005].
- Larry Constantine, a UI consultant, says "some minimum up-front design is needed for the UI to be well-organized and to present users with a consistent

---

2.   There are zealots in both camps who claim that UCD and Agile/XP are incompatible.

Figure 8.4

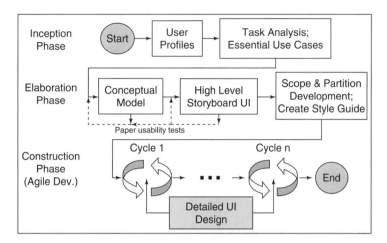

User-centered design with Agile development [adapted from Meads, 2007].

and comprehensible interface." With Carolyn Lockwood, he developed a streamlined "usage-centered" design methodology that they claim fits well into the Agile/XP process [2002].

■ Jon Meads, a UI consultant, finds that UCD fits with Agile methods if the design work (and iteration) occurs mainly in the Inception and Elaboration phases of a project, while the Agile code–test–revise cycles occur in the Construction phase (Figure 8.4).

■ Lynn Miller presents case studies of using UCD on projects that use Agile/ XP methods and concludes that Agile/XP development's emphasis on incorporating user input enhances UCD [2005].

These efforts demonstrate that Agile/XP and UCD can be combined to obtain the benefits of both, as long as Agile/XP practitioners concede that some up-front design is needed to ensure coherence and consistency, and UCD practitioners concede that the UI design will evolve.

Developers are publishers, and should act like it

You are in the publishing and media business—get used to it. Like all others in that business, you need design standards, conventions, guidelines, and, above all, development processes that produce consistent interaction style, layout, formatting, fonts, terminology, writing style, use of color, and so on. To develop easy-to-use software, you need design guidelines that go beyond the minimal conformance requirements for your GUI platform.

Seeing yourself as a publisher also helps clarify the difference between "it works" and "it's ready to ship." The gap between these two states may be as large as the gap between "here's an idea" and "it works." Imagine if *The New York Times* or *National Geographic* were sent to subscribers as soon as all the journalists turned in their stories and photographs. Suppose the first rough cut of Alfred Hitchcock's "The Birds" or Peter Jackson's "Lord of the Rings" had been released. Software is a media product, and developers need to realize that it pays to "sweat the details," just as it does with movies, TV shows, newspapers, and magazines.

Quality UIs require investment

Software development companies should invest in:

- training programmers on principles of user-centered design;
- hiring interaction/UI designers and usability testers;
- providing programmers with GUI and Web guidelines books for their reference, especially industry-standard platform style guides such as Windows, Mac, Java, AJAX, and Flash;
- developing departmental or company UI style guides and standards;
- ensuring that company and industry style guides and standards are followed;
- using GUI toolkits and templates that support UI standards;
- including UI design and revision in development schedules;
- having a project architect responsible for ensuring consistency between different parts of the software;
- putting all text displayed by the software in message files;
- having technical writers and editors review all text messages and labels used in the software;
- conducting usability tests;
- revising designs based on usability test results.

 Layers of GUI standards

UI standards are multilayered, with inner layers having ever-narrower scope (Figure 8.5). There are industry-wide standards. There are platform-specific ones, e.g., for Windows, Macintosh, and Java. Some companies develop corporate standards so their products have a distinctive brand-identified look and feel. Also, products in a particular product line may look and work more alike than do the company's products in general. Finally, standards can be developed for a specific product, to foster consistency between different parts of it. The inner layers augment, rather than contradict, the outer ones.

Figure 8.5

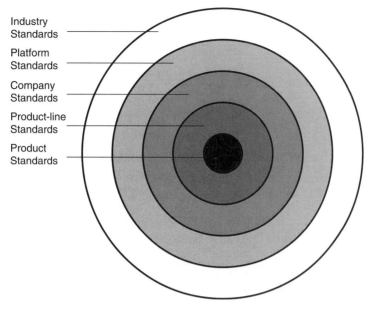

Industry Standards
Platform Standards
Company Standards
Product-line Standards
Product Standards

Multiple layers of GUI design standards applied simultaneously to a product.

Give UI experts more clout

Give UI designers and usability test engineers more authority to declare usability problems to be showstoppers. The easiest way to achieve this is for more UI designers to become managers. UI experts can also gain clout by serving as advisors to managers, helping them foresee the business implications of UI design decisions and flaws.

Once a development team has decided on a UI design, the programmers should implement that design. When programmers don't like something in the design, they should lobby to change the design rather than unilaterally coding the GUI however they want.

Take responsibility

Finally, management can help overcome anarchic development simply by being more assertive. Who, after all, is ultimately responsible for the success of the products?

Blooper 68: No task expertise on the team

Many managers in the software industry don't understand that designing an effective UI for a software product requires a detailed understanding of the work the intended users do and the work environment in which the software will be used. They believe a brief introduction to the software's target task is all a designer or programmer needs in order to create a suitable UI. Development teams therefore often include no one who really understands the tasks, and many teams make no effort to acquire such understanding.

Developers assume they are task-domain experts

One reason for this is historical. Computer-based products were formerly intended and designed only for technically trained users: scientists, engineers, and other programmers [Grudin, 1991; Norman, 1998]. Developers designed for people like themselves. Even when the intended users were not software engineers, the designs sort of worked because the users were technically savvy enough to be able to adapt to technocentric designs.

Today software intended for techno-geeks is only a tiny part of the software market. Software products and services are mainstream. The Internet is a household concept. The users are now workers in every type of business and consumers in homes around the world—even in the developing world. The assumption that software developers can design usable products without needing to import task-domain expertise is now completely invalid, even if it ever was valid.

Even with software being developed for a nontechnical audience, developers may assume they know more about the task domain than they actually do know. They balance their bank account every month, so they think they understand accounting. They were students recently, so they think they know what teachers need. They've been to a clinic, so they believe they can design software for nurses. Overrating one's knowledge is not a problem; it's just human nature; but when managers buy into developers' overrated self-assessments, they are committing a blooper.

© 1996 Greg Howard, distributed by King Features Syndicate.

Discounting users' task knowledge

A second reason for a lack of task-domain expertise on development teams is a lack of regard for task knowledge. Developers know about technology, and technology is what they are developing. So what else is there to know? Knowledge of the task domain is discounted: users don't know about technology, so they don't know anything.

One can see this attitude in the labels software developers often use to talk about the users for whom the software is being designed. Expertise is a linear scale, going from "novice" or "naïve" users, who don't know much about computers, up to "expert" users, who are full-fledged engineers like the developers. The scale is based on knowledge of computer technology. Expertise in a task domain plays no role in positioning a person on the scale.

Three types of knowledge affect a person's effectiveness in using a software product: knowledge of the product's target task domain, knowledge of the particular software product, and knowledge of computer technology in general (Basic Principle 1, page 8). A person can be low, medium, or high on each type, independently.

Similarly, different kinds of expertise are also required to *design* usable and useful products. Software developers usually have only technical expertise. They aren't usually experts in the software's target task domain, limiting their ability to produce successful products for it.

 Complex applications developed without UI or task expertise

Some companies develop applications that are highly specialized or very complex. Designing an effective UI for an air traffic control system, a hospital intensive-care monitoring system, or a stock trading system requires more task-domain knowledge than does designing a desktop calendar or an e-mail reader. Here are three complex applications that companies initially developed without any UI or task-domain experts.

- *Equities trading.* Workstation for professional stockbrokers, stock traders, and their support staff. The developer had received feedback from current and prospective customers that the software was overly complicated and "amateurishly designed." They initially wanted me to simplify the user interface radically, within a few months. We soon settled on the lesser goal of bringing the application's windows and dialog boxes into compliance with design guidelines. Only after eight months of working with them did I feel competent to suggest deeper improvements.

- *Tracking cancer cases.* Many U.S. states keep track of cancer cases in order to spot significant clusters and to provide cancer researchers with epidemiological data. A software company that supplied cancer-tracking software to a state hired me to help improve the usability of its software. The assignment began as a "quick UI review," but soon grew into a lengthy redesign project. To gain some knowledge of the task domain, we conducted an observation and interview study of users, who knew a great deal about cancer, its treatment, and how it is tracked, despite being "clericals" with no formal medical training.

■ *Biomolecular experiments.* A biological instrument company hired me to improve the usability of software for controlling a complex protein-assay instrument. They initially wanted me to quickly review their software and sketch new designs for its screens. However, the main problem was that the software was designed in terms of how the instrument worked internally (e.g., drop extraction needles into sample wells, flow sample from well 1 over test site A2), rather than what biologists wanted to accomplish with it (e.g., compare reaction of proteins A, B, and C to enzyme X). Redesigning the software to match biologists' needs required a great deal of domain knowledge, collected by soliciting input from biologists and even including one in our weekly design meetings.

Importing task expertise is hard

A third reason for a lack of task knowledge on development teams is that importing it, whether by bringing users onto the team or by sending developers out to learn from them, is not easy. Grudin [1991] lists obstacles that even well-meaning organizations encounter:

■ It is sometimes not entirely clear who the users of a product will be. The Segway personal transporter was supposed to be for everyone, but its main use in 2007 is mail delivery.

■ Getting useful feedback or suggestions from task experts before one has a product to show is not straightforward; it requires concerted effort and creativity. Often by the time a product is "showable," it's too late for suggestions from users to have much of an impact on the design.

■ Incorporating input from task experts requires lots of revisions in the design. That requires the cooperation of the entire team because it affects implementation, documentation, schedules, and budgets. Getting buy-in from the entire team, including management, is difficult.

■ Business realities sometimes stymie developers' efforts to seek input from potential users of a software product. Obstacles to user involvement can be found both in software development organizations and in customer organizations.

Often those designing a product's UI would welcome input from task-domain experts, but find getting it frustratingly difficult. Task-domain experts may be very busy and/or prohibitively expensive (Blooper 66, page 341). Perhaps the developers are not allowed to contact potential users for organizational or legal reasons. Software companies are rarely set up to facilitate direct contact between developers and users. Many limit or forbid it.

Years ago, several companies partnered to develop an online video service for schools. The plan was to allow teachers in a certain school district to find and show educational videos online. Teachers would no longer have to order tapes and DVDs in advance from the district's video library or worry about whether the one they needed for their class was checked out.

We were a subcontractor in the project. Our role was to design the UI for finding and showing videos. The prime contractor didn't want to "confuse the school district by presenting them with representatives from multiple companies" and so banned us from contacting the school district or any of its teachers.

We felt that it was impossible to design a UI without knowing how teachers select, order, and use videos. We circumvented the ban, contacting a *different* school district and conducted interviews and focus groups with its teachers. We asked teachers how they selected and ordered videos for their classes, how they showed them, and what they liked and didn't like about the process. We also described possible capabilities and designs for an online video system and asked the teachers to comment. Here are some of our findings:

- Teachers categorize videos by educational "unit," "subject," and "lesson," not by a simple topic/subtopic hierarchy.

- Teachers often choose videos by what is *in* them. A video about sharks might include a clip of a fishing boat and so might be used in a lesson on boats.

- Teachers show videos both to support what they are teaching and as entertainment for rainy days or rewards. Videos for the lesson are planned long in advance. Videos for entertainment are selected on the spur of the moment.

- Teachers preview videos before showing them in class. Cassettes and DVDs allow teachers to take videos home to preview. An online service that didn't allow that would be unpopular.

- Teachers edit videos to match their class's attention span and to present relevant segments. They also pause videos to discuss them. A service that didn't allow that would be ignored.

- Teachers share information about videos. "Video buffs" serve as resources for their colleagues, offering large personal collections and knowledge about videos and equipment.

- Many teachers had given up using the district's video library and instead used their own collections. The online service would compete with those as well as with the district's library.

Without access to task-domain experts—in this case, teachers—we would have had to design our UI "in the dark."

User involvement in development can also be hindered by *customer* organizations [Grudin, 1991]. Managers at a customer company may balk at diverting personnel from their normal work to help a software development effort. Most will need to hear how they will benefit before consenting. This is especially true when the software will be sold on the open marketplace:

> "You want me to loan you one of my employees two days a week for six months to help you develop software that you will then sell not only to us but also to our competitors? I ... don't ... think ... so!"

Whether the barriers keeping developers and users apart are in your organization or the customer's, failing to overcome them reduces the chances of your product being usable and so is a blooper.

Avoiding Blooper 68

Recall the mother of all UI design principles: focus on the users and their tasks, not on the technology (Basic Principle 1, page 8). (If you haven't read that principle yet, now would be a good time.)

Focusing on the users and their tasks means making it a high priority to understand and meet user requirements. Understanding user requirements includes understanding the software's target task domain, which, in turn, requires that the team have at its disposal a *source* of task-domain knowledge. That knowledge can be obtained by using designers who understand the supported activity or by involving prospective users in the design as advisors, test participants, and codesigners.

Let's break that down a bit.

Users' task-domain expertise is a crucial ingredient

Developers—managers as well as programmers—would produce better software if they revised their attitudes about task domain vs. technical expertise. Users are not ignorant; they are experts in the task domain. Developers of course play a critical role in software development as the writers of the code, but should admit their ignorance of most task domains, and of human–computer interaction, and either work to overcome their ignorance by learning from the experts or work around it by inviting the experts to join them on the team or both. This is crucial in order to design successful software products and services in today's hypercompetitive marketplace.

Before designing anything, talk with users. Do it in one-on-one interviews, in which each participant's comments are uninfluenced by the comments of others. Also do it in focus groups, in which participants' ideas, thoughts, and reactions contradict and complement each other. Find out how those who might eventually use the planned product do their work now, what they like and don't like about it, and how they could imagine it being better.

Early in the design process, send team members to immerse themselves in the task domain: observing users, hanging out with them, and, if possible, actually doing some of their work. At the least, the team's UI designer should be well exposed to the work the users do.

Even better—but harder to arrange—bring users onto the design team. *Warning:* It is not easy getting users to contribute effectively once you have some of their time. Just letting them sit in on project meetings with programmers and managers won't work. Most will hesitate to contribute because they feel out of place. Even if they muster the courage to speak, they don't think or talk like developers, so there may be miscommunication, mistrust, and even lack of respect. On the other hand, treating users as second-class team members also won't work. It must be made clear to them that they are needed because of their *task-domain* expertise, which the developers lack. Structured sessions—led by a facilitator who also serves as interpreter—are required. Sessions could focus on:

- analyzing the current workplace, yielding a breakdown of the tasks users perform and the problems they currently have;
- developing a conceptual model and lexicon, i.e., what are the concepts of the task domain and what are they called;
- developing scenarios of people using the planned product, expressed at a high conceptual level (called "user stories" in Agile/XP development);
- distilling the task analysis and scenarios down to produce the most important use cases;
- envisioning possible designs for the product, yielding initial sketches;
- showing users designs or prototypes and asking for feedback and suggestions;
- enacting roles in a simulated workplace, using initial prototypes.

Agile/XP development requires the participation of task-domain experts—users—in the weekly project scrums. Their role is to ensure that all critical requirements are covered and to keep the design focused on the tasks. Teams that follow Agile/XP methods can use any of the above-listed structured ways to ensure that users contribute their expertise. Teams using traditional development methods can also use these types of structured meetings to get users to participate effectively.

Here are good guides for how to enlist and engage users successfully:

- Greenbaum and Kyng, *Design at Work: Cooperative Design of Computer Systems* [1991]
- Schuler and Namioka, *Participatory Design: Principles and Practices* [1993]
- Holtzblatt et al., *Rapid Contextual Design: A How-to Guide to Key Techniques for User-Centered Design* [2004]

Most books on Agile/XP development should also provide advice on how to get users to contribute their task-domain expertise effectively. The current popularity of Agile/XP methods has created an almost overwhelming selection of such books.

Overcome organizational obstacles to user involvement

If you encounter hurdles in trying to bring developers together with users, use your management skills to overcome or circumvent them. If some customers won't participate, find ones who will. If the user's manager is the obstacle, escalate the request to higher management in that organization. If you really can't get access to real users, find surrogates who share characteristics with your users. If all else fails, assign someone on your team to become a user.

Use dedicated designers for complex, specialized applications

Companies developing complex, highly specialized applications should have a dedicated UI designer on staff as a full-time employee. After a year on the job, the designer might actually know something about the company's target task domains. If a development team continually brings in new designers from outside, it will either continually have to pay the cost of teaching them about the task domain or continually have products designed by people who don't understand what they are designing.

Hire dual experts if you can find them

Sometimes it is possible to hire software engineers who are also experts in the target task domain. For example, the music software industry hires programmers who are also musicians. This approach has limitations because programming skill plus task-domain skill does not equal UI design skill, but it is better than having *no* task-domain expertise on the team. Sometimes it can work extremely well. For example, a company that developed medical equipment and software had on its staff an engineer who was also a medical doctor. The products his team developed were very successful. Of course, people with dual expertise are very hard to find.

Blooper 69: Using poor tools and building blocks

It is difficult to build high-quality products using poor-quality tools or shoddy materials. This is as true for software as it is for furniture, houses, and pottery. It is particularly true for GUIs.

The tools for designing and building GUIs for interactive software include GUI toolkits, interactive GUI builders, Web page editors, graphics libraries, query languages, scripting languages, and declarative specification languages. You want to choose the best and most appropriate tools for your development effort. Many criteria must be considered when evaluating GUI tools. One important one is the usability of the GUIs that can be built.

The problem is, those who choose an organization's GUI tools usually lack the skills needed to evaluate that factor. Neither development managers, who usually decide which GUI tools to buy, nor GUI programmers, who build GUIs and advise managers about what tools to buy, are GUI design experts. The criteria they use to choose GUI tools typically do not include the usability of the GUIs that can be built. Instead, managers and developers focus on these criteria:

1. How easy the tool is for programmers to learn
2. How quickly programmers can develop GUIs using the tool
3. How easy the resulting GUIs are to maintain
4. How well the tool fits into the organization's development processes
5. How compatible the tool is with other development tools the team uses
6. Whether the tool runs on the operating system the developers use
7. How compatible the resulting GUIs are to back-end software and existing components
8. Whether the tool is already owned by the company
9. Whether the tool has been previously used in the company by this or other organizations
10. How much code or computer memory the resulting GUIs require
11. Whether the programmer used the tool in a previous job
12. How much the tool costs
13. Whether the toolmaker charges royalties on products made with the tool
14. Whether the tool is currently in fashion or considered "cool" in the software industry

Except for No. 14, these are important criteria. Criteria 1–5 are about usability, but of the tool itself rather than the GUIs it produces. The problem is that because managers and programmers typically decide and advise about GUI tools, criteria 1–14 get much more weight than criteria related to the usability of the GUIs that can be built using the tools, such as the following:

15. How compliant GUIs developed with the tool are with standards for the target application platform, such as Windows, Macintosh, Java, and Web

16. How compliant GUIs developed with the tool are with general GUI design standards

17. Whether the tool guides programmers toward GUIs that conform to design guidelines and avoid bloopers

18. Whether the tool provides all the GUI controls that are needed for the application or allows programmers to easily create them

19. Whether the tool allows appearance details to be fine-tuned to conform to a desired company or application suite look and feel

20. Whether the tool provides communication between GUI controls and semantic or back-end components that is rich enough for users to get accurate and timely feedback for their actions

21. Whether GUIs developed using the tool are sufficiently responsive (see Chapter 7)

22. How easy GUIs developed with the tool are to internationalize and localize

23. How accessible GUIs developed with the tool are to various types of users, such as people who prefer a keyboard to a mouse or are elderly or disabled (e.g., sight, hearing, or motor impaired)

Few managers and programmers have the background to evaluate tools based on criteria 15–23. However, the usability, and hence the perceived quality, of the resulting products depends at *least* as much on these criteria as on criteria 1–14.

Developers, including managers, focus more on their own development costs and benefits than on the costs and benefits that the resulting product will generate for others [Grudin, 1991]. "Others" includes people who sell and support the product (both in the developers' company and outside of it) and those who use it. A product's lifetime is (hopefully) many times longer than its development time, and the number of sales and product support people and users far exceeds the number of developers. Therefore, focusing on development costs and benefits when selecting development tools is a misweighting of criteria.

The experts who are in a position to evaluate tools based on the second set of criteria are UI designers and usability testers. However, they are rarely involved in choosing GUI construction tools. This is especially true in companies that have no UI professionals in-house and instead bring in external consultants when they need a UI designed, reviewed, or tested. The tools are chosen long before the consultant is hired.

The result is that many design recommendations made by UI designers and usability testers are rebuffed by developers because "the development tool won't let us do that" or because "that would be too hard to do on this platform."

The following are cases in which usability was hampered by development tools.

Example 1: *Menus that violate users' muscle memory*

A company had developed software that made heavy use of dropdown menus. Users should be able to operate such menus by either of two methods:

1. Place pointer over menu, press mouse button down to display all choices, drag pointer to desired choice (i.e., move pointer while holding button down), release mouse button.

2. Place pointer over menu, click (i.e., press and release mouse button) to display all choices, move pointer to desired new value, click to choose value and close menu.

Option menus in this software worked only by method 2. The developers could do little about this problem, because the dropdown menus provided by the GUI toolkit their managers had selected did not allow method 1 of operation. Strangely, *menubar* menus, from the same GUI toolkit, worked both ways.

Menu operation is a muscle-memory action: people don't think about it once they've learned it. Some people use method 1; others use method 2. Menus that work only one way violate the muscle memory of users who learned the other way. There was therefore a serious usability flaw in the GUI toolkit the team had chosen. Project leaders refused to ask the toolkit vendor to fix the problem because they were too busy and lacked support channels, and they didn't think it was important anyway because there was another way to operate the menus. The product did not survive long in the marketplace.

Example 2: *Unresponsive controls*

A client was developing an application using GUI controls that was extremely slow to respond to user actions. Buttons would take many seconds to acknowledge being clicked, scrollbars would not respond to mouse movements until after the scrolled window content had scrolled, window-sizing and -moving actions took up to a minute to take effect, and so forth. This is a serious problem because these are hand–eye coordination tasks requiring tight visual feedback (see Chapter 7). The developers' excuse was that the GUI toolkit they were using was slow and would remain so until its next release. Unfortunately, they had to release their product based on the *current* toolkit release, guaranteeing it a reputation of being slow.

Example 3: *Inadequate navigation feedback*

A usability test showed that users were getting lost in an application's online Help documentation. One reason was that the links between topics did not indicate whether the user had already visited the linked section. Several test participants suggested that the links should change color once they had been followed. This suggestion was given to the developers, but they said that the toolkit used to build the Help documentation did not support that.

Usability flaws caused by the choice of a GUI tool can add up. If using a particular tool produces GUIs that have too many problems, one would expect project managers to reconsider their decision to use it. That almost never happens.

Avoiding Blooper 69

It is difficult to give good advice on how to avoid this blooper because so many GUI development tools and toolkits are so bad. This section explains how to evaluate and select the tools and controls it will use to develop GUIs.

 The trouble with GUI components

> A problem common to most GUI development tools is that they force developers to begin by deciding how the GUI *looks*, rather than how it *functions* in the application. For example, developers have to decide up front how a choice will be presented: as a menu or a set of radio buttons. This is because most GUI tools classify controls by their appearance (e.g., menu, text field, radio buttons, checkbox). Developers also usually have to worry about layout issues early in development, because most GUI tools require that each control be explicitly positioned. This leads to endless fiddling and twiddling with widgets and layout, distracting programmers and designers from more important design work: deciding what users of the application need to be able to set and control to accomplish their work.
>
> GUI toolkits can be designed so programmers choose controls based on their function (e.g., one-from-N choice, ON/OFF setting, number in range) rather than their appearance. In such a toolkit, a dropdown menu and a set of radio buttons are not two different types of control, but rather the same type (one-from-N choice) presented in two different ways [Johnson, 1992].   ⊕

Most important criterion for choosing a GUI tool: How usable are the resulting GUIs?

When evaluating and comparing tools, place significant weight on criteria 15–23 above. Your customers don't care how you built your product or what parts it is built from; they care only about the product as a whole. Is it good enough for them, or isn't it? If your product's usability is poor because of the GUI tools you used, the loser isn't the tool developer; after all, you already bought their product. They won. The loser is you.

DILBERT © Scott Adams/Dist. by United Feature Syndicate, Inc.

When developing an application, set responsiveness criteria for each function. Parts of the application that don't meet their responsiveness goals should be considered showstoppers, whether the problem is in your own team's software or in the GUI controls you are using. Don't say, "Those problems are in the GUI controls, not in our software, so we can't fix them." You can fix them: demand improvements from the GUI control developer, get different controls, or build your own. If you ship with unresponsive GUI controls, it is your sales that will suffer, not those of the control vendor.

The best qualified people to judge how well a particular GUI tool or toolkit meets criteria 15–23 are your UI designers (you do have some of those, don't you?), so make sure they are involved in the decision. Criteria 1–13 should be considered by management and the programmers. Criterion 14 should simply be ignored.

If the UI designers can't try the tools directly (e.g., because the tools are just libraries of controls), the programmers will have to implement some of the GUI using the tools and then let the UI people evaluate the results. When shopping for the GUI tools your team will use to build its applications, try to implement crucial parts of the GUI using the various candidate tools. This of course takes time, but then again, choosing GUI-development tools is a big decision because once your programmers learn a tool, you have a significant investment in it and so are unlikely to change tools soon. Therefore, choose your GUI development tools very carefully.

Tools can't design software; only designers can do that

Some managers in the software industry believe that using interactive GUI development tools enables less skilled employees to design professional-quality GUIs. That is just marketing hype, wishful thinking, or both.

Interactive GUI and Web development tools simply allow less skilled people to create UIs, most of which will be of amateur quality. Knowing how to use tools does not imply knowing what to do with them. Enabling developers to build GUIs by dragging controls instead of programming does not ensure that the resulting GUIs will be good. The tools are too unconstrained. Also, as Cooper [1999] points out, the fact that a GUI was constructed does not mean it was *designed*.

Drag-and-drop GUI construction tools are not and will never be the solution to the problem of difficult-to-use software. Indeed, it is more likely that increased use of interactive GUI and Web development software will bring about an overall *decrease* in the quality of applications, as more people who don't know what they are doing develop software. If you want successful software make sure that the people designing it know what they are doing.

Blooper 70: Giving programmers the fastest computers

This may be the most controversial blooper in this book. Nonetheless, the common practice of giving developers the fastest computers and highest speed Internet connections is one important cause of the responsiveness bloopers described in Chapter 7.

Justifications

Management often goes to considerable expense to give software engineers the latest, fastest computers and fastest available connections to the Internet. This is done for several reasons:

- Engineers like speed. They like having the fastest computers available. They like being able to download files from the Web instantly.
- Fast computers and network connections maximize programmer productivity, especially when development involves much compiling or script-driven building or testing of new versions.
- Computer companies like to have their own programmer employees using their latest hardware as one way of shaking out flaws.
- Computer companies like to build software for their newest models because it encourages customers to upgrade.

Costs

One cost of always giving programmers the fastest computers and network connections is that their systems will be faster than those of most customers. Customer adoption of new technology typically follows a bell-curve distribution (Figure 8.6): a few risk takers take the plunge immediately, then adoption of the new technology by old and new customers accelerates, then the market saturates and the sales curve begins falling, and finally the last few holdouts bite the bullet and catch up with everyone else. The important part of the bell curve is the middle; that's where most of the customers are.

Figure 8.6

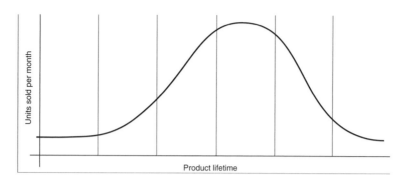

Market adoption of new computer models over time.

Another cost of giving programmers the latest hardware and net connections is that they become accustomed to frequent upgrades and so view performance and responsiveness problems as only temporary, "until the next upgrade." Customers don't upgrade nearly as often because computers and Internet connections cost them real money. They have to wait to upgrade until their accountants have amortized the cost of the last purchase down to the level at which upgrading can be justified. In contrast, upgrading programmers' computers costs *them* nothing. Therefore, they tend to be unsympathetic to customer complaints about performance and/or responsiveness: "Just upgrade your computers and the software will be fast enough."

Net connections: The masses are way behind the technology elite

Internet connection speed is another area in which the general public lags behind the technology elite. Surveys conducted in late 2006 and early 2007 found that between one-fifth and two-fifths of home Internet users in the United States were still using dial-up connections of 56 kbaud or less:

- Consumer Affairs (www.consumeraffairs.com), September 2006: 44% dial-up
- Pew Internet & American Life Project (www.PewInternet.org), December 2006: 29% dial-up
- Website Optimization (www.websiteoptimization.com), February 2007: 21% dial-up

Similarly, an international study published in 2005 found that about one-third of all Internet users (including business users) still had dial-up connections.[3]

Furthermore, an analysis of the trends published in Horrigan [2005] suggests that uptake of broadband Internet access in U.S. homes, which was slow

---

3. Ipsos News Center Press Release, March 2005 (www.ipsos-na.com/news/pressrelease.cfm?id = 2583).

until about 2000 but rose steeply through mid-2005, began slowing again in late 2005 and early 2006. Apparently, market saturation was beginning to set in, as those who wanted or needed broadband got it, and those who use the Internet mainly for e-mail remained satisfied with dial-up.

Even the so-called "high-speed" Internet connections that most people have in their homes and small businesses—mainly DSL and cable—are slow compared to the T3, fiber-optic OC3, and other super-fast Internet connections typically found in technology development firms.

Most of a computer or software company's customers will not have the most powerful computers or fastest Internet connections for many months or years. By then, many software developers will have already upgraded to the *next* new models and net connections. As a result, software that is acceptably responsive on programmers' computers will often not be so on the customers'.

Avoiding Blooper 70

Don't be too quick to upgrade programmers' computers

Without question, programmers need access to fast machines for compiling and building software. But compiling and building can be done on servers. The computers on which developers *run* and *test* the software they develop should be like those that most customers are using. Otherwise, the programmers will produce software that customers will find sluggish and unresponsive. Former Apple user interface designer Peter Bickford shares my opinion. In his book *Interface Design* [1997], he wrote:

> "There's a school of thought that says that programmers should be forced to work on the least-powerful systems in their target market, instead of the high-end workstations they tend to use. While this seems a bit like cruel and unusual punishment to me, I've seen programmers … rewrite routines to work 20 times faster when they were forced to run their applications on the department secretary's machine."

Test on slower computers

Engineering teams should at least have slower machines to test on. Furthermore, testing on computers like those customers have should be mandatory, with firm criteria for deciding whether the software is responsive enough to release.

Test it with slow net connections

Although I do not advocate forcing software developers—especially Web developers—to use slow Internet connections, I do advocate requiring them to test Web applications and Web sites using connection speeds that are typical of their customers. That of course requires finding out what sort of network connections customers have.

Appendices

Appendix A: Glossary

For readers new to UI design, here are terms that are commonly used in the UI field.

- ***Application, software application:*** software designed to help users perform a task, solve a problem, or achieve a goal. Application software contrasts with system software, which controls the internal operation of a computer. Application software is the software most computer users encounter directly. The term comes from the idea that software is applied to a task or set of tasks.

- ***Back end:*** software services used by *applications* to provide content and *task-domain* logic. Back ends store and retrieve data, perform big computations, route communications, etc. Back-end software often runs on computers called servers.

- ***Conceptual model:*** a high-level description of how an application is organized and operates. It specifies the concepts that the application exposes to users and how they are organized. The purpose of a conceptual model is to provide a basis for users to understand how the application works in order to use it effectively.

- ***Conceptual objects:*** the things in a *task domain* that people manipulate. When people talk about a task domain, the conceptual objects are the nouns. (The verbs are the actions that people perform on the objects.) Examples of objects in the task domain of organizing digital photos are photo album, slide show, photo, caption.

- ***Control:*** an element or component of a graphical user interface that computer users interact with to input data to software, or a component that presents data from the software for users. Examples of controls are dialog box, checkbox, text field, slider. Also called a *widget*.

- ***Dialog box:*** a type of software window that opens temporarily to display a message, let users set options on a pending command, or let users set an object's properties. Dialog boxes typically have "OK" and "Cancel" buttons in addition to whatever controls and data fields they need.

- **Display inertia:** a UI design principle stating that when a user edits something on the display, the effect of the change should be kept as local as possible, so most of the display stays as it was. When this principle is violated, users are confused by too much movement.

- **Focus group:** a meeting convened by a product development organization to show customers or users new products, prototypes, or design ideas to get their feedback. Attendees react in groups, so feedback from different people is not independent, but rather builds on feedback from other attendees.

- **GUI toolkit:** a set of *controls* (components) from which *applications* are constructed. Usually the controls in a GUI toolkit embody a specific look and feel, but some GUI toolkits can be switched to present different appearances. Examples of GUI toolkits are Java Swing and Windows ActiveX.

- **Heuristic evaluation:** a method of reviewing the usability of software to find potential problems. Reviewers go through the software systematically with a list of UI design guidelines in hand, noting places where the software's UI violates the guidelines.

- **Interactive system:** any device or computer software that people can operate and that can respond in complex ways. A hammer would not be called an interactive system, but a mobile phone would, and a washing machine might be, depending on how complex it is.

- **Inside-out thinking vs. outside-in thinking:** thinking inside-out is (wrongly) assuming that users of an application know what the designers know and therefore can interpret what they see in the UI as the designers intended. Thinking outside-in is (correctly) assuming that users do not know what designers know, so the UI must be designed to be unambiguously interpretable.

- **Metaphor:** designing a UI to be similar in certain ways to something users already know, so they can transfer their learning from the other thing to the new software UI. Examples of metaphors used in computer systems to expedite learning are computer desktop, trash can for delete, on-screen copies of hand-held calculators.

- **Mode:** a state of a computer *application* in which certain user actions have a particular effect, whereas in a different mode, the same actions have a different effect. For example, on a computer keyboard, the Shift Lock key turns ON a mode that makes the letter keys type capital letters until Shift Lock is turned OFF. Modes allow a system to have more functionality without more keys or buttons.

- **Moded, modal:** the term for an *interactive system* that has *modes.* Moded systems have advantages, but are harder to learn to use.

- **Modeless:** the term for *interactive systems* that don't have *modes,* i.e., every user action always has the same effect.

- **Object/action analysis:** a listing of the *conceptual objects* that people working in a *task domain* encounter. The enumeration specifies how objects are related to each other, e.g., type/subtype, container/containee, whole/part. The analysis also lists actions that can be performed on each type of object and attributes of the object. This analysis is the most important part of a *conceptual model*. The result of object/action analysis is sometimes called an *ontology*.

- **Persona:** a *user profile* elaborated into a detailed description of a person, with relevant details about lifestyle, economic status, education, and *task domain* knowledge and often a photograph or sketch of the user.

- **Primary window:** a window in a *software application* that is "home" for the application as a whole or at least for a certain part of its functionality. Primary windows usually remain displayed for a significant amount of time, in contrast to secondary windows (e.g., dialog boxes), which are usually transient.

- **Product lexicon, dictionary, nomenclature, terminology standard, vocabulary, glossary:** a list of the terminology used in an application and its documentation, with terms and their meanings.

- **Progressive disclosure:** a design technique that simplifies UIs by hiding details or seldom-used controls until the user needs them. In some cases, hidden controls appear when users click a "Details" or "More" button; in others, they appear when other changes in the software make them relevant.

- **Responsiveness:** the ability of software to keep up with users and keep them informed of what it is doing.

- **Secondary window:** a software window that is designed to be displayed temporarily, either to present a message to a user or to collect input from the user. Most secondary windows are *dialog boxes*. Contrasts with *primary window*.

- **Task analysis:** studying the tasks in a *task domain* to understand what all the tasks are, which tasks are common vs. rare, what the steps of each task are, what goes into a task, and what results from it.

- **Task domain:** a set of tasks in which all the tasks concern the same general topic. Examples of task domains are business accounting, bank account maintenance, shopping for a car, the game of chess, taking photographs. Software applications are usually designed to support not just a single task, but rather many tasks in a task domain.

- **Usability test:** a test in which representative users are observed while they use software. Usability tests are conducted to find usability problems. There are many different ways to conduct usability tests.

- **User analysis:** studying the intended users of an *application* or Web site to understand their needs.

- **User profile:** a brief description of one type of user that an *application* is designed for. Several user profiles are usually created for each product, each one representing a distinctive category of important users. When user profiles are elaborated with names and made-up details to define a stereotypical user, they are called *personas*.

- **Visual hierarchy:** a way to design displays so that users can quickly see which information (or functionality) is in which part of the display. This allows users to quickly drill down to the information or functionality that they need, while virtually ignoring the rest of the display.

- **Wizard:** a multistep dialog box that breaks a complex process or collection of options down into simpler parts. Users are led through the steps, but can back up or quit at any time.

Appendix B: How this book was usability tested

Second edition: Improvements based on feedback from first-edition readers

This is release 2.0. Release 1.0 was explicitly usability tested and improved before it was released (see below). The result was a useful book (as indicated by sales), but one that still had usability problems.

Those problems were pointed out by readers in review articles for magazines, in comments posted at online booksellers and in online discussion groups, and in notes sent to me. The most important flaws of *GUI Bloopers* 1.0 were the following:

- *Lack of figure captions:* Figures in *GUI Bloopers* had no captions, just numbers, making it hard for readers to get information by flipping through the book looking at figures.

- *Cross-references were not exact enough:* In the first edition, the publication process did not allow us to have cross-references be exact page numbers; instead, cross-references provided blooper or section numbers.

- *Too wordy:* Many readers complained that the first edition was too verbose.

- *Anti-programmer tone:* In release 1.0, I tried to explain that not all GUI bloopers are the fault of programmers, and those that are nominally committed by programmers are often due to faulty tools, unrealistic schedules, poor management, or a lack of GUI design training. Nonetheless, a few readers complained of an anti-programmer tone.

To correct the first three problems, we did the obvious: we added figure captions, we changed cross-references to page numbers, and we cut excess verbiage. We also removed two chapters few people ever mentioned; they only added to the book's bulk and price. Eliminating the anti-programmer tone wasn't as straightforward, but in revising the book I tried very hard (again) to do that.

First edition testing

This book recommends testing the usability of software as early as possible in development and as often as is feasible along the way. Indeed, it lambastes developers who don't usability-test their products before releasing them. It would be hypocritical to publish this book without first testing it on people who are representative of the intended readers.

Reviewing is not usability testing

When the first edition of this book was proposed to the publisher and while it was being written, outlines and drafts were sent to reviewers to evaluate and comment upon. The reviewers were, in general, experienced UI professionals. Some were professors and industrial researchers; others were UI designers or usability testers working either for companies or as consultants. All had years of experience reviewing books and articles, as well as having their own writings reviewed. Getting input from an author's professional peers is standard practice for technical books. However, such reviews are not a valid usability test of this book, for two reasons:

1. The reviewers used by the publisher are not really the intended readers of this book. The intended readers are software developers who often work without professional UI support, development managers, and new UI designers. Getting feedback from people representing the upper echelons of the Human–Computer Interaction field is very different from testing the book on its intended audience.

2. Asking someone to read a book and comment on it is not the same as asking someone to use it—or consider how they would use it—in their work.

Getting developers to test the book

We asked several professional programmers (some of whom were also managers) to read the manuscript and either use it in their work or consider how they would use it. Some actually did use the book to help find and clean up bloopers in their organization's software. Others just read it and imagined how they would use it. In addition to accepting whatever feedback they gave us, we asked them to answer questions about the book's content and organization. Although this testing was informal, it was extremely valuable in guiding the design of the book as we revised the first draft into the published version.

What we learned from testing

- *Make it more random access.* Programmers did not want to have to read the book from front to back. They wanted to be able to look up bloopers to answer their specific design questions. They wanted each blooper and how to avoid it either to be totally self-contained or to point exactly to where additional information could be found. They wanted the book to be more—in one programmer's words—"random access." No such recommendations came from the academics and researchers who reviewed the book. In response to this feedback, we revised the bloopers to make each one self-contained. Where that wasn't possible, we tried to make it easy to follow cross-references, by referring to blooper and section numbers (not just chapter numbers) and adding a comprehensive table of contents and a detailed index.

- *Make important points stand out.* Programmers did not like it when important points were buried in the middle of paragraphs. They wanted to be able to browse or flip through the book and still get useful information. Based on this feedback, I made more use of headings, emphasis, tables, and bullet points and worked with the publisher to format and lay out the book to make it easier to scan for information.

- *Explain why the bloopers are bloopers.* Programmers asked for explanations of why the bloopers are considered bloopers, as well as for the principles underlying the design rules for avoiding bloopers. The programmers wanted these explanations up front, *before* the bloopers. Early drafts of release 1.0 started with the bloopers, on the assumption that GUI programmers would want to focus on concrete design mistakes and avoid abstract principles and theory. Design principles were scattered as needed around the book—mainly in the design rules for avoiding bloopers. Testing showed that that approach was wrong, so Chapter 1 was added.

- *Give more examples.* A not-so-surprising request from several programmers was "more examples, more screen images." The same request came from regular reviewers. Early versions of the manuscript had a lack of illustrative screen images. Partly as a result of this feedback and partly based on the preexisting plan, many more examples were added, and some bloopers for which good examples could not be found or sketched were deleted.

- *Mark examples as "good" or "bad."* Programmers wanted the visual examples of bloopers and correct design to be clearly marked as "good" or "bad." They didn't want to have to read the text around a figure to find out whether it was an example of a blooper or a good design. We conducted paper tests of various symbols for "good" and "bad" and settled on hands with thumbs up and down for "good" and "bad," respectively.

- *Don't "dis" programmers.* Several programmers criticized early drafts of the book for blaming programmers for committing bloopers. Sometimes, they said, bloopers are the fault of the tools or building blocks that the programmer has to use or of the development process the programmer must follow. I agree. GUI programmers work very hard and do good work. I am using the bloopers format as an instructional device to get developers to learn to recognize common GUI mistakes and how to avoid them. So as not to offend my primary audience, I tried to make the book less critical of the *people* and more critical of the development *process*.

Appendix C: Task analysis of creating slide presentations—questions

The complete list of questions used in task-analysis interviews described in the sidebar on pages 14–15 is as follows:

1. What is your role in producing slide presentations?
    1.1 Do you produce slides yourself or do you supervise others who do it?
        1.1.1 What sort of training or experience is required to do the job you do?
        1.1.2 [If supervises others] What is the skill level of your employees?
    1.2 How much of your total job involves producing slide presentations?
    1.3 For whom do you produce these slide presentations?
        1.3.1 Who is the customer (i.e., who approves the slides)?
        1.3.2 Who is the audience for the presentations?
    1.4 What quality level is required for the slides?
        1.4.1 How important are elaborate special effects (e.g., animation, dissolve)?
        1.4.2 Who decides on appearance and quality, you or the customer?
        1.4.3 Are there different kinds of presentations with different quality requirements?
    1.5 Do you (your department) follow slide formatting standards?
        1.5.1 How do you ensure that slides adhere to those standards?
        1.5.2 Does your slide-making software help with standardization of presentations?
2. What software do you use to create slide presentations?
    2.1 Who decides what software you use for this?
    2.2 Do you use one program or a collection of them?
        2.2.1 [If many] What are the different programs used for?

2.3 Do you use general-purpose drawing software or slide-making software?

    2.3.1 Why?

2.4 What do you like about each of the programs you use?

2.5 What do you dislike about each one; what would you like to see changed?

    2.5.1 Describe some of the things you do to "work around" limitations of the software.

2.6 How easy is the software for new users to learn?

    2.6.1 How do they learn the software (classes, manuals, using, asking)?

    2.6.2 How did you learn it?

2.7 What other software have you used, tried, or considered for making slides, either here or in previous jobs?

    2.7.1 Why don't you use it now?

3. What is involved in making slides?

    3.1 Describe the complete process of producing a presentation, from when you take the assignment to when you deliver it to the customer.

        3.1.1 How much revision is usually required before a presentation is considered done?

    3.2 Do you usually create new slide presentations?

        3.2.1 What is hard and what is easy about creating new material, i.e., what goes quickly and what takes time and work?

    3.3 Do you reuse old slides in new presentations?

        3.3.1 What is hard and what is easy about reusing old material, i.e., what goes quickly and what takes time and work?

    3.4 How do you (your department) organize and keep track of slides and presentations?

        3.4.1 Is each slide a separate file, or are all the slides in a presentation together in one file?

        3.4.2 How do you organize your material?

        3.4.3 How do you name your slide (or presentation) files?

        3.4.4 Do you ever fail to find a slide you know you have?

        3.4.5 How does your software hinder you in reusing material?

        3.4.6 How easily can you include a single slide in several different presentations?

    3.5 What kinds of revisions are often required in the process of preparing a presentation?

        3.5.1 Which are easy and which are hard?

3.5.2 Are the same revisions easy and hard for each slide-making program you use?

3.5.3 Specific important cases:

3.5.3.1 A slide used in multiple presentations is changed.

3.5.3.2 A logo or standard border must be added to all slides in a presentation.

3.5.3.3 The order of slides in a presentation must be changed.

3.5.3.4 Round bullets throughout a presentation must be changed to square ones.

3.5.3.5 The font used throughout a presentation must be changed.

3.5.3.6 Each point on a slide must be expanded into a separate slide.

Appendix D: Illustrating simplicity—the object/action matrix

The conceptual model for any interactive software can be illustrated as a matrix of objects and actions. Objects are listed down the left edge; actions are listed across the top (Figure A.1). For the moment, we are ignoring the object *type* hierarchy and simply listing the objects. The more objects, the taller the matrix; the more actions, the wider.

Constructing such a matrix lets you visualize the simplicity and coherence of a conceptual model. It shows how consistent or inconsistent it is—how easy it is for users to transfer learning about one part to another. A small, dense matrix indicates a design that will be easy to learn: few objects, few actions, and most actions apply to most objects (Figure A.2A).

A large, sparse matrix reflects an incoherent design that will be hard to learn and remember because every concept works differently (Figure A.2B).

Figure A.1

Object/action matrix shows which actions apply to which objects.

Figure A.2

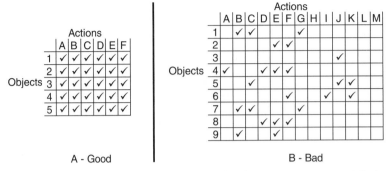

A - Good   B - Bad

Object/action matrices for easy-to-master vs. hard-to-master conceptual designs.

Such a conceptual design will seem confusing and arbitrary to users no matter what GUI is plastered on it.

The larger the matrix, the *more* there is to learn. A tall matrix indicates a lot of objects to master; a wide one indicates many actions to learn. A good rule of thumb is to simplify the conceptual model so that the matrix representing it is as small and dense as possible.

A small matrix, however, reflects very limited functionality. Achieving a small matrix is difficult when the application is anything more complicated than, say, a personal phone directory or a Web site for looking up postage rates. But everything is relative. For any desired functionality, you can design conceptual models of varying complexity. Just aim for the simplest conceptual model and the most compact object/action matrix for the required functionality.

Also, although easy-to-learn, easy-to-use systems often have small, compact object/action matrices, they can have other matrix configurations as well. Consider a system in which all functionality is accessed through five or six generic actions that apply to all objects. Such a system could have a large number of objects without much negative impact on learnability, because all objects work the same way. The object/action matrix for such a system, although tall, would be narrow and dense. This approach has been used to design many highly functional systems.

If we include the object *type* hierarchy in the matrix, we can see another sort of conceptual model that is easy to learn: one in which objects fall clearly into *categories,* with each category having its own actions, perhaps with a few actions that apply to all objects (Figure A.3). The matrix for such a model isn't small or dense, but it also isn't scattered. It has a regularity that aids learning and retention. An example of this would be a real estate service offering both commercial and residential properties, with different actions for each property as well as actions for all properties.

Figure A.3

Objects		Type-Specific Actions												Common Actions
		A	B	C	D	E	F	G	H	I	J	K	L	M
X	1	✓	✓	✓	✓									✓
X	2	✓	✓	✓	✓									✓
X	3	✓	✓	✓	✓									✓
Y	4					✓	✓	✓	✓					✓
Y	5					✓	✓	✓	✓					✓
Y	6					✓	✓	✓	✓					✓
Z	7									✓	✓	✓	✓	✓
Z	8									✓	✓	✓	✓	✓
Z	9									✓	✓	✓	✓	✓

Object/action matrix for a more realistic type of easy-to-master conceptual design.

Appendix E: Usability tests for every time and purpose

Usability tests can be categorized along two dimensions (Basic Principle 9, page 48):

1. The point in development at which they are conducted
2. The formality of the testing method

Implementation stage of testing

First let's consider the point in development at which testing is done. It helps to divide this dimension into three categories:

- *Before development:* Before anything has been implemented, developers can test a design using mock-ups. Mock-ups can be storyboards—hand-drawn sketches of the design on paper that are shown to users in the order they would occur in the running product. They can be screen images created using interactive GUI building tools, printed out onto paper, and placed in front of users with a person acting as "the computer" as the user "clicks" the controls shown on the screens. They can be "cardboard computers" with rear projection screens that show images simulating the display (see the chapter "Cardboard Computers" in the book by Greenbaum and Kyng [1991]). Finally, they can be "Wizard of Oz" systems in which the display on the computer screen is controlled by a person in another room who watches what the user does and changes the user's screen accordingly.
- *During development:* A development team can use prototyping software (e.g., Flash) to create working mock-ups of an application. GUIs prototyped

with such tools would be only prototypes; their underlying code would not be used in the eventual implementation. Alternatively, some GUI building tools allow user interfaces to be partially wired together and "run." This allows early versions of the GUI to be tested even before any back-end code has been written. Another way to test during development is to test parts of the planned application in isolation, to resolve design issues. For example, one could test a table control used in an application long before any of the rest of the application was ready.

- *After development:* Many usability tests are conducted when most of the product has been implemented and it is being prepared for release. At this late stage, it is rare for the results of usability tests to have much of an impact on the pending release because the development organization is usually ready to ship it. One reason for conducting usability tests at this stage is to provide guidance for a preshipping cleanup of minor usability problems. Nonetheless, such testing can also uncover "showstopper" problems that are deemed important enough to delay the release. A second reason for testing "completed" software is to get feedback on how to improve *future* releases. This sort of testing can be conducted after a release, when the schedule is not so frantic and the team is beginning to think about the next release.

Formality of testing

The second dimension along which usability testing can be categorized is the formality of the testing method. Usability test formality has to do with the degree of control the tester exerts over what people do in the test session and whether the measurements are qualitative or quantitative. Again, it is helpful to divide this dimension into three categories:

- *Informal:* This type of testing includes situations in which users are interviewed about the software, for example, how they use it, what they use it for, how they like it. Sometimes this is done in front of a computer with the software running so the user can show what he or she is talking about, and sometimes it isn't. Informal testing also includes situations in which users are observed while they do their real work or while they explore the software in an unguided fashion. The observers note the users' expressed likes and dislikes and record any problems they notice users having. The session may be videotaped or audiotaped. The observations are qualitative. It is best to start each test session with simple tasks and give the test participant progressively harder tasks over the course of the session.

- *Quasi-formal:* In this type of testing, users are asked to do tasks that have been predetermined by the testers, who also prepared the necessary materials and data files and set up the software as required. In other words, users aren't just exploring the software or doing their own work; they are doing what the tester asks them to do. However, as in informal testing, the measurements are mainly observational. The testers record (and count) any errors users make, as well as situations in which users need help (either from online help documents or from the testers). The testers also record the time required to complete each of the tasks. The session may be videotaped.

- *Formal:* This is the type of usability testing that is most similar to the psychology experiments many people remember from their college days. They are true "controlled experiments," conducted to compare alternative designs (e.g., control layouts A versus B) or to determine an optimal value of a design parameter (e.g., number of cascading menu levels). The tasks that test participants are asked to perform are highly prescribed, and their relation to real-world tasks often seems tenuous (e.g., use the mouse to hit a sequence of randomly positioned targets on the screen; find a file using this file browser). In fact, the materials or software used for the test often are devised purely for the test itself, rather than being part of a pending product. The data collected are mainly quantitative (e.g., user reaction or completion time, number of errors) and are analyzed statistically. Often, the data are collected automatically, by the same computer that is running the test software. In addition, such sessions are usually videotaped.

Each level of formality has a place in product development. It is important to realize that the formality of a test is independent of the point in development at which the test is conducted. At any stage of development, one can devise usability tests at any level of formality. Some examples are given in the discussion of Blooper 66 (page 341).

Table A.1 provides examples of tests exhibiting each possible combination of the three development stages and three levels of formality.

Predevelopment tests provide great value

Test before development when possible. It's low tech, it's cheap, it's easy, it provides valuable feedback, and it is early enough to have a major impact on the design. Preimplementation testing allows you to test ideas before the development team goes to the expense of coding them.

For example, to test whether the graphical labels on toolbar buttons convey their intended meanings to users, print them in color or put them on a Web page and ask people to match them with a list of function names. To find out if the location and naming of items in the menubar menus make sense to users, print out the menubar and the menus (or even handwrite them) and ask people to find specified items. Preimplementation testing is good for testing issues of comprehension, navigation, and overall task flow, but of course bad for testing complex interaction and responsiveness issues.

Table A.1   Usability tests conducted at various stages of development and varying in formality

Formality of test method	Development stage		
	Before	*During*	*After*
Informal: interviews, surveys, field studies, observing users in normal work environments	Interviews and focus groups were conducted with teachers to learn how they use videos in the classroom and what they like and dislike about the current (noncomputerized) system for finding, choosing, and showing videos. This was done in preparation for designing an online video locator and viewing service for classroom use. For details, see Blooper 6 (page 77).	During the development of a Web application for recording and tracking voting problems in the 2004 U.S. election, sessions were observed in which volunteer users were trained on early versions of the application. Aspects of the UI that were hard for instructors to explain as well as those about which trainees asked many questions were noted and used to guide design improvements [Johnson and Marshall, 2005].	On election day 2004, legal volunteers in call centers who were using the Election Incident Reporting System (EIRS) were videotaped and interviewed. The field observations and users' comments provided valuable input for improving EIRS for the 2005 and later elections [Johnson and Marshall, 2005].
Quasi-formal: predefined tasks given by test moderator; observers note problems, completion time, assists	A static HTML prototype of a corporate Web site was used to test how easily people could navigate to desired information. Six participants were shown the home page and asked to find answers to specified questions. The test results helped guide the design and implementation of the actual site.	Early builds of a browser-based graphical application for managing groups of servers were tested. Eight experienced system administrators were videotaped and timed performing specified server management tasks. The test was conducted in a corporate usability lab. The results prompted significant changes in the UI.	A released version of a hand-held Internet appliance was tested on 10 people to find usability problems and suggest improvements for the next release. Test participants performed brief tasks dictated by the tester. Test sessions were conducted in vacant offices. Observers took notes, but the sessions were not taped.

Table A.1

(Continued)

Usability tests conducted at various stages of development and varying in formality

Formality of test method	Development stage		
	Before	*During*	*After*
Formal: true experiment, quantitative measurement, statistical analysis, often A vs. B comparison	Desktop icons for an office workstation were tested. Test participants were asked both to guess the meaning of icons and to match icons with function names. The icons were presented on paper. The responses were analyzed statistically to yield "confusability" matrices indicating which icons tended to be confused with one another and which icons were easy to recognize. For details, see Miller and Johnson [1996].	To evaluate a new touchpad remote control for operating on-screen controls for interactive television services, a test compared the prototype remote control with traditional pointing devices. Test participants used the pointing devices to try to hit randomly selected buttons arrayed on a TV screen. The time for participants to hit the target button was recorded. Test sessions were in a formal usability lab and were videotaped. For details, see Johnson and Keavney [1995].	A test compared three methods of finding Help documentation in a Windows applications: (a) content list, (b) index, and (c) search. Test participants sought answers to prespecified questions using each of the methods. Quantitative measures recorded included success/failure, task time, number of clicks, number of documents visited, and others. Statistical analyses were used to check for significant differences between the information-seeking methods.

Snyder's book *Paper Prototyping* [2003] provides a good overview of the possibilities for preimplementation testing. Johnson [1998] describes a project in which budget and time constraints required usability tests to be conducted on paper before anything was developed.

Testing during development can also be cheap

Sometimes usability people are brought in after development has already started. If there isn't much budget or time for usability testing, you may have to be creative in how you test the software's usability.

Johnson and Marshall [2005] describe how low-cost, quick-and-dirty tests were used to evaluate designs and resolve design issues in a project that had no budget or time for usability testing. Krug's book *Don't Make Me Think* [2005] also explains how to test cheaply. Recommended testing methods include:

- testing on users using partially working software or semifunctional prototypes;
- using fellow employees who aren't on the project as test participants;
- giving the software to users or usability experts and asking them to review it and report problems;
- observing training sessions to see aspects of the software that trainees have trouble understanding or instructors have trouble explaining.

Bibliography

Ambler, S. 2005. "The Agile System Development Lifecycle." Ambysoft online article: http://www.ambysoft.com/essays/agileLifecycle.html.

Apple Computer, Inc. 2006. *Apple Human Interface Guidelines*. On the Web at http://developer.apple.com/documentation/UserExperience/Conceptual/OSXHIGuidelines/index.html.

Bankston, A. 2001. "Usability and User Interface Design in XP." CC Pace Systems, on the Web at http://www.ccpace.com/Resources/documents/UsabilityinXP.pdf.

Barber, R., and Lucas, H. 1983. "System Response Time, Operator Productivity, and Job Satisfaction." *Communications of the ACM* 26(11): 972–986.

Beck, K., and Andres, C. 2004. *Extreme Programming Explained: Embrace Change*, 2nd edition. Reading, MA: Addison Wesley.

Berkun, S. 2005. *The Art of Project Management*. Sebastapol, CA: O'Reilly Media.

Beyer, H., and Holtzblatt, K. 1998. *Contextual Design: Defining Customer-Centered Systems*. San Francisco: Morgan Kaufmann Publishers.

Bias, R. G., and Mayhew, D. J. 2005. *Cost-Justifying Usability, Second Edition: An Update for the Internet Age*. San Francisco: Morgan Kaufmann Publishers.

Bickford, P. 1997. *Interface Design: The Art of Developing Easy-to-Use Software*. Chestnut Hill, MA: Academic Press.

Brady, J. T. 1986. "A Theory of Productivity in the Creative Process." *IEEE Computer Graphics and Applications* 6(5): 25–34.

Brinck, T., Gergle, D., and Wood, S. D. 2001. *Usability for the Web: Designing Web Sites That Work*. San Francisco: Morgan Kaufmann Publishers.

Brooks, F. 1995. *The Mythical Man-Month: Essays on Software Engineering*, 20th Anniversary Edition, Reading, MA: Addison-Wesley.

Brown, C. M. 1988. *Human–Computer Interface Design Guidelines*. Norwood, NJ: Ablex Publishing.

Card, S. 1996. "Pioneers and Settlers: Methods Used in Successful User Interface Design." In M. Rudisill, C. Lewis, P. Polson, and T. McKay, eds., *Human–Computer Interface Design: Success Cases, Emerging Methods, Real-World Context*. San Francisco: Morgan Kaufmann Publishers.

Card, S., Moran, T., and Newell, A. 1983. *The Psychology of Human–Computer Interaction*. Hillsdale, NJ: Lawrence Erlbaum Associates.

Carroll, J., and Rosson, M. 1984. "Beyond MIPS: Performance Is Not Quality." *Byte Magazine* 9(2): 168–172.

Conklin, P. F. 1996. "Bringing Usability Effectively into Product Development." In M. Rudisill, C. Lewis, P. Polson, and T. McKay, eds., *Human–Computer Interface Design: Success Stories, Emerging Methods, Real-World Context.* San Francisco: Morgan Kaufmann Publishers.

Constantine, L. 2002. "Process Agility and Software Usability: Toward Lightweight Usage-Centered Design." *Information Age* Aug/Sep.

Cooper, A. 1999. *The Inmates are Running the Asylum.* Indianapolis: SAMS (a division of Macmillan Computer Publishing).

Cooper, A., Reimann, R. M., and Cronin, R. 2007. *About Face 3: The Essentials of Interaction Design.* New York: John Wiley and Sons.

Courage, C., and Baxter, K. 2004. *Understanding Your Users: A Practical Guide to User Requirements Methods, Tools, and Techniques.* San Francisco: Morgan Kaufmann Publishers.

Dayton, T., McFarland, A., and Kramer, J. 1998. "Bridging User Needs to Object Oriented GUI Prototypes via Task Object Design." In L. Wood, ed., *User Interface Design: Bridging the Gap from Requirements to Design.* Boca Raton, FL: CRC Press, pp. 15–56.

Dix, A. 1987. "The Myth of the Infinitely Fast Machine." In *People and Computers III: Proceedings of HCI'87.* Cambridge, UK: Cambridge University Press, pp. 215–228. [www.soc.staffs.ac.uk/~cmtajd/papers/hci87]

Duis, D. 1990. *Creating Highly Responsive Interactive Software despite Performance Limitations.* Masters Thesis, Cambridge, MA: Massachusetts Institute of Technology.

Duis, D., and Johnson, J. 1990. "Improving User-Interface Responsiveness despite Performance Limitations." In *Proceedings of IEEE CompCon'90,* San Francisco, CA: IEEE Computer Society. pp. 380–386.

Flanders, V. 2001. *Son of Web Pages That Suck: Learn Good Design by Looking at Bad Design.* Indianapolis: Sybex.

Flanders, V., and Willis, M. 1998. *Web Pages That Suck: Learning Good Design by Looking at Bad Design.* San Francisco: Sybex. [See also WebPagesThatSuck.com]

Fowler, S., and Stanwick, V. 1998. *GUI Design Handbook.* New York: McGraw–Hill. [Also online at http://fast-consulting.com/GUI%20Design%20Handbook/GDH_FRNTMTR.htm]

Fowler, S., and Stanwick, V. 2004. *Web Application Design Handbook.* San Francisco: Morgan Kaufmann Publishers.

Galitz, W. 2007. *The Essential Guide to User Interface Design: An Introduction to GUI Design Principles and Techniques,* 3rd edition. New York: John Wiley and Sons.

Garrett, J. 2005. "AJAX: A New Approach to Web Applications." Adaptive Path online essay: http://www.adaptivepath.com/publications/essays/archives/000385.php.

Gentner, D., and Grudin, J. 1990. "Why Good Engineers (Sometimes) Create Bad Interfaces." In *Proceedings of ACM Conference on Computer–Human Interaction (CHI'90)*, Seattle, ACM Press, pp. 277–282.

Gnome Project. 2006. *Gnome Human Interface Guidelines*. GNU Foundation: http://developer.gnome.org/projects/gup/hig/.

Greenbaum, J., and Kyng, M. 1991. *Design at Work: Cooperative Design of Computer Systems*. Hillsdale, NJ: Lawrence Erlbaum Associates.

Grudin, J. 1989. "The Case against User Interface Consistency." *Communications of the ACM* 32(10): 1164–1173.

Grudin, J. 1991. "Systematic Sources of Suboptimal Interface Design in Large Product Development Organizations." *Human Computer Interaction* 6: 147–196.

Hinckley, K., Pausch, R., Proffitt, D., and Kassell, N. F. 1998. "Two-Handed Virtual Manipulation." *ACM Transactions on Computer–Human Interaction* 5(3): 260–302.

Hoffman, P. 1999. "Accommodating Color Blindness." *Usability Interface* 6(2). [Also available at http://www.stcsig.org/usability/newsletter/9910-color-blindness.html]

Holtzblatt, K., Wendell, J. B., and Wood, S. 2004. *Rapid Contextual Design, First Edition: A How-to Guide to Key Techniques for User-Centered Design*. San Francisco: Morgan Kaufmann Publishers.

Horrigan, J. B. 2005. "Broadband Adoption at Home in the United States." In *Proceedings of the 33rd Annual Telecommunications Policy Research Conference*. Arlington, VA. [Also available from PewInternet.com]

Isaacs, E., and Walendowski, A. 2001. *Designing from Both Sides of the Screen: How Designers and Engineers Can Collaborate to Build Cooperative Technology*. Indianapolis: SAMS (a division of Macmillan Computer Publishing).

Johnson, J. 1990. "Modes in Non-computer Devices." *International Journal of Man–Machine Studies* 32: 423–438.

Johnson, J. 1992. "Selectors: Going beyond User-Interface Widgets." In *Proceedings of ACM Conference on Computer–Human Interaction (CHI'92)*, Monterey, CA: ACM Press, pp. 273–279.

Johnson, J. 1996a. "The Information Highway: A Worst-Case Scenario." *Communications of the ACM* 39(2): 15–17. [Also available at www.uiwizards.com, under Publications]

Johnson, J. 1996b. "R ↔ D, not R&D." *Communications of the ACM* 39(9): 32–34.

Johnson, J. 1998. "Simplifying the User Interface of an Interactive Movie Game." In *Proceedings of the ACM Conference on Computer–Human Interaction (CHI'98)*, Los Angeles, CA. ACM Press, pp. 65–72.

Johnson, J. 2003. *Web Bloopers: 60 Common Web Design Mistakes and How to Avoid Them*. San Francisco: Morgan Kaufmann Publishers.

Johnson, J., and Beach, R. 1988. "Styles in Document Editing Systems." *IEEE Computer* 21(1): 32–43.

Johnson, J., and Henderson, A. 2002. "Conceptual Models: Begin by Designing What to Design." *Interactions* Jan/Feb: 25–32.

Johnson, J., and Keavney, M. 1995. "A Comparison of Remote Pointing Devices for Interactive TV Applications." In *A Collection of Papers from FirstPerson, Inc.* Technical Report SMLI TR-95-41. Mountain View, CA: Sun Microsystems Laboratories.

Johnson, J., and Marshall. C. R. 2005. "Convergent Usability Evaluation: A Case Study from the EIRS Project." In *Proceedings of ACM Conference on Computer–Human Interaction (CHI 2005)*, Portland, OR, ACM Press, pp. 1501–1504.

Johnson, J., and Nardi, B. 1996. "Creating Presentation Slides: A Study of User Preferences for Task-Specific versus Generic Application Software." *ACM Transactions on Computer–Human Interaction* 3(1): 38–65.

Johnson, J., Roberts, T., Verplank, W., Smith, D. C., Irby, C., Beard, M., and Mackey, K. 1989. "The Xerox Star: A Retrospective." *IEEE Computer*, 22 (9), 11–29.

King, A. 2003. *Speed Up Your Site: Website Optimization*. Indianapolis: New Riders. [See also WebsiteOptimization.com]

Koyani, S. J., Bailey, R. W., and Nall, J. R. 2006. *Research-Based Web Design & Usability Guidelines*. U.S. Department of Health and Human Services, http://www.usability.gov.

Kraut, R., ed. 1996. "The Internet @ Home." Special section of *Communications of the ACM* 39(12): 33–74.

Krug, S. 2005. *Don't Make Me Think: A Common Sense Approach to Web Usability,* 2nd edition. Indianapolis: New Riders.

Lambert, G. 1984. "A Comparative Study of System Response Time on Program Developer Productivity." *IBM Systems Journal* 23(1): 407–423.

Landauer, T. K. 1995. *The Trouble with Computers: Usefulness, Usability, and Productivity*. Cambridge, MA: MIT Press.

Lewis, C., Polson, P., Wharton, C., and Rieman, J. 1990. "Testing a Walkthrough Methodology for Theory-Based Design of Walk-Up-and-Use Interfaces." In *Proceedings of the 1990 ACM Conference on Human Factors in Computing Systems (CHI'90)*, Seattle, ACM Press, pp. 235–247.

Lynch, P., and Horton, S. 2002. *Web Style Guide: Basic Design Principles for Creating Web Sites*. New Haven: Yale University Press. [See also http://www.webstyleguide.com]

Mandel, T. 1997. *The Elements of User Interface Design*. New York: John Wiley and Sons.

Mayhew, D. 1999. *The Usability Engineering Lifecycle: A Practitioner's Handbook for User Interface Design*. San Francisco: Morgan Kaufmann Publishers.

McInerney, P., and Li, J. 2002. "Progress Indication: Concepts, Design, and Implementation." IBM Developer Works Web site: http://www-128.ibm.com/developerworks/web/library/us-progind//.

Meads, J. 2007. "Usability & Product Development: A Usability Course for Management." ACM Conference on Computer–Human Interaction (CHI'07) tutorial, San Jose, CA.

Microsoft Corporation. 2006. *Windows Vista User Experience Guidelines*. On the Web at http://msdn.microsoft.com/library/?url=/library/en-us/UxGuide/UXGuide/Home.asp.

Miller, L. 2005. "Case Study of Customer Input for a Successful Product." In *Agile 2005 Conference Proceedings,* Denver, pp 225-234.

Miller, L., and Johnson, J. 1996. "The Xerox Star: An Influential User-Interface Design." In M. Rudisill, C. Lewis, P. Polson, and T. McKay, eds., *Human–Computer Interface Design: Success Stories, Emerging Methods, Real-World Context.* San Francisco: Morgan Kaufmann Publishers.

Miller, R. 1968. "Response Time in Man–Computer Conversational Transactions." In *Proceedings of AFIPS Fall Joint Computer Conference, Vol. 33, pp 267–277.*

Mirel, B. 2004. *Interaction Design for Complex Problem Solving: Developing Useful and Usable Software.* San Francisco: Morgan Kaufmann Publishers.

Muller, M. J., Haslwanter, J. H., and Dayton, T. 1997. "Participatory Practices in the Software Lifecycle." In H. Helander, T. K. Landauer, and P. Prabhu, eds., *Handbook of Human–Computer Interaction,* 2nd edition. Amsterdam: Elsevier Science.

Mullet, K., and Sano, D. 1995. *Designing Visual Interfaces: Communications Oriented Techniques.* Mountain View, CA: SunSoft Press.

Nardi, B., and Johnson, J. 1994. "User Preference for Task-Specific vs. Generic Application Software." In *Proceedings of the 1994 ACM Conference on Human Factors in Computing Systems (CHI'94),* Boston, MA, ACM Press, pp. 392–398.

Newman, W. M., and Sproull, R. F. 1979. *Principles of Interactive Computer Graphics.* New York: McGraw–Hill.

Nielsen, J. 1993. *Usability Engineering.* San Diego: Academic Press.

Nielsen, J. 1999a. "User Interface Directions for the Web." *Communications of the ACM* 42(1): 65–71.

Nielsen, J. 1999b. "'Top Ten Mistakes' Revisited Three Years Later." On the Web at www.useit.com/Alertbox.

Nielsen, J. 1999c. "The Top Ten *New* Mistakes of Web Design." On the Web at www.useit.com/Alertbox.

Nielsen, J. 1999d. *Designing Web Usability: The Practice of Simplicity.* Indianapolis: New Riders. [See also UseIt.com]

Nielsen, J. 2002. "Flash and Web-Based Applications." UseIt.com, at http://www.useit.com/alertbox/20021125.html.

Nielsen, J. 2005. "The Top-Ten Web Design Mistakes of 2005." UseIt.com, at http://www.useit.com/alertbox/designmistakes.html.

Nielsen, J., and Loranger, H. 2006. *Prioritizing Web Usability.* Indianapolis: New Riders.

Nielsen, J., and Tahir, M. 2001. *Homepage Usability: Fifty Websites Deconstructed*. Indianapolis: New Riders.

Norman, D. 1983. "Design Rules Based on Analysis of Human Error." *Communications of the ACM* 26(4): 254–258.

Norman, D. A. 1988. *The Design of Everyday Things*. New York: Basic Books.

Norman, D. A. 1999. *The Invisible Computer*. Cambridge, MA: MIT Press.

Norman, D. A., and Draper, S. W. 1986. *User Centered System Design: New Perspectives on Human–Computer Interaction*. Hillsdale, NJ: Lawrence Erlbaum Associates.

Penzo, M. 2006. "Label Placement in Forms." *UX Matters*. On the Web at http://www.uxmatters.com/MT/archives/000107.php.

Perfetti, C. 2005. "iHotelier: Demonstrating the Potential of Flash for Web App Design." User Interface Engineering, on the Web at http://www.uie.com/articles/potential_of_flash/.

Pirolli, P. L, and Card, S. K. 1999. "Information Foraging." *Psychological Review* 106(4): 643–675.

Raskin, J. 2000. *The Humane Interface: New Directions for Designing Interactive Systems*. Reading, MA: Addison Wesley.

Redish, G. 2007. *Letting Go of the Words: Writing for the Web*. San Francisco: Morgan Kaufmann Publishers.

Roberts, T. L., and Moran, T. P. 1983. "The Evaluation of Text Editors: Methodology and Empirical Results." *Communications of the ACM* 26: 265–283.

Robertson, G., Card, S., and Mackinlay, J. 1989. "The Cognitive Co-processor Architecture for Interactive User Interfaces." In *Proceedings of the ACM Conference on User Interface Software and Technology (UIST'89)*. New York: ACM Press, pp. 10–18.

Robertson, G., Card, S., and Mackinlay, J. 1993. "Information Visualization Using 3D Interactive Animation." *Communications of the ACM* 36(4): 56–71.

Rosenfeld, L., and Morville, P. 2002. *Information Architecture for the World Wide Web,* 2nd edition. Sebastapol, CA: O'Reilly and Associates, 2002.

Rosson, M. B., and Carroll, J. 2001. *Usability Engineering: Scenario-Based Development of Human Computer Interaction*. San Francisco: Morgan Kaufmann Publishers.

Rudisill, M., Lewis, C., Polson, P., and McKay, T. 1996. *Human–Computer Interface Design: Success Stories, Emerging Methods, Real-World Context*. San Francisco: Morgan-Kaufmann Publishers.

Rushinek, A., and Rushinek, S. 1986. "What Makes Users Happy?" *Communications of the ACM* 29: 584–598.

Schuler, D., and Namioka, A. 1993. *Participatory Design: Principles and Practices*. Hillsdale, NJ: Lawrence Erlbaum Associates.

Shneiderman, B. 1984. "Response Time and Display Rate in Human Performance with Computers." *ACM Computing Surveys* 16(4): 265–285.

Shneiderman, B., and Plaisant, C. 2004. *Designing the User Interface: Strategies for Effective Human–Computer Interaction,* 4th edition. Reading, MA: Addison Wesley.

Smith, S. L., and Mosier, J. N. 1986. "Guidelines for Designing User Interface Software." Technical Report ESD-TR-86-278. Springfield, VA: National Technical Information Service.

Snyder, C. 2003. *Paper Prototyping: The Fast and Easy Way to Design and Refine User Interfaces.* San Francisco: Morgan Kaufmann Publishers.

Spool, J., Scanlon, T., Schroeder, W., Snyder, C., and DeAngelo, T. 1999. *Website Usability: A Designer's Guide.* San Francisco: Morgan Kaufmann Publishers.

Strunk, W., and White, E. B. 1999. *The Elements of Style,* 4th edition. New York: Macmillan Publishing Co.

Sun Microsystems. 2001a. *Java Look and Feel Design Guidelines,* 2nd edition. Reading, MA: Addison Wesley. [Web: http://java.sun.com/products/jlf/ed2/book/index.html]

Sun Microsystems. 2001b. *Java Look and Feel Design Guidelines: Advanced Topics.* Reading, MA: Addison Wesley. [Web: http://java.sun.com/products/jlf/at/book/]

Tesler, L. 1981. "The Smalltalk Environment." *Byte Magazine* 6(8): 90–147.

Thadhani, A. 1981. "Interactive User Productivity." *IBM Systems Journal* 20(4): 407–423.

Thimbleby, H. 1982. "Character-Level Ambiguity: Consequences for User-Interface Design." *International Journal of Man–Machine Studies* 16: 211–225.

Tidwell, J. 2005. *Designing Interfaces: Patterns for Effective Interaction Design.* Sebastapol, CA: O'Reilly and Associates.

Tufte, E. R. 1990. *Envisioning Information.* Cheshire, MA: Graphics Press.

Tufte, E. R. 2001. *The Visual Display of Quantitative Information,* 2nd edition. Cheshire, MA: Graphics Press.

Ullman, E. 1995. "Out of Time: Reflections on the Programming Life." In J. Brook and I. A. Boal, eds., *Resisting the Virtual Life: The Culture and Politics of Information.* San Francisco: City Lights Books, pp. 131–144.

Van Duyne, D. K., Landay, J. A., and Hong, J. I. 2002. *The Design of Sites: Patterns, Principles, and Processes for Crafting a Customer-Centered Web Experience.* Boston: Addison Wesley.

Wharton, C., Rieman, J., Lewis, C., and Polson, P. 1994. "The Cognitive Walkthrough: A Practitioner's Guide." In J. Nielsen and R. L. Mack, eds., *Usability Inspection Methods.* New York: John Wiley and Sons.

Wolfmaier, T. 1999. "Designing for the Color-Challenged: A Challenge." ITG Publication 2.1. On the Web at http://www.internettg.org/newsletter/mar99/accessibility_color_challenged.html.

Zarmer, C., and Johnson, J. 1990. "User Interface Tools: Past, Present, and Future Trends." HP Laboratories Technical Report HPL-90-20.

Index

About the Author

Jeff Johnson is President and Principal Consultant at UI Wizards, Inc., a product usability consulting firm that offers UI design, usability reviews, usability testing, and training. He has worked in the field of Human-Computer Interaction since 1978. After earning B.A. and Ph.D. degrees from Yale and Stanford Universities, he worked as a user-interface designer and implementer, engineer manager, usability tester, and researcher at Cromemco, Xerox, US West, Hewlett-Packard Labs, and Sun Microsystems. He has published numerous articles and book chapters on a variety of topics in Human-Computer Interaction and the impact of technology on society. He frequently gives talks and tutorials at conferences and companies on usability and user-interface design. He assisted in the design and evaluation of the Election Incident Reporting System, a Web-based system for reporting and voting problems, which was used to monitor the 2004 and 2005 U.S. elections. In addition to authoring *GUI Bloopers* and *GUI Bloopers 2.0,* he wrote *Web Bloopers: 60 Common Design Mistakes and How to Avoid Them* (2003).